Fourth Edition

Juvenile Delinquency

Fourth Edition

Juvenile Delinquency

A Justice Perspective

Ralph A. Weisheit
Illinois State University

Robert G. Culbertson
University of Wisconsin — Platteville

WAVELAND
PRESS, INC.
Prospect Heights, Illinois

For information about this book, write or call:
    Waveland Press, Inc.
    P.O. Box 400
    Prospect Heights, Illinois 60070
    (847) 634-0081
    www.waveland.com

Contents

Preface

There is considerable public concern about "the youth of today." There is a perception that juvenile crime is more frequent and more serious than ever and that our system of justice is slow to respond and generally ineffective. Having failed to attain most of the broad objectives established by the creation of the first juvenile court more than 100 years ago, we have witnessed an increasing sense of frustration. On the one hand the public is angered by delinquency, but on the other hand there is little consensus as to what should be done with juvenile offenders.

Early efforts concentrated on the offender and the broad issues related to causation. However, since the U.S. Supreme Court became involved in the delinquency problem in 1965, there has been a growing interest in studying both the juvenile offender and the formal system which identifies and processes offenders. This change is well illustrated in the merger of courses on juvenile delinquency with those on juvenile justice. The distinction between theoretical and policy concerns is becoming increasingly blurred. Ironically, our "progress" in the study of delinquency brings us full circle. The earliest significant American work on delinquency was conducted in the twenties and thirties by individuals who similarly blended theory and policy concerns and, in the process, laid the foundation for decades of both "academic" and "practical" work.

This reader was developed to reflect the changes in the study of juvenile delinquency and juvenile justice, and to meet several needs in this important field. First, we have produced a supplementary text that reflects an interdisciplinary perspective. Second, the reader supplements the general discussions presented in textbooks with more in-depth coverage of specific issues in delinquency. Third, the articles chosen for this reader not only reflect a range of issues, but they take very different approaches to understanding the problem of delinquency and the proper societal response.

Mirroring changes in the study of juvenile delinquency and juvenile justice, this book has evolved and changed with each new edition. This fourth
edition is a substantial revision, reflecting substantial changes in the field.
Over half of the articles are new to this edition, and some of the ideas and
terms presented in this edition were practically unknown when the previous
edition was assembled. Some of these new articles focus on the juvenile
offender, including such issues as recognizing the importance of early life
experiences on the biology of children and on their subsequent behavior,
school crime, the influence of early sexual abuse on later delinquency, and
features of gang violence. Other articles focus on the justice system itself,
including cycles of juvenile justice, the role of an offender's family in
shaping juvenile court decisions, the movement toward "restorative justice," the rise of "therapeutic justice," treating juvenile offenders, and the
debate about whether the juvenile court should be abolished. All of the
articles reflect changing sentiments about delinquency, both among members of the general public, and among professionals who study and work
with juvenile offenders.

Our ultimate objective is to stimulate the interest of students in one of the
more complex and fascinating aspects of deviant behavior. That behavior
and our response to it have serious implications for the offenders and for
society as a whole. Students will find the articles concise, informative, and
clearly presented.

R.A.W.
R.G.C.

Section I

The Delinquency Problem and the Justice System

For as long as there have been young people there has been a problem with youthful crime and misbehavior. The names for this misbehavior, what we now call juvenile delinquency, have changed as have the particular behaviors that most concern us, but the perception of a youth crime problem has persisted over centuries.

Despite having generations to consider the youth crime problem and to experiment with a variety of official responses, there is still little agreement on the role of the state in preventing and responding to juvenile crime. On the one hand are those who believe the state should have little involvement in the lives of children, except in those instances when the behavior constitutes a serious violation of the law. On the other hand are those who believe the state has a significant responsibility to respond to juvenile misconduct regardless of the nature of that misconduct.

The first two chapters of this book focus on the historical context for our current responses to juvenile misconduct. In "Delinquency and Social Policy: A Historical Perspective," Paul Lerman addresses the complexities of this debate and identifies competing and conflicting ideological perspectives. Tracing our current problems back to 1660, Lerman identifies the sources of confusion which have contributed to the lack of a clear distinction between problems related to poverty, welfare and dependency, and those related to crime. The end result of a long history of child saving is

1

that youth can easily lose their freedom for long periods of time for behaviors that are not criminal. Since publication of Lerman's work, problems have become even more complicated as the juvenile justice system continues to reach out to "help" children through the use of long-term institutionalization and jailing. Even in those states where detaining youth for status offenses violates the law, judges have found a way to circumvent the law through contempt proceedings. That is, while a judge may not be able to jail a child for failing to attend school, judges are jailing youth after they hold them in contempt of court for failing to obey a court order to attend school. This practice underscores Lerman's contention that each reform movement results in the incarceration of more children, not less. Because we do not have consistent policy statements, serious offenses can be treated much too lightly and trivial offenses much too harshly.

In "The Cycle of Juvenile Justice" Thomas J. Bernard further elaborates on change and continuity in the juvenile justice system. He identifies six aspects of juvenile delinquency and juvenile justice that have remained constant for at least 200 years. Included among these constants throughout our history has been a public perception that delinquency is more serious today than it was only thirty or forty years ago, and that the policies of the past will correct our current problems. Related to this is the relatively constant belief that we are in the midst of a juvenile crime wave unlike any experienced in the past. Bernard argues that recurring concerns throughout history have led to a cycle of juvenile justice. We not only look longingly to an imaginary past, but we adopt "new" policies and programs that have long been abandoned. A cycle of juvenile justice approach is useful for placing current concerns about juvenile delinquency in perspective. The approach also encourages us to look to history before assuming that our "new" approaches have never been tried.

Both Lerman and Bernard make a powerful case for examining our current delinquency problem in a larger historical context. The old saying that "history repeats itself" has never been more true than in the case of juvenile delinquency. Accurately understanding the delinquency problem and making good policy choices for responding to it require a consideration of both where we have been and where we want to be in the future. This book begins with a look at the past and concludes with a look to the future, while covering contemporary issues in between.

1

Delinquency and Social Policy
A Historical Perspective

Paul Lerman

Delinquency Definition and the Ideal of Liberty

Many Americans, when they think about delinquency, probably conjure up an image of criminal behaviors. However, the actual American definition of delinquency, as revealed by our correctional practices and statutes, ever since the founding of the Plymouth Bay Colony, has always included other reasons for legally punishing or incarcerating youth.

As might be expected, the colonists used the law of their native land as a basis for forming an American response to wayward youth. According to English law, juveniles above the age of seven were subject to criminal statutes and sanctions; however, both in England and in the colonies, youth under fifteen were usually treated less severely than adults. Beginning about 1660, the laws of the Massachusetts colony began to invoke the criminal process to support adult authority. A preamble to one of the 1660 laws stated:

> It appeareth, by too much experience, that diverse children and servants doe behave themselves disobediently and disorderly, towards their parents, masters, and Governors. . . .[1]

Based on a speech delivered Feb. 22, 1976, at Rutgers University, at the Conference on Juvenile Justice and Delinquency Prevention.

Paul Lerman, "Delinquency and Social Policy: A Historical Perspective," *Crime and Delinquency*, 23:4 (October 1977), pp. 383–393. Copyright © 1977 by Sage Publications, Inc. Reprinted by permission of Sage Publications, Inc.

The law gave a magistrate the power to summon before him "any such offender, and upon conviction of such misdemeanors, . . . sentence him to endure such corporal punishment, by whipping or otherwise, as in his judgment the merit of the fact shall deserve, not exceeding ten stripes for one offense."[2]

The laws of 1660 also made lying by children and failure to observe the Sabbath punishable offenses. Besides these laws, Massachusetts and other colonies had special laws regarding indentured servants and apprentices, so that masters could apply to the courts for measures to control youth who fornicated, contracted to marry, or gambled at cards or dice. In addition to these special restrictions on youth, juveniles were also subject to the Poor Laws which condemned idleness, begging, and vagrancy and used criminal penalties to enforce obedience.

These kinds of behaviors were included in the first attempt at a correctional definition of "delinquency" by the House of Refuge founded in 1825, the first institution specifically designed for juvenile offenders. In a memorial to the public appealing for funds, the Society for the Reformation of Juvenile Delinquents, the founding organization, stated:

> The design of the proposed institution is, to furnish, in the first place, an asylum, in which boys under a certain age, who become subject to the notice of our Police, either as vagrants, or houseless, or charged with petty crimes, may be received . . . [and] subjected to a course of treatment, that will afford a prompt and energetic corrective of their vicious propensities. . . .[3]

New York legislation granted the institution a state charter and gave the self-perpetuating managers the right to "receive and take into the House of Refuge . . . all such children as shall be taken up or committed as vagrants, or convicted of criminal offenses. . . ." Committing bodies could include judges, police magistrates, and the commissioner of the Almshouse and the Bridewell, providing the youth were "proper objects."[4] The New York legislature thereby concurred in the broad correctional definition set forth by the reformers in their public appeal.

In 1826 Boston established a House of Reformation for Juvenile Offenders. The incorporation act gave the House directors the power,

> . . . at their discretion, to receive and take into said house all such children who shall be convicted of criminal offenses or taken up and committed under and by virtue of an act of this Commonwealth "for suppressing and punishing of rogues, vagabonds, common beggars, and other idle, disorderly and lewd persons," and who may . . . be proper objects therefor. . . .[5]

Both the Boston and the New York statutes authorized the use of jails and prisons for youth who were not deemed "proper objects." However, by

1857, when the first national convention of refuge superintendents (from New York, Boston, Rochester, Cincinnati, Philadelphia, New Orleans, Baltimore, Pittsburgh, Chicago, and St. Louis) met in New York, there were seventeen juvenile reformatories, housing about 20,000 children admitted under policies and statutes that comprehended virtually every childhood misfortune.[6]

By the onset of the Civil War, a juvenile classified as a "proper object" of reformation could be covered by statutes that stemmed from three sources: (1) American adaptation of Elizabethan poor laws that covered idleness, begging, vagrancy, and destitution; (2) Puritan-inspired definitions of offenses peculiar to childhood and the apprentice status—in modern sociological language, juvenile status offenses; and (3) state adaptations of common-law criminal offenses. These three sources contributed, in actual correctional practice, to the lack of clear distinction between the problems of poverty, child welfare, and crime. In general, young America used the coercive power and punitive sanctions of the criminal law to handle many problems that were clearly noncriminal. In the nineteenth century, the reformatory performed the social functions of a juvenile almshouse, a workhouse, and a house of correction.

Sympathy for the plight of children whose fathers had been killed in the Civil War fostered a movement to build special asylums for poor and homeless youth, thereby diverting some youth from a reformatory experience. In addition, the "placing out" system, particularly in rural areas, was used to rescue children from "corrupting" living conditions. The spread of the free common schools also served to occupy some idle youth during the day. While these efforts may have diverted many idle and dependent youth from reformatories, the earlier statutes remained on the books in the older states, and the new Midwest and Western states, early in their statehood, enacted a broad correctional conception of delinquency through a variety of statutes that legitimated institutionalization in specific facilities.[7]

With the creation of the first juvenile court in Chicago, at the turn of the twentieth century, there was an attempt to codify existing Illinois statutes by adding a dependency and neglect category distinct from a criminal delinquency classification. In actual practice, however, distinctions among dependents, neglected children, status youth, and criminal offenders were often blurred: all categories could be—and actually were—detained in the same institution, even though the legislation and some judges gave a new emphasis to reforming "worthy" children in their own homes. The 1899 law, for example, made it possible for a youth to be held in detention or sent to a state training school if he was destitute; or if he was homeless, abandoned, or dependent; or if he had improper parental care; or if he was begging or receiving alms; or if he was living in a house of ill fame or with any vicious or disreputable person; or if he was in an unfit place.[8]

Following the lead of Illinois, other states also made certain that the jurisdiction of the court was sufficiently broad to encompass, as a "proper object" for detention or reformation in a training school, a broad array of poor law, juvenile status, and criminal characteristics. These broad terms were justified in 1901 by a Chicago child-saving committee, which urged that the legal definition of "condition of delinquency" be amended to include items that were implicit in the original dependency and neglect category or had been used in practice—"incorrigible"; "growing up in idleness and crime"; or "knowingly associating with thieves or vicious or immoral persons." The committee argued that "the amendment is intended to include all children that are in the need of government and care."[9] Since the use of local jails and prisons was forbidden, any separate juvenile correctional facility was deemed to be a place of government and care of the incorrigible and idle as well as a place of custody for the criminal offender. The reformers were successful in enacting a statutory definition of delinquency that had been implicit in practice for about 250 years.

The reformers believed that by deliberately equating the delinquent with any child "in need of government and care" they could use the police powers of the state to save children who might escape a narrow legal construction of dependency and neglect. To provide this control and care, they pushed through the legislature the creation of the first all-juvenile detention facilities, establishment of a truancy and parental school, provisions for paid probation officers, and state subsidies to existing religious institutions. They also initiated, before World War I, the creation of small pensions for worthy widows to allow them to keep their children at home. The court, with its broad jurisdictional boundaries, was primarily designed to serve the intake functions of a coercive welfare agency within the context of a modern juvenile quasi-criminal court.

Until the early 1960s, no statute in any state explicitly acknowledged the legal or correctional difference between status offenders and criminal offenders. About fifteen years ago a new legal category, Person in Need of Supervision, known as PINS, was created in New York and California as a noncriminal basis of juvenile court jurisdiction, distinct from a narrower definition of dependency and child neglect. By 1974 thirty-four states distinguished between criminal-type delinquency and at least some of the status offenses, but only eleven states explicitly prohibited institutionalizing status offenders in state training schools that housed criminal offenders.

The movement to remove the vestiges of Poor Law and juvenile status characteristics from the correctional definition of "delinquency" recently received added support from the federal Juvenile Justice and Delinquency Prevention Act of 1974. A state receiving block grants under the Act must give assurance that, within a specified time, no status offender will be detained in or committed to an institution set up explicitly for criminal delinquents. While this movement to narrow the boundaries of delinquency definitions and practices is laudable, whether youth will actually fare better under the new labels is still uncertain. Recent evidence indicates that PINS youth are more likely than delinquent youth to be detained in a facility as part of their court processing, are detained longer, and, if institutionalized, stay for longer periods. Whether Americans can learn to treat all arrested truant, idle, incorrigible, promiscuous, and runaway youth less harshly than their truly delinquent brothers and sisters is still uncertain at this time.[10] In a country that prizes the ideal of liberty, it is ironic that youth can still lose their freedom so easily, and for such lengthy periods, for behaviors that are clearly not criminal and that would not even be admitted before an adult criminal court.

Delinquency and Justice for All

The evidence that noncriminal delinquents can be, have been, and are dealt with harshly is related to another American theme, "justice for all." Since 1824, when the House of Refuge was empowered to institutionalize a variety of youth—without distinction between the criminal and the noncriminal—for indeterminate periods, American juvenile laws and practices have flouted two basic components of a reasonable conception of justice: (1) Any deprivation of liberty, or other state-imposed penalty, should be graded proportionately to the degree of social harm a person has done or clearly threatens to do to members of a community. (2) Offenses or harms that are comparable should be dealt with by punishments that are equal.[11]

Before the Revolution of 1776, juveniles were treated like adults. In the reform legislation that swept the former colonies immediately after the War of Independence, imprisonment and fines replaced the pillory, the stocks, and other forms of corporal punishment. Borrowing ideas from European classical criminology (associated with Beccaria) and the general environment of the Enlightenment, Americans reformed their criminal codes with the aim of securing equality of judicial handling. Children benefited from these reforms, even though they were also thrust into the same local jails and prisons as adults.[12]

About 1820, when the House of Refuge was under discussion administrators of the local Bridewell were trying to separate youth from adults during the day, furnish some in-jail instruction in reading and writing, and care differently for their younger charges.[13] According to the keeper of the Bridewell, the period of confinement ranged from a few days to a year or more, with many remaining several months. Though the charges were mainly for "trifling offenses," many remained longer than customary "because of a want of residence."[14]

Instead of seeking residences for the vagrant, apprenticeships for the unemployed, and schools for the ignorant, the Society for the Reformation of Juvenile Delinquents decided to attack the problems of child welfare, poverty, and delinquency with a new social invention—an all-purpose workhouse and reformatory designed to reshape moral character coercively and render children obedient to their superiors. Only after a child had met the strict reform standards of the Refuge superintendent—during a stay ranging from a year to three years—would he be bound out as a laboring apprentice or sent out on a whaling ship. The reformers argued that agents of government should be the "fathers of the people," should "stand towards the community in the moral light of guardians of virtue."[15] In carrying out their guardianship inside the Refuge, they were not reluctant to use the stripes, solitary confinement, bread and water, and other correctional penalties.

In exchange for receiving a new and quite punitive "father," juveniles gave up their traditional rights under criminal law. Commitment to the Refuge meant that vagrancy and "trifling offenses" could be dealt with the same as more serious offenses since they could be viewed as signs of "vicious propensities." Many resolutions were proposed at the first national convention of House of Refuge superintendents in 1857 but only one was chosen for adoption—for fear of stifling any autonomous correctional initiatives. Not surprisingly, the superintendents agreed that they should have "unqualified control over the treatment and disposition of inmates for the length of their minority."[16] Children were deprived of legal restraints on the type, degree, and duration of punishment that agents of government could impose, and all parental rights were abrogated for the duration of the child's minority. In many cases, parents did not even know where youth had been placed after a long stay at Refuge.

Juvenile court legislation at the turn of the twentieth century continued this tradition of deliberately refraining from establishing any definition of degrees of delinquency or limits on the type, degree, and duration of penalties. While the indeterminate sentence has, in some jurisdictions, given way to eighteen-month renewable placements (or sentences) or three-year dispositions, no state has enacted legislation that limits its power in accordance with traditional norms of justice.

The historical legacy continues to confound the handling of juvenile status and trivial, petty offenders, the bulk of the delinquency population, and it neutralizes the commonsense moral distinction made by most Americans when they compare the harm done by a mugger of the elderly to a shoplifting spree at a local store. We have devised a system where the serious offense can be treated much too lightly and the trivial much too seriously. We now have 150 years of evidence that relinquishing substantive justice in exchange for a correctional regime that does not correct is a bad bargain. Even if our institutional programs were effective, one could still argue that just dispositions should take precedence over efforts at reformation. Recognition of the legal and moral concept of degrees of criminal delinquency could promote the ideal of "justice for all," including children.

The Modern Social Control System: The Ideal and the Actual

The overreach of the delinquency definition and the failure to specify degrees of offense highlight the profound discrepancy between formal declarations of liberty and justice and our societal practices. This disparity between the ideal and the actual deserves to be examined further, since the current degree of discrepancy tells us a good deal about the modern American approach to controlling, regulating, and treating delinquency.

Enforcement of the law in America is local and has always varied in scope and degree. As a result, many youthful misbehaviors have been either overlooked by police or ignored by judges. In practice, police and judges have exercised discretion in softening the breadth and harshness of our laws. Until recently, reformers were usually not satisfied with this tendency toward underenforcement since identifying, correcting, and reforming youth at the earliest possible age was deemed important. The founders of the House of Refuge complained that local judges were reluctant to convict youth because they were unwilling to mix the young with older, hardened criminals. Seventy-five years later, when the modern juvenile justice system was created in Chicago, reformers complained that judges were reluctant to correct youth because they had to send youngsters to jails pending disposition of their cases. If the laws were not strictly enforced how could "guardians of virtue" become "fathers of the people" or take legal control of all children "in need of government and care"?

Both of these important movements in juvenile reform, the refuge movement and juvenile court movement, did help to separate youth from workhouse and criminal adults. But in the process of doing this, they created new forms of broad social control over youth. It is quite likely that *more* youth were incarcerated *after* each reform than *before* it. The Refuge Movement founders were the initiators of our reformatories, industrial and training schools, truancy and parental schools, and other *long-term* juvenile correctional facilities. The juvenile court movement founders were the initiators of *short-term* detention facilities, where youth could be properly studied and governed before a determination of whether they needed longer government and care.

Given the breadth of our nation's definition of juvenile delinquency and a continual growth in youth population, the juvenile court's available resources were continually strained to meet the demand for coercive child saving. Underenforcement, informal adjustment of cases, and high probation caseloads were adaptive mechanisms utilized to deal with the fundamental problems of a potentially limitless demand for reformation of the young and the limited supply of resources. Other aids to the overburdened juvenile social control system were inadvertently provided in the support programs of Aid to Dependent Children, mental health, and child welfare, which siphoned off Poor Law and juvenile status offenders who comprised part of the potential "delinquent" population. States and counties, of course, have varied in their use of alternative resources and underenforcement mechanisms, so that many juvenile facilities still house a mixed population of delinquent, dependent, neglected, and status offense children.

Accompanying all of these diverse trends have been assertions by correctional leaders that we have moved progressively from a policy of revenge and restraint to rehabilitation and reintegration of the juvenile offender. Some academics also have given support to this assessment.[17] Unfortunately, the disparity between these lofty intentions and actual practice is much greater than we have wished to believe.

Summary and Conclusions

We continue to compound the original delinquency problem by permitting systems of juvenile control to expand under broad laws that operate under arbitrary discretionary standards. Many of the standards and the outcomes appear unreasonable and unjust when subjected to close scrutiny. Left to operate according to the unstated policy, the system tends to result in a dominance of social control. Merely adding more fiscal and organizational resources to the existing system—as during the last decade—can only further the relative dominance of social control over efforts at treatment. This incremental policy of merely adding more resources has resulted in excessive expense—in both dollars and social values—without offsetting benefits.

During the first seventy-five years of this century, we created a modern juvenile control system to regulate the conduct and character of America's youth. We accomplished this while believing that we were primarily engaged in saving or rehabilitating youth. The image of a nonrestraining society was set forth while we constructed new institutions that were classified as detention facilities, residential schools, diagnostic centers, and reception clinics. During this time we also created probation and other less coercive services, but the dominance of our continued reliance on institutionalization is clearly revealed by national and state data. In the last quarter of this century will we continue to maintain the discrepancy between reality and our intentions, or will we begin the troublesome task of determining where arbitrary social control ends and justice and non-coercive help begin?

Footnotes

[1] Joseph M. Hawes, *Children in Urban Society: Juvenile Delinquency in Nineteenth Century America* (New York: Oxford University Press, 1971), p. 14.

[2] *Id.*, p. 41.

[3] Society for the Reformation of Juvenile Delinquents, *House of Refuge Documents* (New York: Mahlon Day, 1832), p. 21. Hereafter cited as *Refuge Documents*.

[4] Hawes, *op. cit. supra* note 1, p. 41; Robert S. Pickett, *House of Refuge* (Syracuse, NY: Syracuse University Press, 1969), p. 58.

[5] R. H. Bremner, J. Barnard, T. K. Hareven, and R. M. Mennel, *Children and Youth in America: A Documentary History,* 2 vols. (Cambridge, MA: Harvard University Press, 1970), Vol. 1, p. 681.

[6] David Rothman, *The Discovery of the Asylum* (Boston: Little, Brown, 1971), p. 209.

[7] Bremner et al., *op. cit. supra* note 5, Vols. I, II.

[8] *Id.*, Vol. II, p. 507.

[9] Hawes, *op. cit. supra* note 1, p. 185.

[10] P. Lerman, "Child Convicts," *TransAction,* July–August 1971, pp. 35–44, 72.

[11] P. Lerman, "Beyond *Gault:* Injustice and the Child," in Paul Lerman, ed., *Delinquency and Social Policy* (New York: Praeger, 1970), p. 237.

[12] Rothman, *op. cit. supra* note 6, pp. 30–57.

[13] Pickett, *op. cit. supra* note 4, p. 57.

[14] Refuge Documents, *op. cit. supra* note 3, p. 15.

[15] *Id.*, p. 13.

[16] Rothman, *op. cit. supra* note 6, p. 293.

[17] L.T. Empey, *Alternatives to Incarceration* (Washington, DC: U.S. Dept. of Health, Education and Welfare, 1967).

Juv crime is down over past 25 yrs
Juv arrests have increased in past 25 yrs
Poor people arrested more - effect of support systems
generally police will call parents - Not judge

2

The Cycle of Juvenile Justice

Thomas J. Bernard

What Stays the Same in History?

This chapter examines aspects of juvenile delinquency and juvenile justice that have stayed the same for at least two hundred years. Some of these aspects have remained unchanged for a much longer time, even since the dawn of recorded history. This is one-half of the question being asked about history: "What aspects of juvenile delinquency and juvenile justice have stayed the same for at least two hundred years, and what aspects have changed?"

Five aspects of juvenile delinquency and juvenile justice have stayed the same for at least two hundred years:

1. Juveniles, especially young males, commit more crime than other groups.
2. There are special laws that only juveniles are required to obey.
3. Juveniles are punished less severely than adults who commit the same offenses.
4. Many people believe that the current group of juveniles commit more frequent and serious crime than juveniles in the past—that is, there is, a "juvenile crime wave" at the present time.

Bernard, Thomas J. 1992. *The Cycle of Juvenile Justice.* New York: Oxford University Press. (Excerpt from book: Chapter 3: What Stays the Same in History?)

5. Many people blame juvenile justice policies for the supposed "juvenile crime wave, "arguing that they are too lenient (serious offenders laugh at "kiddie court") or that they are too harsh (minor offenders are embittered and channeled into a life of crime).

Although these five aspects have stayed the same for at least two hundred years, at each point in time people generally believed that things were different only thirty or forty years ago. Thus, these five unchanging aspects are often associated with a "myth of the good old days" and with the optimistic view that the "juvenile crime wave" would end if we only implemented the juvenile justice policies we had back then.

These five aspects give rise to a sixth aspect that has stayed the same for at least two hundred years—what I call the "cycle of juvenile justice." This cycle arises from the fact that, at any given time, many people are convinced that the problem of high juvenile crime is recent and did not exist in the "good old days." These people conclude that the problem lies in the policies for handling juvenile offenders, whether those are harsh punishments or lenient treatments. The result is a cycle of reform in which harsh punishments are blamed for high juvenile crime rates and are replaced by lenient treatments, and then lenient treatments are blamed for high juvenile crime rates and are replaced by harsh punishments.

The Behavior of Youth, Especially Young Males

Regardless of whether crime is high or low at a particular time or place, young people (and especially young males) commit a greater proportion of the crime than would be expected from their proportion in the population.[1] For example, juveniles between the ages of 13 and 17 are about 8% of the population of the United States at present.[2] If they were arrested at the same rate as everyone else, they would account for about 8% of arrests. Instead, they account for almost twice as many arrests, including twice as many for serious violent crimes and almost four times as many for serious property crimes.

Recent Changes in Juvenile Crime in the United States

Prior to 1952, juvenile arrest rates in the United States were fairly low and fairly stable. In 1951, for example, juveniles accounted for 4.5% of all arrests, including 3.7% of arrests for serious violent crimes and 14.6% of arrests for serious property crimes. With some minor fluctuations, such as a temporary increase during World War II, these figures had been fairly stable at least back to the beginning of the century.[3]

While low by today's standards, juvenile crime was considered a serious problem at the time. A textbook published in 1954 included the following statement:

Nowhere does the failure of crime control show up more clearly than among our youth. Even before World War II, according to one study, national statistics indicated that some two million of forty-three million boys and girls in the United States below the age of eighteen years came to the attention of the police annually. Youth plays a top-heavy part in the traditional crimes that feed the headlines and for which arrests are made. They frequently commit the familiar crimes against property, often with attendant violence, and their inexperience and lack of judgment make them relatively easy to apprehend.[4]

Juvenile arrests began to rise in 1952 and continued until they peaked in 1974.[5] In that year, juveniles accounted for 45% of all arrests, including 22.6% of those for serious violent crimes and 50.7% of arrests for serious property crimes. That was also the year in which the total juvenile population (i.e., everyone in the country who is younger than 18 years old) peaked at about 34 million. Since then, the juvenile population has declined to about 28 million, a decrease of about 20%.

The decline in the juvenile population has been accompanied by a decline in the proportion of arrests that involve juveniles. In 1989, juveniles accounted for 15.5% of all arrests, including 15.4% of arrests for serious violent crimes (murder, forcible rape, robbery, and aggravated assault), and 32.7% of arrests for serious property crimes (burglary, larceny-theft, motor vehicle theft, and arson). While this represents a drop of about one-third in the *proportion* of arrests that involve juveniles, the *rate* of juvenile arrests (i.e., the number of arrests adjusted for the number of juveniles in the population) has remained relatively constant.[6]

Juvenile Crime in Earlier Times

Even when juvenile arrest rates were what we now consider low, people were concerned about how much crime juveniles committed. For example, in 1938, England was alarmed by a report that found that convictions of males peaked at age 13, and that the probability of conviction was greater from ages 11 to 17 than at any other age.[7] In the United States, a report in 1940 pointed out that "young people between 15 and 21 constitute only 13% of the population above 15, but their share in the total volume of serious crime committed far exceeds their proportionate representation."[8] Extensive publicity about the "juvenile crime wave" followed in 1941 and 1942.[9] The FBI supported this publicity with statistics that showed big increases in delinquency, but the Children's Bureau, a government agency that also monitored delinquency, said that the increases were due to changes in reporting practices by police and court agencies.

These concerns are not confined to our century. In the middle of the

1800s, many young men roamed around the "Wild West" with guns strapped to their hips looking for trouble. Although stories about people like Billy the Kid were exaggerated into legends, it was still an exceptionally violent period.[10]

In the early 1800s, there were a large number of stories in the press about the extensive criminality of youth.[11] For example, a commentator on the problems of crime in London was alarmed by the volume of juvenile crime:

> It is a most extraordinary fact, that half the number of persons convicted of crime have not attained the age of discretion.[12]

About that time, there were 3,000 prisoners in London under the age of 20, half of whom were under 17 and some of whom were as young as 6.[13] These convictions were not merely for minor offenses or youthful misbehaviors. In 1785, the Solicitor-General of England stated in the House of Commons that eighteen out of twenty offenders executed in London the previous year were under the age of 21.

Gang fights are often viewed as a modern phenomenon, but Shakespeare's play *Romeo and Juliet,* set in fifteenth-century Italy, revolves around what we would now call a gang fight. The young men of the Montagu family, which included Romeo, had been in running battle with the young men of the Capulet family, which included Juliet. On a hot summer day with "the mad blood stirring," the two groups happened to run into each other on the street. In the initial exchange, a polite greeting ("Gentlemen, good day: a word with one of you") was answered by a challenge to fight ("And but one word with one of us? couple it with something: make it a word and a blow"). After a few more exchanges, the fight began and two youths, both about 16 years old, were killed.

The events in this story were placed in fifteenth-century Italy, but they could have been situated in the United States in modern times. In fact, the play and movie *West Side Story* were based on Romeo and Juliet but set in New York City in the 1950s. If the play were written for today, it might take place in Los Angeles. This illustrates that stories about the criminality of young people, and of young males in particular, are not unique to any particular time or place.

We could continue this tale back to the first crime recorded in the Bible, in which Cain (the eldest son of Adam and Eve) killed his younger brother Abel. Ever since then, young people in general, and young men in particular, have been committing crimes at a greater rate than other people. We are always aware of this phenomenon but tend to lose track of the fact that it has always been this way.

What Explains Juvenile Crime?

Why is it that young people in general, and young men in particular, commit such a large proportion of crime? Is it their biological makeup, with large volumes of hormones running through their systems? Is it their psychological state of mind, generated by the conflicts of adolescence? Is it socialization into roles, with expectations that young men will be strong and in control, but never weak or "chicken"? Various explanations of this phenomenon are presented in texts on juvenile delinquency,[14] but those explanations are not reviewed here.

For whatever reason, young people in general and young men in particular have always committed more than their share of crime. Thus, we should expect that this will continue in the future. Some people may argue that if we only implement a particular policy (e.g., death penalty, psychoanalysis, lengthy prison sentences, education, or employment training), then juveniles will stop committing more than their share of crime. The lessons of history suggest that these people are wrong.

Special Laws for Juveniles

A second aspect that has stayed the same for at least two hundred years (and seems to have remained constant over recorded history) is that certain offenses apply only to youths, not adults. At the present, these are called *status offenses*, since they only apply to people with the status of being a juvenile. The most common of these laws today are laws against running away from home, refusing to attend school (truancy), and refusing to obey parents (incorrigibility). Other common status offenses involve drinking alcoholic beverages, violating curfew, and engaging in consensual sexual activities.

Adults are allowed to do all these things, but juveniles who do the same commit punishable offenses. Adults who do not like their family can move out, but a juvenile who moves out may be arrested by the police. Adults can quit school or quit their job, but a juvenile who quits school may be taken to juvenile court and placed on probation. Adults are free to engage in most consensual sexual activities, but juveniles who engage in the same activities may be sent to a juvenile institution.

Status Offenses in Earlier Times

Originally, offenses that applied solely to youths focused on the duties that people held for their parents. In the Code of Moses in the Bible, for example, there were severe penalties including death for striking or cursing your parents,[15] although these severe punishments were rarely carried out in practice.

The Puritans made these Biblical passages the basis for a "stubborn child" law in 1646.[16] That law "served as a direct or indirect model for legislation enacted by every American state making children's misbehavior a punishable offense." It was substantially modified through the years but remained in force in Massachusetts until 1973. Since the days of the Puritans, there has been a continual expansion of attempts to control the non-criminal but "offensive" behavior of children through legal means.

Decriminalization? Deinstitutionalization?

Today, considerable debate exists about how to handle these offenses. Some people argue that the laws against these activities should be repealed: *decriminalization* of status offenses. People who favor decriminalization argue that status offenses are harmful to the youths who engage in them, but that handling these offenses in juvenile court takes a bad situation and makes it worse. They argue that voluntary social service agencies, not the juvenile court, should intervene with these youths.

Other people argue that juveniles who commit status offenses should be handled in juvenile courts but should never be locked up for such offenses. These people favor *deinstitutionalization* of status offenses. This is generally considered a more moderate response, since the offenses remain subject to the juvenile court.

In practice, however, deinstitutionalization is not much different from decriminalization. Imagine a juvenile who is brought into juvenile court for truancy, and the judge orders her to go to school. But if status offenses are "deinstitutionalized," then the judge cannot send her to an institution and can only place her on probation. If she still refuses to go to school, the judge can do nothing.

In effect, deinstitutionalizing status offenses means that the juvenile court has no power to enforce these laws. If you are going to do that, then you might as well repeal the laws—that is, decriminalize status offenses.

Status Offenses as an Aspect That Stays the Same

The lessons of history suggest that neither decriminalization nor deinstitutionalization will work in the long run. Status offenses go back to the beginning of recorded history. Because this appears to be something that has stayed the same over this long span, it seems unlikely to change in the future.

In fact, in states that have decriminalized status offenses, such as Washington, there has been a tendency for status offenders to be "redefined" as criminal offenders so that they still could be processed through the juvenile courts.[17] Almost every status offender does something that can be defined as a criminal event for the purpose of sending the juvenile to an institution. For example, before the law was changed, a youth who refused to obey his parents could have been brought into court on a charge of incorrigibility, but he would have only been sent to an institution if court officials thought it was in his "best interests." After the law was changed, that youth could not be sent to an institution at all. But if court officials thought it was in the youth's "best interests" to be sent to an institution, then they could charge the youth with some criminal offense. For example, if he threatened a parent or teacher (but did not harm them in any way), he could be charged with simple assault. The youth then could be sent to an institution (since it was in his "best interests"), but would now be labeled a criminal offender rather than a status offender.

The more modest effort to "deinstitutionalize" status offenders has also resulted in redefining status offenders as criminal offenders. This idea was originally embodied in a federal policy that guided the provision of federal funds for juvenile justice to the states. Early figures suggested almost all status offenders were redefined as criminal offenders, so they continued to be institutionalized.[18] Despite this tendency, many judges opposed the policy because they felt they needed the power to institutionalize status offenders directly.[19]

In response to their concerns, federal policy was modified so that a violation of a condition of probation would be considered a criminal offense. Under this modification, a youth charged with a status offense could be brought into court and placed on probation. One of the conditions of probation would be that the youth not commit the status offense again. Youths who committed additional status offenses would be considered to have violated their probation, which would be defined as a criminal offense. These youths then could be sent to an institution.

To some extent, these changes have made the institutionalization of status offenders "invisible."[20] Kids are still institutionalized for truancy, but they are no longer defined as status offenders. They either are charged with some minor criminal offense and institutionalized for that, or school attendance is made a condition of probation so that further truancy is defined as a criminal offense.

It might seem to be a good idea to remove jurisdiction for status offenses from the juvenile court, but the lessons of history suggest that this will never occur—there have been separate laws for juveniles for as far back as history records.

Mitigation of Punishments for Juveniles

A third aspect that has stayed the same for at least two hundred years (and indeed over history) is that juveniles are treated more leniently than adults when they commit the same offenses. That is, when a juvenile is convicted of a crime, the punishment is not as severe as when an adult is convicted of the same crime.

Mitigation in Earlier Times

The Code of Hammurabi, written over 4,000 years ago, indicated that juveniles were to be treated more leniently than adults. In ancient Jewish law, the Talmud specified the conditions under which immaturity was to be considered for more lenient punishment. Under these provisions, there was no corporal punishment before the age of puberty, which was set at 12 for females and 13 for males, and no capital punishment before the age of 20. Similar leniency was found among the Moslems, where children under the age of 17 were generally exempt from retaliation and the death penalty, although they could be corrected.

Roman law also included a lengthy history of mitigated punishments for children. As early as the Twelve Tables (about 450 B.C.), there was absolute immunity from punishment for children below a certain age. Originally, immunity applied only to children who were incapable of speech, but eventually it was applied to all children below the age of 7. In addition, children below puberty have been given reduced punishment under Roman Law since around the year A.D. 500. Justinian, for example, established puberty at 14 for boys and 12 for girls. In between age 7 and puberty, criminal responsibility was made dependent on age, nature of offense, and mental capacity.

Under ancient Saxon law, a child below the age of 12 could not be found guilty of any felony, and a child between 12 and 14 might be acquitted or convicted on the basis of natural capacity. After 14 there was no mitigation.

English common law had acquired its modem form by about the middle of the 1300s, and was summarized by Blackstone in 1769.[21] In general, the law at that time was based on the following framework for mitigating punishments:

Below the age of seven, juveniles have no responsibility for their actions and therefore cannot be punished for any crimes they commit.

From seven to 14, juveniles are presumed to lack responsibility for their actions, but the prosecution can argue that they should be punished in spite of their youth.

From 14 to 21, juveniles are presumed to be responsible for their actions, but the defense can argue that they should not be punished, despite their age.

After the age of 21, everyone is responsible for their actions and therefore is punished to the full extent of the law.

Mitigation in the Juvenile Court

Today, the juvenile court embodies the concept of less responsibility, and therefore less punishment, for juveniles. In most states, juveniles below the age of 18 are sent to juvenile court when they commit offenses, and the punishments given there are generally more lenient than those in adult courts for similar offenses. A few states have higher or lower ages of juvenile court jurisdiction. For example, in New York State, only juveniles 15 and younger are sent to juvenile court, while those who are 16 and older are tried in adult court.

Juveniles normally sent to juvenile court may be tried instead in adult courts when they commit serious or frequent offenses. Such a procedure goes by a variety of names, including waiver, transfer, certification, and direct filing.[22] Under these provisions, juveniles are treated the same way that youths aged 7 to 14 were treated under English common law: it is presumed that they are not fully responsible for their actions, but the prosecutor can argue that there are special reasons in this case why they should be tried in adult court. If the judge agrees, then the youth is sent to adult court for the full punishment that any adult would receive.

In addition, in some states, certain offenses are not within the jurisdiction of the juvenile court at all, no matter what the child's age. For example, in Pennsylvania, jurisdiction for all homicides lies in criminal courts. Youths charged with homicide are taken directly to criminal court, regardless of how young they are. There, the defense lawyer can argue that, because of immaturity, the youth should be handled in juvenile court. If the judge agrees, the youth can be transferred. These youths are treated the way youths aged 14 to 21 were treated under English Common Law: that is, they are presumed responsible for their actions but the defense may attempt to prove otherwise.

Mitigation as an Aspect That Stays the Same

The specific rules for mitigating punishments for juveniles have changed throughout history. At some times and places, mitigation extends all the way to age 21, while at others only to age 12 or 14. At some times and places, punishments for juveniles are greatly reduced or even eliminated, and at others they are only slightly reduced.

In the future, we can expect that the specific rules for mitigating punishments of juveniles will continue to change, but the mitigation of punishments itself will remain. Whether we provide greater reductions in punishments or lesser, to more juveniles or to fewer, mitigation of punishments will remain a feature of any system for processing juvenile offenders.

Views of Adults about the Behavior of Youth

According to Donovan, "every generation since the dawn of time has denounced the rising generation as being inferior in terms of manners and morals, ethics and honesty." [23] The view that adults have of juveniles is separate from how juveniles actually behave. This view goes as far back as history records, so it probably will remain the same into the future.

Many adults today complain about how rotten kids are, but this was true in Colonial America as well. Harvey Green says:

> One of the most consistent and common themes in the history of relations between American parents and their children is criticism of the younger generation. From almost the moment the settlers of Jamestown and Plymouth stepped off their boats in the early seventeenth century, there arose the cry that children were disobeying their parents as never before.[24]

This phenomenon is not confined to America. Over two thousand years before the Pilgrims, Socrates had his own complaints about youth:

> Children now love luxury. They have bad manners, contempt for authority, they show disrespect for elders and love chatter in place of exercise. They no longer rise when their elders enter the room. They contradict their parents, chatter before company, gobble up dainties at the table, and tyrannize over their teachers.[25]

We can go back even further than that. Fourteen hundred years before Socrates, a Summarian father wrote to his son:

> Because my heart had been sated with weariness of you, I kept away from you and heeded not your fears and grumblings. Because of your clamorings, I was angry with you. Because you do not look to humanity, my heart was carried off as if by an evil wind. Your grumblings have put an end to me; you have brought me to the point of death. . . . Others like you support their parents by working. . . . They multiply barley for their father, maintain him in barley, oil, and wool. You're a man when it comes to perverseness, but compared to them you are not a man at all. You certainly don't labor like them—they are the sons of fathers who make their sons labor, but me, I didn't make you work like them.[26]

Juveniles as Serious Criminals

Most of the above quotes apply to what we now call status offenses. Perhaps kids today are engaged in serious, horrifying crimes, terrible offenses. Today, you might argue, many kids are the worst kind of criminals. There may have been a lot of minor delinquencies in the past, but the serious, hard-core juvenile crime of today is new.

For example, in 1989, *Time* Magazine described "the beast that has broken loose in some of America's young people."[27] The following series of quotations gives a sense of the article while omitting numerous examples presented to illustrate each point:

> More and more teenagers, acting individually or in gangs, are running amuck. . . . To be sure, teenagers have never been angels. Adolescence is often a troubled time of rebellion and rage. . . . But juvenile crime appears to be more widespread and vicious than ever before. . . . Adolescents have always been violence prone, but there are horrendous crimes being committed by even younger children. . . . The teen crime wave flows across all races, classes, and life-styles. The offenders are overwhelmingly male, but girls too are capable of vicious crimes. . . . What is chilling about many of the young criminals is that they show no remorse or conscience, at least initially. Youths brag about their exploits and shrug off victims' pain.

The author suggested that this recent "upsurge in the most violent types of crimes by teens" began in 1983.

However, five years before this juvenile crime wave apparently began, *Time* magazine seemed to be just as alarmed about the juvenile crime problem:

> Across the U.S., a pattern of crime has emerged that is both perplexing and appalling. Many youngsters appear to be robbing and raping, maiming and murdering as casually as they go to a movie or join a pickup baseball game. A new, remorseless, mutant juvenile seems to have been born, and there is no more terrifying figure in America today.[28]

The author of the 1989 article must have neglected to read this 1978 article. How could the wave of juvenile violence start in 1983 if *Time* had already carried an article about it in 1978?

Views of Adults in Earlier Times

These quotations from *Time* magazine occur during a time in which juvenile crime, including serious violent and property crime, declined by about one-third. Similar quotations can be found during times when juvenile crime is rising. For example, in 1964, the long-time head of the FBI J. Edgar Hoover was similarly convinced that things had changed:

> In the Twenties and Thirties, juvenile delinquency, in general, meant such things as truancy, minor vandalism and petty theft. Today, the term includes armed robbery, assault and even murder. . . . We should not permit actual crimes to be thought of in terms of the delinquencies

of a past era. I am not speaking of the relatively minor misdemeanors usually associated with the process of growing up. It is the killings, the rapes and robberies of innocent people by youthful criminals that concern me.[29]

Ten years earlier, in 1954, a New York City judge made a similar statement in *Newsweek,* except that he described the low juvenile crime as being in the 1900s and 1910s, rather than in the 1920s and 1930s:

Back before the first world war, it was a rare day when you saw a man under 25 up for a felony. Today it's the rule. And today when one of these kids robs a bank he doesn't rush for a businesslike getaway. He stays around and shoots up a couple of clerks. Not long ago I asked such a boy why, and he said: "I get a kick out of it when I see blood running." [30]

The article was entitled: "Our Vicious Young Hoodlums: Is There Any Hope?"

That same year, *Time* magazine ran an article about the "teenage reign of terror (that) has transformed New York City's public school system into a vast incubator of crime in which wayward and delinquent youngsters receive years of 'protection' while developing into toughened and experienced criminals."[31] It said that in some schools, half the pupils carried switchblades or zipguns, others carried homemade flame throwers or plastic water pistols filled with blinding chemical solutions, and other students threatened or beat up teachers who gave them poor grades. It suggested that this behavior had begun "in the past few years."

Views of Adults as an Aspect That Stays the Same

Similar alarms were raised in the 1940s, 1930s, and 1920s.[32] At those times, people believed (as they do today) that the country was being overwhelmed in a rising tide of juvenile delinquency and crime, and that it had not been a serious problem only forty or fifty years ago. Juvenile crime itself seems to go up and down, but the quotations about how terrible juveniles are seem to stay the same. Whether juvenile crime is high or low, many people believe that it is worse today than ever before.

Belief That Juvenile Justice Policy Increases Crime

A fifth aspect of juvenile delinquency and juvenile justice that has stayed the same for at least two hundred years is a belief that the system for processing juvenile offenders increases juvenile crime. This belief seems to be widely held at all times and all places, whether a lot of delinquency or only a little occurs, and whether juveniles are harshly punished or leniently treated.

Presently, widespread concern exists that lenient treatment increases juvenile crime. But that concern tends to alternate in history with the opposite concern: that harsh punishment increases juvenile crime. Let us look at these two concerns historically.

Concern That Leniency Increases Juvenile Crime

People have always been concerned that lenient treatment increases crime among juveniles. This was a major point in the 1978 *Time* magazine article quoted above:

> When [a juvenile offender] is caught, the courts usually spew him out again. If he is under a certain age, 16 to 18 depending on the state, he is almost always taken to juvenile court, where he is treated as if he were still the child he is supposed to be. Even if he has murdered someone, he may be put away for only a few months. He is either sent home well before his term expires or he escapes, which, as the kids say, is "no big deal." Small wonder that hardened juveniles laugh, scratch, yawn, mug and even fall asleep while their crimes are revealed in court.[33]

Several years earlier, Ted Morgan argued a similar point in an article entitled "They Think, 'I Can Kill Because I'm 14'."[34] Ten years before that, J. Edgar Hoover similarly warned against the "misguided policies which encourage criminal activity, resulting in the arrogant attitude: "You can't touch me. I'm a juvenile!"[35]

Concern about Leniency in Earlier Times

Today, many people believe that leniency causes juvenile crime and blame the juvenile justice system for this leniency. They suggest that if juveniles were tried in adult courts and sent to adult institutions, the problem would be solved. But the juvenile justice system was originally established because the adult courts were believed to be too lenient on juveniles. This suggests that sending juveniles to the adult system will not necessarily result in harsher treatment.

Before the establishment of the first juvenile institution in New York City in 1825, only adult prisons were available for punishing juveniles. These were viewed as very harsh places that would increase the likelihood that juveniles would commit more crime. Prosecutors, judges, and juries in the criminal courts all naturally tried to avoid sending juvenile offenders to these institutions, with the result that many were freed with no punishment at all.[36]

The chief judge in New York was concerned that freeing these juveniles without any punishment encouraged them to commit further crime. He helped establish the first juvenile institution to receive these youngsters who otherwise would get off scot-free. One year after the establishment of the institution, the New York City District Attorney stated that the new institution had solved the problem.[37]

Around that same time, a "Report of the Committee for Investigating the Causes of the Alarming Increase of Juvenile Delinquency in the Metropolis" was issued in London that expressed similar concerns.[38] The problem, as it existed in both London and New York, was that only harsh punishments were available in the adult system, but that the natural tendency to provide more lenient treatments to juveniles resulted in many of them being let off without any punishment whatsoever. The juvenile justice system was originally invented to correct this problem: its goal was to provide some punishments for those who were receiving no punishments at all from the adult system.

Concern about Harshness Increasing Crime

Just as there have been concerns for a long time that leniency increases juvenile crime, there also have been concerns that harsh punishments increase juvenile crime. For example, many law-abiding adults committed at least some crimes when they were juveniles for which they might have been sent to an institution. Most of them were not caught or, if caught, received lenient treatment. Most of them then quit committing crimes, since their behavior was part of growing up.

Now suppose instead of this lenient treatment, they had been sent to an institution. Such harsh punishment might have increased the likelihood that they would continue to commit crimes in the future, rather than simply growing out of it. This is the purpose of leniency—to allow juveniles to "get out while the getting is good."

Concern about Harshness in Earlier Times

This has not just been a concern in recent times. For example, the judge in New York City in the early 1820s was quoted above as being concerned that letting juveniles off scot-free would encourage them to commit crime. That same judge was also concerned that sending juveniles to the prisons and jails would be "a fruitful source of pauperism, a nursery of new vices and crimes, a college for the perfection of adepts in guilt."[39] That is, this judge had to choose between providing harsh punishments or doing nothing at all, and he believed that both choices increased crime among juveniles.

A similar concern about harshness later provided the motivation for establishing the first juvenile court in Chicago in 1899. Because of an Illinois Supreme Court decision in 1870, lenient handling of juvenile offenders was severely restricted. This meant that juvenile justice officials faced the same dilemma as the earlier officials in New York City: they either had to provide harsh punishments to juvenile offenders or they could do nothing at all. Like the New York City judge, they believed that both choices increased crime among juveniles. The juvenile court was invented partly to provide lenient treatments for juveniles who were being harshly punished in Chicago's jails and poorhouses, and partly to provide lenient treatments for juveniles for whom nothing was being done at all in the adult courts.

Concern about Juvenile Justice Policy Stays the Same

If you think about the problem faced by officials in New York and London in the early 1800s and in Chicago in the late 1800s, then it becomes apparent that the concern that leniency causes juvenile crime and that harshness causes juvenile crime are really two sides of the same coin. Their relation is described by what Walker calls the "law of criminal justice thermodynamics":

> An increase in the severity of the penalty will result in less frequent application of the penalty.[40]

This "law" explains the basic problem faced by these officials.[41] Only harsh punishments were available to respond to juvenile crime. Some juveniles received those punishments, but others were let off because the punishments seemed inappropriate and counterproductive. In terms of the above "law," the penalties were so severe that they were infrequently applied.

Another way to phrase it is to say that *certainty and severity are enemies.* If you increase the severity of a penalty, you usually decrease the certainty with which it is applied. If you want to increase the certainty with which a penalty is applied, usually you must reduce its severity. This is exactly what criminal justice officials in London, New York, and Chicago did: they reduced the severity of penalties for juveniles in order to increase the certainty of applying them. That is, they established a "lenient" juvenile justice system.

The continual concern about the effectiveness of juvenile justice policies arises from this relationship between certainty and severity. If juvenile justice policies provide harsh punishments, then some juveniles will receive those punishments but others will receive no punishment at all because the punishments seem inappropriate and counterproductive. Concern about the effectiveness of these policies arises because both of these two choices are thought to increase crime.

But if the policies provide lenient treatments, then many juveniles receive the treatments but some laugh and feel free to commit serious crime with impunity. Concern about the effectiveness of these policies arises because people believe that if we had only "gotten tough" with these juveniles earlier, then the serious crimes would never have occurred.

The Cycle of Juvenile Justice

Juvenile offenders always are treated more leniently than adults who commit the same offenses, and juveniles who initially commit minor offenses are treated very leniently by the justice system. At least some of these juveniles go on to commit serious crimes. Many people conclude that these serious crimes would not have occurred *if* the juvenile had been punished severely for the earlier offenses. They argue that leniency encourages juveniles to laugh at the system, to believe they will not be punished no matter what they do, and to feel free to commit more frequent and serious crimes.

In response to these views, justice officials begin to "toughen up" their responses to juvenile offenders, and the "lenient" responses become less available. Some minor offenders receive the harsh punishments, but others are released because the harsh punishments seem ineffective and counterproductive.

Despite "getting tough," juvenile crime rates remain high (as they always do). Some minor offenders who received harsh punishments go on to commit serious crimes, along with some of those who were let off. This generates increased efforts to provide even harsher punishments. But as the penalties become more severe, they are less frequently applied: even more minor offenders are released with no punishment at all. The juvenile crime rate still remains high.

Throughout all of this, many people remain convinced that the "juvenile crime wave" began only recently, that it did not exist back in the "good old days," and that it can be ended through proper justice policies. Eventually, enough time passes so that the "good old days" was before the whole "get tough" movement began, when juvenile offenders were treated leniently.

Since they are now convinced that there was no problem of serious juvenile crime back then, they conclude that harsh punishments actually increase juvenile crime. Like the reformers in New York and London in the early 1800s and in Chicago in the late 1800s, they argue that these punishments embitter the juveniles, cut off their legitimate options, and teach them the ways of crime. They also argue that harsh punishments indirectly increase juvenile crime because so many juveniles are let off when only harsh punishments are available.

The juvenile system then is reformed to take account of this argument, and juvenile offenders once again receive lenient punishments. But juvenile crime rates remain high, adults remain convinced that the problem is recent and that it did not exist in the "good old days," and that it can be solved through proper justice policies. Eventually, enough time passes so that the "good old days" are back when officials "got tough" with juvenile offenders. Because people are now convinced that there was no problem with serious juvenile crime back then, they naturally conclude that the problem lies in the leniency with which juvenile offenders are now treated. A new reform movement then reintroduces harsh punishments.

The "cycle of juvenile justice" arises from the fact that juvenile crime rates remain high, regardless of justice policies that are in effect at the time. But many people arc always convinced that these high rates only occurred recently, that back in the "good old days" juvenile crime was low, and that juvenile crime would be low again if only we had the proper justice policies in effect. These people then generate continual pressure to abandon whatever justice policies are in effect at the time and replace them with new policies. Because only a limited number of policies are possible to begin with, the result is that the juvenile justice system tends to cycle back and forth between harshness and leniency.

This cycle cannot be broken by any particular juvenile justice policy since every conceivable policy confronts the same dilemma: after it is implemented, many people will continue to be convinced that juvenile crime is exceptionally high, that it was not a serious problem in the "good old days," and that it would not be a serious problem today if we only had the proper justice policies in effect.

This dilemma confronts not only our current juvenile justice system but also any conceivable organizational arrangement for processing juvenile offenders. Earlier organizational arrangements for processing juvenile offenders grappled with (and were discarded because of) the same dilemma. New and different organizational arrangements that might be created in the future to process juvenile offenders would soon confront the same dilemma.

Notes

[1] Travis Hirschi and Michael Gottfredson, "Age and the explanation of crime," *American Journal of Sociology*, 89:552–84 (1983). See also Frank R. Donovan, *Wild Kids*, Stackpole, Harrisburg, 1967 and Wiley B. Sanders, ed., *Juvenile Offenders for a Thousand Years*, University of North Carolina Press, Chapel Hill, 1970.

[2] Paul Strasburg, *Violent Juvenile Offenders: An Anthology*, NCCD, San Francisco, 1984.

[3] Negley K. Teeters and David Matza, "The Extent of Delinquency in the United States," pp. 2–15 in Ruth Shonle Cavan, ed., *Readings in Juvenile Delinquency*, Lippincott, Philadelphia, 1964;

Sophia M. Robison, *Juvenile Delinquency,* Holt, Rinehart and Winston, New York, 1960, Chapter 2; Walter C. Reckless and Mapheus Smith, *Juvenile Delinquency,* McGraw-Hill, New York, 1932, Chapter 2.

[4] Clyde B. Vedder, *The Juvenile Offender,* Doubleday, Garden City, NY, 1954, p. 26.

[5] The year 1952 was the first one in which the tables were labeled as representing arrests in cities with 2,500 or more population. This raises the possibility that some of the rise in the proportion of juvenile arrests might result from changes in data collection. See Teeters and Matza, op. cit.

[6] Philip J. Cook and John H. Laub, "Trends in Child Abuse and Juvenile Delinquency, " in Francis X. Hartmann, ed., *From Children to Citizens: The Role of the Juvenile Court,* Springer-Verlag, New York, 1987.

[7] Hibbert, op. cit., p. 433.

[8] Quoted in Teeters and Matza, op. cit., p. 4.

[9] James Gilbert, A *Cycle of Outrage,* Oxford, New York, 1986, pp. 24–26.

[10] James A. Inciardi, Alan A. Block, and Lyle A. Hallowell, *Historical Approaches to Crime,* Sage, Beverly Hills, 1977, pp. 59–89.

[11] These articles are described in Archer Butler Hulbert, "The Habit of Going to the Devil," *Atlantic Monthly* 138:804–6 (December, 1926). See Teeters and Matza, op. cit.

[12] Sanders, op. cit., p. 135.

[13] Hibbert, op. cit., p. 432.

[14] E.g., see Curt R. Bartol and Anne M. Bartol, *Juvenile Delinquency,* Prentice-Hall, Englewood Cliffs, 1989. For a review of theories of crime generally, see George B. Vold and Thomas J. Bernard, *Theoretical Criminology,* Oxford, New York, 1986.

[15] Exodus 21:15; Leviticus 20:9.

[16] John R. Sutton, *Stubborn Children,* University of California Press, Berkeley, 1988, p. 11. See also Lee E. Teitelbaum and Leslie J. Harris, "Some Historical Perspectives on Governmental Regulation of Children and Parents," in Teitelbaum and Aiden R. Gough, eds., *Beyond Control: Status Offenders in the Juvenile Court,* Ballinger, Cambridge, MA, 1977, pp. 1–44.

[17] Thomas C. Castellano, "The Justice Model in the Juvenile Justice System: Washington State's Experience," *Law & Policy* 8(4):479–506 (October, 1986).

[18] Ira M. Schwartz, *(In)justice for Juveniles,* D. C. Heath, Lexington, 1989, pp. 2–3.

[19] Gordon A. Raley and John E. Dean, "The Juvenile Justice and Delinquency Prevention Act: Federal Leadership in State Reform," *Law & Policy* 8(4):397–418 (October, 1986).

[20] Frederic L. Faust and Paul J. Brantingham, *Juvenile Justice Philosophy,* West, St. Paul, 1979, p. 460.

[21] Sir William Blackstone, *Commentaries on the Laws of England, IV,* London, 1795, p. 23.

[22] See H. Ted Rubin, *Juvenile Justice,* Random House, New York, 1985, Chapter 2.

[23] Donovan, op. cit., p. 11.

[24] Harvey Green, "Scientific Thought and the Nature of Children in America, 1820–1920," in A *Century of Childhood, 1820–1920,* Strong Museum, Rochester, NY, 1984, p. 121.

[25] Quoted in Gary F. Jensen and Dean G. Rojek, *Delinquency.* Heath, Lexington, 1980, p. 2.

[26] Samuel Noah Dramer, "A Father and His Perverse Son," *Crime and Delinquency* 3(2):169–73 (April, 1957).

[27] Anastasia Toufexis, "Our Violent Kids," *Time,* June 12, 1989, pp. 52–58. See also the editorial "Meltdown in our Cities," in *U. S. News and World Report,* May 29, 1989, for similar arguments.

[28] "The Youth Crime Plague," *Time* July 11, 1979, pp. 18–28.

[29] Hoover, op. cit. For a similar article written one year earlier, see Judith Viorst, "Delinquency! National Crisis," *Science News Letter,* 84:202–3 (September 28, 1963).

[30] "Our Vicious Young Hoodlums: Is There Any Hope?" *Newsweek Magazine* 44:43–44 (September 6, 1954).

[31] "The New Three Rs," *Time* 63(6):68–70 (March 15, 1954). This is based on a special series appear-

ing in the New York *Daily News* the preceding week.

[32] E.g., J. Edgar Hoover, "The Crime Wave We Now Face," *The New York Times Magazine,* April 21, 1946, pp. 26–27; "Children Without Morals," *Time* 40:24 (October 5, 1942); Leonard V. Harrison and Pryor M. Grant, *Youth in the Toils,* Macmillan, New York, 1939; Clyde A. Tolson, "Youth and Crime," *Vital Speeches* 2:468–72 (April 20, 1936); and "Youth Leads the Criminal Parade," *The Literary Digest,* 113:20 (April 23, 1932). For alarms raised in even earlier times, see Hulbert, op. cit.

[33] "Youth Crime Plague," op. cit.

[34] *New York Times Magazine,* January 19, 1975. A similar article appeared in the same magazine thirteen years earlier, but with an emphasis on the social causes of delinquency rather than on lenient treatment. See Ira Henry Freeman, "The Making of a Boy Killer," *New York Times Magazine,* February 18. 1962, pp. 14ff.

[35] Hoover, op. cit., p. 668.

[36] Robert M. Mennel, *Thorns and Thistles,* University Press of New England, Hanover, NH, 1973, pp. xxv–xxvi.

[37] Bradford Kinney Peirce, *A Half Century with Juvenile Delinquents,* Patterson-Smith, Montclair, 1969, p. 79.

[38] Sanders, op. cit., p. 111.

[39] Quoted in Peirce, op. cit., pp. 41–42.

[40] Samuel Walker, *Sense and Nonsense About Crime,* 2nd ed., Brooks/Cole, Pacific Grove, 1989, pp. 46–48.

[41] We face similar problems today. For example, homicide is punished more severely than any other crime. Franklin Zimring, Sheila O'Malley, and Joel Eigen ("Punishing Homicide in Philadelphia," *University of Chicago Law Review* 43:252, Winter, 1976) found that homicide defendants who did not receive a very severe punishment typically received little or no punishment at all. They concluded: "The problem is not that our system is too lenient or too severe; sadly, it is both." At the other end of the scale, minor delinquencies are punished the most leniently, and often result in diversion from the juvenile justice system. The problem here has been that, because the punishments are so lenient, they have tended to be very broadly applied. The phrase used to describe this is "widening the net"—i.e., diversion programs are compared to a fishing boat dragging an ever-widening net that sweeps up more and more fish. See James Austin and Barry Krisberg, "Wider, Stronger, and Different Nets," *Journal of Research in Crime and Delinquency* 18:165–96 (1981).

Section II

Sources of Delinquency

Why some youth become delinquent and others do not remains a mystery. What is increasingly clear is that simple explanations are inadequate. The causes of human behavior, including delinquency, are complex, and predicting whether any one child will become delinquent is nearly impossible. It is true, however, that we have a better understanding of those influences that increase the risk of delinquency or protect children from it. These include early life experiences, events that take place in the school, the way in which children are treated by their parents, and the influence of peers. The chapters in this section consider these influences and their implications for delinquency and antisocial behavior.

Recent evaluations of delinquency prevention programs suggest the importance of very early childhood experiences and of early intervention. In "Tracing the Roots of Violence," Robin Karr-Morse and Meredith S. Wiley show that experiences in the first two years of life not only shape later behavior, but influence the "wiring" of the brain. By permanently changing the way the brain works, these early experiences have an impact that can last a lifetime. By the time a child has reached adolescence, a biological pattern may have been set that can be difficult to change through either treatment or punishment.

School occupies a large part of the lives of most adolescents. Although most kids are probably safer in school than in their homes, school crime has drawn national attention. Richard Lawrence's chapter "School Crime and Juvenile Justice" shows that the issue of schools and delinquency has many dimensions. Lawrence begins by considering whether schools are a source of delinquency or simply reflect problems that young people face in their communities and their homes. He then describes the extent of school crime and the link between offending and victimization in the schools. The impact of dropping out of school on delinquency and the role that schools can play in responding to the delinquency problem are also considered, as are the problems associated with balancing the rights of students with society's interest in school safety. This chapter makes clear that understanding and responding to school crime are difficult and complex tasks.

In "Private Pain and Public Behaviors," Robin Robinson uses interviews with delinquent girls to illustrate the link between childhood sexual abuse and delinquency. The observations of these delinquent girls not only reveal the devastating impact of abuse, but they also show how the line between victim and offender can be blurry for many juvenile offenders. This research also reminds us of the great challenges facing juvenile justice and the difficulty of "fixing" intractable problems.

In the final article in this section, "Features of Gang Violence," Scott Decker draws on a three-year field study of gangs to consider the role of violence in both the origins and the growth of gangs. This chapter also examines the circumstances under which gangs engage in violence, noting that violence in a particular gang is not continuous, but ebbs and flows. Decker suggests a seven-step process to explain cycles of gang violence, and he considers structural factors in the gang that shape any particular gang's involvement in violence. Finally, the chapter makes clear that violence can serve many functions in the life of a gang, such as increasing the solidarity of gang members and the forming of new gangs as offshoots of existing ones.

3

Tracing the Roots of Violence

Robin Karr-Morse and Meredith S. Wiley

Seemingly normal at birth, Chelsea was born more than forty years ago in a small coastal town in the Pacific Northwest. But unknown to her parents— and to a host of doctors who by school age evaluated her as retarded— Chelsea was deaf. She was isolated in school, where she was classified as being of low intelligence. It wasn't until she was thirty-one years old that a neurologist recognized her real disability and had her fitted with a hearing aid. Now Chelsea is an active member of her community. She works in a veterinary clinic. The only problem is that after fifteen years of therapy and with normal intelligence, she still cannot speak intelligibly. Chelsea is living testimony to the lesson that in human brain development, there is a critical period for spoken language. Because her brain was deprived of the sounds she needed to hear at a crucial time, the physical connections necessary for organizing speech in coherent sentences have forever been lost to her. Chelsea will never master normal sentence construction.[1]

Ryan was born to an unmarried college student who decided that the best future for her baby would be secured by placing him with married parents through adoption. However, the adoption agency, unaware at that time of the importance of earliest attachment, was concerned about Ryan's irregular heartbeat. A response to anesthesia his mother had received for her cesarean delivery, the arrhythmia disappeared fairly quickly. But since medical assurances were paramount to the agency, it placed Ryan in a

Karr-Morse, Robin and Meredith S. Wiley. 1997 *Ghosts from the Nursery: Tracing the Roots of Violence.* (Excerpt from book: Chapter 2: Grand Central: Early Brain Anatomy and Violence)

private foster home where, without the social worker's knowledge, the foster mother was taking care of nine other children under age three.

Ryan lay in a crib day after day. He drank cold milk from bottles that were propped to feed him. He heard the sounds of the other children, but he rarely saw an adult face. He was handled infrequently; his diapers went unchanged for most of the day. He developed a full-body rash, a bleeding diaper rash, cradle cap, ear infections in both ears, and, most fearsome, an unwillingness to be held or to look at an adult face. At nine weeks, when Ryan was finally placed in his adoptive home, he would turn away from efforts to engage him, staring instead at a bright light or shining object. He had gained weight normally and, in spite of his rash, was a handsome, red-haired baby. But he did not want to be touched. If he cried, he preferred to lie on a flat space, where he would comfort himself. Ryan was not autistic. He was twice separated from major caregivers and severely neglected. What his brain had missed was touch, trust, and reciprocal contact with a parent. Now twenty-five years old, Ryan looks normal. He is a college student and works full-time. But he is still somewhat withdrawn, and his relationships with people, while improving each year, are superficial and lack spontaneity. Trust is still precarious for Ryan. Touch is still measured.

Neither Chelsea nor Ryan is a violent individual in spite of early losses. Both were raised in loving homes and environments that were protective and prosocial. But Chelsea and Ryan remind us that there are "critical periods" and sensitive periods for several key aspects of human development, including the ability to trust or to feel connected to other people. While we might like to believe that given sufficient opportunity we can reverse any damage done to children, the research tells us that the effects of some early experiences cannot be undone.

Scientists use two terms to describe these specifically timed processes. "Critical periods" is a phrase used to describe a window of time in which a specific part of the brain is open to stimulation, after which it closes forever. In human development, neurobiological researchers have confirmed two functions that develop in such critical periods—vision and spoken language. Both fall into a very specific "use it or lose it" opportunity in early life. "Sensitive periods" is a phrase used primarily by psychologists to describe a less precise period of time when it appears that key functions are strongly affected but may not be lost forever. Examples of these functions include the acquisition of a second language and math and logic development.

The enormous power of human experience in shaping the brain has only been gradually accepted following the pioneering work of Dr. David Hubel and Dr. Torsten Wiesel, done nearly forty years ago. The doctors sewed shut one eye of newborn kittens to test the effects of sensory deprivation. When the sewn eyes were opened a few weeks later, they were permanently blinded. But the eyes that had remained open could see better than normal eyes. No amount of visual stimulation following this experience could restore sight in the blind eyes. The same procedures performed in adult cats did not result in this rewiring. The doctors received a Nobel Prize for their landmark finding that sensory experience is essential to teach developing brain cells their jobs and that there is a short and early critical period for connecting the retina to the visual cortex, beyond which the opportunity is forever lost.

Babies born with cataracts have taught us that this dependence on environmental input is also true for humans in the development of vision. Babies with cataracts who did not receive surgery in the earliest months grew up blind because the brain cells that would normally process vision died or were called to work elsewhere. By four months of age, babies totally deprived of vision from birth are blind. Children who grow up alone or in the wild without exposure to language until age ten cannot ever learn to speak. In addition, when a baby is deprived of hearing human voices, the connections that allow brain cells to process sound, and consequently language, can become ineffectual. Instead of the neat columns of cells that are characteristic of normal brain structure, the cells are scrambled. The resulting aberrant formation of the cells that provide the biological underpinnings of speech may cause language disorders and in some cases may result in childhood seizures and epilepsy.[2]

While the last decade has shown that the developing brain retains great "plasticity," including the ability to offset damages in most areas, there are exceptions. And the exceptions primarily occur with key systems developing in earliest childhood. We used to believe that the brain and its activity were set on course and developed on a path controlled entirely by heritable genetic programming. From this perspective, we believed that the brain like any other organ grew to its genetically predestined size and function uninterrupted from the outside world except by injury or disease or the influence of drugs. A burst of new research in the last decade has shown us conclusively that this is far from reality. To the surprise of no one who has specialized in observing the rapid pace of fetal and newborn development, the new technologies show the rest of us some previously unimaginable truths about human brain growth.

The most amazing result of all has been the portrait that emerges of the brain itself. Far from the preset, isolated, and independently functioning organ pictured in our biology texts of a decade ago, the brain is, in fact, a dynamic organism that is constantly reflecting and adjusting to the environment the individual is experiencing. While genetics do set the broad parameters, actual matter in the brain is built—or not—by sound, sight, smell, touch, and movement from the outside environment. By the eighteenth week of gestation, when the brain is still primitive, the fetus has developed all of the one hundred to two hundred billion basic brain cells or neurons that it will ever have in a lifetime. But by birth, connecting structures (dendrites and synapses) between those nerve cells have just started to form. Those connections now depend on the outside environment for completion. Stimulation from the baby's world actually generates the building of the corresponding systems to process that stimulation in the baby's brain. Seeing people and objects, for example, generates the building of dendritic and synaptic growth in the visual cortex; hearing sounds builds the auditory cortex; and so forth.

Both the matter of the brain and to some degree the function this matter performs are generated by exposure to stimulation. Because we are each different genetically and because each of our environments is different, no two brains are exactly alike. Babies who are talked to and read to or who are exposed to more than one language are building a different set of connections than those who are receiving primarily large-muscle stimulation—patty-cake, prewalking games, etc. While there are scientists such as Dr. Frank Kiel of Cornell University who believe that the brain comes prewired with some concepts, such as a preference for a human face over inanimate objects, there is general agreement in the scientific community that even before birth the brain is shaped by stimulation from the environment. After birth, development is an interactive process between the baby's physiology and his or her environment.

The dependence of the human brain on the environment for its growth begins to make sense when one considers the purpose of the brain in all organisms. The primary goal of the brain is to enable the organism to survive. The key to survival and to human dominance on the planet is our ability to adapt to the kind of environment in which we find ourselves. Live video photographs can now show us that both the organic matter and the chemistry of the human brain change in response to our environments to allow us to cope with variables in our worlds. The parts of the brain that grow and the parts that don't depend on the baby's experience. Dr. Bruce Perry calls this phenomenon "use-dependent development."

So the genes provide the blueprints and lay down the basic framework of the brain. But the shaping and finishing within that framework is facilitated by the environment. As Ronald Kotulak said in his Pulitzer Prize-winning series on brain development published in 1993 in the *Chicago Tribune*:

> They work in tandem, with genes providing the building blocks, and the environment acting like an on-the-job foreman, providing instructions for final construction. . . . Sounds, sights, smells, touch— like little carpenters—all can quickly change the architecture of the brain, and sometimes they can turn into vandals. . . . The discovery that the outside world is indeed the brain's real food is truly intriguing. The

brain gobbles up its external environment in bits and chunks through its sensory system: vision, hearing, smell, touch and taste. . . . The digested world is reassembled in the form of trillions of cells that are constantly growing or dying, or becoming stronger or weaker, depending on the richness of the banquet.

Our familiar global measures of children's systematic development, like head circumference and behavioral milestones such as crawling, walking, and talking, are now validated and enhanced by new graphic, computer-generated techniques that enable us to view precise functions in the developing brain. What we are now able to see is the physiology that accompanies and shapes these behavioral milestones. The newly achieved behaviors in turn catalyze the next round of physiological development. Behavior and neurobiological activity are inextricably linked and are, in a sense, two aspects of the same happening.

Perhaps the greatest advantage of the neurophysiological research is its potential to predict or anticipate corresponding behavioral changes. Dr. Harry Chugani of the University of Michigan uses PET scans to measure the metabolism of glucose by the developing brain. He has learned that high rates of glucose use in regions of the brain correspond with periods of rapid overproduction of synapses and nerve terminals. When glucose metabolism declines, this signals the selective elimination, or "pruning," of excess connections and marks a decline in developmental plasticity. This pattern of proliferation and pruning is then followed by a period of reorganization, when newly formed connections are integrated into existing systems. Dr. Geraldine Dawson of the University of Washington and Dr. Kurt Fischer of Harvard University describe at least thirteen of these levels or stages of brain development. They believe that one stage builds directly on the last, so that later infancy skills are built on those established in early infancy and so on. More than half of these levels occur in the first twenty-four months of life.[3]

The implications of this new understanding are both promising and discomforting. While the human baby is born with literally trillions of unprogrammed circuits just waiting to be stimulated into great poetry or science or music, there is the reality that for many key capacities, circuits not used may die. The experiences of a child will determine the circuits connected. In an article published in February 1996 in *Newsweek,* Sharon Begley, having interviewed several prominent neurobiologists, wrote, "They suggest that, with the right input at the right time, almost anything is possible. But they imply that if you miss the window, you're playing with a handicap."

When What You See Is What You Get

Like a tapestry constantly being woven, the brain responds to the world around it. While this adaptability is clearly an evolutionary asset, the brain's dependence on the environment can also have devastating results. When the stimulation is nonexistent or aberrant, opportunities can be lost or muted. While there presently are only a few known critical periods for the development of key capacities, research is showing that the first thirty-three months is the most profound time of opportunities. Scientists are now measuring and documenting these opportunities—or the lack of them—not just in discernible behavioral differences but also in concrete terms such as brain weight.

Several years ago, Dr. William Greenough at the University of Illinois at Champaign-Urbana exposed young rats to enriched environments full of toys, exercise equipment, food, and playmates. On autopsy he found that the enriched rats had 25 percent more connections between brain cells than those rats raised in standard laboratory cages. The brains were actually larger and weighed more. Dr. Craig Ramey at the University of Alabama found that he could produce similar results with studies done on children. Beginning with babies as young as six weeks of age, he exposed a group of impoverished inner-city children to a daily environment that included learning, toys, playmates, and good nutrition. The enriched children were found to have higher IQs than the control group of children from a similar background. The study also found a lower rate of mental retardation and developmental difficulties in the enriched group.

In an interview with the authors, Ramey stated:

> In at least eleven separate studies [comparing high-risk children with those who do not receive intervention], we have data to show that, if you do not intervene before twenty-four months, these children will be seriously developmentally delayed.[4] And we have no data to show that we can reverse the majority of these delays.[5]

In three related studies spanning thirty years of research, Ramey has demonstrated that the timing and targeting of early intervention makes all the difference. Concerned about the lack of sustained gains in follow-up studies on children in Head Start, where gains in IQ tend to fade after about three years, Ramey makes a strong case for beginning earlier, in the first months of life, when the neurological circuits for learning words and sound are being built. He began his Abecedarian project in 1972 as an experiment to test whether mental retardation coming from inadequate environments could be prevented. The interventions included intensive high-quality pre-school programs combined with medical and nutritional supports beginning shortly after birth and continuing until children entered kindergarten. The researchers assigned children from 120 impoverished families into one of four groups: intensive early education in a day care center from age four months to eight years; from four months to five years; from five to eight years; and none (control group).

Among these families, all of whom were poor, the researchers discovered that the factors that most placed children at risk of cognitive delays or mental retardation had to do with the parents' educational histories and their intellectual and language abilities. The single strongest predictor of all is the mother's tested level of intelligence. In the Abecedarian project, of the control-group children, all of whom had mothers with IQs less than seventy, all but one child emerged in grade school retarded or of borderline intelligence. In the intervention groups, children who, beginning at four months, participated in the program five days a week, fifty weeks a year, all tested within the normal range by age three—an average of twenty points higher than children in the control group. When children did not receive intervention until after age five, 86 percent tested below an IQ of eighty-five. Ramey's research has conclusively shown that interventions that begin at birth and are provided during the preschool years, but not later, have a measurable impact on children's development, which is sustained to age fifteen. In a recent follow-up study with Dr. Frances Campbell, Ramey reported that children who were enrolled early in the Abecedarian project still scored higher in reading and in math by five points at age fifteen than did children who did not receive intervention. Ramey believes that early enrollment in the enriched day care is key to these enduring gains. Children enrolled after the age of five showed no sustained gains in IQ or academic performance. In an interview reported by Ronald Kotulak in his *Chicago Tribune* brain development series, Ramey stated:

> The quality of the environment and the kind of experiences children have may affect brain structure and function so profoundly that they may not be correctable after age five. If we had a comparable level of knowledge with respect to a particular form of cancer or hypertension or some other illness that affected adults, you can be sure we would be in action with great vigor.

Neurobiologists studying how the brain develops give us insight into how Ramey's observations occur biologically. Dr. Charles Nelson of the University of Minnesota studies how the brain changes from experience. As mentioned earlier dendritic and synaptic nerve connections are overproduced and the brain "prunes" those not properly reinforced by stimulation. Nelson refers to this process of overproduction, selective stimulation, and pruning as an "information capture mechanism." This learning process allows the organism to shape itself in accordance with the variables consistently occurring in the environment and to specialize its responses accordingly. If the information is distorted, so is the development.

Dr. Greenough explains critical periods—such as that for vision—in terms of Nelson's information capture mechanisms. The critical period occurs because the cells for capturing certain information are there on a time-limited basis before they are pruned or used elsewhere. Greenough postulates that information capture mechanisms may also be set in place neurologically to allow the animal to adapt and incorporate the responses appropriate to specific social environments. He believes that if inappropriate experiences (e.g., abuse) occur or if appropriate experiences do not occur—especially when these are combined with biological factors such as attention-deficit/hyperactivity disorder—later behavior is likely to reflect this early programmed distortion on a sustained basis. Dr. H. F. Harlow's classic work with monkeys is one example of the information capture process at work in the arena of social development. Baby monkeys separated from their mothers at birth, nursing from a cloth-covered wire substitute mother, were deprived of mutual emotional exchanges with a live, nursing, mother monkey. Although the little monkeys received adequate nutrition, the neurons available for reciprocal social communication were not stimulated. As a result, wire-mothered baby monkeys became agitated and withdrawn and had difficulties relating to other monkeys. This pattern of social incompetence continued throughout their lives.

Building upon the work of Dr. Nelson, Dr. Greenough postulates that the brain not only adapts but also orchestrates a pattern of changes throughout the organism in response to repetitive stimulation. Learning a new athletic skill is an example of this process; a series of changes occur beyond physical conditioning. Greenough's studies on rats show that when something new is learned, there is a synaptic reorganization of the brain. In the motor cortex, nerve cells begin to form additional connections that encode the general skill. Tissue and blood cells are added, making the whole brain better equipped for new skills. The changes that occur are not limited to the brain; they also affect the spinal column and muscles. The brain adapts to the specific changes by orchestrating a cascading pattern of changes.

The size of a toddler's vocabulary is a more concrete example of the early developmental opportunities afforded by the information capture process. Dr. Janellin Huttenlocher of the University of Chicago has demonstrated that when socioeconomic factors are equal, babies whose mothers talk to them more have a bigger vocabulary.

At twenty months, babies of talkative mothers knew 131 more words than the infants of less talkative mothers. At twenty-four months the difference was 295 words. Regardless of the words used, exposure to the sounds of human speech builds the circuitry in the infant brain that creates the path for more words to be absorbed. Repeated exposure actually builds the physiological capacity. The more words the child hears by age one, the larger vocabulary at age two.[6]

The cognitive advantages of early intellectual stimulation carry forward as a child reaches school age. From the earliest months of life, babies who are encouraged by caregivers to take an interest in their environments and to explore their world through vision, touch, and hearing score higher on cognitive and language tests both at preschool and at grade school. Dr. Peter Huttenlocher, also at the University of Chicago, has shown that the power of a brain grows in direct relationship to the number of neurons and the number of connections between the cells it contains. The linkages between neurons (synapses) are the connections that make the brain work. Huttenlocher counted these connections during autopsies and found that a tissue sample the size of the head of a pin from a twenty-eight-week-old fetus contains 124 million connections. A newborn sample has 253 million connections, while a sample from an eight-month-old has 572 million. Connections are the most prolific in the beginning of life and start to slow down in production at the end of the first year, tapering off at 354 million connections per sample at age twelve.[7]

The fetal stage and the first two years of life are the period of most rapid brain growth. During early development the brain produces many more cells and connections than it can use. Which cells survive and what a brain can or cannot do are determined by what a child learns in the first decade of life. Proceeding cumulatively from the beginning, the opportunity to nurture synaptic growth and retention is at its greatest during this early time. It is at this time that we have the greatest possible potential to directly enhance the quality of brain power ultimately applied to language or music or social, emotional, math, or logic skills. Yet the educational system in this country begins at age five. The fundamental wiring of the brains of our future workforce occurs—or not—before we are paying attention.

The last decade of brain research has clearly demonstrated that the best time for children to learn a second language is in early grade school, not high school. As we learn about brain systems and their maturation, there is growing evidence that preschool rather than higher education ought to be the focus of our most creative educational strategies, including interventions to stem emotional and cognitive disabilities that can undermine learning from the time of birth.

In a recent television interview on *Prime Time Live,* Diane Sawyer discussed the subject of critical periods in brain development with Dr. Michael Phelps, who co-invented the brain-imaging technique called the PET scan. Phelps was quoted by Sawyer as saying: "The development years are not just a chance to educate, they're actually your obligation to form a brain and if you miss these opportunities then, you've missed them—forever."

The program concluded with poignant images of caged songbirds while in voiceover Sawyer said: "At Rockefeller University, there is a birdcage and it's quiet. The scientists tell us that they've learned that when baby song-birds like these don't hear a parent singing, when they grow up, they will never learn to sing."[8]

From the Bottom Up

Anatomically, the brain can be divided into four basic parts: the brain stem, the midbrain, the limbic brain, and the cortex. These parts develop in a hierarchical progression, starting with simple and gradually moving to more complex functions. This development begins with the brain stem, which controls the basic and most essential functions necessary to sustain life, including involuntary functions like blood pressure, heart rate, and body temperature. Next to develop is the midbrain, which controls appetite and sleep, among other things. Then comes the limbic brain, which is the seat of emotion and impulse. And, finally, the cortex, where logic, plan-ning, and cognition—the executive functions—take place, is developed. Each of these parts of the brain is responsive to the environment, or use-dependent, according to Dr. Perry, and will be shaped by the individual's unique experience of his or her surroundings.

When we seek to understand violent behavior from the perspective of brain anatomy, we find some surprising realities. First of all, violent impulses are generated in the lower parts of the brain, particularly the limbic system. Under conditions of extreme threat or rage, when the brain is flooded with stress hormones, the "fight or flight" human is not under the governance of the analytical cortex, the seat of rationality and wisdom. Under those extreme conditions, it is the limbic brain and midbrain which are quickest to respond to mobilize the individual. This biological process is well understood by the army. The constant drill and practice in boot camp to prepare for combat is deliberately directed at the limbic brain. The training of new recruits for war conditions, where instantaneous and pre-cise action is called for, must bypass the analytical and time-consuming cortical functions. Even those of us who have never served in the military have our own experiences with the body's response to emergency or threat and can recall moments of freezing or running when normal rational thoughts were totally unavailable to us until fear or fury subsided. Dr. Perry succinctly explains that our ability to think before we act is related to the ratio between the excitatory activity of the primitive areas of the brain and the moderating efforts of the cortical or higher areas:

> Any factors which increase the activity or reactivity of the brainstem
> (e.g., chronic stress) or decrease the moderating capacity of the limbic

or cortical areas (e.g., neglect) will increase an individual's aggressivity, impulsivity and capacity to display violence.[9]

This understanding of the stress response system and its impact on brain development has huge implications for working with people with attentional or impulsive disabilities. For children with developmental disabilities or damage (e.g., attention-deficit/hyperactivity disorder or post-traumatic stress disorder), cognitively based therapies may be an exercise in futility. To be effective, interventions need to be directed at the limbic and midbrain levels.

Violent behavior is most likely to occur when a young child's experiences result in lack of adequate stimulation to the cortex—the system for modulation and control—together with overstimulation of the alarm system. The check-and-balance system in the brain may be thrown off. According to Perry, if those experiences are chronic and occur early enough, a state of hyperarousal or of numbing may become a permanent trait in a child, setting the stage for a host of learning and behavioral problems. This is when we build the blueprint. These months are the time of greatest access and potential—and vulnerability—for creating competent and balanced responses to the stressors all children to one degree or another will face in our society.

Alarm Central: The Limbic System

The limbic system lies wrapped at the center of the protective layers of the cortex. The cortex, with its more advanced rational and uniquely human capacities, sits above the limbic brain ready to edit, adapt, and analyze the impulsive behavior originating from this ancient source of fight-or-flight mobilization. Central to the limbic system is the amygdala, from the Greek word for almond. This structure generates strong emotional signals, acting, according to neurophysiologist Joseph LeDoux, as an "emotional guardian." LeDoux's research on the role of the amygdala has clarified how impulsive behavior can occur without rational processing or even awareness. According to LeDoux, under conditions of great emotional excitement, signals from the amygdala may, by design, bypass the neocortex, the rational and strategic part of the brain. This seems to be nature's insurance in case of a need for immediate action in the face of serious threat. In a description of this process in his book *Emotional Intelligence*, Daniel Goleman writes: "In the brain's architecture, the amygdala is poised something like an alarm company where operators stand ready to send out emergency calls to the fire department, police, and a neighbor whenever a home security system signals trouble."[10]

When a sight or a sound signals a strong negative or painful association such as Dad's entry into the bedroom at night followed by sexual violation, the amygdala won't necessarily wait for analysis by the thoughtful neocortex before, upon again hearing Dad's footsteps in the room, it floods the brain with neurochemicals for fight or flight. The more the painful connection is experienced, the more quickly the limbic alarm response will be triggered. The entry of any man into the bedroom at any time may come to trigger the response. If stimulated intensely or often enough, this alerting system may not subside. Hypervigilance may be the result, so that the individual becomes extremely sensitive to associated cues—such as the sound of heavy footsteps—that warn of oncoming threat. Dr. Perry believes that this kind of trauma occurring often enough or intensely enough can rob a very young child of the ability to learn normally by pulling circuitry meant for other tasks to monitoring for threatening cues in the environment. Initially, these occurrences induce chronically fearful states of hyperarousal in children. If the child is too young to be able to run or resist, she or he will develop a "surrender" or dissociative response. Neurochemical and hormonal responses enable children to go numb or freeze and remove themselves emotionally. Over time, such states may become integrated as traits in the developing child. These can be difficult neurological patterns to change and may inflict permanent damage depending on the age of the child and the type, intensity, frequency, and duration of the trauma.[11]

Impairment or injury may also affect the activity of the limbic system. In normal individuals, the emergency response generated by the amygdala is held in check by the neocortical process, specifically the left prefrontal lobe. Goleman refers to the role played by this area of the brain as a "neural thermostat." Impairment or injury may result in an inability to modulate the signals from the amygdala and related limbic structures. The consequence is highly impulsive behavior, unchecked momentarily by reason. People whose behavior is affected by this neurobiological abnormality are at great risk for school failure, drug abuse, and criminality—not because they lack intelligence, but because they have a limited ability to control their behavior. Strong negative emotions like rage or jealousy can suddenly heat up and overrun the entire system—emotion can overtake rationality.

Researchers, including Dr. Frank Wood of Wake Forest University and Dr. Adrian Raine of the University of Southern California, assert that they can see a characteristic pattern of underactivation of the prefrontal lobe together with excessive activity in the region of the limbic system in the brains of impulsive killers. Emotionally charged memories may be stored in the limbic system and may be restimulated—often years later. The neural alarm system is often imprecise or out of date, and, since it acts without rational (cortical) screening, behavior may appear totally out of context in the present circumstances.

There is a great deal of speculation about the possible causes of this kind of brain abnormality. The hypotheses range from injury to the prefrontal lobes to genetic causes. What we know is that children with early discernible impulse-control problems, such as attention-deficit/hyperactivity disorder (ADHD), are at considerably higher risk of later violent behavior when the problem is left untreated, or is treated only by stimulant medication. Negative outcomes for these children are greatly increased when ADHD is exacerbated by familial or environmental factors such as maternal rejection, child abuse, or the modeling of violent solutions to everyday problems.

The Mind Body Synthesizer: The Orbitofrontal Cortex

An area of the brain that is receiving increasing attention in relation to infant development is the orbitofrontal cortex. This part of the brain connects the cortex to the limbic system and is critically involved in the regulation of emotions. Here sensory input of all kinds—vision, hearing, touch, taste, and smell—is connected with our visceral body sensations. This is the area responsible for our "gut reactions" to people and events—our earliest associations between experiences in the outside world and our internal physical responses. Dr. Allan Schore, of the Department of Psychiatry and Biobehavioral Sciences at the UCLA School of Medicine, views the orbitofrontal cortex as the key area involved in both infant attachment and emotional regulation, the failure of which can result in impulsive violence.

The orbitofrontal cortex (so called because it sits just above the orbit of the eyes) is positioned at the undersurface and between the two cerebral hemispheres.[12] This area represents a central point of convergence of the cortex and subcortex. Because of its unique anatomical location, it receives both sensory stimulation (vision, touch, sound, smell) from the external social environment and visceral information concerning the body's internal environment, so that interpersonal experiences can be associated with emotional and motivational states.

According to Schore, all of the connections between the cortex and the subcortex are regulated by this particular area. As a result, sensory information from the environment, such as the expression on the mother's face and the tone of her voice, is associated in the baby's experience with the physical sensations the baby is simultaneously experiencing, such as intense pleasure and excitement or fear and discomfort. When this goes awry, for example, when a baby "fails to thrive" or fails to gain weight, stops growing, and seems to lose interest in living, this is the area of the

brain responsible for the linkages between sensual and emotional deprivation and the physical symptoms that result.

The orbitofrontal areas contain neurons that are especially sensitive to
the emotional expressions on the human face, which is a primary source of
information sent and received in social situations. The orbitofrontal cortex
is particularly expanded in the right hemisphere, which connects deeply
into the limbic system, where positive and negative emotions are generated.
In fact, this part of the cortex sends direct connections to all the lower
limbic areas, including the amygdala. Because it is the only part of the
cortex that projects directly to the hypothalamus and autonomic centers
deep in the brain stem, the orbitofrontal cortex acts as a central control
center over both the sympathetic and the parasympathetic nervous systems,
which generate the bodily components of emotional behavior.

Schore points out that the critical period for the development of this
system exactly coincides with the time period extensively investigated by
attachment researchers. He emphasizes that the maturation of the orbitofrontal system is experience dependent: it is directly influenced by the
nature of the attachment relationship. The child's first relationship, typically with the mother, acts as a template for the imprinting of circuits in the
child's developing, emotion-processing right brain. Schore believes that
this is the biological root of the shaping of the individual's adaptive or
maladaptive capacities to enter into all later emotional relationships. If
Schore is right, an early relationship with an emotionally attuned primary
caregiver who regulates the baby's physical and emotional states provides a
growth-promoting environment for the infant's developing orbitofrontal
cortex. Conversely, early experiences with an emotionally unresponsive or
abusive caregiver can inhibit the maturation of this system. Schore concludes that a negative early relationship can lead to a lifelong limited
ability, especially under stress, to regulate the intensity, frequency, and
duration of primitive negative states such as rage, terror, and shame. Schore
states:

> There is now evidence that the orbitofrontal areas show a preferential
> vulnerability to a spectrum of later forming psychiatric disorders,
> including sociopathic and character disorders that display antisocial
> behaviors and problems with impulse control.[13]

We did not understand the significance of the orbitofrontal cortex until
the 1940s, when lobotomies were performed experimentally for a time to
control extremely emotional individuals. A lobotomy essentially amounts
to the disconnection of the orbitofrontal area and results in the total loss of
emotionality. While intelligence is unaffected by a lobotomy, the individual
loses his or her "personality"—and the ability to relate emotionally. Nor-

mal emotional responses are flattened or absent.

Recently this area of the brain has been highlighted in studies of Vietnam veterans who suffer from post-traumatic stress disorder (PTSD). Dr. J. Douglas Bremner, a psychiatrist at Yale, showed slides of Vietnam battle scenes to two groups of veterans, one group of whom suffered from PTSD and one of whom did not. Computerized x-rays (PET scans) that measure the rate of glucose metabolized in different areas of the brain were used to indicate which parts of the brain were functioning during the viewing of the slides. By contrast to those with PTSD, the orbitofrontal area in non-traumatized veterans was highly active, enabling them to distinguish "real" from reenacted scenes. Dr. Bremner explained this process in a recent article published in *The New Yorker.*

> The orbitofrontal region is the part of your brain that evaluates the primal feelings of fear and anxiety which come up from the brain's deeper recesses. It's the part that tells you that you're in a hospital watching a slide show of the Vietnam War, not in Vietnam living through the real thing. The vets with PTSD weren't using that part of their brain. That's why every time a truck backfires or they see a war picture in a major magazine they are forced to relive their wartime experiences: they can't tell the difference.[14]

Gone But Not Forgotten: The Amygdala and Memory

Since babies have neither language nor reason and since most of us have no conscious memories of our lives before age two, it would seem to make sense that this time has little influence on our present functioning. This is the logic we have traditionally used to dismiss the role of our earliest experiences. But neuroscientist Dr. Joseph LeDoux points out that the amygdala, together with the hippocampus in the limbic brain, may explain what analysts have been telling us for years: that the events in early life, particularly those experienced with strong emotion, can and do remain an influence throughout our lives. Memory, as it turns out, is not just a matter of rational or even verbal recall. We also have a nonverbal, essentially emotional memory, particularly for experiences, events, and people that carry a strong emotional valence.

Sensual experience (auditory, visual, tactile, and olfactory) typically travels first to the neocortex for analysis. But when perceptions are accompanied by strong emotional impact, particularly those perceived as life threatening, they may bypass the neocortex and send a message directly to the amygdala, which mobilizes the organism for fight or flight. All of this can happen in an instant—and without input from rational processing by the neocortex.

Studies done by Dr. LeDoux in 1989 that exposed rats to fear-inducing visual stimuli provide strong evidence that the amygdala matures very early in life, so that emotional messages can be processed before cognition. In addition, LeDoux found that these fear-based associations experienced early were difficult to erase, even when the sensory cortex was later completely severed. According to LeDoux, early experienced precognitive emotions continue to play out in later life even though the individual may have no conscious memory of the association.[15]

Dr. George Engel documented this process at work in a thirty-year longitudinal study of "Monica."[16] Monica was a child born with congenital atresia of the esophagus, a condition that precluded her being fed by mouth. For the first two days after birth she choked and regurgitated her feedings. On the third day a feeding tube was inserted into her stomach. For two years she was fed through the tube while lying flat on her back without holding or contact of any kind. She was in fact frequently fed "while crying, fussing or playing" and did not participate in the process. A tube placed in her neck to continuously drain the saliva limited how Monica could be held. Her mother subsequently became depressed and withdrew from her baby. Monica became unresponsive and for a while showed a failure to thrive.

At age two, Monica was hospitalized for nine months while her esophagus was reconstructed. She began to receive oral feedings either lying flat on her back or propped in her crib. Her mother and the nurses still rarely held her. After she returned home, she was able to eat normally. She grew up with no conscious memories of her early tube feedings; she was told by her mother much later that she had been fed by a tube in her abdomen as a baby.

Engel and his associates continued to observe Monica as she grew. As a little girl she fed her dolls in the exact position she herself had experienced, flat on their backs without holding or contact of any kind. Engel also noted that her conversations with the dolls indicated preconscious memories of her earlier experiences. She would place the dolls down on the bed and stand at their side. At four years of age she said to one, "Poor baby, you ain't got a mouth." She also talked about the dolls "leaking at the neck," where she herself had experienced the early drainage tube.

When Monica babysat as a teenager, she fed her charges in the same strange way. When she had children of her own, in spite of having observed her mother feeding her younger siblings normally, Monica seldom, if ever, held their bottles during their feedings. Her mother, husband, and a sister all coached her to hold her babies enfolded in a face-to-face position. Although she was generally compliant with requests from others, she consistently refused close body or face-to-face contact with her babies while feeding them. Instead, clearly acting from early and enduring preverbal memory, she lay them flat across her lap and replicated her own experience.

Infant memory is the subject of much current research at several universities, including the University of Massachusetts. Drs. Rachel Clifton and Nancy Myers, both psychologists, have successfully documented the capacity of two-and a half year old children to exhibit learning they experienced at age six months.[17] Originally researching motor and hearing skills, Dr. Clifton placed sixteen six-month-old babies in a pitch dark room with objects that made different sounds and used infrared cameras to capture how and when infants reached for the objects. After the initial experience, the stimuli were not repeated until follow-up testing two years later. At that time, the original children were paired with a control group of thirty-month-old toddlers who had not had the original experience. "All of the children were again placed in a dark room with the same objects making the same sounds. The children who had the prior experience reached for the objects without signs of fear." Fewer of the control group reached for the objects, and many cried. Clifton and Myers believe that the babies, when put into a situation similar to their earlier experience, were able to access memories of a time when they were six months old and the task appeared less frightening.

A growing number of scientists believe that the limbic memory does not wait until birth to begin. Dr. David Chamberlain, a psychologist who was one of the founders of the Association for Pre- and Perinatal Psychology and Health, finds increasing evidence of a primitive memory stored at the sensory level beginning during late gestation. Chamberlain refers to these memories as "cellular" because they are unconscious and preverbal and are often held and expressed in specific parts of the body.[18]

Dr. Lenore Terr, a child psychiatrist at the University of California Medical Center in San Francisco, studied children under the age of five who had experienced serious trauma from birth to thirty-four months. Verifiable proof of the trauma the children experienced was recorded in photos, police reports, statements from eyewitnesses, confessions, or corroborating injuries. This is presumed to be a time when little or no verbal memory exists. Yet these children clearly showed that they had retained behavioral memories of their trauma, which Terr found to be reenacted in part or in entirety in their play. Terr believes that traumatic events—especially those experienced early—create "burned-in" images that last a lifetime.

Pease Porridge Hot, Pease Porridge Cold

It was only a game. Even though it was for science—it was only a game.

The first person who hit the button after the light flashed got to zap his partner with an electric current. The winner could pick a charge ranging from one, a light twinge, to eight, a jolt of pain. These were college students at McGill University in Montreal. They usually picked low dosages of electricity, giving what they got, exchanging only the level of pain they received. That was before the drink. Scientists deliberately raised the aggression level of participants by giving them a dose of amino acids that lowered their levels of the brain chemical serotonin. Soon the game changed. Volunteers began zapping their partners with higher and higher numbers in spite of receiving lower charges themselves. Next, the students were given another snack, this time a dose of tryptophan, an essential ingredient for the brain to produce serotonin. As the serotonin levels rose, the choice of painful jolts diminished. An Orwellian experiment, perhaps, but proof positive that the manipulation of neurochemicals can alter levels of aggression.[19]

Serotonin-reducing chemicals such as certain amino acids lower the threshold for aggressive tendencies. In rodents, serotonin-reducing drugs were first viewed as aphrodisiacs because the rats became very sexually active under their influence. But aggression soon followed. Handlers were bitten and other rats were attacked just for coming close—behaviors previously unseen in the animals.[20]

The role of the neurotransmitter serotonin in aggressive behavior has been under study since the mid 1970s when Marie Asberg, at the Karolinska Hospital in Stockholm, observed the linkage between low serotonin and violent suicides, suicides involving guns, knives, ropes, or jumping from high places. Soon criminals with a history of violence were discovered to also have low levels of serotonin. But the effect of serotonin can only be understood in relation to a counterbalancing neurotransmitter, noradrenaline.

While serotonin is known to be key to modulating impulsive behaviors at the neocortical level of the brain, noradrenaline is the alarm hormone designed to alert the system to respond to danger. Together they have a teeter-totter type of relationship: in normal people, serotonin is higher during sleep and decreases during wakefulness, while noradrenaline is higher during wakefulness and lower during sleep. The balance between the two is the key to normal function. For most of us there is a balance, enabling us to react in reasonable ways. But, as with the McGill students, our functional levels can be altered, at least temporarily. Alcohol and extremely stressful environments can have similar effects to the students' initial drink of amino acids. When these exposures occur to a developing fetus or infant, the levels of serotonin and noradrenaline are just being built, shaping lifetime patterns.

Violent behavior is roughly of two types: impulsive and premeditated. Most acts of violence are impulsive. "Cold-blooded" or premeditated acts are far less common and are typically enacted by a very different personality than the "hot-blooded" crime. When environmental experiences early in life cause noradrenaline levels to be too high and serotonin levels too low, the result, in the presence of later emotional triggers, may be impulsive violence. Conversely, very low levels of noradrenaline together with low levels of serotonin result in underarousal, which may generate an appetite for high-risk behaviors to achieve arousal, setting the stage for predatory violence or premeditated crimes. Interestingly, very high levels of serotonin are not a means of counteracting this effect. Excessively high serotonin levels result not in well-being, but in rigidity or obsessive-compulsive behavior, like Lady MacBeth's repetitive hand washing. The balance of neurochemicals in either scenario is thought to be set primarily by early experience.[21] When babies develop in an atmosphere of terror or trauma, these neurochemicals can be called upon to enable them to survive. But that which enables survival may also create permanent and lethal imbalances.

Low levels of serotonin may be the result of a genetic error. A single gene inherited by some people from their fathers results in an inability to adequately convert tryptophan from common foods into serotonin. The individual inheriting this gene may have no problem unless there is an additional stressor, primarily alcohol. In affected individuals, alcohol briefly raises, then drastically lowers, serotonin levels. At the latter point, the individual is prone to acting out aggressively. This gene is common— affecting 40 percent of the Swedish population tested at random.[22] With 48 percent of the homicides in the United States committed under the influence of alcohol, the role of this interaction is clearly of concern.

Normal serotonin and noradrenaline levels are extremely important to balanced functioning. Without realizing it, our culture is creating more and more individuals with an imbalance in this delicate equation in the brain. Alcohol, drugs, and other toxic exposures such as lead are being implicated in damage to the genes responsible for these neurochemicals. So are conditions after birth such as abusive, terrifying, or war-torn environments, in which impulsive or reactive behaviors are essential to survival. Researchers suspect that conditions of child neglect, child abuse, gang warfare, and domestic violence are—without our awareness—biologically, as well as socially, feeding the cycle of violent crime. As Ron Kotulak stated in his series on the brain:

> Underlying the scientific quest, which has revealed genetic and environmental links to abnormal brain chemistry, is the growing suspicion that society may unwittingly be feeding the nation's epidemic of murder, rape and other criminal acts by making childhood more dangerous than ever.[23]

Abuse and neglect in the first years of life have a particularly pervasive impact. Prenatal development and the first two years are the time when the genetic, organic, and neurochemical foundations for impulse control are being created. It is also the time when the capacities for rational thinking and sensitivity to other people are being rooted—or not—in the child's personality.

Endnotes

[1] The story of Chelsea was originally presented on *Prime Time Live* by Diane Sawyer, aired January 25, 1996, "Your Child's Brain." (Kate Harrington, producer)

[2] Kotulak, "The Roots of Violence."

[3] Dawson, G., and Fischer, K.W., eds. (1995), *Human Behavior and the Developing Brain*, Guilford Press, New York, (pp. 22–23).

[4] "High-risk children" are defined in Dr. Ramey's studies by the social attributes of the family and the biological condition of the children.

[5] Telephone interview with Dr. Craig Ramey, November 4, 1995.

[6] Kotulak, "Unlocking the Mind."

[7] Ibid.

[8] Diane Sawyer, "Your Child's Brain," January 25, 1996.

[9] Perry, B. (1997), "Incubated in Terror: Neurodevelopmental Factors in the Cycle of Violence," *Children in a Violent Society*, Osofsky, J.D. (ed.), Guilford Press, New York, (pp. 124–149).

[10] Goleman, D. (1995), *Emotional Intelligence: Why It Matters More Than IQ*, Bantam, New York, (p. 16).

[11] For more in-depth information on Dr. Perry's concept of "traits to states," see chapter 7 of Karr-Morse and Wiley (1997), *Ghosts from the Nursery: Tracing the Roots of Violence*, New York: Atlantic Monthly Press.

[12] The information from Dr. Allan Schore is drawn from his written works, and from both phone and personal interviews. Schore, A.N. (1994), *Affect Regulation and the Origin of the Self: The Neurobiology of Emotional Development*, Lawrence Erlbaum and Associates, Hillsdale, New Jersey; Schore, A.N., (1996), "The Experience-Dependent Maturation of a Regulatory System in the Orbital Prefontral Cortex and the Origin of Developmental Psychopathology," *Development and Psychopathology* 8: 59–87.

[13] Interview with Dr. Allan Schore, March 7, 1997.

[14] Gladwell, M. (March 3, 1997), "Damaged," *The New Yorker.*

[15] LeDoux, J. (1993), "Emotional Memory Systems in the Brain," *Behavioral and Brain Research* 58.

[16] Engel, G., Ruschman, F., Harnay, V., and Wilson, D. (1985) *Parental Influences in Health and Disease*, Little Brown, Boston.

[17] Goldberg, J. (July 1993), "The Amazing Minds of Infants," *Life*, Special Issue: "Babies Are Smarter than You Think."

[18] Chamberlain, D. (1987), "The Cognitive Newborn: A Scientific Update," *British Journal of Psychotherapy* 4:30–71.

[19] This story and the information on the research is drawn from Ron Kotulak's article, "How Brain's Chemistry Unleashes Aggression," published in the special section, "The Roots of Violence."

[20] Ibid.

[21] Perry, "Incubated in Terror."

[22] Ibid.

[23] Kotulak, R. (1993), *Chicago Tribune*, Series: "Unlocking the Mind," April 11–15, and special section: "The Roots of Violence: Tracking Down Monsters within Us," December 12–15.

4

School Crime and Juvenile Justice

Richard Lawrence

No study of juvenile delinquency would be complete without an examination of delinquency in schools. The presence of disorder and delinquency in schools and on school grounds is a growing problem. Most secondary schools have some students who disrupt the classroom and threaten the safety of other students and teachers. A related issue is the presence of juvenile delinquents in school. Youths who have been adjudicated for delinquent conduct are usually required to attend school as a requirement of probation. Juvenile offenders who have served time in a correctional facility are also encouraged by a parole officer to enroll in school again following their release to the community. In this chapter we will address a number of questions: How extensive and serious is school crime? How many students and teachers report being victims of crime at school? To what extent do school experiences contribute to delinquent behavior? What can schools do to help prevent delinquency? How can schools, law enforcement, and juvenile justice agencies combine their efforts to reduce delinquency?

The public perception of most inner-city junior and senior high schools is that they are dangerous places for students and teachers, that drugs are rampant, and that growing numbers of students carry guns and other weapons. Media attention has increased public fears and concerns about delinquency in schools. Newspapers and magazines rivet our attention on school

Lawrence, Richard. 1998. *School Crime and Juvenile Justice.* (Original chapter)

problems with headlines about "more kids bringing weapons to school," "America's schools confronting violence," and "classrooms as killing grounds." School violence occurs more frequently in inner-city schools, but suburban and smaller-city schools are now experiencing similar problems.

Schools are a reflection of the community. As crime has increased in cities and communities, it has also increased in the schools. The problem no longer is restricted to inner-city schools, or to neighborhoods characterized by lower socioeconomic levels. The types of crimes most often committed in schools involve drug and alcohol possession, theft, and vandalism. Weapons possession and violent crimes are less common but receive a great deal of publicity when they happen, and create a climate of fear among students and teachers. The extent and nature of school crime and violence have been a major focus of government-funded research, such as the Safe School Study Report to Congress (National Institute of Education, 1978; Gottfredson and Gottfredson, 1985) and more recent research funded jointly by the U.S. Departments of Education and Justice (Kaufman, et al., 1998).

School Crime: Community Problem or School Problem?

Some have suggested that school violence is simply one manifestation of violence in society. Others believe that school crime is caused by school structure and policies. This raises the question of whether school crime is simply a reflection of crime in the community, or whether it is a function of problems within the school itself. In short, the question is whether school crime is an internal or an external problem.

An Internal Problem

According to the Safe School Study, school crime is not merely a reflection of social ills in society. The National Institute of Education (NIE) study concluded that schools can do much to reduce school disruption and crime by treating students fairly and equally, improving the relevance of courses to suit students' interests and needs, and having smaller classes (National Institute of Education, 1978). If indeed school crime is primarily an internal problem, then schools are responsible for improving the school climate, student discipline policies, and other changes that may reduce crime and disruption. The Safe School Study found that many variables which are not under the school's control such as unemployment, poverty, and neighborhood conditions are not necessarily important in school crime. These findings are supported by those of a recent study in which it was concluded that individual student characteristics such as effort, belief in rules, and positive peer associations exert stronger influences on student conduct (Welsh, Greene, and Jenkins, 1999:106).

The study also found that outsiders are not responsible for most school crime and violence. Except for cases of trespassing and incidents of breaking and entering during non-school hours, most offenses (74 to 98 percent) are committed by youths enrolled in the school. This finding is contrary to the claim of many that school dropouts and intruders are responsible for most school crime and has a direct bearing on the types of security programs that school districts and individual schools should develop. If school administrators instituted security programs on the belief that their schools were more at risk from outside trespassers, then those programs may be misdirected and ineffective. The overall implication of school crime as an internal problem is that schools may not have much to fear from the type of neighborhood in which they are located. According to this view, schools can do much to reduce disruption, crime, and violence, but it also means that schools are responsible for dealing with their own crime problems.

An External Problem

School crime as an external problem views the school in the context of the community. Schools are a microcosm of society, and they reflect our culture. What happens in the community and on the streets invariably spills into schools. Crime does not occur in the schools in isolation from crime in the rest of society. Much of what is called "school crime" is really crime committed by young persons who are enrolled in school or who commit the crime on the way to or from school. Gold and Moles (1978) analyzed data from the 1972 National Survey of Youth and concluded that delinquent behavior that occurs in school is not an isolated phenomenon, but rather is the same kind of behavior that takes place outside of school, and tends to be committed by the same individuals. They claim that the amount of delinquency occurring in school is proportionately less than the amount of time youths spend there, since youths spend about 20 percent of their waking hours in school, but 13 percent of their offenses are committed in school (Gold and Moles, 1978:115).

To view school crime as an external rather than an internal problem is to see school crime as inseparable from, and a function of, crime in the community. This view has important implications for explaining and preventing school crime. Viewing school crime as an internal problem is to place the blame squarely on the schools, and to hold schools responsible for solving what may be more of a community problem. McDermott (1983:278) noted two unfortunate consequences of this approach: (1) the blame is placed solely on the school administrators and teachers, and (2) schools are expected to offer solutions such as better teachers, smaller classes, fair and equal treatment of students, relevant subject matter in courses, and tighter discipline. Policies such as these may help minimize school disruption, and they are positive steps toward quality education. However, if school crime is primarily a reflection of crime in the community, then relying on improved teaching and discipline may not significantly reduce levels of school crime. If crime in schools does not exist apart from crime in the community, this has important implications for school crime prevention efforts. If this is so, then concentrating efforts in the school probably will not have a significant impact in the long run for those schools located in high-crime communities.

McDermott also questioned the assumption that offenders and victims are different groups, with one preying on the other. In a study of delinquency in the school and the community, she presented evidence that three groups of young people—offenders, victims, and the fearful—were not mutually exclusive (1983:281). Some youths who became offenders had been victimized and were themselves fearful of crime. The fear experienced by victims of crime often drives them to actions that are unlawful. Some students unlawfully bring weapons to school for self-protection and do not intend to use them offensively.

The consensus from research is that viewing school crime as an internal problem is incomplete and inaccurate. School crime as a reflection of community crime receives support from other researchers. In a reanalysis of the Safe School Study data, Gottfredson and Gottfredson (1985:188) presented evidence that school crime was as much a reflection of community disorganization and crime as it was of internal school problems. A longitudinal analysis using National Crime Survey data examined victimization of juveniles in schools, homes, streets, and parks. More assaults, robberies and larcenies occurred in homes than in schools, streets, or parks. The authors concluded that one of the causes of victimization in schools is the community surrounding the school, and they suggested that increases or decreases in victimization rates outside schools would be reflected by increases or decreases inside schools (Parker, Smith, Smith and Toby, 1991). Concentrating crime prevention efforts only on the school is unlikely to have a long-term significant impact, especially for schools located in high-crime communities. School policies which focus on tighter security, stricter discipline, and similar crime control approaches may well reduce disruption and crime in the school but simply displace the problems to the community. Likewise, suspending or expelling disruptive students without referral to an alternative program simply puts them out on the street with nothing to do. If concerted efforts aimed at both school and community crime do not occur, then schools will continue to face problems of disruption, crime and victimization in the hallways and on the school grounds. Crime in schools must be seen as an extension of crime in communities. That means we must view it as a larger social problem. It is not just the responsibility of the school board, administrators and teachers. School crime, like crime in the community, must become the responsibility of citizens, parents, and students as well as police and juvenile court officials.

Measuring the Extent of School Crime

Research on delinquency in school has been limited by imprecise and incomplete methods of measuring the extent of the problem. The FBI Uniform Crime Reports list the number of juvenile arrests each year, but they do not specify the number of crimes committed at school. Police statistics do indicate that a substantial number of juvenile crimes are committed on school property. More than half (56 percent) of the property and violent crimes against youth aged 12–15 occurred at school, and 37 percent of all violent crimes against that age group in 1991 occurred in school or on school grounds (Whitaker and Bastian, 1993). Ten percent of all public schools reported at least one serious violent crime to the police; another 47 percent reported a less serious violent or nonviolent crime (a fight, theft, or vandalism); and 43 percent of public schools did not report any of these crimes to the police (Kaufman, et al., 1998:14). School officials reporting few crime incidents tended to be from suburban areas or smaller cities, located in neighborhoods with little crime.

Victim surveys are more complete measures of the true extent of crime than police statistics, since many persons do not report their victimization experiences to police. Many students who have been victims of crime at school do not report the incidents to school officials, who are responsible for notifying police of crime incidents. The first nationwide measure of the extent of school crime was the Safe School Study conducted in 1977 (National Institute of Education, 1978). A total of 11 percent of secondary school students reported being victims of theft; 1.3 percent reported being attacked at school; and one-half of 1 percent reported having money or property taken from them by force. About 12 percent of teachers were estimated to have had something worth more than $1 stolen from them, and about one-half of 1 percent of teachers reported being physically attacked (National Institute of Education, 1977:2–3).

The School Crime Supplement of the National Crime Victimization Survey (NCVS) provides the best current measure of the extent of school crime, based on a representative sample of students throughout the United States. The NCVS is an ongoing household survey that gathers information on the criminal victimization of household members aged 12 and older. The School Crime Supplement focuses on the percent of students who report that they have been victimized one or more times. The results of the 1989 and 1995 surveys are summarized in Table 1 and Figure 1, showing the percent of students who reported being victims of violent crimes and property crimes tabulated by student and school characteristics. There was little or no change between the two studies in the percent of students reporting property victimization at school, but students reporting violent victimization increased from 3.4 percent to 4.2 percent. Fewer female students reported being victims of property crime in 1995, but the proportion of females who were victims of a violent crime increased from 2 to 3.3 percent. The same pattern is observed when comparing property and violent crimes in schools in central cities, suburbs, and nonmetropolitan areas: property crimes decreased slightly, while violent crimes increased in all

Table 1: Percent of Students Aged 12–19 Reporting Victimization at School by Student and School Characteristics

Student and School Characteristics	*1989*		*1995*	
	Violent[1] Crime	*Property[2] Crime*	*Violent[1] Crime*	*Property[2] Crime*
Total	3.4	12.2	4.2	11.6
Males	4.8	12.1	5.1	12.0
Females	2.0	12.3	3.3	11.2
Central city	3.9	13.4	4.7	11.3
Suburbs	3.5	11.3	4.4	11.5
Nonmetro. area	2.9	12.3	3.5	12.0

[1]Violent crimes include physical attacks or taking money or property by force, weapons, or threats.
[2]Property crimes include theft of property from a student's desk, locker, or other locations.

Source: Adapted from Chandler, Chapman, Rand, and Taylor. 1998. *Student's Reports of School Crime: 1989 and 1995*. Washington, DC: U.S. Departments of Education and Justice.

three categories of schools. There is little difference in victimization of students in central cities, suburban, or nonmetropolitan area schools.

More students reported that drugs (marijuana, cocaine, crack, or uppers/downers) were available at school (63.2 percent in 1989 to 65.3 percent in 1995). Survey results indicate that reports of drugs, guns, and gangs in schools are associated with more property and violent crimes in schools. Methodological differences between the first nationwide measures of school crime in 1977 and the NCVS statistics limit our ability to make accurate comparisons. It is clear, however, that there have been more student reports of gangs, guns, and violent victimization experiences in schools since 1977, and a slight increase from 1989 to 1995.

Teachers also report an increase in victimization experiences. In a survey conducted for the National Center for Education Statistics, a national sample of 1,350 public school teachers responded to questions concerning school crime and discipline problems. Highlights of the survey report were that:

- Student alcohol use was considered a problem by 23 percent of the teachers.
- Student drug use was considered a problem by 17 percent of the teachers.
- Nineteen percent of teachers reported verbal abuse by a student in the past four months, eight percent had been threatened with injury in the past 12 months, and two percent had been physically attacked in the past 12 months (Mansfield, Alexander, and Farris 1991:iii).

In summary, the best available measures indicate that a significant number of students are victims of crime in schools and on school property, and the presence of drugs, gangs, and weapons is a growing problem at many schools. However, victim surveys show that few serious violent crime incidents occur in most schools. Most crimes that occur at school are petty theft, damage to school property, or minor assaults. Violent schools are not the norm. Students and teachers are safer in most schools than they are in most other parts of the community. There is nevertheless a widespread perception that schools are violent, dangerous places. A number of factors contribute to this perception. First, student and teacher reports of being victims of verbal abuse and threats create a climate of fear. Second, violent

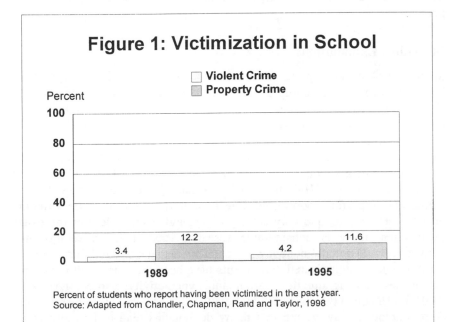

Percent of students who report having been victimized in the past year.
Source: Adapted from Chandler, Chapman, Rand and Taylor, 1998

school crime incidents receive widespread publicity. Incidents such as assaults, students in possession of guns, and threats or "hit lists" are widely publicized, and national coverage via television, newspapers, and magazines gives the impression that the problem is widespread. Although students are statistically safer in school than in other places, the fear of being victimized poses a problem when it disrupts the learning process and contributes to absenteeism. Many students report that they have stayed home one or more days because of threats and a fear of being attacked; nine percent of students (or 2.1 million) aged 12 through 19 reported that they avoid one or more places at school out of fear for their safety (Kaufman, et al. 1998:32). Crime and delinquency in schools is a significant problem for victims but also for other students and school staff, because it creates a climate of fear and disrupts the educational process.

Explaining Delinquency in Schools

Criminologists have developed numerous theories to explain juvenile delinquency. Explanations have ranged from those that focus on the individual to those that locate the origins of crime in social processes and the structure of society. Theoretical explanations that include young peoples' school experiences as a factor in delinquency causation are individual explanations, structural-strain theories, social process theories, and the labeling perspective.

Individual Explanations

Social scientists attempting to understand human behavior have studied individual differences among persons, including intelligence, learning disabilities, and psychological characteristics. Research results indicate that juvenile delinquents tend to have lower IQ scores than nondelinquents. Some interpret this to mean that lower intelligence leads to more delinquent involvement, while others believe that it may mean that youth with lower IQ scores are simply more likely to be apprehended by police. Other interpretations of the IQ-delinquency relationship are that youth with low verbal ability perform poorly, become frustrated with school, are vulnerable to peer pressure, and may act out accordingly. Regardless of the exact explanation, there is considerable research support for a relationship between low IQ and delinquency. Researchers also have found that a significant number of adjudicated delinquents have been diagnosed with learning disabilities such as attention deficit and hyperactivity disorder (ADD or ADHD). The third type of individual explanation is personality differences, as psychologists have found that many delinquents tend to be more emotionally unstable, impulsive, suspicious, hostile, irritable, and self-centered than nondelinquents. Psychological learning theories of behaviorism, social learning, and moral development have contributed to understanding delinquent involvement of some youth (cf. Lawrence, 1998:39–44).

Structural-Strain Theories

Social structure and strain explanations of delinquency focus on the social and cultural environment in which adolescents grow up or on the subcultural groups in which they become involved. Social structure explanations claim that delinquent acts are often an expression of frustration resulting from limited educational and employment opportunities, particularly for lower-income and disadvantaged youth. Albert Cohen (1955) observed that many lower-class youths (especially boys) do poorly in school, and that school performance is related to delinquency. He explained it as a result of lower-class youth having to perform according to middle-class expectations and values. Structure theorists note that most young people accept middle-class goals and want a middle-class lifestyle, but youth from disadvantaged backgrounds often find that legitimate means for achieving those goals have been blocked to them by such barriers as unequal educational and vocational opportunities. Delinquency is viewed as a reaction to the frustration (or "strain") caused by limited opportunities to succeed through legitimate means.

Social Process Explanations

Social process explanations of delinquency focus on social interactions between individuals and environmental influences that may lead to delinquent behavior. The "differential association" theory of Edwin Sutherland (1970) holds that delinquency is a learned behavior acquired as youth interact closely with other deviant youth. Travis Hirschi (1969) explained delinquency as the absence of social bonds that help youth avoid delinquent involvement. Nondelinquent youth have an "attachment" or positive relationship with their parents, other adults, and with nondelinquent friends; a "commitment" to socially acceptable activities and values, including education and employment goals; "involvement" in conventional activities; and a "belief" and respect for the law and societal norms. Numerous studies have supported this explanation, noting the importance of social bonds in discouraging youth from delinquent involvement.

Labeling Theory

Labeling theorists claim that delinquency often results from societal reaction to minor deviant behavior. The very process of identifying and segregating deviant persons as criminals may increase the likelihood that the behavior will be perpetuated. The theory has been criticized by criminologists because it fails to explain why youth initially engage in deviant behavior, it fails to explain the reasons and motives behind delinquency, and labeling theorists seemingly excuse juveniles' delinquent involvement and blame it on societal overreaction. Some criminologists believe that school tracking, the practice of placing students into groups based on perceived academic ability, is a form of labeling. More minority and lower income students tend to be placed in the basic or lower-ability track. Teachers often expect lower academic achievement and more behavior problems from these students, and their expectations often are met.

Social, Cultural, and Legal Trends as Factors in School Crime

There is no single criminological theory that has been developed to explain delinquency in school or the role of school experiences in contributing to delinquency. The school is an important social institution that is central to the development of youth, however, so no explanation of delinquency is complete without some mention of the role of schools. The basic question is why we are witnessing an increase in disorder and disruption in schools, and in the number of students and teachers being victimized. Popular explanations hold that a greater number of students are violating school rules and committing crimes than in the past because of a lack of adequate discipline in schools. That, however, is an untenable explanation since it simply places the blame on teachers and principals for lax discipline. Most schools have a list of clearly stated rules, and educators have a vested interest in maintaining a safe and orderly teaching environment. A more tenable explanation is that students today seem to be less responsive to disciplinary measures by school staff and get by with misbehavior that was not tolerated in years past. A number of social, cultural, and legal changes have contributed to the growing problem of disorder and delinquency in schools.

Changes in Families

The family is the primary source for nurturing and socializing a child. Parents are role models for children, providing examples for interacting with others, for ethical and legal behavior, for instilling work habits, and for fulfilling responsibilities. Children who grow up in families marked by parental conflict and tension, or with parents who are absent or neglectful or who frequently engage in verbal abuse, are predisposed to factors that promote antisocial and delinquent behavior. Family problems contribute to school truancy, poor school performance and failure, and disruptive and delinquent behavior in school.

The increase in divorce and single-parent families, and the increase in both parents being employed outside the home have made it difficult for parents to fulfill their responsibilities. Single-parent families face more difficulties in discipline, supervision, and economic stability. The quality of the parent-child relationship is more important than family size or whether both parents are present, however. Delinquency is less likely among youths who have a positive "attachment" to their parent(s) (Hirschi, 1969). Parenting skills are important in helping prepare youths to have a positive school experience and to avoid delinquency. Inconsistent parental discipline and limited supervision are strong predictors of delinquent behavior (cf. Lawrence, 1998:60–64).

Schools are also instrumental in changing the parent-child relationship, regardless of family structure, size, or relationships. Since the origin of public education, schools have had the effect of separating children from their families. Schools have now taken over many of the functions that were previously the responsibility of parents. The result has been a distancing of children from parents, as they spend more time with teachers and their peers. Many parents do not take the time or make the effort to be aware of their child's educational achievements or any behavior problems. Parents have mixed reactions upon being notified of problems at school. Some are reluctant to believe their child has school problems; others feel powerless to do much; some don't want to be bothered, believing it is the responsibility of school staff to handle the problems. The absence of communication between teachers and parents allows for distrust and lack of mutual respect to develop.

Peer Influence and Delinquency

At the same time that school attendance separates children from their parents, peers begin to play a larger role in young people's lives. Schools bring large numbers of peers together for extended periods of time. By the time youth reach the junior high years, peers have an equal or greater influence on them than their parents and teachers. Peer relationships are important in encouraging school attendance and achievement, but friends who have no academic or career goals have a negative influence, encouraging disruptive behavior and absenteeism. Youth who have poor relations with their parents and who are not committed to school tend to associate with like-minded peers, and disruption, truancy, and delinquency are encouraged by their association.

The formation of juvenile gangs is an extension of adolescent peer groups. Youth join gangs for a variety of reasons: a need for peer acceptance, belonging, and recognition; for status, safety, or security; for power; and for excitement (cf. Spergel et al., 1994:3). Youths who are especially drawn to gangs include those raised under socially depriving conditions, those who are failing in school and not involved in school activities, and those who are unemployed and who have few if any perceived job goals or opportunities. Most gang members are bored with school and feel inadequate in class. They have not developed effective learning skills and therefore experience frustration and failure in school. They do not identify with teachers and tend to dislike and distrust them. Gang problems in schools often begin in the streets as students who are gang members bring gang attitudes and behaviors into the school. Gang violence generally does not occur in schools, although gang recruitment and planning of gang activities may occur on school grounds. Gang members may claim parts of the school as their turf, leave their marks with graffiti, and intimidate and assault other students (cf. Spergel, et al., 1994). School crime victimization surveys indicate that there is a relationship between gang presence in schools, more reported drugs and weapons, and student reports of fear and victimization (Chandler, et al., 1998).

According to Spergel and his associates (1994), five strategies have been used in dealing with youth gangs:

1. *Neighborhood mobilization.* This approach was used in the 1920s and 1930s to get local citizens, social institutions, and the criminal justice system to work together to socialize youth in general, but it did not specifically target gang youth.
2. *Social intervention.* An approach used in the 1940s and 1950s, social intervention offered counseling, recreation, group work, and social service referrals for street gangs. This approach was not effective in reducing gang delinquency.
3. *Provision of social and economic opportunities.* Concerns about school failure and unemployment of inner-city youth led to the development of special school and job programs, such as Head Start and Job Corps. The programs seem to be effective, but it is not clear to what extent they reduce the youth gang problem.
4. *Gang suppression and incarceration.* Youth gangs in the 1970s and 1980s became more sophisticated and active in criminal activities. This, combined with a decline in outreach efforts and a tighter labor market, led to more reliance on law enforcement, prosecution, and incarceration of gang leaders who were serious offenders.
5. *Organizational development strategy.* The more current, effective approach for dealing with gangs is to combine special police gang units and specialized probation units for gang suppression and intervention, and to work closely with schools and community organizations to

develop programs for at-risk youth who are most susceptible to gang involvement (Spergel, et al., 1994:7–15).

Public schools, particularly middle schools, have perhaps the greatest potential for prevention and intervention into youth gang problems. The most recent comprehensive effort to respond to the problem is the Gang Resistance and Education Training (G.R.E.A.T.) Program, a school-based gang prevention program in which uniformed law enforcement officers teach a nine-week curriculum to middle-school students. Results from a survey of 5,935 eighth-grade students in 11 sites indicate that students completing the program had more prosocial attitudes and lower rates of some types of delinquent behavior than did students in the comparison group (Esbensen and Osgood, 1999).

School Attendance, Expectations, and Dropouts

Public education of all citizens is viewed as essential in a democratic society, and schools have been expected to serve as the primary institution for social change. The school is a structured environment that places demands and expectations on students. Those who are not prepared for these educational expectations act out in frustration. Perhaps the main reason many youth violate school rules is that they do not want to be there. They rebel against the structure and demands of the classroom. They are not there to learn. Their parents have not prepared them for school and do not provide the encouragement and support for educational success. Many homes are void of positive learning models, and the value of education is not promoted by parents. Youth who lack the skills for successful school achievement and who are not committed to educational goals resist the structure and demands of school through tardiness, absenteeism, and truancy, which often escalate to disruptive and delinquent behavior.

The dropout rate in U.S. schools is a serious problem. Nationwide, a total of over 3 million (12.7 percent) persons aged 18 to 24 are high school dropouts; Hispanics had the highest dropout rate (32.7 percent), and the rate for blacks was slightly higher than for whites (16.4 vs. 12.2 percent) (Bruno and Adams, 1994:xiv–xv). Dropout rates in New York are as high as 80 percent, 50 percent in Los Angeles, and 70 percent in Chicago. School dropout is considered a national problem, especially considering the consequences of dropout, which include unemployment, loss in tax revenue, costs of social welfare, increased crime, and the cost of correctional supervision and prison.

Research on dropout and delinquency has reached mixed conclusions. Elliott and Voss (1974) conducted a longitudinal study of 2,617 students from eight schools in California and found that delinquency rates for the dropouts were higher while they were in school. After they dropped out, the rates of delinquency declined. They concluded that the findings supported strain theory—that delinquency is a response to the frustration of negative school experiences—and that dropping out diminishes both the frustration of school and involvement in delinquency. Thornberry, Moore, and Christenson (1985) conducted a similar longitudinal study of Philadelphia youth and found that youth who dropped out at sixteen and eighteen years of age had more arrests following dropout than while they were in school. There was a slight decrease in arrests (22%) for those who dropped out at seventeen, but the decrease in arrests was 55 percent for all those who graduated. Contrary to strain theory, their results were interpreted as supportive of control theory, whereby youths who are committed to education are less likely to engage in delinquency. In a third study of dropout and delinquency, Jarjoura (1993) analyzed data from the National Longitudinal Survey of Youth and controlled for previous offending of dropouts, which was not accounted for in the Thornberry, et al. study. Jarjoura also controlled for gender, race, age, prior misconduct, and school performance. He found that students who dropped out because they disliked school and those who were expelled for misconduct had the highest probabilities of involvement in theft and drug sales after dropping out. Dropping out for personal reasons such as marriage or pregnancy had no effect on later involvement in drugs or theft. Although youth who were expelled for misconduct or delinquent behavior in school reported more subsequent delinquent involvement than graduates, Jarjoura concluded that differences in later criminal behavior were explained by prior misconduct, not by dropping out. These findings underscore the complexities of the dropout-delinquency relationship, and no single theory offers an adequate explanation. It is unlikely that prevention programs for either dropout or delinquency will be very effective until we understand them more fully.

Placed in historical perspective, the proportion of American youth who attend school and graduate is much better than it was at the beginning of the twentieth century, when most youth left school by age 16. The higher percentage of youth staying in school today may not necessarily signify a dramatic positive commitment of most youth toward education, however. As many as a third to a half of students today say that they do not like school, so it is surprising that the dropout rate is not higher. Why do more students not drop out? There are three reasons why most youth stay in school: compulsory attendance laws, dropout prevention programs, and because most of their friends are there.

Compulsory attendance laws were enacted in every state legislature by 1918. The early laws applied to children from eight to fourteen years of age, with some states extending the law to the age of sixteen (Rippa, 1980:170). Such laws underscore the importance we place on education for employment, life skills, and responsible citizenship. Compulsory school attendance can assure that youth are physically in school, but there is no guarantee that they will be mentally engaged in the learning process. The unintended consequence of compulsory attendance is that many students remain enrolled against their wishes and disrupt the learning process for other students and teachers. States' adoption of compulsory attendance also brings with it an obligation to provide alternative educational resources for delinquent students who have been expelled for violation of school rules. Alternative schools have a lower student:teacher ratio and students receive more individual attention than in regular schools, so more resources and funds are needed.

Students who are at risk of dropping out are encouraged to stay in school through dropout prevention programs, which aim to retain students in school until they graduate or reach the age at which they can legally drop out. The programs are promoted in the belief that all youth should be in school, regardless of their commitment to education and the problems that they may cause. Dropout prevention is also in part a response to studies that have noted the negative consequences of school dropout that include unemployment, reduced tax revenues, more demand for social services, increased crime, and poor mental and physical health. The programs have been effective in improving retention and increasing graduation rates. An unintended consequence of retaining resistant students in school, however, is to increase the incidences of school disruption and delinquency. Delinquent involvement in fact is often higher during the school year as frustrated students act out with the support of other antisocial peers. The belief that dropout leads to delinquency now has been questioned by longitudinal research findings. Dropping out for personal reasons has no effect on later delinquent involvement. Youth who are expelled for student misconduct report more subsequent delinquent involvement, but later criminal behavior is explained more by prior misconduct than by dropping out (cf. Lawrence, 1998:99–101).

The third reason some students stay in school despite their lack of commitment to education is because it offers many benefits not available to school dropouts. Their attendance is irregular and their academic performance is unsatisfactory, but by staying in school youth satisfy parental expectations and enjoy more peer associations than they would as dropouts. As students they avoid the negative stigma associated with being a dropout. That does not mean they are positively involved in school, however. They are physically present but mentally absent. These are the youth who cause most of the disruption and delinquency in school.

School Rules and Students' Rights

The increase in disorder and delinquency in school is due in part to a greater emphasis on students' rights than in past years. Students do have rights. In the words of former U.S. Supreme Court Justice Abe Fortas, students do not "shed their rights at the schoolhouse gate." There were abuses by school authorities in past years, but many believe that the present emphasis on students' civil rights and due process requirements has made it difficult to strictly enforce school regulations. The U.S. Supreme Court in *Tinker v. Des Moines* (309 U.S. 506) reminded school boards that schools may not be operated in a totalitarian manner, with absolute authority over students. Given the demands for equal rights among disadvantaged groups in the past few decades, it is not surprising that students have also exerted their rights under the U.S. Constitution. The emphasis on civil rights has encouraged students to emphasize their rights over their responsibilities under the law, and has opened up the threat of litigation by students and their parents. Many school administrators and teachers will at some time in their career be involved in a lawsuit or legal challenge. The result has been that school staff often overlook some disruptive behavior and rule violations, taking disciplinary action only in the most serious cases.

Court rulings on students' rights involve primarily suspension or expulsion, and the conducting of searches in schools. The 1975 U.S. Supreme Court ruling in *Goss v. Lopez* (419 U.S. 565) ordered that schools must provide due process requirements before students can be suspended or expelled: written notice giving grounds for the suspension or expulsion, a description of the hearing process, a statement summarizing the school officials' decision, and the evidence or facts on which the decision was based. In the 1985 case of *New Jersey v. T.L.O.* (105 S.Ct. 733) the U.S. Supreme Court defined students' Fourth Amendment rights and provided guidelines for officials conducting school searches. The Court ruled that the Fourth Amendment prohibition against unreasonable searches and seizures does apply to school officials, who are acting as representatives of the state, and that students do have some expectations of privacy when they bring to school legitimate, noncontraband items. However, the Court also noted that school officials have an equally important need to maintain a safe and orderly learning environment, so officials can conduct searches without a warrant as long as there are sufficient grounds for it and the search is not excessively intrusive. Subsequent court cases have upheld the constitutionality of school locker searches, canine searches, and drug testing (cf. Lawrence, 1998:156–166).

The courts have drawn a reasonable balance between school rules and students' rights, but the due process requirements specifying written documentation of charges, formal hearings where witnesses may testify, and the allowance of legal appeals have affected school officials' discipline policies. The due process requirements seemingly have given more protection to unruly students than to school staff, contributing to a disorderly school climate for teachers and well-behaved students.

Weakening Authority of Teachers

While students seemingly have been given more rights, teachers feel that many of their rights and the authority to control and discipline students have been taken away. Compared with the absolute authority they had in the past, many teachers no longer feel in control of the classrooms and hallways of their schools. Students do not perceive the teachers to be in control. Most youth regularly test the limits of acceptable behavior, and students with little interest in education test the teachers' tolerance levels with minor violations like tardiness and walking the halls without a pass. Minor infractions quickly escalate to littering, writing on walls, smoking in the restroom, and verbal disruptions or threats directed at teachers. The growth of disobedience, disruption, and delinquency has been attributed to a "marshmallow effect" (Devine 1996). When students push a rule, the system—like a marshmallow—gives way. Personal stereos, beepers, hats, bandannas, hoods, and jewelry, for example, are all officially forbidden but unofficially tolerated. When students are challenged by a teacher, they respond only momentarily or not at all and walk away. Hats and other forbidden clothing have become symbols of students' control, as teachers have found it easier to ignore minor rule violations than to face the challenges of students (and often their parents). When students get by with minor rule violations, they are less hesitant to challenge more serious rules like alcohol and drug possession or threats and assaults against fellow students and teachers. A related factor in the growth of school disruption and delinquency is the reality of the street culture in the school hallways. Like drug dealers who fear each other more than they fear the police, students fear one another more than they fear the teachers or even the school security officers. It is this fear, and the need to appear tough, that explains the carrying of weapons (Devine 1996:105).

Teachers' authority is also more frequently challenged by parents than in the past. Many parents have grown to tolerate their children's behavior and style of dress as part of the youth culture, and it becomes difficult to enforce restrictions on their children's behavior when "their friends are doing it." To maintain order in schools that house hundreds of students in crowded conditions, educators must set more limits on behavior and dress styles. Some school regulations are viewed by students and their parents as overly restrictive, and teachers' attempts to enforce the regulations are often challenged by students and their parents.

Strategies for Preventing Delinquency in Schools

Most schools do not have a great deal of serious violent crime, but all schools have some students who are disruptive and engage in delinquency.

The potential for students to act out their frustrations exists in every school. School personnel, law enforcement officials, community leaders, and policymakers must work together to make schools safe places for students and school staff. Just as it "takes a village to raise a child" it also requires a concerted, coordinated effort of many individuals and organizations to prevent delinquency in schools.

Federal and State Legislation

Schools are local institutions that must have local autonomy, but school delinquency cannot be reduced without federal and state legislation that addresses three issues: the ready availability of guns in the hands of youth, compulsory school attendance laws, and the creation of smaller schools.

Gun control is a controversial issue in the United States on which lawmakers have been unable to pass much legislation, despite a majority of voter support. A series of school shooting incidents that resulted in numerous injuries and fatalities has served as a stark reminder to lawmakers that stronger regulations are needed to keep deadly handguns out of the hands of teenagers. It will require more than the threat of harsher punishment and lengthy prison sentences to deter many youth who see deadly weapons as the answer to solving their personal conflicts. Prevention must accompany the threat of harsh punishment for possession of deadly weapons.

State and federal lawmakers must also carefully examine the effects of compulsory school attendance and allow school administrators to enforce school regulations through expulsion of repetitively delinquent and violent students. Compulsory attendance seems to be treated as more important than safe and orderly schools. Compulsory attendance laws place an obligation on the state to provide educational resources for all students, even after they have been expelled for delinquent behavior. If we are to maintain safe and orderly schools, the right to public education should be conditional on students' compliance with minimum behavioral standards. Jackson Toby (1983) has long been an advocate for lowering the age of compulsory school attendance, and he maintains that this would not result in thousands of teenagers dropping out and engaging in delinquency. Most youth, if given the choice of school attendance with minimum behavioral standards, would continue to enroll or would return when they recognize the need for an education (Toby, 1983:44). Delinquency in schools is forcing lawmakers to rethink public education and make difficult decisions. Creating safe and orderly schools where students can attend without fear of being victimized is worthy of some tough decisions.

It is common practice in public education to create huge schools in metropolitan areas and to consolidate smaller city schools into single large ones. Administrators defend this practice not only for economical but also for curricular reasons. Large schools can provide more educational resources at less cost. Now more educational researchers are acknowledging that smaller schools would be safer and more productive learning centers than the larger ones and would be more cost effective in the long run. One step in this direction is the development of smaller "schools within schools." The next step must be to replace our huge overcrowded schools with smaller schools of about 500 students. This is admittedly an idealistic proposal, given that educational resources are already being stretched thin and must compete with other demands for revenue. Restructuring schools is a necessary step for preventing delinquency, however, and is a sound long-term investment. The success of alternative schools with at-risk students is evidence that smaller schools are more effective than large ones (cf. Devine, 1996:211).

School Administration Policies

Most school administrators have taken some steps to make schools orderly and safe, but many of the security measures are incomplete and poorly coordinated. A complete school safety plan should include an assessment of security needs, a school security plan that is appropriate to each school, a clear statement of school policies and regulations that is communicated to students and parents, school staff training to improve skills in discipline and classroom management, a system for recording and reporting all school crime incidents, regular communication and a close working relationship with law enforcement and juvenile court officials, and a clear definition of the roles and responsibilities of school resource officers and security officers.

The omission of metal detectors and security cameras in the above list was not an oversight. Many experts agree that relying on physical security devices and technology is not an adequate solution to school violence. We need "mental detectors" more than just metal detectors. That is, all school staff must stay in touch with students, listening to their concerns and fears and communicating with each other. Devine (1996) notes that teachers' role as disciplinarians has been relinquished to security guards. Behavioral standards are as important as educational standards. Teachers must be given the authority to discipline students, with support from administrators and parents.

Business and Community Support

We conclude this chapter where we began: school crime is a reflection of crime in the community and will not be solved only through the efforts of teachers and school principals. School crime and violence reflect the cul-

74 Richard Lawrence

ture of violence on the streets that is too often accepted as "normal" by many citizens. School crime is a community problem. Unless and until community leaders and parents get as incensed about school crime as they do about drugs, guns, and violence in the media, little attention and few resources will be directed to reducing the problem. Educators must be given the authority to maintain discipline and the resources necessary to maintain crime-free schools. Failure to do so will mean the erosion of public education.

References

Chandler, Kathryn A., Christopher D. Chapman, Michael R. Rand, and Bruce M. Taylor. 1998. *Students' Reports of School Crime: 1989 and 1995*. Washington, DC: U.S. Department of Education and U.S. Department of Justice.

Cohen, Albert. 1955. *Delinquent Boys*. New York: Free Press.

Devine, John. 1996. *Maximum Security: The Culture of Violence in Inner-City Schools*. Chicago: The University of Chicago Press.

Elliott, Delbert S. and Harwin H. Voss. 1974. *Delinquency and Dropout*. Lexington, MA: Lexington Books.

Esbensen, Finn-Aage, and Wayne Osgood. 1999. "Gang Resistance Education and Training (G.R.E.A.T.): Results of the National Evaluation." *Journal of Research in Crime and Delinquency*, 36:194–225.

Gottfredson, Gary D. and Denise C. Gottfredson. 1985. *Victimization in Schools*. New York: Plenum Press.

Hirschi, Travis. 1969. *Causes of Delinquency*. Berkeley, CA: University of California Press.

Jarjoura, G. Roger. 1993. "Does Dropping Out of School Enhance Delinquent Involvement? Results from a Large-Scale National Probability Sample." *Criminology*, 31:149–171.

Kaufman, P., X. Chen, S.P. Choy, K.A. Chandler, C.D. Chapman, M.R. Rand, and C. Ringel. 1998. *Indicators of School Crime and Safety, 1998*. Washington, DC: U.S. Departments of Education and Justice.

Lawrence, Richard. 1998. *School Crime and Juvenile Justice*. New York: Oxford University Press.

Mansfield, Wendy, Debbie Alexander, and Elizabeth Farris. 1991. *Teacher Survey on Safe, Disciplined, and Drug-Free Schools*. Washington, DC: National Center for Education Statistics.

National Institute of Education. 1978. *Violent Schools—Safe Schools: The Safe School Study Report to the Congress, Vol. I*. Washington, DC: U.S. Department of Health, Education, and Welfare.

Parker, Robert N., William R. Smith, D. Randall Smith, and Jackson Toby. 1991. "Trends in Victimization in Schools and Elsewhere, 1974–1981." *Journal of Quantitative Criminology*, 7:3–17.

Rippa, S. Alexander. 1980. *Education in a Free Society: An American History*. New York: Longman.

Spergel, Irving, David Curry, Ron Chance, Candice Kane, Ruth Ross, Alba Alexander, Edwina Simmons, and Sandra Oh. 1994. *Gang Suppression and Intervention: Problem and Response: Research Summary*. Washington, DC: Office of Juvenile Justice and Delinquency Prevention.

Sutherland, Edwin H. and Donald R. Cressey. 1970. *Principles of Criminology*. New York: J.B. Lippincott.

Thornberry, Terence P., Melanie Moore, and R.L. Christenson. 1985. "The Effect of Dropping Out of High School on Subsequent Criminal Behavior." *Criminology*, 23:3–18.

Toby, Jackson. 1983. "Violence in School." In *Crime and Justice: An Annual Review of Research*, vol. 4, pp. 1–47, edited by M. Tonry and N. Morris. Chicago: The University of Chicago Press.

Welsh, Wayne, Jack Greene, and Patricia Jenkins. 1999. "School Disorder: The Influence of Individual, Institutional, and Community Factors." *Criminology*, 37: 73–115.

Whitaker, Catherine J. and Lisa D. Bastian. 1993. *Teenage Victims: A National Crime Survey Report.* Washington, DC: U.S. Government Printing Office.

5

Private Pain and Public Behaviors
Sexual Abuse and Delinquent Girls

Robin A. Robinson

Katharine: The [court petition] got filed because I stopped going to school when I was eleven and a half, twelve . . . quit halfway through sixth grade. . . . I was a straight-A student . . . . I just flew through school. Until my life started cracking down.

Interviewer: What was the first thing that cracked?

Katharine: My brother started sexually abusing me when I was eleven. I just started doing drugs and began drinking and I stopped going to school. I couldn't deal with that. . . . At school it was just too much pressure. I couldn't work on my own problems. I couldn't handle everything.

Katharine was a patient in an acute adolescent psychiatric unit of a state facility when I interviewed her. She came into the room clutching a stuffed animal in her right hand and wearing a diamond engagement ring on her left hand. Katharine, who was committed to juvenile corrections for operating under the influence of alcohol and driving to endanger, began her career with the youth authorities for truancy, as a child in need of services under the jurisdiction of the Massachusetts child welfare agency, following the onset of sexual abuse by her older brother (unknown to the agency). Katharine felt inadequate and blamed herself because she could not cope simultaneously with the trauma of the ongoing abuse and the requirements of school, her alcoholic mother, and stepfather, so her response was to "crack down," lose herself in drugs and alcohol. She ran away from home 6 months later and became a street prostitute to support herself. The prostitution continued for a couple of years, on and off, as she ran between home and the streets. She reported that she spent time in several treatment programs, including secure treatment and five psychiatric inpatient admissions, that focused on numerous suicide attempts (including jumping from the roof of a three-story building), prostitution and other sexual activity, running away, and finally, the sexual abuse. Katharine offered me the following poem as a testament of her ordeals:

Tears of Guilt and Shame

Giving up on life seems so easy to do
'Cause of all the pain and hurt you have put me through.

I used to keep the pain and hurt buried inside
I never knew it was nothing to hide.

None of the tears I cried those nights and days
Helped me feel I wasn't to blame.

I do not feel as confused
Because I am not the only one to be sexually abused.

I turned to drugs and walked the street,
Not knowing help was right at my feet.

But now I know I am not the one to blame,
So now, no more tears of guilt and shame.

Katharine represents, in many ways, girls involved with youth authorities. They are likely to be in their early to mid teens; have a personal as well as a family history of drug and/or alcohol use; be sexually active, usually with multiple partners; have been physically and sexually abused; and sexually revictimized; and have problems in school. Typically, the girls come from households headed by single mothers, in which the girls assume early responsibility for mothering siblings and often their own mothers. Girls faced with such personal and family characteristics as described here may act in ways that hurt mostly themselves, such as sexual acting out, drug and alcohol use, and other potentially self-destructive actions, including suicide attempts, running away, truancy, and lawbreaking. Socially unacceptable behaviors may bring girls to the attention of authorities who are responsible for restoring or guiding them to normative behavior (Hudson, 1989; Koroki & Chesney-Lind, 1985; Peacock, 1981).

Social policy attention is focused on girls' public behaviors, often driven by a mystique about the perceived power of their emerging sexuality. Policymakers, social workers, other service providers, and social scientists are often both captivated and perplexed by the possible outcomes of that sexuality, including a high level of sexual activity, prostitution and other sex work, and teenage pregnancy and motherhood. In recent years, the mystique has extended to the delinquency of adolescent girls. Some research has focused on female involvement in gang activity (Campbell, 1981), and occasional news stories focus on cases in which adolescent girls are violent perpetrators. But violent events are not the norm among female offenders—most are apprehended for petty property crimes such as shoplifting, other larceny, and motor vehicle offenses (Chesney-Lind, 1989; Chesney-Lind & Shelden, 1991; Robinson, 1990) and the public behaviors of female delinquents are not well understood (Hudson, 1989; Koroki & Chesney-Lind, 1985; Robinson, 1990).

Little empirical research analyzes the meanings of delinquent behaviors to girls themselves. Concern with public actions, both sexual and delinquent, misses the troubles in the girls' private lives, descriptions of which can enrich understanding and point to policy recommendations (Hudson, 1989). Seldom have the girls' stories been heard in their own voices.

In 1989, I began a study of female delinquents and their needs relative to particular life stories. In the larger study (not reported here), I sought to discern the differences between girls who had been adjudicated delinquent, that is, convicted of criminal offenses by the juvenile courts, and those who had been placed by juvenile courts under the jurisdiction of child welfare agencies to monitor and manage their behavior. I chose Massachusetts as the site for the study, the state that has been touted nationally and internationally for 20 years by juvenile justice practitioners and researchers as the pioneer in juvenile deinstitutionalization and in progressive programs for juvenile offenders. The study included delinquent girls under the jurisdiction of the Department of Youth Services (DYS) and girls designated children in needs of services (CHINS) under the jurisdiction of the Department of Social Services (DSS). I reasoned that to study female juvenile offenders in an agency environment that operated on a progressive philosophy and agenda would protect, to some extent, the findings of such a study from the confounding influence of harsher, more punitive agency protocols that some other jurisdictions may employ.

I began the research with a conviction that female delinquency would be understood best by examining life stories told by delinquent girls, placing delinquent events in the context of those stories. I assumed that the offenses the girls had committed were but moments in the span of their brief but troubled lives (Hagan & Palloni, 1988), but they were socially significant. Girls had gained the offender label based on unlawful actions, effectively relegating to lesser importance other experiences and moments. After gaining approval from both departments to interview 30 girls, review their official records, and speak with their caseworkers, social workers, and program workers, I sought to recreate the contexts in which the momentary offenses had occurred and to build, as the data allowed, a theoretical model describing the elements of the female delinquent's life context (see Robinson, 1990). The analysis here examines the content of narrative accounts by the girls of their experiences. I discuss the dominant theme of the effects of sexual abuse.

Theoretical Framework

Historical Context

Virtually no primary scholarly literature exists prior to the 20th century to describe what were believed to be the causes of female children's delinquency; what remain are religious tracts for children that admonish duty and obligation to parents, God, scripture, and country. From these, we can extrapolate the characteristics and behaviors "naughty" and delinquent children were thought to have. We know, for example, that in the early days of the Massachusetts colony, children's disobedience to parents could be a capital offense. Similarly, the "visionary girls" of Salem witch trial notoriety in the 17th century were initially perceived by parents and community as delinquents, but were later seen as victims of the deviant wiles of the Goodwives charged with witchcraft. Later analysis of the Salem witch period suggests that the girls may have been participants in activities connected with sexuality, religious practice, and healing powers beyond the norms of the community; the girls invented stories to cover their actions and were thereafter perceived as victims. Witchcraft was highly associated with suspected, unacceptable sexuality (Karlsen, 1981).

What also survive are admonitions in the form of pamphlets designed to lure farm children, particularly girls, to burgeoning industrial centers in the early- to mid-1800s to take jobs as much-needed mill and factory workers (Dublin, 1981). The girls came to the towns and cities, as young as age 10, to live in dormitories and work in the mills for 12 to 15 hours per day. The girls' lives were supervised by the women who operated the dormitories; specific codes of behavior that survive suggest what the definitions of delinquency might have been. Most rules relate to respect for elders, obedience, chastity, rules of work, rules of property, and prohibition of alcohol consumption. Sexual indiscretion was a principal prohibition.

The history of the female status offender and female delinquent in Massachusetts is chronicled by Brenzel (1983) in *Daughters of the State: A Social Portrait of the First Reform School for Girls in North America, 1856-1905*. The school, located in Lancaster, Massachusetts, was the first of its kind in the country and served as a model; definitions for appropriate candidates for commitment carry through to today, though legislatively the mandates have changed. . . .

Many a girl went to the State Industrial School for Girls in Lancaster as a "stubborn child," which only ceased in 1972 to be a legal foundation for commitment to the Massachusetts Department of Youth Services. The concept "stubborn child" continues to this day as a tacit (if not statutory) basis for commitment. Brenzel's argument—the purpose of the Lancaster school was to mold morally or culturally recalcitrant girls to the normative values and behaviors of the dominant culture—parallels the beliefs of many DYS and DSS practitioners today. Female status offenders and juveniles guilty of criminal offenses are randomly labeled and placed throughout the youth service system, with social control as the tacit goal.

Frameworks for Analysis

Contemporary empirical research on female offenders (for example, Chesney-Lind, 1973, 1978, 1982, 1989; Chesney-Lind & Rodriguez, 1983; Hudson, 1989) finds gender bias against females operates at all levels of the criminal and juvenile justice systems, from initial police contact to corrections. Social service networks may perpetrate a punitive surveillance of adolescent females who behave in ways unacceptable to the norms of the dominant patriarchal culture. As in the past, tacit offenses are often sexual in origin and/or nature (Chesney-Lind & Shelden, 1991). . . .

Recent research has begun to explore the causal relationship between physical/sexual abuse and delinquent activity among girls (Koroki & Chesney-Lind, 1985). Using DSS case-file data, a study of delinquent youth in Massachusetts found 38% of the girls were sexually abused and 57% physically maltreated. These data were generated by officially reported and substantiated cases of sexual and physical abuse, not on self-reports by the children (Guarino, 1985).

The juvenile court, since its inception, has viewed girls as particularly vulnerable to moral corruption. The courts are slow to commit girls to delinquent status, but once committed, harsh punishments protect them. Girls are as likely as boys to run away from home, but are more often referred to court for the behavior. Shelden, Horvath, and Tracy (1989) report that girls are two to five times less likely to escalate to more serious crime than boys after a status offense, and that "more often than not, girls are being victimized at home and hence require a completely different response by the court." The discretionary nature of the juvenile court relative to the offenses most often committed by girls allows a wide range of sanctions and exhibits the active practice of paternalism and protection.

The work of Jean Baker Miller (1976) contributes additional understanding to the problem of sexual abuse in girl offenders. In relationships of temporary inequality, such as the relationship between parent and child, the power differential serves as a tool for the development of the subordinate, and the power equation shifts as the child matures. Permanent inequality, on the other hand, is galvanized by sustained subordination and dominance. Girls may succumb to powerlessness in situations in which they should be building increasing reserves of personal power and resources. Parent-daughter and other adult-girl relationships that should be temporarily unequal may be scarred by sexual abuse or other physical violence. The psychological burdens of a shift from temporary to permanent inequality block the normal course of development of the female adolescent. . . .

I suggest that girls' struggles to maintain affiliation with abusers create crises in the context of inequality with their caretakers. Those who come to the attention of youth authorities do so as they begin to exhibit self-determination; they make decisions to leave abusive homes, attempt to support themselves (albeit through illegal and unacceptable means), and challenge the rules and constraints that have been placed on them as girls. They defy acceptable standards of girl behavior as they seek to remove themselves from abusive and neglectful situations. In their stories, girls describe the ways they are proactive, including using drugs and alcohol as means of self-anesthesia to cope with abusive situations.

My framework builds on others' work and focuses on four principal elements: (a) Sexually abused girls may feel the perpetrator has betrayed trust, as have other adults and persons of authority (Browne & Finkelhor, 1986); (b) girls' self-blame and guilt are part of a process of self-stigmatization; (c) girls *survive* by running away from home, and commit *crimes of survival* to live on the street or to find shelter; and (d) they struggle with powerlessness (Browne & Finkelhor, 1986). I suggest that powerlessness is of two kinds: *true powerlessness*, including behavioral manifestations over which the girl has no control or ability to change, such as nightmares, phobias, and depression; and *intermediate powerlessness*, which exists in temporary situations that the girl can change once she escapes the abusive situation or makes a decision to act in some way that makes sense to her given her life circumstances, such as running away, truancy, and delinquency.

As W. I. Thomas (1923) argues in *The Unadjusted Girl*, individuals act according to what makes sense given the particulars of the situation:

> If now we examine the plans of action carried out by children and men (sic) with reference to social values, whether they are good or mischievous, we find that the general intellectual pattern of the plan, the quality of ingenuity, is pretty much the same in any case. When, for example, children have escapades, run away, lie, steal, plot, etc., they are following some plan, pursuing some end, solving some problem as a result of their own definition of the situation. (p. 234)

Thomas' work provides an additional theoretical lens for viewing the sense adolescent girls make of the behaviors that bring them to the attention of the agencies.

Research Method

This was a descriptive, qualitative study of the life stories of delinquent girls as told to me in interviews. My goal was to describe life events and characteristics of the girls from their own perspective, including what led to agency jurisdiction. The research was informed by feminist theory, which privileges the voices of the women studied. It was informed also by the research literature and theoretical perspectives presented earlier.

Three research objectives guide the study: (a) to gain from the girls an understanding of the life experiences and events that led them to the unacceptable behaviors for which they were referred for agency services; (b) to determine the prevalence of abuse in this population of girls receiving agency social services; and (c) to explore what differences existed, if any, between delinquent girls and girls receiving services as children in need of services.

I interviewed 30 girls, 15 adjudicated delinquents and 15 children in need of services, located across Massachusetts. The girls were located for the study by random selection of current cases in representative areas of the state. Face-to-face interviews, depending on the skill of the interviewer, provide an opportunity to develop rapport in the course of the interview, thus provoking more candid responses (Bradburn, 1983) and an opportunity to observe and carry through on cues from the respondent (DeLamater, 1982).

The particular offending behaviors for which the girls had been placed under agency jurisdiction were, in large part, responses to life events; the girls had acted in ways that made sense to them, within their ability to choose and act. To understand their actions, the context of life events was explored for possible or likely meanings. Official agency records rarely capture a life history from the perspective of the client when the client is an offender. Although my study was not intended to be a large-scale prevalence study of child sexual abuse, the rate of such abuse was determined for the sample.

Operational definitions of sexual abuse are not consistent in the research literature (Bass & Davis, 1988). The definition for this study was based on the subjective experiences of the girls themselves. I broached the issue with each girl who related a suggestive incident. When I felt there was a cue, I probed the subject. When a girl responded that she thought she had been sexually abused, I asked her to talk about the kind of abuse, how it felt abusive to her, the identity of the abuser(s) (though I didn't ask for names), and whether she had disclosed it to anyone. Any stories about abuse emerged from these questions, with the extent of discussion controlled by the girls. In the analysis of the 30 interviews, I examined recurrent themes about abusers and the responses of others in stories the girls told.

I began each interview with the following, open-ended question: "Tell me about your family? With whom do you live?" For girls in placement, I amended the question to: "With whom did you live before you came here or went to any other placement?" The open nature of the question prompted a wide range of responses. Each of the family members listed provided a relationship that I explored with the girl. I observed facial expressions, body language, words used to describe people and relationships, and her overall affect. Usually, family stories intermingled with information about school, drug and alcohol use, relationships with parents, other authority figures, peers, sexual activity, and other topics, including official delinquent behavior. In some cases, the girls developed accounts of physical and sexual abuse in their response to my initial question. For example, 15-year-old Diana in secure treatment (locked residential) responded:

> Tell you about my family? Well, my father, he's an alcoholic, and my mom, she's very, very nervous. And she always used to go out and get him beer, and she always used to say . . . "he ain't gonna drink real heavy and nothing can happen" and I couldn't deal with it anymore, and I couldn't deal with

my dad drinking and my mom always going out and getting it for him. . . .
It didn't hit me 'til I was around ten or eleven, that my father's drinking began
to affect me and stuff, because he began to get real violent, and beat me and
my mom up.

Katharine responded to the same question at the beginning of the interview:

There was, like, problems with my brother. [What was that?] Sexual abuse.
When I was younger. And my mother had an alcohol problem and she just
blew me off the wall. [What do you mean?] She never listened. She was never
there for me. The only time she wanted something is when she wanted one
of us to go to the store or something. She was a real idiot.

I allowed each interview to flow as a conversation, probing as the girls raised
issues in different areas of their lives. In some cases, a girl dropped hints that
she wanted to tell something but didn't know how. I drew the girls out slowly,
allowed them the opportunity to retreat and proceed as they felt comfortable.
Usually the hints centered around one or more abuse incidents that either she didn't
know how to articulate or was afraid to disclose.

Sexual victimization was not the only subject demanding empathy and support.
The girls' stories described other events and circumstances in their lives that evoked
psychological pain and fear: tales of running away, experiences with illicit drugs
and alcohol, satanic cults and ritualistic torture, suicide attempts, self-mutilation,
relationships of conflict and betrayal with parents, other loved and trusted adults,
troubled peer relationships, and reproductive health problems, especially miscar-
riages and abortions. I prepared for the interview process by reading related studies,
and I also read works of fiction and drama that have similar subjects as themes,
listening to the dialogue and acclimating to discussion of the painful issues. I wanted
to ensure that I would be well-prepared for the interviews, that neither shock,
dismay, nor judgment would censor the girls' stories (Finkelhor, 1986, pp. 222-223).

The Private Pain: Meanings of Sexual Abuse

Sexual abuse and other disruptive traumas combined with the usual developmental
tasks of growing up. Often, sexually abusive incidents served as points of initiative
for the girls to take action, as they moved from silence to subjective knowledge,
as described by Belenky, Clinchy, Goldberger, and Tarule (1986). What follows
are excerpts from the life stories of some of the girls in the study who represent
recurrent themes across the sample.

Of the 30 girls, 23 reported that they had been sexually abused, 10 by more
than one person. Six spoke of abuse by their fathers as well as by some other
individual(s), and 14 by at least one male relative. Eight had been sexually abused
by family friends, neighbors, or foster family members. Among the abusers was
one female, a cousin. None recounted abuse by strangers.

Sexual abuse with a close family member constitutes a breach of trust. The closer the relative is, the greater the sense of betrayal. Girls who reported being sexually abused by their fathers expressed feelings of devastation, not always at the time, but often later as they reconstructed their lives. In several cases, sexual incidents continued well into early adolescence; as the girls grew older, their awareness was heightened that something was dreadfully wrong.

Annie, a 14-year-old committed to the youth services authority for breaking and entering, had been sexually abused by her father and by "so many other people . . . it's hard to separate them all." Annie was very small and childlike, soft-spoken though animated as she became caught up in the story she was relating. She recounted an early memory of abuse by her father:

> I didn't see my dad much growing up. The last time I saw him I was 12 years old . . . and before that I didn't see him since I was, like, five. . . .I was scared of him . . . because when I was younger, I was molested by him, and a lot of things that happened then, it's hard to believe now, but it happened. Do you know what I mean? I was four when that happened . . . it was my weekend home. It was the weekend my sister and I went there together . . . and he lived in a one-bedroom apartment . . . and my sister went outside to play, and my dad started touching me, and he did some pretty horrid things. . . . It scared me, but I know it happened, but I can't remember what exactly did happen because there were so many other people who molested me in my life, too. So, it's hard to separate them all, do you know what I mean? Cause I see all these pictures, and everybody doing it to me, but the faces really don't come clear.

Annie wrote a poem about her father. She recited it to me, from memory, during the interview:

Love Is Blind

When I'm with you, you don't see my love.
When we're together, you don't see my trust.
We both have to accomplish what's there to be.
Like a blind seagull drifting its way to sea,
Not wondering when and if it awakes.
Love is a four-letter word,
But someone somehow got the wrong meaning.

The transcript from Annie's interview recounts a sequence of sexual victimizations, beginning with her father's molestation of her when she was four, continuing with a stepfather, a friend of one of her stepfathers, a male babysitter, the babysitter's brother, and a foster brother. There was physical abuse and neglect from her mother and first stepfather, and she was placed in a series of foster homes, interspersed with trial stays at home that never worked out. Annie spoke little of her feelings about the incidents, directing attention instead to trying to remember details, names, and places. She did recount that the night she was arrested for breaking and entering a neighbor's house (who was on vacation) she was running away from home because her stepfather had been beating her. She hid under the dining room table in the neighbor's house, and waited for the police to find her. She said she wanted the police to come, so they would take her out of her stepfather's house. She reasoned that if she committed a crime, they would take her away permanently.

Angela, a 15-year-old CHINS (for running away), related the story of how her father had been absent from her life until she met him when she was 12 years old. She spoke of feeling abandoned by her birth father, her grief at finding out at the age of 12 that her first stepfather was not her "real" father, and anger and mistrust toward her birth father when, soon after they met, he sexually abused Angela and her sister.

Angela (R): I've had two stepfathers. Well, one really raised me. I call him my real father. . . . F_____ was my natural birth father but he was never around for me. He left me when I was 10 months old. So I don't consider him my real father.

Interviewer (Q): Did you ever know him?

R: Yeah, I know him now. . . . I don't know, I like him I guess because he's my father, but I don't really talk to him that much.

Q: When did he come back into your life?

R: When I was 12.

Q: What happened that made him do that?

R: My mother wanted to tell us sooner but she didn't want us to know that my real father was alive. She didn't want us to know. . . . The father of the three little kids, I lived with him since I was 10 months old and I always thought he was my natural birth father. And when I turned 12, my mother told me he wasn't my real father. . . . And that's when I started having problems. When I was 12 years old.

Q: Do you think it had anything to do with the problems?

R: I think it had to do with all the abuse that was going on, and my mother, and the things that were going on with my stepfather [physical abuse of Angela and her mother as well as his heavy drug use in the home]. . . . I have feelings for my father, but I never trusted him. When he came back, my sister loved him, but I never did, cause he abused me and my sister.

Q: How?

R: Sexually. He molested me and my sister. Because this show he was looking at in his work . . . where fathers were showing their daughters how to have sex and mothers were showing their sons how to have sex. And he said that he wanted me to try it out, and that he won't hurt, that I didn't have to worry about getting pregnant if I was worried about that. You know, he tried it with me but it wouldn't work. I kept saying, no, I don't want to.

Q: He tried with you physically?

R: Yeah! And I told him over and over, no, I don't want to. And good thing my sister walked back in, cause he stopped. Then, when we spent the night over his house, with his wife, he tried everything with my sister, and my sister didn't know no better and my sister let him cause she loved him. She didn't want to get taken away from him. So she did whatever he told her to. I didn't. Because I knew it was wrong. And I told my mother about that, and my mother called DSS and told them. And they pressed charges against him. But he lied and he said he didn't do it. And that's what got me so mad at him, that's why I never trusted him again . . . and my sister even lied, too. She lied because she loved him. I wouldn't lie about nothing like that. Just to save his behind. Yeah.

Angela had learned from her experience with her second stepfather, who was physically violent with her, her mother, and her sister, to be wary. In the case of her second stepfather, DSS had removed the children from the home when claims of abuse, filed by an adult friend and neighbor of Angela's, were substantiated. Angela had lived in a foster home for a while, then returned to her mother. Around the same time, she was told about and met her "real" father. Her second stepfather, by that time, had been incarcerated for cocaine possession and was out of the home. A year later, he returned home, the beatings resumed, and Angela ran away to live with a boyfriend. She continued to go to school throughout the sequence of events, because "getting schooling is the only way out." She became pregnant, had a miscarriage, and returned home. During the time she was gone, her mother filed a CHINS petition. Angela's social worker from DSS, hearing of the miscarriage, went back to the court that had issued the CHINS petition and requested Angela be sent to a residential group placement. I interviewed Angela at the group home.

The violence Angela experienced confused her. She perceived that she had followed the rules: She did excellent work in school and tried to take care of her mother and younger siblings. Her stepfather beat them regardless. The discovery at the age of 12 that her biological father had abandoned her when she was an infant, the introduction to him, and the subsequent sexually abusive incidents further confused her and challenged the developmental tasks she faced at adolescence, including finding a place for herself as a self-determining individual. Running away from the abusive situation seemed to make the most sense of any alternative she could fathom.

When Annabelle was 3 years old, her mother left her and her older brother at their grandmother's house, and, with no explanation that Annabelle heard, did not return until Annabelle was five years old. Annabelle quickly came to identify grandmother as mother, not knowing who her mother was until she appeared to reclaim her. Annabelle's story revealed not only physical abandonment, but emotional abandonment subsequently when she left her grandmother's home to live with her mother, stepfather, and older brother. Her brother began to sexually abuse her when she was 11 years old. He would come to her room at night; she responded by staying out most of the night, hanging out in the local park. Because she felt betrayed by her mother and had no one else she felt she could trust, she kept the reason for her nighttime absences secret. Annabelle said her mother assumed she was out all night, partying and having sex with boys. Finally, her mother filed a CHINS petition, charging that Annabelle was a runaway.

> **R:** My brother was doing things that I never told about.
> **Q:** To you?
> **R:** Yeah. So I would stay out at night so it wouldn't happen.
> **Q:** What kinds of things?
> **R:** Sex. Rape. Cause our rooms were right next to each other upstairs and our parents' room was downstairs. . . . So I stayed out at nighttime so I wouldn't be near him.
> **Q:** And you never told anybody about that?
> **R:** Not until . . . last year.
> **Q:** So you were involved with CHINS for 4 years and they never knew about the abuse from your brother?
> **R:** No.
> **Q:** You never told your mom or anyone?
> **R:** No . . . I just started staying out late and my mom got really mad about it. . . . And plus when I was home I would go out more often. Because when you're 12 you start doing things with your friends, you know? And my mother didn't like that. She called me a little slut and everything.

The actions Annabelle took to protect herself antagonized her mother to the point that Annabelle became the object of derision in the household for almost everything. Eventually, she did run away, back to her grandmother's house. She told her mother where she was going, but her mother went to court for a warrant anyway. The police apprehended her at her grandmother's house. The subsequent court appearance resulted in the first of 19 placements over the next 4 years, including residential placements, foster homes, inpatient psychiatric units, and detention units.

Over the 4 years of placements, Annabelle stated that she made a conscious decision to divorce herself completely from any relationship with her mother, stepfather, and brother. She attempted suicide several times, lived with a man for several months by whom she became pregnant, was imprisoned by the same man (he stabbed her on two occasions when she tried to leave him), suffered a miscarriage, and finally ran away. She was subsequently arrested (for contempt of court, again, for running away), spent time in yet another detention and inpatient psychiatric unit, and then was placed in yet another foster home. At the time of the interview, she was living in a temporary foster home and claimed to have contact with no family members except her grandmother.

Annabelle expressed frustration with the legal technicalities that retained her mother as legal parent and guardian; the only nurture she had ever experienced was from her grandmother, yet she was thwarted repeatedly from staying with her in a place where she felt safe, wanted, and loved. No child abuse or neglect petitions had ever been filed against the mother. Annabelle believed that her constant running away focused the family problems onto her, and the mother's proactive pursuit of Annabelle kept her in the position of offender. The sexual abuse by her brother had continued over 4 years, every time Annabelle was sent or taken home, and continued up to 5 months before I interviewed her:

> **R:** [In the context of a discussion of her attempted suicides and in response to a question about whether she really wanted to die] I don't know. The world's fucked up. I mean, I don't want to hang around here forever, but, I suppose if the world was great and no one wanted to die there'd be a population problem. But I don't want to hang around forever and I don't want to die today so, take it as you want. . . . Every time I went back to my mother's my brother would do it again. He's been doing it all along up until 5 months ago. Every time I tried to get out, I'd get arrested and sent to some place to "improve" me. Last time, the court order wanted to send me to another assessment. And I hated it. I ran . . . went back, did my time, stayed on the highest level. Got out. And I went to court, they tried to talk this bullshit about residential. It was fucked. I wouldn't go. But, so, I stayed with my mother, which obviously didn't work out . . . my brother was still doing it. So, I'm like . . . What? I talked to my social worker. . . . I didn't have anywhere else I could go.
>
> **Q:** So you went back to your mom's?
>
> **R:** Yeah. I called [my social worker], I was having problems. "Well, I don't have anyplace for you." I said, well, can I go stay with my friend [to get away from my brother]? "Yeah, fine," she said, "give me the phone number and the address," she told me. So I went and stayed there. Gave her the phone number, the address, the mother's name, everything. Three days later I find out I have a warrant out for my arrest for runaway. From my mother . . . *and my social worker!*

In addition to a sense of "badness" the girls felt within themselves, they also expressed differentness and separateness from peers, especially, and from adults. They spoke of difficulties they had relating to others, the need to keep troubles within, self-doubts about how others perceived them. Some related stories of a single, close friendship with another girl who had shared similar troubles. Many could reveal their pain to no one.

I interviewed Lisa, a 14-year-old committed to DYS for larceny of a motor vehicle, in a residential placement. Early in the interview, Lisa spoke of her alienation from the group of girls there because of her personal history, and their rejection of her for wanting to talk about it:

> I'm not allowed to talk about my sexual abuse in group, not that and not the Satanism. I'm not allowed to talk about anything I don't feel comfortable talking about, or anything the group is uncomfortable talking about. . . . Some girls here had an attitude toward me about the Satanism and I said to them, please don't let my past get in the way of our relationship.

Feeling marginalized, Lisa's story (the content of which was independently documented from other sources) is informative in several ways. She had been sexually abused by male family members; her uncle and brother dominated her

stories on the subject. Her earliest recollection of sexual abuse was an incident
that happened when she was 5 years old. Several people over the next 6 years
sexually abused her until she was 11. (Revictimization is a common theme in the
life stories of the girls and is supported by the literature on sexual abuse [see
Herman, 1992; Russell, 1984].)

> Nobody cared. . . . I did what I wanted, how I wanted. When I wanted it
> . . . I wasn't allowed to do anything when I was little. I wasn't allowed to
> play with my friends well, I really didn't have any friends. . . . I was, kind
> of, basically on my . . . by myself. When I tried to have friends, I'd get into
> a fight or something like that . . . it just wouldn't work out, having friends.
> So I basically just grew up having one friend. . . . She lived up the street.
> She was quite a few years older than I was. And she did drugs, and she got
> pregnant at 16. . . and I didn't see her for a while.

Lisa became involved with DSS when a child abuse and neglect petition was
filed against her mother. Lisa never disclosed the sexual incidents throughout her
years of involvement with DSS, though she told me her social workers had asked.
She denied because she did not want to be perceived as the deviant she already
had labeled herself. She was embarrassed that her mother's neglect was known
to the agency, and she didn't want to admit to any other abuse. The fears and secrecy
she harbored kept her from seeking friendships.

At the age of 12, Lisa ran away from home with a girl she knew after they had
met and become involved with a group of Satanic cultists. Lisa said she felt she
didn't belong anywhere, and the Satan worshippers were attractive because they
seemed to have power, something Lisa lacked in her own life.

> **R:** And when I was 12, I had gotten involved in a little Satanism. I was *involved*
> with Satanism. . . . And we started hanging around with these people . . .
> they were in a cult. . . . We basically went there at first just to party. All's
> I did was coke the first night that I ever met any of them . . . about thirty
> people . . . only six girls. After hanging around with them for about a week,
> me and my friend ran away from home. . . . I saw them as people who had
> a lot of power, cause anything they said was done. The leader, he had power.
> . . . He had control. I saw that and I wanted it. . . . We had to do some
> pretty gross things . . . and sex was always expected. Now, I feel gross, and
> I didn't like it back then.
> **Q:** Why did you do it?
> **R:** For the power. Cause the more that you did with the group, the more power
> you got.
> **Q:** Did you feel the power? Or did you keep hoping you'd get it? Or what?
> **R:** You feel . . . [long silence]. It's a different feeling. I don't know how to explain
> it. You could really, actually, pretty much feel the power. You could feel,
> I don't know, something more than what I had before. I used to do a lot of
> acid when I was doing this. It was . . . oh . . . it was sick.

Q: What kind of "more" did you feel? More control over yourself? Other people? Smarter? Braver? Sexier? What more was it?

R: Like I could do anything. You know? No one's going to stop me.

Q: And what did you do with the power?

R: I did what I wanted to do, and how I wanted to do it.

Q: And at that time, what was it?

R: Party. Have sex. Fuck off. Oh, God, it was all so sick.

Ironically, living at the margin of family acceptance led Lisa to seek power from a group that would accept her, if she provided sex. Lisa ended up feeling yet another kind of difference, the stigma of being involved in a Satanic cult. But she acted in a way that made sense to her: She felt powerless and joined a group that she perceived as powerful. Lisa summarized her story:

> Oh, there's definitely a connection between my mom and her boyfriends beating on me and my brother and my uncle molesting me, and my drinking and the drugs and the cult and all. Get stoned, forget about it all.

Conclusion

There is minimal focus on girls in trouble as worthy subjects of social policy (Hudson, 1989), yet research suggests an association between female delinquency and child sexual abuse. As children and as females, female delinquents and status offenders who have been sexually abused are "victims as well as offenders, [whose] backgrounds and current situations require specialized services that overburdened and underfunded social service and correctional systems will be hard pressed to deliver" (Chesney-Lind & Rodriguez, 1983).

The lack of a public voice that women can use to share common experience in a public forum is a troubling deficiency, especially for adolescent female offenders. The secrecy of abuse feeds the effects of the abuse, encouraging self-stigmatization. Known strategies for change—exit and voice (Hirschman, 1970)—were rarely possible for the girls in my study, except in ways that either labeled them as deviant or jeopardized their safety. Heilbrun (1989) decries the lack of a public voice: "male power has made certain stories unthinkable." Living in isolation and fear, lacking the "sight of a possible life," girls could find a common voice, make sense of their experiences, and find personal power by sharing experiences with others (Herman, 1992). . . .

Research suggests a strong association between abuse, particularly sexual abuse, and the offending behaviors of girls (Chesney-Lind, 1989; Hudson, 1989; Koroki & Chesney-Lind, 1985), which my study also finds. . . . The stories I collected suggest the strength girls find, ultimately within themselves, to challenge dangerous and abusive situations and to leave. The stories also reveal the remnants of volition the girls retain in the face of horrendous experiences. The accounts draw attention to affiliation and care in the development and behavior of girls, and on the loyalty they may feel to others to the detriment of their own well-being. My research questions the widespread belief that adolescent girls are offenders needing to be controlled and reformed. The control of adolescent female sexuality—a tacit goal of the juvenile courts and the agencies that serve girls committed to their care—misses the mark.

The ideal of the sexually innocent adolescent girl, perpetuated over millennia, seems to be incongruous with the lives of adolescent girls in current American society, certainly with those in my sample. Popular media and current events militate against an ideal of sexual innocence; adolescent girls are challenged *not* to absorb the messages of easy sexuality promoted in the popular culture. Childhood and early adolescent experiences of sexual abuse may further exacerbate the confusion of appropriate sexual behavior that girls who experience such abuse may have.

Still, the girls who were the subjects of my study were rulebreakers, by their own admission and by the determination of the juvenile courts. It is difficult to distinguish the meanings society holds of their rulebreaking relative to the meanings the girls convey. An understanding of the meanings the girls give for their behavior may serve to enlighten policymakers and practitioners who work in the agencies that serve girls like these. Understanding the girls' actions, in the context of their experiences with family, may aid service workers.

Because girls constitute a minority of the total population in the juvenile courts and related services, it is difficult, though essential, to organize resources to deal specifically with them. Concern with boys has dominated the theories and research guiding program philosophy and standards, perception of juvenile crime and risk, and assumptions about the needs and characteristics of juvenile offenders. The special life issues and characteristics of girls suggest that they are a special population with special needs, which are addressed ineffectively by traditional programs.

Four major areas of policy reform are suggested by my study:

1. Routine screening and treatment by specially trained personnel for girls who have experienced sexual abuse
2. Universal discussion of and education about sexual abuse in schools and community programs, to target the age groups at greatest risk (primary grades through junior high school)
3. Legislative, juvenile court, and agency reformulation of response to juvenile female offending, particularly in cases of nonviolent and other victimless crimes
4. Development of ongoing, interagency collaboration between decision makers and street-level practitioners to focus on the needs of girls and their families

It is tempting to say that society must change the way it views girls, as objects to be controlled, whether the views are intended to be benevolent, punitive, or abusive. It is tempting to say that no social control is better than harmful or stigmatizing social control. But otherwise how do we provide aid and guidance to children who grow up with inadequate nurture or experience profound violations? How do we honor and support girls' individual talents, will, and volition? Given the findings of my study, perhaps the best course is to focus on policy change in existing agencies that provide services, so that they can more closely respond to needs as voiced by the girls themselves.

References

Bass, E., & Davis, L. (1988). *The courage to heal: A guide for women survivors of sexual abuse.* New York: Harper & Row.

Belenky, M. F., Clinchy, B. M., Goldberger N. R., & Tarule, J. M. (1986). *Women's ways of knowing: The development of self, voice, and mind.* New York: Basic Books.

Bradburn, N. M. (1983). Response effects. In P. H. Rossi, J. D. Wright, & A. B. Anderson (Eds.), *Handbook of survey research.* New York: Academic Press.

Brenzel, B. M. (1983). *Daughters of the state: A social portrait of the first reform school for girls in North America. 1856-1905.* Cambridge: MIT Press.

Browne, A., & Finkelhor, D. (1986). Initial and long-term effects: A review of the research. In D. Finkelhor & Associates, *A sourcebook on child sexual abuse* (pp. 143-179). Beverly Hills: Sage.

Campbell, A. (1984). *The girls in the gang.* Oxford, UK: Basil Blackwell.

Chesney-Lind, M. (1973). Judicial enforcement of the female sex role. *Issues in Criminology, 3,* 51-71.

Chesney-Lind, M. (1978). Young women in the arms of the law. In L. H. Bowker (Ed.), *Women, crime, and the criminal justice system.* Lexington, MA: Lexington Books.

Chesney-Lind, M. (1982). Guilty by reason of sex: Young women and the juvenile justice system. In B. R. Price & N. J. Sokoloff (Eds.), *Criminal justice system and women* (pp. 77-104). New York: Clark Boardman.

Chesney-Lind, M. (1989). Girls' crime and women's place: Toward a feminist model of female delinquency. *Crime & Delinquency, 35*(1), 5-29.

Chesney-Lind, M., & Rodriguez, N. (1983). Women under lock and key: A view from the inside. *Prison Journal, 63*(2), 47-65.

Chesney-Lind, M., & Shelden, R (1991). *Girls, delinquency, and crime.* Pacific Grove, CA: Brooks-Cole.

DeLamater, J. (1982). Response effects of question content. In W. Dijkstra & J. van der Zouwen (Eds.), *Response behavior in the survey-interview.* London: Academic Press.

Dublin, T. (1981). *Women at work: The transformation of work and community in Lowell, Massachusetts, 1826-1860.* New York: Columbia University Press.

Finkelhor, D. & Associates. (1986). *A sourcebook on child sexual abuse.* Beverly Hills, CA: Sage.

Guarino, S. (1985). *Delinquent abuse and family violence: A study of abuse and neglect in the homes of serious juvenile offenders* (14, 020-200-74-2-86-CR). Boston: Executive Office of Human Services, Dept. of Youth Services.

Hagan, J., & Palloni, A. (1988). Crimes as social events in the life course: Reconceiving a criminological controversy. *Criminology 26*(1), 87-100.

Heilbrun, C. (1989). *Writing a woman's life.* New York: Norton.

Herman, J. (1992). *Trauma and recovery.* New York: Basic Books.

Hirschman, A. O. (1970). *Exit, voice, and loyalty: Responses to decline in firms, organizations, and states.* Cambridge: Harvard University Press.

Hudson, A. (1989). "Troublesome girls:" Towards alternative definitions and policies. In M. Cain (Ed.), *Growing up good: Policing the behaviour of girls in Europe*. London: Sage.

Karlsen, C. F. (1981). *The devil in the shape of a woman: The Witch in seventeenth century New England*. Unpublished doctoral dissertation, Yale University, New Haven, CT.

Koroki, J., & Chesney-Lind, J. (1985). *"Everything just going down the drain:" Interviews with female delinquents in Hawaii*. (Youth Development and Research Center. Report No. 319) Manoa: University of Hawaii.

Miller, J. B. (1976). *Toward a new psychology of women*. Boston: Beacon Press.

Robinson, R. (1990). *Violations of girlhood: A qualitative study of female delinquents and children in need of services in Massachusetts*. Unpublished doctoral dissertation, Brandeis University, Waltham, MA.

Russell, D. E. H. (1984). *Sexual exploitation*. Beverly Hills: Sage.

Shelden, R. G., Horvath, J. A., & Tracy, S. (1989). Do status offenders get worse? Some clarifications on the question of escalation. *Crime and Delinquency 35* (2), 202-216.

Thomas, W. I. (1923). *The unadjusted girl*. Boston: Little, Brown.

6

Collective and Normative Features of Gang Violence

Scott H. Decker

In 1927 Frederic Thrasher observed that gangs shared many of the properties of mobs, crowds, and other collectives, and engaged in many forms of collective behavior. Despite the prominent role of his work in gang research, few attempts have been made to link the behavior of gangs to theories of collective behavior. This omission is noteworthy because, despite disagreements about most other criteria—turf, symbols, organizational structure, permanence, criminality—all gang researchers include "group" as a part of their definition of gangs. Gang members are individuals with diverse motives, behaviors, and socialization experiences. Their group membership, behavior, and values, however, make them interesting to criminologists who study gangs.

In this paper we explore the mechanisms and processes that result in the spread and escalation of gang violence. In particular, we focus on contagion as an aspect of collective behavior that produces expressive gang violence. Collective behavior explanations provide insights into gang processes, particularly the escalation of violence, the spread of gangs from one community to another, and increases in gang membership in specific communities.

Decker, Scott H. 1996. Features of Gang Violence. *Justice Quarterly,* 13:2:243-264.

Gang Violence

Violence is integral to life in the gang, as Klein and Maxson (1989) observed, and gang members engage in more violence than other youths. Thrasher (1927) noted that gangs developed through strife and flourish on conflict. According to Klein (1971:85), violence is a "predominant 'myth system'" among gang members and is constantly present.

Our analysis of gang violence focuses on the role of threat, actual or perceived, in explaining the functions and consequences of gang violence. We define threat as the potential for transgressions against or physical harm to the gang, represented by the acts or presence of a rival group. Threats of violence are important because they have consequences for future violence. Threat plays a role in the origin and growth of gangs, their daily activities, and their belief systems. In a sense, it helps to define them to rival gangs, to the community, and to social institutions.

Katz (1988) argues that gangs are set apart from other groups by their ability to create "dread," a direct consequence of involvement in and willingness to use violence. Dread elevates these individuals to street elites through community members' perceptions of gang members as violent. In many neighborhoods, groups form for protection against the threat of outside groups (Suttles 1972). Sometimes these groups are established along ethnic lines, though territorial concerns often guide their formation. Sanders (1993), in a 10-year study of gangs in San Diego, argued that the mix of conventional values with underclass values—spiced by the realities of street culture—was a volatile combination. Hagedorn (1988) found that conflicts between the police and young men "hanging out" on the corner led to more formalized structures, and ultimately to gangs. Both Suttles (1972:98) and Sullivan (1989) underscored the natural progression from a neighborhood group to a gang, particularly in the face of "adversarial relations" with outside groups. The emergence of many splinter gangs can be traced to the escalation of violence within larger gangs, and to the corresponding threat that the larger gang comes to represent to certain territorial or age-graded subgroups. Sullivan (1989) documented the expressive character of most gang violence, and described the role of fighting in the evolution of cliques into street gangs. Because this occurs at a young age, the use of group violence attains a normative character.

Threat also may contribute to the growth of gangs. This mechanism works in two ways: through building cohesiveness and through contagion. Threats of physical violence increase the solidarity or cohesiveness of gangs within neighborhoods as well as across neighborhoods. Klein (1971) identified the source of cohesion in gangs as primarily external—the result of intergang conflict; Hagedorn (1988) also made this observation. According to Klein, cohesion within the gang grows in proportion to the perceived threat represented by rival gangs. Padilla (1992) reported a similar finding, noting that threat maintains gang boundaries by strengthening the ties among gang members and increasing their commitment to each other, thus enabling them to overcome any initial reluctance about staying in the gang and ultimately engaging in violence. Thus the threat of a gang in a geographically proximate neighborhood increases the solidarity of the gang, motivates more young men to join their neighborhood gang (see Vigil 1988), and enables them to engage in acts of violence that they might not have committed otherwise.

The growth of gangs and gang violence contains elements of what Loftin (1984) calls "contagion." In this context, contagion refers to subsequent acts of violence caused by an initial act; such acts typically take the form of retaliation. Violence—or its threat—is the mechanism that spreads gangs from one neighborhood to another, as well as contributing to their growth. From Loftin's perspective, the concept of contagion can be used to explain the rapid growth, or the "spikes," that occur in violent crime. He argues that three conditions must be present if contagion is to occur: (1) a spatial concentration of assaultive violence, (2) a reciprocal nature to assaultive violence, and (3) escalations in assaultive violence. These conditions apply to our use of the concept of threat in explaining gangs. Gangs have a strong spatial structure; they claim particular turf as their own and are committed to its "defense" against outsiders. The specter of a rival gang "invading" their turf and violating its sanctity is likely to evoke a violent response, leading to the spatial clustering of violence.

The reciprocal nature of gang violence explains in part how gangs form initially, as well as how they increase in size and strength. Klein and Maxson (1989:223) demonstrated that fear of retaliation was three times more likely to characterize gang homicides than other homicides involving juveniles. The perceived need to engage in retaliatory violence also helps to explain the increasing sophistication of weapons used by gang members. As Horowitz (1983) observed, gang members arm themselves in the belief that their rivals have guns; they seek to increase the sophistication of their weaponry in the hope that they will not find themselves in a shootout with less firepower than their rival. This process was documented by Block and Block (1993) in their explanation of the increase in street gang homicides in Chicago.

The threat of attack by a group of organized youths from another neighborhood is part of the gang "myth" or belief system, and helps to create the need for protection as well as to generate unity in a previously unorganized group of neighborhood youths. The origin and spread of such beliefs explain, among other things, the viability of the gang. Threat performs an additional function: it enhances the mythic nature of violence in the gang by increasing the talk about violence and preparedness for violent engagements.

The threat of violence also "enables" gang members to engage in violent acts (especially retaliatory violence) that they might not have chosen under other circumstances. The need to respond effectively to rival gang violence escalates weaponry and increases the "tension" that often precedes violent encounters between gangs. Many gang members reported to Padilla (1992) that they joined their gang out of fear of violence at the hands of rival gangs. The concern that a rival gang is considering an attack often compels a peremptory strike (particularly drive-by shootings) from the gang that considers itself under threat.

Loftin's (1984) third element of contagion, rapid escalation of assaultive violence, explains the sudden peaks in gang violence. These peaks can be explained in part by the retaliatory nature of gang violence (Decker and Van Winkle 1996), a finding in the data from Chicago gangs (Block and Block 1993).

Threat has an additional function, however. As gangs and gang members engage in acts of violence and create "dread" (Katz 1988:135), they are viewed as threatening by other (gang and nongang) groups and individuals. Also, over time, the threats that gang members face and pose isolate them from legitimate social institutions such as schools, families, and the labor market. This isolation, in turn, prevents them from engaging in the very activities and relationships that might reintegrate them into legitimate roles and reduce their criminal involvement. It weakens their ties to the socialization power and the controlling norms of such mainstream institutions, and frees them to commit acts of violence.

Collective Behavior

Collective behavior and social organizations such as gangs share many common elements, including group behavior, collective processes, and group structure. Thus it is productive to view collective behavior on a continuum with social organizations rather than regarding them as separate topics of study. Thrasher (1927) observed that collective behavior processes operated within the gang, and could be used to account for the emergence of collective violence. Such processes included games, fights, meetings, and defining common enemies. His theoretical formulation, and the supporting distinctions between gangs and other forms of social organizations (e.g., groups, mobs, crowds, publics),[1] make clear the role that he perceived for collective behavior explanations of gang activity.

We adopt our definition of collective behavior from McPhail (1991), who identified three elements of collective behavior: (1) group, (2) behavior, and (3) common actions that vary on one or more dimensions such as purpose, organization, or duration. McPhail observed that gang violence is a form of collective behavior because it emerges from a group process involving common actions that have a defined purpose. This view of collective behavior is agnostic with regard to motives; that is, such behavior may have either well-defined instrumental goals or more expressive goals. Most research has characterized gang motives as expressive, but Sanchez-Jankowski (1991) argued for a more instrumental orientation. On the basis of his 10-year observation of gangs in three cities, he described gangs as "formal-rational" organizations; he contended that gangs have rules, roles, and goals, and function as highly differentiated and purposive social organizations. Sanchez-Jankowski's research, especially with regard to gang violence, stands alone in its conclusions.

Ironically, the view of gangs as a form of collective behavior may be explicated most fully not in original research on gangs, but in Pfautz's (1961) reconceptualization of Yablonsky's (1959) research on violent gangs. Yablonsky described the gang as a near-group, and attributed much of its violent behavior to the leadership of members who were emotionally disturbed and lacked effective controls against participating in violence. Pfautz argued that it is more productive to view gang violence as the outcome of collective behavior; he noted that some forms of collective behavior are more likely to emerge in the face of a weakened social structure.[2] In reviewing the gang literature, Pfautz observed that gangs lack structure, goals, and techniques. Therefore they act on the basis of what he identified as "associational characteristics," the strength of membership ties or bonds. According to this view, violent behavior by gangs is an expressive response to objective social circumstances (poverty, racism, and other pressures of the underclass) rather than a symbolic expression of "manhood," "low self-esteem," or lack of group solidarity. Gang violence, however, is not a purposive attempt to alter social structure. It emerges as a collective response by members of the underclass to organize around neighborhood affiliations.

Short (1974) attempted to develop theoretical links between several aspects of gang behavior and collective behavior. By observing that gangs emerge out of typical adolescent activities—activities that lack organization, involve groups ripe for collective action, and entail only weakly held group goals—he argued that they originate in collective behavior. Conflict between gangs is particularly important to this process because such disputes help to establish boundaries between groups and reinforce the ties between members. Short agreed with Pfautz that most gang delinquency is expressive, especially gang violence, which frequently reflects the gang's attempt to enforce its particular definition of a situation on another gang. The gang's collective liability for wrong done to rival members expands the pool of potential victims and

increases the threats of retaliatory violence. These characteristics underscore
the utility of collective behavior approaches in accounting for gang violence.

Data and Methods

This paper is based on the results of a three-year study of gangs conducted
in St. Louis between 1990 and 1993. Our work is consistent with other
research (Hagedorn, 1988, 1991; Moore 1978; Padilla 1992; Vigil 1988)
that used field techniques to understand gang members' perspective. We
agree with Hagedorn (1991) that one can understand this perspective most
fully by contacting gang members directly in their communities. We contacted gang members directly on the street and conducted interviews at a
neutral site.[3] This procedure was consistent with our goal of learning about
gang activities in the words and terms used by gang members to describe
them. Our working definition of a gang includes age-graded peer groups
that exhibit permanence, engage in criminal activity, and have symbolic
representations of membership. Field contacts with active gang members
were made by a street ethnographer, an ex-offender himself, who had built
a reputation as "solid" on the street through his work with the community
and previous fieldwork. The street ethnographer had been shot several
years earlier, and now used a wheelchair. The combination of his reputation
in the community and his experience in contacting and interviewing active
offenders enhanced the validity of the responses. Using snowball sampling
procedures (Biemacki and Waldorf 1981; Wright et al. 1992), the research
team made initial field contacts with gang members, verified membership,
and built the sample to include more subjects.

Our sampling strategy was designed to interview members from a variety
of gangs and to gain a broader perspective into gang activity. Like most
field studies, the pace of our study was often erratic; in some months we
held several interviews, while in others we had none. Individuals who met
our criteria, acknowledged gang membership, and agreed to an interview
were included in our sample. We verified membership through information
from previous subjects, our own observations, or both. The field ethnographer played a key role in this process by comparing responses from the
interview to street conversations. Our final sample of 99 active gang members was the outcome of more than 500 field contacts initiated with gang
members. Members of the final sample were selected on the basis of extensive involvement in the gang and their willingness to participate in the
study.

A semistructured questionnaire, based on a number of unstructured interviews conducted before the beginning of the study, was used to guide the
interviews. We promised confidentiality to each subject, and did not record
their real names. Interviews were conducted by six members of the

research team; each was familiar with the gang literature, was knowledgeable about gangs in St. Louis, and had conducted several practice interviews. Each interview was tape-recorded and transcribed for analysis. Interviews generally lasted two hours; they asked for information about joining the gang, the nature of gang organization, illegal activities (especially violence), legal activities, links to other gangs, and ties to traditional institutions. A specific set of questions addressed the ties between gang members and their families. We also observed a number of gang activities and individual gang members in the field. We spoke regularly with these individuals and recorded notes to supplement the interviews.

We interviewed individuals from several gangs. According to our interviews and observations, gangs in St. Louis appear to have strong ties to their neighborhood but also claim affiliation with a larger gang that extends well beyond neighborhood boundaries. The bond between gang members and their own subgroup within the gang, however, was usually stronger than the attachment to the larger gang. This finding is consistent with our observations that gangs in St. Louis were organized rather loosely. Few gangs whose members we interviewed had identifiable leaders, roles, or rules.[4] Most of our subjects identified themselves as "regular" members, though 10 individuals told us they were either leaders or "OGs" (original gangsters). We observed little variation between their responses and those of regular members.

We interviewed 99 active gang members representing 29 different gangs. Sixteen of these gangs, accounting for 67 of our 99 subjects, were affiliated with the Crips. Gang members affiliated with the Bloods accounted for the remainder of our sample, and included 13 gangs and 32 members. Field techniques cannot provide a representative sample, but our subjects varied considerably in age, gang affiliation, and activities, thus assuring that we received information from a variety of gang members. As a result, it was unlikely that our respondents revealed information about only a narrow segment of gang activity.

Although our data were collected over a three-year period, they are not longitudinal in the sense that they followed a single individual or group of individuals over time. We were sensitive to the dynamic nature of gangs in St. Louis during our study period, and incorporated those concerns into questions about how the gang had changed over time. In addition, we compared responses recorded early in the study with those of subjects interviewed in the later stages. Finally, near the end of our study, we recontacted several individuals whom we had interviewed in the early phases of the project. We noted any changes in gang violence that occurred during the course of the study.

We identified six different "constellations" of gangs in our sample, four with the Crip designation and two groups of Bloods. We use the term *constellation* to refer to a larger gang that may be composed of many gang subgroups. For example, the Genevive Thrush Posse is affiliated with the Rolling Sixties, a larger gang of Crips. We found no important differences between these constellations on any of the dimensions of violence we examined. This finding adds credence to the claim that members of our sample knew about a wide range of activities within their gang.

Ages for members of our sample ranged from 13 to 29, with an average age of 17. The majority were black (96%) and male (93%). On average, the gang members we interviewed had been active members for three years. More than three-quarters of our subjects told us that their gang existed before they joined; the average age of gangs in our sample was six years. An average of 213 gang members were involved in the larger gang; subgroups ranged from six to ten members. Ninety percent of our sample reported that they had participated in violent crime; 70% reported that they had committed a property crime. Thus it is not surprising that our subjects also had extensive experience with the criminal justice system: 80 percent reported an arrest, and the average number of arrests was eight.

Collective Violence Processes within the Gang

Gang violence includes a number of acts and is most likely to involve assaults and the use of weapons. Although the motives for these acts are diverse, much gang violence (as discussed above) is retaliatory. This quality is evident in the disproportionate number of assaults and shootings committed in response to the acts of other gangs. This finding is similar to those of other gang researchers including Hagedorn (1988), Klein and Maxson (1989), Maxson, Gordon, and Klein (1985), Moore (1978), Sanders (1993), and Vigil (1988). Initial interviews made clear that a number of violent acts were committed by gang members outside the gang. It would be inappropriate to classify these acts as gang-related, even though they were committed by gang members. Our classification of gang violence included only those acts committed by gang members which were organized by gang members and motivated by gang concerns, especially revenge, retaliation, reputation, and representation of membership. This classification corresponds to the more restrictive of the two definitions applied by Maxson and Klein (1990).

The centrality of violence to gang life was illustrated by counts of the times a topic was mentioned during an interview.[5] Except for drugs (which were mentioned more than 2,000 times), our subjects mentioned violence more often than any other topic. They referred to violence 1,681 times, including hundreds of references to specific acts such as killing or murder (246), assault (148), and robbery (71). As further evidence of the importance of violence, nine of our 99 subjects have been killed since the study began in 1990; several showed us bullet wounds during the interview.[6] As stated earlier, this group had extensive arrest histories: 80 percent had been arrested at least once, the mean number of arrests per subject was eight, and one-third reported that their most recent arrest was for assault or weapons violations.

Other incidents also illustrate the salience of violence in the lives of gang members. One day three gang members were sitting on their front porch, waiting for the field ethnographer to pick up one of them for an interview. As he drove up their street, he heard shots and saw the three subjects being shot in a drive-by. Their wounds were superficial, but this incident underscored the daily potential for violence as well as our ability to observe it firsthand. During the course of our research, several gang members offered to demonstrate their ability to use violence, typically by inviting us to accompany them on a drive-by shooting or to drop them off in rival territory and watch them shoot a rival gang member. We declined all such invitations, but they are not uncommon in field research (Wright and Decker 1994). On a few occasions during interviews, gang members displayed a firearm when asked whether they possessed a gun. Most subjects reported beginning their life in the gang with a violent encounter; usually they were "beaten in" by members of the gang they were joining. The process of leaving the gang was also described in violent terms: by being "beaten out," leaving through fear of violence, suffering serious injury, or death.[7]

The research reported here attempts to provide a framework for understanding the peaks and valleys of gang violence. As Short and Strodtbeck (1974) observed, efforts to understand gang violence must focus both on process variables (such as interactions) and on situational characteristics (such as neighborhood structure, age, race, and sex). For these reasons we concentrate on stages in the gang process that illustrate important aspects of gang violence, and we examine such violence in the context of five spheres of gang activity: (1) the role of violence in defining life in the gang, (2) the role of violence in the process of joining the gang, (3) the use of violence by the gang, (4) staging grounds for violence, and (5) gang members' recommendations for ending their gang.

The Role of Violence in Defining Life in the Gang

A fundamental way to demonstrate the centrality of violence to life in the gang is to examine how gang members defined a gang. Most answers to this question included some mention of violence. Our subjects were able to distinguish between violence within the gang and that which was unrelated to the gang.[8]

INT: What is a gang to you?

007: A gang is, I don't know, just a gang where people hang out together and get into fights. A lot of members of your group will help you fight.

INT: So if you just got into a fight with another girl because you didn't like her?

007: Then it would be a one-on-one fight, but then like if somebody else jump in, then somebody would come from my side.

INT: Why do you call the group you belong to a gang?

046: Violence, I guess. There is more violence than a family. With a gang it's like fighting all the time, killing, shooting.

INT: What kind of things do members of your organization do together?

085: We have drive-bys, shootings, go to parties, we even go to the mall. Most of the things we do together is dealing with fighting.

Most often the violence was protective, reflecting the belief that belonging to a gang at least would reduce the chance of being attacked.

INT: Are you claiming a gang now?

046: I'm cool with a gang, real cool.

INT: What does that mean to be cool?

046: You don't got to worry about nobody jumping you. You don't got to worry about getting beat up.

Other subjects found the violence in their gang an attractive feature of membership. These individuals were attracted not so much by protection as by the opportunity to engage in violence.

INT: Why did you start to call that group a gang?

009: It's good to be in a gang cause there's a lot of violence and stuff.

INT: So the reason you call it a gang is basically why?

101: Because I beat up on folks and shoot them. The last person I shot I was in jail for five years.

INT: What's good about being in a gang?

101: You can get to fight whoever you want and shoot whoever you want. To me, it's kind of fun. Then again, it's not . . . because you have to go to jail for that shit. But other than that, being down for who you want to be with, it's kind of fun.

INT: What's the most important reason to be in the gang?

057:   Beating Crabs.[9] If it wasn't for beating Crabs, I don't
       think I would be in a gang right now.

Whether for protection or for the opportunity to engage in violence, the members of our sample attached considerable importance to the role of violence in their definition of a gang. Many of the comments evoke what Klein (1971) termed "mythic violence"—discussions of violent activities between gangs that reinforce the ties of membership and maintain boundaries between neighborhood gangs and those in "rival" neighborhoods. In this sense, violence is a central feature of the normative system of the gang; it is the defining feature and the central value of gang life.

Violence in Joining the Gang

Most gangs require an initiation process that includes participation in violent activities. This ritual fulfills a number of important functions. First, it determines whether a prospective member is tough enough to endure the level of violence he or she will face as a gang member. Equally important, the gang must learn how tough a potential member is because they may have to count on this individual for support in fights or shootings. The initiation serves other purposes as well. Most important, it increases solidarity among gang members by engaging them in a collective ritual. The initiation reminds active members of their earlier status, and gives the new member something in common with other gang members. In addition, a violent initiation provides a rehearsal for a prospective member for life in the gang. In short, it demonstrates the centrality of violence to gang life.

Three-quarters of our subjects were initiated into their gangs through the process known as "beating in." This ritual took many forms; in its most common version a prospective gang member walked between lines of gang members or stood inside a circle of gang members who beat the initiate with their fists.

020:   I had to stand in a circle and there was about ten of them.
       Out of these ten there was just me standing in the circle.
       I had to take six to the chest by all ten of them. Or I can
       try to go to the weakest one and get out. If you don't get
       out, they are going to keep beating you. I said "I will
       take the circle."

One leader, who reported that he had been in charge of several initiations, described the typical form:

001:   They had to get jumped on.
INT: How many guys jump on em?
001:   Ten.

INT: And then how long do they go?
001:   Until I tell em to stop.
INT: When do you tell em to stop?
001:   I just let em beat em for bout two or three minutes to see
       if they can take a punishment.

The initiation also communicates information about the gang and its activities.

099:   I fought about four people at one time.
INT: Fought who?
099:   I fought some old Gs.
INT: How long did you have to fight them?
099:   It seemed like forever.
INT: So they beat you down or you beat them down?
099:   It went both ways because I knocked that one mother-
       fucker out.
INT: So that was your initiation?
099:   Yeah. And then they sat down and blessed me and told
       me the sixteen laws and all that. But now in the new
       process there is a seventeenth and eighteenth law.

Other gang members reported that they had the choice of either being beaten in or "going on a mission." On a mission, a prospective member had to engage in an act of violence, usually against a rival gang member on rival turf. Initiates often were required to confront a rival gang member face-to-face.

041:   You have to fly your colors through enemy territory.
       Some step to you; you have to take care of them by
       yourself; you don't get no help.
084:   To be a Crip, you have to put your blue rag on your head
       and wear all blue and go in a Blood neighborhood—that
       is the hardest of all of them—and walk through the
       Blood neighborhood and fight Bloods. If you come out
       without getting killed, that's the way you get initiated.

Every gang member we interviewed reported that his or her initiation involved participating in some form of violence. This violence was rarely directed against members of other gangs; most often it took place within the gang. Then, in each successive initiation, recently initiated members participated in "beating in" new members. Such violence always has a group context and a normative purpose: to reinforce the ties between members while reminding them that violence lies at the core of life in the gang.

The Use of Gang Violence

To understand gang violence more clearly, it is critical to know when such violence is used. In the four following situations, gang members did not regard themselves as initiating violence; rather, because its purpose was to respond to the violent activities of a rival gang. Retaliatory violence corresponds to the concept of contagion (Loftin 1984) as well as to the principle of crime as social control (Black 1983). According to this view, gang violence is an attempt to enact private justice or wrongs committed against the gang, one of its members, or a symbol of the gang. These wrongs may be actual or perceived; often the perceived threat of impending violence is as powerful a motivator as violence itself.

This view of gang violence helps to explain the rapid escalation of inter-gang hostilities that lead to assaults, drive-by shootings, or murders between gangs. Such actions reflect the collective behavior processes at work, in which acts of violence against the gang serve as the catalyst that brings together subgroups within the gang and unites them against a common enemy. Such violent events are rare, but are important in gang culture. Collective violence is one of the few activities involving the majority of gang members, including fringe members. The precipitation of such activities pulls fringe members into the gang and increases cohesion.

When violence comes to the gang. We asked gang members when they used violence. Typically they claimed that violence was seldom initiated by the gang itself, but was a response to "trouble" that was "brought" to them. In these instances, the object of violence was loosely defined and was rarely identified; it represented a symbolic enemy against whom violence would be used. These statements, however, indicate an attempt to provide justifications for gang violence.

INT: How often do gang members use violence?
005:   When trouble comes to them.
INT: When do you guys use violence?
018:   When people start bringing violence to us. They bring it to us and set it up. We take it from there.
INT: When do members of the gang use violence?
037:   When somebody approaches us. We don't go out looking for trouble. We let trouble come to us.
INT: When do you guys use violence?
042:   Only when it's called for. We don't start trouble. That's the secret of our success.

The view of gang members passively sitting back and waiting for violence to come to them is inconsistent with much of what we know about gang life. After all, many gang members reported that they joined the gang expressly for the opportunity to engage in violence; many lived in neighborhoods where acts of violence occurred several times each day; and most had engaged in violence before joining the gang. Even so, unprovoked violence against another gang is difficult to justify; retaliatory actions against parties that wronged them can be justified more easily. Also, such actions are consistent with the view of the gang as a legitimate social organization serving the legitimate purpose of protecting its members—a central value in the gang's normative structure.

Retaliation. A number of gang members told us that they used violence to even the score with a specific group or individual. Unlike the subjects above who reported generalized responses, these individuals identified a specific target for their violence: someone who had committed a violent act against them or their gang in the past.

> 002: I had on a blue rag and he say what's up cuz, what's up blood, and I say uh, what's up cuz, just like that, and then me and him got to arguin' and everything, and teachers would stop it, and then me and him met up one day when nobody was round. We got to fightin. Naw, cause I told Ron, my cousin, my cousin and em came up to the school and beat em up. And the next day when he seen me, he gonna ask me where my cousin and em at. I say I don't need my cousin and em for you. They just came up there cause they heard you was a Blood. And they whooped em. Then me and him had a fight the next day, yeah. And then I had to fight some other dudes that was his friends and I beat em up. Then he brought some boys up to the school and they, uh, pulled out a gun on me and I ran up in the school. And then I brought my boys up the next day and we beat on em.
>
> INT: What happened yesterday?
>
> 039: This dude had beat up one of our friends. He was cool with one of my friends but he had beat up another one of my friends before. They came back and busted one of my friends' head. We was going to get him.

Specific examples of retaliation against rival gangs were mentioned less frequently than was general gang violence. This point underscores the important symbolic function of gang violence, a value that members must be ready to support. The idea that rival gangs will "bring violence" to the gang is an important part of the gang belief system; it is pivotal in increasing cohesion among members of otherwise loosely confederated organizations.

Graffiti. A third type of gang violence occurred in response to defacing gang graffiti. Organizational symbols are important to all groups, and perhaps more so to those whose members are adolescents. The significance of graffiti to gangs has been documented by a number of observers in a variety of circumstances (Block and Block 1993; Hagedorn 1988; Moore 1978; Vigil 1988). In particular, graffiti identify gang territory, and maintaining territory is an important feature of gang activity in St. Louis and other cities. As Block and Block observed in Chicago, battles over turf often originated in attempts by rival gangs to "strike out" graffiti. Several gang members told us that attempts to paint over their graffiti by rival gangs were met with a violent response, but no gang members could recall a specific instance. Claiming to use violence in response to such insults again reflects the mythic character of gang violence; it emphasizes the symbolic importance of violence for group processes such as cohesion, boundary maintenance, and identity. Further, such responses underscore the threat represented by rivals who would encroach on gang territory to strike out gang graffiti.

> INT: What does the removal of graffiti mean?
> 043: That's a person that we have to go kill. We put our enemies up on the wall. If there is a certain person, we "X" that out and know who to kill.
> INT: What if somebody comes and paints a pitchfork or paints over your graffiti? What does that mean to your gang?
> 046: First time we just paint it back up there, no sweat. Next time they come do it, we go find out who did it and go paint over theirs. If they come back a third time, it's like three times you out. Obviously that means something if they keep painting over us. They telling us they ready to fight.

Territory. Most gang members continued to live in the neighborhood where their gang started. Even for those who had moved away, it retained a symbolic value. Protecting gang turf is viewed as an important responsibility, which extends well beyond its symbolic importance as the site where the gang began. Our subjects' allegiance to the neighborhood was deeply embedded in the history of neighborhood friendship groups that evolved into gangs. Thus, turf protection was an important value.

When we asked gang members about defending their turf, we received some generalized responses about their willingness to use violence to do so.

> INT: If someone from another gang comes to your turf, What does your gang do?
>
> 019: First try to tell him to leave.
>
> INT: If he don't leave?
>
> 019: He'll leave one way or the other—carry him out in a Hefty bag.
>
> INT: What was your interest in it (the gang)?
>
> 036: We started out, we didn't want nobody coming out and telling us, walking through our neighborhood cause we grew up in this hood and we was going to protect it even if it did mean us fighting every day, which we done. We fought every day. If you walked through the neighborhood and we didn't know you or you didn't know where you was going in the neighborhood, we would rush you.

In other instances, however, the responses identified an individual or an incident in which the gang used violence to protect its turf.

> INT: What kind of things does the gang have to do to defend its turf?
>
> 013: Kill. That's all it is, kill.
>
> INT: Tell me about your most recent turf defense. What happened, a guy came in?
>
> 013: A guy came in, he had the wrong colors on, he got to move out. He got his head split open with a sledgehammer, he got two ribs broken, he got his face torn up.
>
> INT: Did he die from that?
>
> 013: I don't know. We dropped him off on the other side of town. If he did die, it was on the other side of town.
>
> INT: If someone from another gang came to you-all turf, what happens? What do your gang do?
>
> 068: We shoot. If it's a lot, we gonna get organized and we shoot.

Staging Grounds for Violence

Gang members expect that when they go to certain locations they will be the targets of violence from other gangs or will be expected by members of their own gang to engage in violence. In some cases, large-scale violence will occur. Other encounters result only in "face-offs." These encounters highlight the role of situational characteristics in gang violence. Most often the staging grounds are public places such as a restaurant.

> INT: Do they ever bring weapons to school?
>
> 011: No, cause we really don't have no trouble. We mainly fight up at the White Castle. That's where our trouble starts, at the White Castle.

In other instances, the encounters may take place at the skating rink.

> INT: What kind of fights have you guys had lately?
>
> 057: Yeah, last Saturday at Skate King.
>
> INT: Do you go there to skate or were you just hanging?
>
> 057: We used to skate a long time ago, but we just all the sudden went [crazy]. Crabs started hanging out there. Usually all Bloods up there but the Crabs started hanging out there so we had to get rid of them.

Dances are not new locations for youthful violence. Members of our sample identified them as locations that produced violent encounters between rival gangs.

> INT: Do you go to dances?
>
> 017: Yeah. That's when we mostly get into the gang fights. Yeah, we go to dances.
>
> INT: What about the last fight? What was that about?
>
> 031: That was at a dance. It was some Slobs[10] there. They was wanting to show they colors and just didn't know who they was around. They weren't really paying attention.
>
> INT: How often do you guys use violence?
>
> 033: Only if we go out to a dance or something.

The expectation of violence at certain locations was so strong that some members avoided going to those places.

> INT: Do you go to dances or parties?
>
> 047: I don't. I stay away from house parties. Too many fights come out of there.

According to another gang member, violence at house parties had reached such a level that many hosts searched their guests for weapons.

> 074: Sometimes people wait until they get out of the party and start shooting. Now at these parties they have people at the door searching people, even at house parties.

In general, gang members reported that they "hung out" in small cliques or subgroups and that it was rare for the entire gang to be together. This reflects the general character of social organization in the gangs we studied. An external threat—usually from another gang—was needed to strengthen cohesion among gang members and to bring the larger gang together. Many members of our sample reported that they did not go skating, to the mall, or to dances alone or in small groups because they knew that gang violence was likely to erupt at such locations. Thus the gang went en masse to these locations, prepared to start or respond to violence. These expectations contributed to the eventual use of violence. In this way, the gang's belief system contributed to the likelihood of violent encounters.

Ending Gangs

When we asked for gang members' perspectives on the best way to end gangs, we expected to find a variety of recommendations targeted at fundamental causes (racism, unemployment, education) as well as more proximate solutions (detached workers, recreation centers, job training). Instead the modal response reflected the centrality of violence in the gang. Twenty-five of our 99 subjects told us that the only way to get rid of their gang would be to use violence to get rid of the members. This response was confirmed by gang members in their conversations with the field ethnographer. For many gang members, life in the gang had become synonymous with violence; for one respondent, even job offers were not sufficient to end the gang.

> INT: What would be the best way to get rid of your gang, the
>   Rolling Sixties?
> 033:   Smoke us all.
> INT: Kill you all?
> 033:   Yeah.
> INT: We couldn't give you guys jobs?
> 033:   No, just smoke us.

Others recommend using extreme violence to get rid of their gang.

> INT: What would it take to get rid of your gang?
> 035:   Whole lot of machine guns. Kill us all. We just going to
>   multiply anyway cause the Pee Wees gonna take over.
> INT: What would be the best way to get rid of the Sixties?
> 042:   Kill us all at once. Put them in one place and blow them
>   up.

Violence is so central a part of gang culture that even the members' recommendations about ending gangs include elements of violence.

The Process of Gang Violence

The analysis above suggests a model that accounts for the escalation of gang violence and is consistent with the nature of gang process and normative structure: it reflects the lack of strong leadership, structure, and group goals. The key element is the collective identification of threat, a process that unites the gang and overcomes the general lack of unity by increasing cohesion. This occurred in response to threats against the gang, either real or perceived, by rival gangs. The role of mythic violence is particularly important in this context; it is the agent through which talk about violence most frequently unites gang members.

We suggest that a seven-step process accounts for the peaks and valleys of gang violence. The key to understanding violence is the nature of organization within gangs. Most gangs originate as neighborhood groups and are characterized by loose ties between their members and the larger gang. These groups generally lack effective leadership; cohesion in small cliques is stronger than the ties to the larger gang. Against this backdrop, symbolic enemies are identified when subgroups interact with other gangs near them. Threats from those groups—whether real or perceived—expand the number of participants, and may increase cohesion among members and heighten their willingness to use violence. Violence between gangs is most often the result of a mobilizing event that pushes a ready and willing group beyond the constraints against violence. Such events may include the deployment of gang members to protect or attack certain locations, to engage in actions in cars, or simply to act "loco." Violent encounters typically are short-lived and de-escalate rapidly. This de-escalation, however, may be only a respite before the next retaliation. The process moves through the following seven steps:

1. Loose bonds to the gang;
2. Collective identification of threat from a rival gang (through rumors, symbolic shows of force, cruising, and mythic violence), reinforcing the centrality of violence that expands the number of participants and increases cohesion;
3. A mobilizing event possibly, but not necessarily, violence;
4. Escalation of activity;
5. Violent event;
6. Rapid de-escalation;
7. Retaliation

This model is generally consistent with McPhail's (1993) description of individual and collective violence. His explanation distinguishes between outcome violence and intended violence. The former is characterized by attempts to manage what McPhail calls "disturbances to self-perception."

Examples would include challenges to status that are repelled with actions which do not originate with a violent intent, but result in a violence (Athens 1992; Luckenbill and Doyle 1989). Participants in intended violence, on the other hand, enter a setting or interaction with a predisposition toward violence. In its collective form, this type of violence generally involves two opposing groups, many of whose members play interchangeable roles of victim, perpetrator, and witness of violence. The collective violence of gangs described in our research fits McPhail's conceptual scheme: "Not only do purposive actors act alone to match their perceptions to their reference signals for violent individual goals, they occasionally act together with other members of their groups to achieve violent collective goals" (1993:17). McPhail points to the need to analyze the "planning preparations, rehearsal and implementation of collective violence" (1993:17). We believe that the current analysis and model of the collective behavior process of gang violence supports McPhail's model.

Conclusion

Gang violence, like other gang activities, reflects the gang's organizational and normative structure. Such violence, especially retaliatory violence, is an outgrowth of a collective process that reflects the loose organizational structure of gangs with diffuse goals, little allegiance among members, and few leaders.

If gangs are composed of diffuse subgroups, how is violence organized? Our answer to this question is "Not very well and not very often," because most gang violence serves important symbolic purposes within the gang. In addition, most gang violence is retaliatory, a response to violence—real or perceived—against the gang.

Gang violence serves many functions in the life of the gang. First, and most important, it produces more violence through the processes of threat and contagion. These mechanisms strongly reflect elements of collective behavior. Second, it temporarily increases the solidarity of gang members, uniting them against a common enemy by heightening their dependence on each other. When gang violence exceeds tolerable limits, a third function may be evident: the splintering of gangs into subgroups and the decision by some individuals to leave the gang.

Endnotes

[1] The chart (Thrasher 1927:70) depicting these distinctions is a classic, and provides considerable insight into the level of organization in gangs today. This chart has received little attention from criminologists, however.

[2] This argument is consistent with contemporary arguments that link the reemergence of gangs in the

1980s to the growth of the urban underclass. In this context see Hagedorn (1988), Jackson (1992), Moore (1978), and Vigil (1988).

[3] Each gang member was transported to and from the interview site, usually an office at the university, by the fieldworker. This trip offered the opportunity to speak informally about gang and non-gang matters. It also provided the chance to discuss the nature of the interview, both before and after it was administered. The field ethnographer and the interviewer compared notes, particularly in cases where a subject displayed "excessive" bravado, to ensure that responses reflected the ethnographer's knowledge of the subject, based on his own contacts and observations.

[4] In these respects, St. Louis gangs resemble those in Los Angeles (Klein 1971; Klein, Maxson, and Cunningham 1991; Vigil 1988), Milwaukee (Hagedorn 1988), Chicago (Block and Block 1993; Short and Strodtbeck 1974), and San Diego (Sanders 1993).

[5] These counts were derived from GOFER, the qualitative software package used for organizing much of the analysis of the transcribed interviews.

[6] Since this manuscript was first submitted to JQ in November 1994, two more members of our sample have been killed, raising the total to 11.

[7] Despite these claims, a sample of 24 ex-gang members gave little evidence that their exit from the gang was accompanied by violence. The claim that one can end the gang only through violence may reflect the mythic character of violence identified by Klein (1971). The threat of violence toward those interested in leaving the gang discourages such actions and reinforces the cohesion between members.

[8] Quotes are used to illustrate major substantive categories of the collective and normative features of gang behavior. INT denotes the interviewer; the number (e.g., 007) is the subject's identification number.

[9] This is a derogatory term used by Blood gang members to refer to Crips.

[10] This is a derogatory term used by Crip gang members to refer to Bloods.

References

Athens, L. 1992. *The Creation of Dangerous Violent Criminals.* Urbana: University of Illinois Press.

Biernacki, P. and D. Waldorf. 1981. "Snowball Sampling: Problems and Techniques of Chain Referral Sampling." *Sociological Methods and Research* 10:141–63.

Black, D. 1983. "Crime as Social Control." *American Sociological Review* 43:34–45.

Block, C. R. and R. Block. 1993. "Street Gang Crime in Chicago." *Research in Brief* (December). Washington, DC: National Institute of Justice.

Decker, S. H. and B. Van Winkle. 1996. *Life in the Gang: Family, Friends and Violence.* New York: Cambridge University Press.

Hagedorn, J. 1988. *People and Folks.* Chicago: Lakeview Press.

———. 1991. "Back in the Field Again: Gang Research in the Nineties." Pp. 240, 259, *Gangs in America,* edited by R. Huff. Newbury Park, CA: Sage.

Horowitz, R. 1983. *Honor and the American Dream.* New Brunswick, NJ: Rutgers University Press.

Jackson, P. I. 1992. "Crime, Youth Gangs and Urban Transition: The Social Dislocations of Postindustrial Development." *Justice Quarterly* 8:379–98.

Katz, J. 1988. *The Seductions of Crime.* New York: Basic Books.

Klein, M. 1971. *Street Gangs and Street Workers.* Englewood Cliffs, NJ: Prentice-Hall.

Klein, M. and C. Maxson, 1989. "Street Gang Violence." Pp. 198-234 in *Violent Crimes, Violent Criminals,* edited by N. Weiner. Beverly Hills: Sage.

Klein, M., C. Maxson, and L. Cunningham. 1991. "Crack,' Street Gangs, and Violence. *Criminology* 29:623-50.

Loftin, C. 1984. "Assaultive Violence as Contagious Process." *Bulletin of the New York Academy of Medicine* 62:550–55.

Luckenbill, D. and D. Doyle. 1989. "Structural Position and Violence: Developing a Cultural Explanation." *Criminology* 27:419–36.

Maxson, C., M. Klein, and M. Gordon. 1985. "Differences between Gang and Nongang Homicides." *Criminology* 21:209–22.

Maxson, C. and M. Klein. 1990. "Street Gang Violence: Twice as Great or Half as Great?" Pp. 71–102 in *Gangs in America,* edited by R. Huff. Newbury Park, CA: Sage.

McPhail, C. 1991. *The Myth of the Madding Crowd.* New York: Aldine.

———. 1993. "The Dark Side of Purpose: Individual and Collective Violence in Riots." Presidential address, Midwest Sociological Society, Chicago.

Moore, J. 1978. *Homeboys.* Philadelphia: Temple University Press.

Padilla, F. 1992. *The Gang as an American Enterprise.* New Brunswick, NJ: Rutgers University Press.

Pfautz, H. 1961. "Near-Group Theory and Collective Behavior: A Critical Reformulation." *Social Problems* 9:167–74.

Sanchez-Jankowski, M. 1991. *Islands in the Street.* Berkeley: University of California Press.

Sanders, W. 1993. *Drive-Bys and Gang Bangs: Gangs and Grounded Culture.* Chicago: Aldine.

Short, J. 1974. "Collective Behavior, Crime, and Delinquency." Pp. 403–49 in *Handbook of Criminology,* edited by D. Glaser. New York: Rand McNally.

Short, J. and F. Strodtbeck. 1974. *Group Process and Gang Delinquency.* Chicago: University of Chicago Press.

Sullivan, M. 1989. *Getting Paid: Youth Crime and Work in the Inner City.* Ithaca: Cornell University Press.

Suttles, G. 1972. *The Social Construction of Communities.* Chicago: University of Chicago Press.

Thrasher, F. 1927. *The Gang.* Chicago: University of Chicago Press.

Vigil, D. 1988. *Barrio Gangs.* Austin: University of Texas Press.

Wright, R., S. H. Decker, A. Redfern, and D. Smith. 1992. "A Snowball's Chance in Hell: Doing Field Work with Active Residential Burglars." *Journal of Research in Crime and Delinquency* 29:148–61.

Wright, R. T., and S. H. Decker, *Burglars on the Job: Streetlife Culture & Residential Burglary.* Boston: Northeastern University Press.

Yablonsky, L. 1959. "The Delinquent Gang as a Near-Group." *Social Problems* 7:108–17.

Section III

Juveniles in the System

As a society we have long had mixed reactions toward adolescents, and this is particularly true for adolescents who get into trouble with the law. On the one hand there are claims that teenagers are mature enough and responsible enough that we should treat juvenile offenders as adults, including the possibility of long prison sentences. At the same time we see them as too immature and irresponsible to entrust with such responsibilities as voting, drinking, or smoking cigarettes. Questions about what should be done with juveniles in the system are the focus of this section. An important element for each chapter is the way in which juveniles as a group are viewed in our society.

In the first article, "Conceptions of Family and Juvenile Court Processes," Charles J. Corley, Timothy S. Bynum, and Madeline Wordes use interviews with juvenile court personnel to determine how the juvenile court uses family variables and how these variables influence the decisions made by the juvenile court. The chapter suggests that family factors have an important influence on court decisions, including the decision to handle the case either through a formal court process or informally through diversion or the dropping of charges. Perceptions of parental involvement and concern were relevant in every stage of the process.

In "Certification to Criminal Court," Joseph Sanborn examines the process of transferring juveniles to adult court. He outlines the mechanisms through which this can happen and looks at the circumstances under which

117

juveniles are likely to be transferred. He concludes that waiver serves a variety of functions and that the use of waivers does not reflect a belief that the philosophy guiding juvenile justice is wrong. Further, those who work with juveniles do not believe that waivers are necessary to protect society. Instead, juvenile justice officials most often see waiver as a tool of last resort, to be used with juveniles who are beyond the rehabilitative capacity of the juvenile court, or who require more resources than are available through the juvenile justice system.

In "Screwing the System and Making It Work," Mark D. Jacobs uses the case of a troubled young man named Larry to illustrate how workers in the juvenile justice system may go out of their way to make the system work in the best interests of the child. The case of Larry also illustrates how early life experiences and forces beyond the control of the justice system can undermine even the best efforts to help kids change. It is a somber reminder that the system does not work in a vacuum, but is only part of the environment that shapes juvenile behavior. This chapter also raises questions about who is properly responsible for delinquency and its correction. As Jacobs observes, such questions are particularly difficult in a "no-fault" society in which no person or agency is prepared to accept responsibility when things go wrong.

Gordon Bazemore's chapter "Restorative Justice: What's 'New' About the Balanced Approach?" clarifies what is meant by restorative justice and how it differs from the juvenile justice system's traditional focus on the best interests of the juvenile. Many states have adopted the language of restorative justice, but Bazemore argues that the balanced approach is much more than simply changing terminology. It requires giving equal attention to punishing the offender, ensuring the safety of the community, and rehabilitating the offender. Unlike more traditional approaches to juvenile justice, restorative justice, as the name implies, also emphasizes restoring losses experienced by victims. Running throughout the restorative justice model is a focus on desired outcomes for the individual, the community, and the victim. Also unlike traditional juvenile justice, restorative justice requires the commitment and involvement of the community, an idea consistent with developments in other parts of the justice system, such as community policing and community courts.

In the final chapter of this section, "Teen Court: A Therapeutic Jurisprudence Perspective," Allison R. Shiff and David B. Wexler describe another alternative to the court's traditionally punitive approach. Teen courts, they argue, are good examples of preserving basic due process rights while also utilizing the justice system toward therapeutic ends. Teen courts are aimed at first-time offenders with the hope of preventing future criminality. As the name implies, teen courts are legal processes conducted primarily by teenagers who reach judgments about other teens. The chapter outlines how teen courts operate and why they provide a good example of therapeutic jurisprudence.

7

Conceptions of Family and Juvenile Court Processes
A Qualitative Assessment

*Charles J. Corley, Timothy S. Bynum
and Madeline Wordes*

The study of the influence of social variables on court dispositions has a long history (Black and Reiss, 1970; Ferdinand and Luchterhand, 1970; Arnold, 1971; Thornberry, 1973; Ageton and Elliott, 1974; Barton, 1976; Cohen and Kluegel, 1979; Elliott and Ageton, 1980; Fagen, Slaughter, and Hartstone, 1987; Bishop and Frazier, 1988; Pope and Feyerherm, 1990). More recently, familial characteristics have been included in these assessments (Carter, 1979; Cohen and Kluegel, 1979; Sieverdes, Shoemaker, and Cunningham, 1979; Horwitz and Wasserman, 1980; Poole and Regoli, 1980; Chein and Hudson, 1981; Fenwick, 1982; Frazier, Richards, and Potters, 1983, Fagen, Slaughter, and Hartstone, 1987). This article examines conceptions of family among juvenile court personnel and their possible influence upon juvenile justice processes.

While juvenile justice sanctions are not solely premised on the characteristics of the families of the youths appearing before the court, familial qualities are of paramount importance. Matza (1964) suggests that the court assesses the abilities of the parent or parents to sponsor correctly a juvenile

Corley, Charles J., Timothy S. Bynum, and Madeline Wordes. 1995. Conceptions of Family and Juvenile Court Processes. *The Justice System Journal,* 18:2:157–172.

on a less intrusive court-derived sanction in response to the child's offensive behavior. Much like the *kadi* in India who distributes justice with great discretion, the juvenile court considers the level of danger and possibility for out-of-court supervision. More specifically, Matza suggests that

> the alternative sentences from which the kadi (read "juvenile court") chooses depend first, on a traditional rule-of-thumb assessment of the total risk of danger and thus scandal evident in the juvenile's current offense and prior record of offenses; this initial reckoning is then importantly qualified by an assessment of the potentialities for "outpatient supervision" and the guarantee against scandal inherent in the willingness and ability of parents or surrogates to sponsor the child (1964:125).

Thus, Matza suggests juvenile courts assess a juvenile's familial characteristics to determine the willingness and ability of the juvenile's parents or surrogates to sponsor adequately the child on less restrictive or less punitive court treatment.

However, other researchers suggest family factors are important to the juvenile court for different reasons. Hirschi and Gottfredson (1993) suggest that the presence of an adult is usually sufficient to prevent crime among children, and it is the family that is primarily responsible for instilling in the child an appreciable level of self-control (Gottfredson and Hirschi, 1990). For children within a certain age range, the commission of criminal acts is prima facie evidence that adult supervision is inadequate (Hirschi and Gottfredson, 1993). Moreover, Gottfredson and Hirschi (1990) suggest that to transmit various elements of self-control (e.g., delayed gratification, respect for the rights and property of others, and impulse resistance) to a child properly, someone must monitor the child's behavior, recognize deviant behavior when it occurs, and correct such behavior.

Both perspectives suggest that the juvenile court uses a familial diagnosis to determine an appropriate sanction. On one hand, Matza (1964) maintains the juvenile court is primarily interested in the parent's willingness to sponsor (work with the court) a juvenile on a less intrusive court-derived sanction. However, Hirschi and Gottfredson (1993) suggest that this familial diagnosis includes an assessment of familial traits pertinent to parental supervision and control that extend beyond Matza's idea of parental sponsorship.

Differences between these two perspectives regarding the importance of family compel us to determine if familial variables are important in juvenile court decision making; investigate whether parental sponsorship, supervision and control, or other familial traits are the focus of the court's interest; and examine the potential effects of familial characteristics on juvenile court processes. Contrary to previous research that has alluded to correlations among certain family variables (i.e., single-parent homes) and juvenile justice sanctions (Arnold, 1971; Meade, 1973; Carter, 1979; Cohen and Kluegel, 1979; Sieverdes, Shoemaker, and Cunningham, 1979; Horwitz and Wasserman, 1980), this work attempts to explain why family variables are important to juvenile court decision makers and how those variables affect juvenile court processes and sanctions.

The Juvenile Court and Individualized Treatment

Reasons for assessing the family characteristics of juveniles are embedded in the "progressive" philosophy of the juvenile court. This philosophy focuses on providing individualized treatment rather than simply sanctioning deviant behavior. Matza (1964:114) notes that the principle of individualized justice implies, at least, that dispositions are to be guided by an understanding of the juvenile's personal and social characteristics and "individual needs." Moreover, the juvenile court's principle of equity or treatment of like cases in a similar manner is overshadowed by its principle of individualized justice.

However, Matza (1964:114) notes that individualized treatment is a mystification that obscures, rather than enlightens, the processes of decision and disposition. More specifically, Matza (1964:114) suggests that the pool of items needed to arrive at individualized treatment is so broad (e.g., age, offense, culpability, risk, and offense history, etc.) that any relationship between criteria of judgment and disposition is unclear. Thus, the juvenile court, with its goal of individualized treatment, relies heavily upon the professional judgment and experience of its personnel to provide personalized treatment. Court personnel must use their wisdom in assigning weights to the various elements of the aforementioned pool of items. While legal variables, such as seriousness of offense and prior offenses, are important in the decision-making process and direct disposition, they are moderated by the court's objective to provide individualized treatment, which, in turn, broadens the pool of items that must be considered to individualize treatment (Matza, 1964).

The Link between Juvenile Court and Family

Because the juvenile court intends to act as a surrogate family for youths who may need its services (Empey and Stafford, 1991), the court must have some conception of what a family is and the functions a family serves. Given the social control functions of the family in American society and the emphasis juvenile courts place upon social control, it is logical that the juvenile perform some form of familial assessment. This appraisal is predicated upon an ideal type of family structure and function believed to exist among middle-class Americans. It is within this context that "traditional families" are defined and legally sanctioned as heterosexual (sexually exclusive) unions with children, where the adult male serves as the provider and ultimate authority figure (Eshleman, 1989).

Since the court serves as surrogate parents for youths who appear to need its services and inculcates law-abiding behavior among such youths, we speculate that the juvenile court's evaluation of the characteristics of a child's familial characteristics is based upon traditional models of family life where an emphasis is placed upon parental supervision and control.

Review of Previous Research

Although previous research has assessed the influence of various social variables (e.g., age, sex, race, social class, etc.) on juvenile justice processes (Black and Reiss, 1970; Ferdinand and Luchterhand, 1970; Thornberry, 1973, 1979; Ageton and Elliott, 1974; Barton, 1976; Hill, 1980; Elliott and Ageton, 1980, Fagen, Slaughter, and Hartstone, 1987; Zatz, 1987; Bishop and Frazier, 1988; Pope and Feyerherm, 1990; Kempf, Decker, and Bing, 1990; Leiber, 1992), fewer studies have included an assessment of the influence of family variables (Arnold, 1971; Meade, 1973; Carter, 1979; Cohen and Kluegel, 1979; Sieverdes, Shoemaker, and Cunningham, 1979; Horwitz and Wasserman, 1980; Poole and Regoli, 1980; Chein and Hudson, 1981; Fenwick, 1982; Fagen, Slaughter, and Hartstone, 1987). Moreover, among those who have included family factors, few go beyond an examination of family structure (Horwitz and Wasserman, 1980; Poole and Regoli, 1980; Frazier, Richards, and Potter, 1983).

Overall, studies have yielded complex, varied, and inconclusive results regarding how family variables influence juvenile court processes and sanctions. For instance, Meade (1973) found that youths from disrupted families were more likely to be exposed to a formal hearing than youths from intact families. However, disrupted-family status had no influence on formal hearing outcomes or likelihood of recidivism. Chused (1973) and Sieverdes (1973) found that juveniles from broken homes received more severe dispositions than youths from intact families. However, the presence of two parents was reported not to be as good a predictor of case disposition (Ferdinand and Luchterhand, 1970; Arnold, 1971; Scarpitti and Stephenson, 1971) as family stability (Frazier, Richards, and Potter, 1983). In addition, Horwitz and Wasserman (1980) found that family and school problems explained more of the variance in case disposition than number of prior arrests and offense seriousness. In their research, youths whose family backgrounds showed the presence of familial conflict experienced more severe dispositions than youths whose family backgrounds did not suggest there was a problem at home.

Thus, among studies that examined the effect of family variables beyond the presence of two parents in the juvenile's home, there is support for the supposition that family variables affect juvenile court processes and sanctions.

However, a review of the literature leaves us to question whether familial influences have been properly examined relative to juvenile justice processes and sanctions. Two issues, in particular, contribute to this conclusion. First, many of the earlier studies focused primarily upon family structure (Arnold, 1971; Fagen, Slaughter, and Hartstone, 1987; Cohen and Kluegel, 1979; Horwitz and Wasserman, 1980; Johnson, 1986). These studies assessed the effect of single-parent status on juvenile court sanctions. However, few studies found that court officials responded more harshly to the indiscretions of youths from single-parent homes than youths from two-parent homes (Arnold, 1971; Johnson, 1986). Yet, this factor alone does not reflect the broader concept of family. For instance, Horwitz and Wasserman (1980) found that the presence of family problems negatively influenced case disposition. Hence, examining family variables beyond structural components may provide greater insight into juvenile justice decision making.

Second, earlier studies did not examine multiple decision points in the juvenile justice process. Pope and Feyerherm (1990) suggest that researchers who attempt to assess the effect of social variables on juvenile justice processes perform a multivariate analysis of each decision point in those processes. Since case dispositions are the result of a process, as much of the process as possible should be included in the examination of juvenile justice decision making. Examining multiple decision points may enable researchers to identify where in the process social variables have an effect.

However, even if these criteria are satisfied, there is still a likelihood that the effect of family variables will not be detected. Although family variables may appear to have an effect early in the juvenile justice process, that effect may be lost or labeled insignificant in the latter stages of quantitative multivariate assessments. Family variables may actually become more important as cases are forwarded through the judicial process, but the quantifiable effects of family variables wane as the characteristics of families involved in the cases become more uniform.

While some studies indicated that family factors affected juvenile justice processes, our review of the literature did not specifically reveal how the characteristics of a juvenile's family affect juvenile court decisions. Furthermore, it was not clear whether family characteristics were assessed in terms of parental supervision and control, parental sponsorship, or other unspecified reasons.

Methodology and Data Collection

Data are derived from personal interviews conducted with various juvenile court personnel (i.e., prosecutors, judges, referees, supervisors, intake staff, and probation officers) across seven counties from a Midwestern state. Two of the seven counties were highly urbanized, three were a mixture of urban and suburban areas, and the remaining two were rural. Almost all of the key decision-making court personnel within each of the selected sites were interviewed. Only a few could not be interviewed because of scheduling conflicts. Ninety-four interviews were conducted with judges, referees, supervisors, intake staff, and probation officers. Fifty-one percent of these interviews were with judges and referees. The average age of court personnel was between 40 and 45 years old. The majority of court personnel were Caucasian. In five of the selected courts, the majority of decision makers were male.

The overall objective of the interview process was to obtain an understanding of the pattern of each court's decision-making process. To that end, questions focused on understanding legal and social factors deemed important to the decision maker for purposes of case processing, determination of sanctions, and placement. To further assist our research efforts, a felony (breaking-and-entering) scenario was presented to each court decision maker. Respondents identified important factors and commented as to their influence on the decision-making process. There were sixteen 3 x 5 inch cards laid in front of each person interviewed for the scenario. On one side of each card was a category of information, and on the reverse were specific circumstances representative of a typical youth who may appear before the court charged with a breaking-and-entering offense. These categories and corresponding circumstances included the juvenile's age, sex, prior offense record, sexual behavior, school performance, attitude, co-offenders, substance abuse profile, living situation, marital status of parents, criminal history of family, primary caregiver's occupation, income, and level of parental control. The value and damage to property, evidence found, and victim profile also were provided.

Interviewers informed each respondent that a juvenile had been referred to court by the police and was charged with a breaking-and-entering offense. Court personnel were then asked to look over the cards and determine the category of information and order they would consider in their processing, disposition, and placement decisions. Additionally, court staff were free to make various comments about the categories and other factors not included on the cards that could influence their decisions as to the processing of a juvenile charged with a breaking-and-entering offense.

While it was preferred that court personnel describe how the factors they identified affected specific stages of the justice process (intake, informal hearing, formal hearing or adjudication, disposition, etc.), court personnel articulated how these factors affected court decisions in general. While the effect of particular variables on specific stages of the juvenile justice process could not be assessed, protocol analysis of the breaking-and-entering scenario shows how family characteristics affect decisions at intake, processing of cases either informally or formally, disposition of cases, and placement decisions.

Our research focused primarily on specific comments regarding the influences of family factors on court proceedings and outcomes. Ethnograph™, a research software package designed to analyze qualitative data, was used to analyze data obtained from interviews. More specifically, Ethnograph was used to search the coded information for text related to family characteristics, processes, sanctions, and placement.

Findings

Analysis of these qualitative data suggests that across all juvenile courts, family factors were important during intake decision making. It is at intake where the court decides whether to intervene in the matter before it. Family characteristics were also examined relative to case processing. Often, the court decides at a preliminary hearing or other informal justice stage to either treat the juvenile in a formal manner with an adjudicatory hearing or divert the youth to some otherwise informal program.

Moreover, conceptions of family and their perceived influence were examined in regard to final disposition and subsequent placement of youth. Overall, these data suggest that court staffs across the seven counties considered family characteristics, such as caregiver control and family structure, important in determining intake decisions, case processing, disposition, and placement.

Although definitions of caregiver control and family structure varied, analyses suggest court personnel generally believed caregiver control to reflect the level of restraint a parent had over the child as well as the level of respect displayed by the child for the parent or caregiver. Court personnel evaluated family structure in terms of occupants, family criminality, value transmittance, and presence of two parents. It should be noted, however, that caregiver control and family structure were often mentioned in relation to one another. Thus, while the results are presented in separate sections regarding their perceived influence, caregiver control and family structure, as discussed by court personnel, were often intertwined.

Additionally, it should be noted that comments made by court staff referred to a felonious breaking-and-entering scenario in which it was assumed that a male juvenile was charged with the offense.

Caregiver Control

Intake staff consistently identified social control and family factors as important considerations in the decision to handle a case either informally (i.e., drop charges, divert) or formally. For instance, one court worker indicated, "A petition probably would not be authorized in a situation where there was evidence of parental control and there would be a greater likelihood that the case would be dropped." This statement suggests that court personnel perceive social control for adolescents to lay within the family and that the family must be evaluated in terms of the parents' ability to control and supervise children. Moreover, youths appearing before the court whose parents exhibited an acceptable level of control and had a cooperative attitude with the court were said to have a greater likelihood of having their cases diverted or dismissed than youths with parents who had little control or were uncooperative. This point of view was reinforced by juvenile court supervisors. For instance, a supervisor mentioned that "a higher level of parental control tends to decrease the formality with which a case is likely to be handled. . . . If the parent is willing to work, then we try something else." Thus, the decision to process either informally or formally a juvenile is, in part, predicated on the perceived level of social control the parent (or parents) has over the youth. In addition, the parent must also display a willingness to work with the court in its efforts to help the child. This would suggest that parental sponsorship is also important in juvenile court processes (Matza, 1964). However, parental sponsorship, as articulated by court personnel (i.e., willingness of the parent to work with the court), was framed within the context of parental control. In short, court personnel were not obliged to invoke the full adjudicatory process in cases where parental control was deemed acceptable and parents were cooperative.

Interviews also revealed that even in cases where a petition was filed and the case set for a preliminary hearing, the courts (particularly suburban courts) attempted to be less intrusive in the lives of juveniles whose parents showed interest in the welfare of their children and maintained an appreciable level of social control over them. This viewpoint was expressed by a majority of court personnel. For instance, a suburban referee noted that . . . an examination of caregiver control will give insight into whether probation will work. . . . My starting philosophy is to look at the problems within the home."

The perception of an acceptable level of interest both in the child and in caregiver control makes other less intrusive options available to the court. This suggests that the more informal mechanisms of social control the juvenile has in his or her life, the more lenient the response from the court. One referee pointed out that "I look at caregiver control to see if there is someone who can work with us on behalf of the kid." Yet another suburban referee elaborated on the importance of assessing caregiver control and interest in the child in terms of providing less officious options. This referee stated:

> I want to know if the parents are stable. . . . Have they thrown-up their hands and given up on the child?. . . If I thought the parents could handle the situation, then I might hold a case in abeyance to see if the parents can deal with the kid at home. . . . You need to know the parents' attitude. . . . Do they want the child?

Court staff frequently indicated that caregiver control and willingness of the caregiver to work with the court were well received and opened various other options such as consent, intensive probation, probation, or in-house arrest for formally processed youths. Thus, the presence of a caregiver who is concerned about the child and has what is perceived to be an appreciable level of control over the youth lessens the harshness of juvenile court sanctions.

The commitment of a juvenile to the department of social services, the juvenile court's harshest sanction, was also influenced by level of caregiver control. Commitment of a juvenile involves placement in a facility or other court-determined home where custody of the juvenile is assigned to the state. While the seriousness of the offense was also a critical consideration in the youth being made a ward of the state, the lack of parental control also influenced the decision to commit. At least one court supervisor responded that "if the parent has no control then you almost always have to enter an order of commitment."

However, court personnel were quick to point out that the majority of juveniles who appear in court do not commit serious offenses and that the court's decision to commit a juvenile to the state is often made after the youth has been in court for previous serious criminal behavior. Additionally, court personnel suggested that the seriousness of an offense committed by a juvenile reflects the level of control that exists in the home. While youths who commit more serious offenses are expected to be treated formally and receive harsher sanctions, more serious offenders are also thought to be in greater need of more formal court-mandated mechanisms of control. Control is believed lacking in the homes of serious offenders. The locus of social control for juveniles is perceived by court personnel to lie within the family. Thus, the decision of the court to invoke even its most intrusive sanction was also influenced by family factors (i.e., level of caregiver control).

Family Structure

Family structure was also mentioned as an important factor in juvenile court processing. However, it should be noted that family structure, as defined by court personnel, encompassed living situations, family composition, family criminality, prioritization of daily activities, and transmittance of values. Moreover, caregiver control and family structure were often intertwined in discussions with court staff.

Court personnel stated a need to have information relative to the youth's overall living situation as well as structure of the home. In particular, court officials wanted knowledge of the occupants and activities of the household. It was indicated that "we need to know exactly who the kid is living with. . . . We assess the youth's living situation in terms of safety, guidance and support." Knowledge of a juvenile's family structure, occupants in the home, and their values was said to be important in judicial processing, sanction, and placement. Youths living with their biological or legally adoptive parents were perceived to have stronger elements of informal social control in their lives than juveniles living with other relatives or friends. Adolescents residing with their parents were thought to be in less need of the court's supervision and were more likely to have their cases dropped, diverted, or otherwise handled in an informal manner than juveniles living with others. Moreover, youths who were living with their parents and had their cases formally processed and received court sanctions were more likely to receive less intrusive sanctions (e.g., restitution or probation) than youths residing with other relatives or friends.

Court interest in the occupants of the household included information about family criminality. However, court staff were more interested in knowledge of the criminal behavior of siblings rather than knowledge of the criminal activities of parents. In particular, it was mentioned that

> I look at the criminal history of the family to see if brothers and sisters are involved in criminal offenses. . . . It can show that a youth is beyond control. . . . It really shows that the home lacks structure.

Many other court personnel believed that homes where more than one child had been involved with the court reflected negatively on the parents' ability to supervise and guide their children.

Court personnel interested in the criminal activities of the parents were concerned about the influence a parental criminal role model could have on an adolescent. It was expressed that there may be a need to find an alternative placement for youths (i.e., foster care) in living situations where the behavior of the parents exposed the youths to a criminal lifestyle. But the criminality of siblings was said to be a clear indication of both the inability of the parents to provide guidance and structure and the need for court intervention.

In addition, both urban and suburban court personnel wanted information about the structure of the home regarding priorities placed upon various family activities and values. For instance, an urban judge asserted, "I want to know what the priorities are in the home. . . . Are the parents committed to the children? Does the mom have a boyfriend there that is more important than her children?" Court personnel felt they could identify family situations where priority was not placed upon the rearing of children. Moreover, homes in which the court perceived a lack of emphasis on child rearing would indicate a need for the court to be more intrusive (e.g., formally process a case, provide a more intensive sanction) in the lives of juveniles.

Concern was also expressed regarding the need for parents to instill in their children "middle-class values." It was not uncommon for respondents to inquire about

> what kind of role model is the parent? . . . What is the parent not working saying to the kid? . . . If values are to be enforced, there has to be someone at home to work with us. . . . It's a waste of time if there is not anyone at home enforcing values.

Court personnel from urban, suburban, and rural jurisdictions were concerned that families both teach their children to value hard work and education and establish a sense of morality. Court personnel thought these characteristics reflected middle-class values essential to the transformation of adolescents to productive adult citizens. Therefore, juveniles appearing in court from homes where "middle-class values" were not enforced were believed to be in need of the court's intervention.

However, court personnel often equated family structure with level of parental control. For instance, it was alleged that

> two parents are in a better position to control and supervise their child than the single parent. . . . If there is a two-parent family, there will be a better chance of success. . . . Unfortunately most of our kids are poor and from single-parent homes.

Not all respondents associated higher levels of parental control with two-parent households. At least one judge responded that "a single parent home can have stability as well; particularly if there is a father or brother around who can assist with the kid." Nonetheless, enough court staff associated two-parent households with higher levels of parental control, which created an apparent pattern in thought among court workers.

Statements that associated caregiver control with family structure were troublesome for two reasons. First, the assumption that two-parent households have more control over their children than single-parent households suggests court personnel may actually be focusing upon family composition rather than parental or caregiver competency. Second, the association of family structure with parental control may bias the court against youths from single-parent households, of which a disproportionate percentage would be economically disadvantaged, minority, or both.

As a case in point, urban and suburban court workers in particular argued that "minority families comprised of single mothers and their children lack basic family structure which explains the greater need for intervention in the lives of minority children." Moreover, more than half of the court workers interviewed in one large urban area postulated,

> If African American adolescents are treated any differently by the court than majority adolescents, it is primarily because of the family surrounding the Black youth. . . . Black families do not have structure. . . . There is no male around.

Definitions of family structure varied across and within jurisdictions. Here, court staff are not simply referring to the physical composition of the juvenile's family. Structure was also used to assess the character of the occupants of the home as well as interpret the quality of supervision within the home.

Family structure was also associated with caregiver control. That is, homes with structure were alleged to have higher levels of parental control over adolescents than homes without structure. Thus, parental control was presumed to be lacking in homes that did not possess structure. The result was that youths from family backgrounds with "appropriate family structures" were said to be treated with leniency because these youths were thought to have solid, informal mechanisms of social control regulating their behavior from within the family.

The perception that differential treatment of juveniles by race (when it occurs) as primarily based on the perceptions of the family surrounding the adolescent suggests that minority or poor juveniles may not have been perceived to be from homes with "appropriate family structures" and, consequently, received more intensive court interventions. Furthermore, court-mandated intervention was also often articulated as the only viable method to obtain free treatment for these youths. Minority juveniles were often perceived to be in need of more formal mechanisms of social control because of their familial and economic backgrounds than their majority counterparts, and court intervention was thought to be the only means of providing them state-funded treatment their parents could not provide or afford.

Similarly, the subsequent removal of youths from the home was found to reflect the court's perception that biological or adoptive parents better control their children, middle-class values are important in the progression to adulthood, criminality among siblings is a manifestation of a lack of parental control, and single-parent homes provide less supervision and structure than two-parent homes.

Discussion

This research suggests that in its attempt to individualize treatment, the juvenile court incorporates family variables into the decision-making process. Moreover, this research shows that the juvenile court relies heavily on professional judgment to assess merits of family characteristics to determine court processes and sanctions (Matza, 1964:114).

Matza (1964) suggests that family variables are included as a means to better assess the needs of the child. More specifically, Matza (1964:114) suggests that family variables are examined by the court specifically to assess the willingness and abilities of parents to correctly sponsor a juvenile on a derived sanction. However, this research suggests that family attributes affect procedural, sanction, and placement decisions and that parental sponsorship as examined by court personnel is conceptualized and assessed within a social control framework. It is not enough that a parent is willing to sponsor a child. The parent must be perceived by the court as having both an appreciable level of control over the juvenile and the ability to provide the youth with a structurally stable home. Thus, this research suggests that while parental sponsorship is important, as Matza suggests, it is framed and assessed within a social control context comparable to Gottfredson and Hirschi's (1990) perspective on delinquency.

Family structure was often equated with social control. This suggests court officials were influenced by actual family composition and not necessarily the ability of the parents to supervise and control. Many court officials believe juveniles from two-parent homes should receive more lenient treatment because two parents were better able to supervise and control an adolescent than a single parent.

Whereas the juvenile court seems supportive of the traditional two-parent functional model of family life, with assigned roles and responsibilities, this model has to a large extent been abandoned by family researchers and scholars. This abandonment has most noticeably occurred since the voluminous entry of women into the labor force during the 1950s (Eshleman, 1989). Juvenile justice decision making based on a model of family composition, rather than parental competency inclusive of the willingness of the parent to sponsor a child, could prove especially detrimental to youths of color and others whose cultural or economic backgrounds support various nontraditional family structures. In comparison to majority adolescents, there are a disproportionate number of minority adolescents raised in single-parent homes. For instance, the National Center for Health Statistics (1989) reported that 62.2 percent of births to African-American mothers occurred among unmarried women, whereas 16.7 percent of births to white females occurred among unmarried women. Moreover, statistics show that African-American children are more likely than white children to live with their mothers alone because of the higher rates of marital dissolution and lower rates of marriage and remarriage among African Americans (Turner and Helms, 1988).

Therefore, a court decision-making model even partially predicated upon ideal traditional family structure and functions places a large number of minority youths at risk for more intrusive juvenile court processing and sanctions (Wordes, Bynum, and Corley, 1994; Corley, Bynum, and Wordes, 1993).

A traditional, structural functional assessment of family life in juvenile justice decision making also yields possible insights into Sampson and Laub's (1993) findings as to how poverty and racial inequalities become associated with increased juvenile justice processing. In brief, the conceptualization and evaluation of family characteristics we found in the juvenile justice system rewards youths from two-parent homes with less officious intervention in their lives, punishes youths from structurally inappropriate backgrounds with more intrusive actions, and substitutes race and class biases by favoring traditional, two-parent families. Thus, as family variables were often used by court personnel in this study, they became class and race surrogates. This occurred, in part, because parental sponsorship was overshadowed by issues of structure and control in such a manner that youths perceived not to be from "structurally appropriate" backgrounds were thought to be in greater need of the court's services.

Additionally, it should be noted that the conceptualization and assessment of a juvenile's family characteristics did not vary across urban, suburban, or rural jurisdictions. In general, court officials (across all seven jurisdictions) believe single-parent homes produce youths who need more social control. This works to the detriment of minority and lower-class youths.

Recommendations

Given the juvenile court's attempts to tailor its sanctions to meet the needs of the individual, it is unlikely that social variables, such as family characteristics, are likely to be excluded from the decision-making process. However, the court may be better able to meet the needs of the child through an assessment of parental competency and legal variables. This could include an evaluation of the caregiver's abilities to negotiate their own complex environment while at the same time establishing linkages and networks that provide legitimate opportunities and mentorships for their children (Rosier and Corsaro, 1993). Then, possibly, the willingness and abilities of the parent or caregiver to sponsor correctly a youth could be assessed outside the realm of family structure and parental control and more in conjunction with parental competency.

Results of this qualitative research should be expanded. Future research should draw on both qualitative and quantitative research methodologies. This may enable the influence of familial traits to be assessed at various stages throughout the justice process. Moreover, gender differences should be examined relative to the effect of family variables on juvenile court processes and sanctions. While the present study examines differences in treatment and family characteristics among male adolescents charged with a felony offense, it would have been an even better study if gender differences could have been examined.

References

AGETON, S., and D. ELLIOTT (1974). "The Effects of Legal Processing on Delinquent Orientations," 22 *Social Problems* 87.

ARNOLD, W. K. (1971). "Race and Ethnicity Relative to Other Factors in Juvenile Court Dispositions," 77 *American Journal of Sociology* 211.

BARTON, W. H. (1976). "Discretionary Decision-making in Juvenile Justice," 22 *Crime and Delinquency* 470.

BISHOP, D. M., and C. E. FRAZIER (1988). "The Influence of Race in Juvenile Justice Processing," 25 *Journal of Research in Crime and Delinquency* 242.

BLACK, D. M., and A. J. REISS (1970). "Police Control of Juveniles," 35 *American Sociological Review* 63.

CARTER, T. J. (1979). "Juvenile Court Dispositions: A Comparison of Status and Nonstatus Offenders," 17 *Criminology* 341.

CHEIN, D. B., and J. HUDSON (1981). "Discretion in Juvenile Justice," in D. Fogel and J. Hudson (eds.), *Justice as Fairness: Perspectives on the Justice Model.* Cincinnati, OH: Anderson Publishing Company.

CHUSED, R. H. (1973). "The Juvenile Court Process: A Study of Three New Jersey Counties," 26 *Rutgers Law Review* 488.

COHEN, L. E., and M. FELSON (1979). "Social Change and Crime Rate Trends: A Routine Activities Approach," 44 *American Sociological Review* 588.

COHEN, L. E., and J. R. KLUEGEL (1979). "The Detention Decision: A Study of the Impact of Social Characteristics and Legal Factors in Two Metropolitan Juvenile Courts," 58 *Social Forces* 146.

CORLEY, C., T. BYNUM, and M. WORDES (1993). "Assess the Impact of Family Variables on Juvenile Justice Processes." Paper presented at the American Society of Criminology meeting in Phoenix, AZ.

DALY, K. (1987). "Structure and Practice of Familial-based Justice in a Criminal Court," 21 *Law and Society Review* 267.

EMPEY, L. T., and M. STAFFORD (1991). *American Delinquency: Its Meaning and Construction.* Belmont, CA: Wadsworth Publishing Company.

ELLIOTT, D. S., and S. S. AGETON (1980). "Reconciling Race and Class Differences in Self-reported and Official Estimates of Delinquency," 45 *American Sociological Review* 95.

ESHLEMAN, J. R. (1989). *The Family: An Introduction.* Boston, MA: Allyn and Bacon, Inc.

FAGEN, J., E. SLAUGHTER, and E. HARTSTONE (1987). "Blind Justice? The Impact of Race on the Juvenile Justice Process," 33 *Crime and Delinquency* 224.

FELD, B. C. (1993). *Justice for Children: The Right to Counsel and the Juvenile Courts.* Boston, MA: Northeastern University Press.

FELSON, M. (1986). "Linking Criminal Choices, Routine Activities, Informal Social Control, and Criminal Outcomes," in R. Clark and D. Cornish (eds.), *The Reasoning Criminal.* New York: Springer-Verlag.

FENWICK, C. R. (1982). "Juvenile Court Intake Decision Making: The Importance of Family Affiliation." 10 *Journal of Criminal Justice* 443.

FERDINAND, T. N., and E. G. LUCHTERHAND (1970). "Inner-city Youth, the Police, Juvenile Court and Justice," 17 *Social Problems* 510.

FRAZIER, C., P. RICHARDS, and R. POTTER (1983). "Juvenile Diversion and Net Widening: Toward a Clarification of Assessment Strategies," 42 *Human Organization* 115.

GOTTFREDSON, M., and T. HIRSCHI (1990). *A General Theory of Crime.* Stanford, CA: Stanford University Press.

HILL, R. (1980). "Black Kids: White Justice," 24 *New Society* 174.

HINDELANG, M. J. (1987), "Race and Involvement in Common Law Personal Crimes," 43 *American Sociological Review* 93.

HIRSCHI, T., and M. GOTTFREDSON (1993). "Rethinking the Juvenile Justice System," 39 *Crime and Delinquency* 262.

HORWITZ, A., and M. WASSERMAN (1980). "Some Misleading Conceptions in Sentencing Research: An Example and a Reformulation in the Juvenile Court," 18 *Criminology* 411.

JOHNSON, R. E. (1986). "Family Structure and Delinquency," 24 *Criminology* 65.

KEMPF, K., S. DECKER, and R. BING (1990). *An Analysis of Apparent Disparities in the Handling of Black Youth Within Missouri's Juvenile Justice Systems.* Technical report, University of Missouri, St. Louis.

KORNHAUSER, R. R. (1978). *Social Sources of Delinquency: An Appraisal of Analytic Models.* Chicago: University of Chicago Press.

LIEBER, M. (1992). *Juvenile Justice Decision Making in Iowa: An Analysis of the Influence of Race on Case Processing in Three Counties.* Technical report, University of Northern Iowa, Cedar Falls.

MATZA, D. (1964). *Delinquency and Drift.* New York: John Wiley and Sons, Inc.

MEADE, A. (1973). "Seriousness of Delinquency, the Adjudicative Decision and Recidivism: A Longitudinal Configuration Analysis," 64 *Journal of Criminal Law and Criminology* 478.

NATIONAL CENTER FOR HEALTH STATISTICS (1989). *Monthly Vital Statistics Report,* November.

PLATT, A. M. (1969). *The Child Savers: The Invention of Delinquency.* Chicago: University of Chicago Press.

POOLE, E. D., and R. M. REGOLI (1980). "An Analysis of the Determinants of Juvenile Court Dispositions," 31 *Juvenile and Family Court Journal* 23.

POPE, C., and W. FEYERHERM (1990) "Minority Status and Juvenile Processing: An Assessment of the Research Literature (Parts 1 and 2)," 22 *Criminal Justice Abstracts* 327 and 527.

REISS, A. J., Jr. (1951). "Delinquency as the Failure of Personal and Social Controls," 16 *American Sociological Review* 196.

ROSIER, K. B., and W. A. CORSARO (1993). "Competent Parents, Complex Lives: Managing Parenthood in Poverty," 22 *Journal of Contemporary Ethnography* 171.

SAMPSON, R. J. (1986). "Crime in Cities: The Effects of Formal and Informal Social Control," in A. J. Reiss and M. Tonry (eds.), *Communities and Crime.* Chicago: University of Chicago Press.

———— (1983). "The Neighborhood Context of Criminal Victimization." Ph.D. diss., State University of New York at Albany.

SAMPSON, R. J., and J. H. LAUB (1993). "Structural Variations in Juvenile Court Processing: Inequality, the Under Class, and Social Control," 27 *Law and Society Review* 285.

SCARPITTI, F. R., and R. M. STEPHENSON (1971). "Juvenile Court Dispositions: Factors in the Decision Making Process," 17 *Crime and Delinquency* 142.

SKOGAN, W. (1986). "Fear of Crime and Neighborhood Change," in A. J. Reiss and M. Tonry (eds.), *Communities and Crime.* Chicago: University of Chicago Press.

SIEVERDES, C. (1973). "Differential Disposition of Juvenile Offenders: A Study of Juvenile Court Labeling." Ph.D. diss., Mississippi State University.

SIEVERDES, C. M., D. J. SHOEMAKER, and O. R. CUNNINGHAM (1979). "Disposition Decisions by Juvenile Court Probation Officers and Judges: A Multivariate Analysis," 4:2 *Criminal Justice Review* 121.

THORNBERRY, T. P. (1979). "Sentencing Disparities in the Juvenile Justice System," 70 *Journal of Criminal Law and Criminology* 164.

——— (1973). "Race, Socioeconomic Status and Sentencing in the Juvenile Justice System," 64 *Journal of Criminal Law and Criminology* 90.

TURNER, J., and D. HELMS (1989). *Marriage and Family: Traditions and Transitions.* Orlando, FL: Harcourt Brace Janovich.

WORDES, M., T. S. BYNUM, and C. J. CORLEY (1994). "Locking Up Youth: The Impact of Race on Detention Decisions," 31 *Journal of Research in Crime and Delinquency* 149.

ZATZ, M. (1987). "The Changing Forms of Racial/Ethnic Biases in Sentencing," 24 *Journal of Research in Crime and Delinquency* 69.

8

Certification to Criminal Court
The Important Policy Questions of How, When, and Why

Joseph B. Sanborn, Jr.

Introduction
The Problem of Studying Certification

Typically, juveniles who commit crimes are subject to the jurisdiction of juvenile court. In a number of situations, however, youths charged with crimes can be tried, instead, in criminal court. This process has been given a variety of names, the most popular of which are transfer, waiver, and certification.

Prosecuting juvenile defendants as adults is the most critical decision for both the juvenile justice system and the youths accused of criminal behavior (Comments 1981; Stamm 1973). On the one hand, this decision represents an acknowledgement that the juvenile court has failed in its mission in that it will not have the opportunity to rehabilitate the young wrongdoers. On the other hand, channeling cases into the adult system exposes defendants to the harsh consequences possible in criminal court sentencing (Braithwaite and Shore 1981; Eigen 1981a, 1981b; Stamm 1973).

From *Crime & Delinquency* (Vol. 40, No. 2, April 1994) pp. 262-281, copyright © 1994 by Sage Publications, Inc. Reprinted by permission of Sage Publications, Inc.

Most publications on certification have been prescriptive, involving armchair observations as to what is wrong with it. Accordingly, most works have been directed at deriving the best formula for transfer (Sargent and Gordon 1963; Schornhorst 1968; Stamm 1973; Reid 1974; Mylniec 1976; Vitiello 1976; Edwards 1977; Gasper and Katkin 1980; Braithwaite and Shore 1981; Feld 1978, 1981a, 1981b, 1983, 1984, 1987, 1989). The empirical research has concentrated primarily on only two items: the characteristics of juveniles transferred to adult court (Hays and Solway 1972; Keiter 1973; Hamparian et al. 1982; Eigen 1981a, 1981b; Bortner 1986; Fisher and Teichman 1986; Fagan, Piper, and Forst 1986; Fagan, Forst, and Vivona 1987; Fagan and Deschenes 1990) and the trial and sentencing experiences of juveniles processed in the criminal court (Greenwood, Petersilia, and Zimring, 1980; Eigen 1981a, 1981b; Bortner 1986; Rudman, Hartstone, Fagan, and Moore 1986).

Thus far, the certification literature has provided policymakers with much contradictory advice and many confusing directions about transferring juveniles to criminal court. The confusion centers primarily around three vital aspects of certification: *how* transfer should occur; *when* transfer should take place; and, relatedly, *why* juvenile courts should be allowed to send some youths to adult court. The purposes of this article are twofold: to address the definitional problems underlying certification and to ascertain if juvenile court workers support or reject allegations made about transfer in the literature.

Definitional Considerations

The How Question (Precisely What Is Certification?)

Certification should be defined as the discretionary decision made by a judge or a prosecutor that a charge involving a defendant, legally defined as a juvenile, will be prosecuted in criminal court instead of in juvenile court.[1] That is, juvenile court would have jurisdiction over the case *but for* the decision of the court official. There are, then, only two types or methods of transfer: judicial and prosecutorial. Judicial transfer involves the discretionary decision-making power granted the juvenile court judge to send certain juveniles, usually defined as those not amenable to treatment in the juvenile justice system, to adult court. Prosecutorial waiver entails the discretion vested in the prosecutor to directly charge the youth as an adult because either concurrent jurisdiction allows this person to choose the appropriate court for all crimes committed by juveniles (i.e., pure prosecutorial transfer), or special, legislatively-designated-offenses statutes permit the prosecutor, via charging those specific crimes (i.e., limited prosecutorial transfer), to avoid or bypass juvenile court jurisdiction. In short, certification involves the selection of youths, who could have been tried in juvenile court, for prosecution in adult court.

The literature has contributed to definitional confusion by suggesting that there is actually a third type of transfer: legislative waiver. However, the legislature by itself cannot certify juveniles to adult court; the most it can do is to empower a court official to transfer a youth. The legislature can reduce the maximum age of juvenile court jurisdiction. Many observers regard this maneuver as legislative waiver (Whitebread and Batey 1977; Zimring 1981; Forst and Blomquist 1991; Comments 1992). But as soon as the new law takes effect, the new inhabitants of criminal court are not referred to as having been transferred. Rather, they are recognized as adult defendants; the parameters of criminal court jurisdiction simply have been expanded so as to include these younger persons, who now cannot possibly be defendants in the juvenile system.

Even more disturbing is the distortion effected by those who employ the legislative label in referring to what is actually limited prosecutorial transfer. Moreover, these individuals assert that this type of waiver is "mandatory" or "automatic" because the legislature designates that certain offenses (perhaps in conjunction with the age and the record of the accused) are to be prosecuted in criminal court (Feld 1978, 1981a, 1981b, 1983, 1984, 1987, 1989; Comments 1981, 1987; Notes 1966b, 1983, 1992; Notes and Comments 1980; Osbun and Rode 1984; Rogers and Mays 1987; Sorrentino and Olsen 1977; Whitebread and Batey 1977; Grundfest, Paskow, Szabo, and Williams 1981; Young 1981; Wizner 1984). This is clearly erroneous because, in this case, transfer becomes mandatory if, and only if, the prosecutor charges the necessary offense. Because this type of transfer is actively controlled by the prosecutor, it should not be called legislative.[2] Because this certification is initiated by the prosecutor's power to charge, which is an incredibly discretion-laden decision, this certification method certainly cannot be labeled mandatory or automatic with any integrity or accuracy (and without the constant use of quotation marks).[3]

The When Question (For Whom Should Transfer Toll?)

Historically, certification has been directed primarily against two populations: those who did not appear to be amenable to juvenile court treatment efforts (i.e., the beyond-rehabilitation group), and those who appeared as worthy candidates for the harsh, punitive consequences possible in the criminal justice system (i.e., the greater-punishment group).

Three questions have been relevant in deciding the transfer fate of the former constituency: (a) would treatment resources be wasted on the youths? (Comments 1966, 1976, 1987, 1991; Bishop, Frazier, and Henretta 1989; Bishop and Frazier 1991; Feld 1978; Fagan and Deschenes 1990; Forst and Blomquist 1991; Edwards 1977; Gasper and Katkin 1980; Browne 1977; Gillespie and Norman, 1984; Grisso, Tomkins, and Casey 1988; Grundfest et al. 1981; Notes 1966a, 1972, 1975; Notes and Comments 1967, 1980; Stamm 1973; Zimring 1981); (b) would these juveniles contaminate others and frustrate the latter's chances of rehabilitation? (Bortner 1986; Comments 1966, 1987, 1991; Feld 1978; Forst and Blomquist 1991; Gasper and Katkin 1980; Grundfest et al. 1981; Notes 1975; Notes and Comments 1980; Significant Developments 1973; Thomas and Bilchik 1985); and (c) does the juvenile system simply lack the necessary resources to deal with these offenders? (Bishop et al. 1989; National Advisory Committee 1976; Mountford and Berenson 1969; Notes and Comments 1980).

Three different considerations have influenced the certification of youths thought to be worthy recipients of punitive sanctions: (a) the desirability of longer sentences possible in adult court (Bortner 1986; Bishop and Frazier 1991; Comments 1991, 1992; Edwards 1977; Fagan and Deschenes 1990; Feld 1978, 1984; Forst and Blomquist 1991; Gasper and Katkin 1980; Gillespie and Norman 1984; Greenwood et al. 1980; Grundfest et al. 1981; Stamm 1973; Wizner 1984; Zimring 1981, 1991); (b) the lack of security in juvenile facilities (Comments 1991; Gasper and Katkin 1980; Gillespie and Norman 1984; Notes and Comments 1980); and (c) the deterrent efforts and public safety provided by an adult record (Bishop et al. 1989; Bortner 1986; Comments 1987, 1991; Gasper and Katkin 1980; Grundfest et al. 1981).

Remarkably, however, the literature has recently been dominated by two movements, which have clouded the question as to when waiver is appropriate. The first involves numerous observers who insist that the only viable candidates for transfer are those from the greater-punishment camp or those youths who have committed the most serious crimes and warrant very lengthy prison terms (Bortner 1986; Comments 1992; Edwards 1977; Champion 1989; Champion and Mays 1991; Gasper and Katkin 1980; Feld 1983, 1984, 1987; Gillespie and Norman 1984; Flicker 1981; Greenwood et al. 1980; Institute of Judicial Administration/American Bar Association 1980; Stamm 1973; Twentieth Century Fund 1978; Zimring 1981,1991; Mays and Houghtalin 1992; Whitebread and Batey 1981).

> The primary justification for waiver is the need for minimum lengths of confinement that are substantially in excess of the maximum sanctions available within the juvenile court. (Feld 1984, p. 33)

> The most pervasive rationale for the remand of juveniles to adult court is that such action provides greater protection to the public than does juvenile justice processing. This is an assumption for which there is little empirical validation. (Bortner 1986, p. 56)

> If the primary objective of transfers is to subject juvenile offenders to more stringent penalties in criminal courts, for committing more serious crimes, then the wrong population is being targeted for waivers here. (Champion 1989, p. 583)

> The justification for waiver is singular: transfer to criminal court is necessary
> when the maximum punishment available in juvenile court is clearly inadequate
> for a particular offender. (Zimring 1991, p. 276)

These individuals, among others, have ignored the fact that juvenile courts have also traditionally targeted for transfer the beyond-rehabilitation population, regardless of either the severity of the crime or the need for lengthy incarceration.

Similarly, the second movement has centered on the notion that because some juveniles fare better with criminal court sentencing than they probably would have done with juvenile court dispositions, the very legitimacy of transfer itself is called into question (Bortner 1986; Champion 1989; Champion and Mays 1991; Edwards 1977; Feld 1984, 1987; Gasper and Katkin 1980; Gillespie and Norman 1984; Sagatun, McCollum, and Edwards 1985).

> There is a certain anomaly when youths are waived from juvenile court because
> they presumably require longer sentences than the juvenile system can provide
> and then are placed on probation as adults. (Feld 1984, p. 36)

> The moderate rate of incarceration is important because it demonstrates the
> discrepancy between the popular rationale for remand and the actual
> consequences of such actions. (Bortner 1986, pp. 57-58)

> If waivers are not resulting in more severe penalties for juveniles, what are
> they accomplishing? These findings suggest that their use in the present
> jurisdictions is primarily cosmetic. (Champion 1989, p. 584)

These statements demonstrate that specious premises lead to specious conclusions, and unreasonably suggest that juvenile court policies must he held hostage to criminal court practices.

There may or may not be a so-called leniency or punishment gap facing some certified juveniles; many research projects have discovered more punitive sanctions in adult court (Barnes and Franz 1989; Dawson 1992; Eigen 1981a, 1981b; Fisher and Teichman 1986; Greenwood, Abrahamse, and Zimring 1984; Houghtalin and Mays 1991; Mays and Houghtalin 1992; Thomas and Bilchik 1985; Rudman et al. 1986). For many, and perhaps most, transfers (i.e., the beyond-rehabilitation group), the punishment gap is mostly irrelevant inasmuch as the juvenile court is not pursuing lengthy terms of incarceration. Even for the greater-punishment population, the failure of the criminal court to deliver a harsh sentence does not retroactively invalidate the transfer. If nothing else, the criminal court fails to meaningfully punish many serious adult offenders as well. More important, the juvenile court cannot significantly punish young offenders without running afoul of its treatment mission and without destroying the delicate due process balance of its adjudicatory hearing (Feld 1984; Zimring 1981, 1991). Therefore, the juvenile court should not be rendering lengthy sentences; extended incarcerations mean that warehousing/punishment is occurring (Forst and Blomquist 1991). Finally, many of the worst juvenile offenders are probably going to be viewed as "virgins" and as being among the least significant adult criminals.[4]

The Why Question (Is Waiver Necessary?)

Closely related to the question of when transfer should occur is the issue as to whether certification is necessary. Here, juvenile court proponents have hoisted themselves on their own petards. Initially, the optimism accompanying the juvenile court experiment went too far in suggesting that all the difficulties of all youths could be resolved in that forum (Mack 1909; Lou 1927). From virtually the first day of its operation, juvenile court relied on transferring its most troublesome cases to the adult system (Flicker 1981, 1983; Hamparian 1981; Stamm 1973; Whitebread and Batey 1981; Wizner 1984). Juvenile court officials recognized and acknowledged early on that they were faced with some youths who had problems and/or had committed wrongs that were beyond the rehabilitative or punitive capacities of the juvenile system; transfer was designed, then, to remove those with problems that the juvenile court could not or would not address.

Nevertheless, a number of observers have been more than unreasonable in their analyses and criticisms of transfer. One tactic has been to thrust the treatment rhetoric back at juvenile court and to suggest that it is inconsistent to be supposedly concerned about young offenders' rehabilitation but yet to send them to the criminal justice system where rehabilitation generally has little support or effectiveness (Notes 1983; Whitebread and Batey 1981). Similarly, others attack juvenile court for not developing satisfactory solutions to the treatment problems of the young (Bortner 1986; Feld 1978; Flicker 1981; Schornhorst 1968; Sorrentino and Olsen 1977; Notes 1983; Stamm 1973).

These challenges are unfair because they hold juvenile court accountable for the failures of criminal court and society. Moreover, they insist that juvenile court must be able to deal with the dysfunctions of all youths, even those who are older and/or perhaps are severely troubled/dangerous, requiring more years of help/control than juvenile court can reasonably/legally provide. This reasoning also forces juvenile court to make an untenable choice: either accept the referrals of all juvenile offenders or acknowledge the inability to help all young criminals, which is translatable, then, as not being equipped to rehabilitate any juvenile delinquents (see Bortner 1986; Flicker 1981).

Juvenile court officials have also been impugned for admitting that transfer can operate as a safety valve to remove the really difficult cases from juvenile court (Feld 1978; Wizner 1984). Critics have seized on this admission as grounds for alleging that certification is nothing more than a method by which juvenile court siphons off societal pressure for retribution (Bortner 1986; Comments 1968a, 1968b, 1969, 1976, 1981; Champion 1989; Keiter 1973; Notes 1966a, 1975, 1983, 1986; Notes and Comments 1967; Sargent and Gordon 1963; Schornhorst 1968; Stamm 1973). These accusations appear implausible for at least two reasons. First, historically, most transfers to criminal court have been relatively innocuous property offenders (Bortner 1986; Champion 1989; Champion and Mays 1991; Feld 1981a, 1981b, 1987, 1989; Bishop and Frazier 1991; Bishop et al. 1989; Nimick, Szymanski, and Snyder 1986). It is difficult to envision the community exerting pressure to certify repeat property offenders. Second, juvenile court operates in relative secrecy. The number of juvenile offenders who attract the community's attention, let alone its hostility, is rather small, and many of them are prosecuted in juvenile court.

Dimensions of the Empirical Study

Research Design and Methodology

The empirical research reported here was conducted to ascertain the perspectives of various juvenile court workers, both as to who should be certified to criminal court, in which manner, and for what reasons, and as to whether the literature has been correct in describing waiver.

Interviewing was chosen as the method of data collection. An open-ended survey interview was employed (Babbie 1989, pp. 244-47); I asked a uniform set of questions to standardize the results and to ensure accurate recording. The answers were mostly open-ended and were often followed by probes, which allowed the interviewee to amplify the meaning of points he or she made (Babbie 1989, pp. 248-49; Fitzgerald and Cox 1987, pp. 102-4). The interviews were administered to 100 juvenile workers between the summer of 1987 and the winter of 1988; each of them lasted approximately 30 minutes.

Research Sites

Three courts were selected for study to determine whether demographic composition or size of the court and its caseload had any bearing on the various perceptions of the juvenile court personnel (Stapleton, Aday, and Ito 1982). The first court was located in a large urban center (Court A), the second was in a suburban setting (Court B), and the third was from rural surroundings (Court C). All three were situated in a northeastern state.

The county in which Court A sat consisted of one major city. In 1987, approximately 11,000 delinquency cases were referred to juvenile court. Certification has been of critical importance to this court where prosecutors have been the primary initiators of transfer actions. Hundreds of juveniles have been sent to the urban criminal court over the last several years (see Table 1). Six judges, 21 assistant district attorneys (including supervisors), and 17 assistant public defenders (including supervisors) were assigned to full-time duty in the urban court; all participated in this study. Court-appointed and privately retained attorneys represented about 25% of the juvenile defendants. A sample of 10 of these lawyers was randomly selected from court lists, which identified the attorneys who appeared most frequently in Court A. Ten of the 130 probation officers in the urban juvenile court were randomly selected to be interviewed. Finally, all six of the social workers who assisted the public defenders in preventing certification also took part in the research.[5]

Court B was located in a county that served as a major suburban outlet for the community in which the urban court was located. There was one formerly industrial city within the county limits, but the predominant character of the county was suburban. There were 1,187 petitions filed in 1987. Probation officers and prosecutors share decision-making power in instituting transfer requests. There has been only moderate certification activity during the past several years (see Table 1). Three judges, three assistant district attorneys and one assistant public defender who handled approximately 70% of the caseload worked part-time in the juvenile court; all participated in this study.[6] Five supervisors conducted all of the certification work for the probation department; all five took part in the research. Five private attorneys were randomly selected for the interview.

Court C was situated in a mostly rural county, which included two major towns. There were 1,145 petitions filed in 1987. Probation officers have mostly decided which youths were subjected to waiver hearings. Certification was not an issue in 1987, and only a handful of youths has been waived to the adult court since then (see Table 1). One judge, one assistant district attorney, and one assistant public defender, who handled 85% of the caseload, were assigned to part-time duty in the rural court; all participated in this study. Five of the 21 probation officers and five private attorneys were selected for the interview.[7]

Research Findings

Appropriate Reasons for Certification

Nearly all of the workers (88%) answered positively that juvenile court needed certification. Only 12 persons believed that juvenile court could operate without

Table 1: Number of Petitions Certified to Criminal Court by the Juvenile Courts, 1987-1992

Year	Court		
	Urban (A)	Suburban (B)	Rural (C)
1987	195	23	0
1988	146	29	1
1989	257	25	4
1990	283	15	3
1991	230	34	2
1992	155	36	2

transfer; all of these individuals were from the defense ranks. The urban court members (85.7%) were only slightly less likely than those of the suburban (94.1%) or rural courts (92.3%) to acknowledge that certification was necessary in the juvenile justice system.

More than three-fourths of the workers who saw a need for waiver declared that some youths have had problems or have presented challenges that were beyond the rehabilitative capacities of the juvenile justice system. Only about one-fourth of the prowaiver respondents maintained that society's protection was better served by sending some juveniles to criminal court and that certain crimes were so heinous that they were beyond the purview of juvenile court. Transferring youths so as to conserve the juvenile system's resources was identified by nearly as many individuals. Certification was also justified for its deterrent effect (see Table 2).

The participants were then asked if the literature had been accurate in its depiction of transfer. Only approximately one-fourth of the workers regarded waiver as either a failure in juvenile justice philosophy or a means of societal retribution. Most of the individuals who voiced these views were from the defense ranks and were more likely to work in Court A. Similarly, approximately one-third of the respondents acknowledged that transfer operates as a safety valve, a mechanism to get the public off the juvenile court's back; defense people dominated this group. According to the vast majority of the participants, certification mostly represented a lack of resources in the juvenile justice system and/or an inability of the juvenile court to handle the problems of certain young people (see Table 3).

Appropriate Candidates for Certification

The juvenile court act that controlled the three courts in the study provided for a maximum jurisdictional age of 18; certification was possible for anyone 14 years of age who committed a felony, including a first offender. Prosecutors had to prove

Table 2: Reasons for Transfer Cited by Percentage of Court Workers Who Saw a Need for Transfer

	Court			
Reasons	Urban (A)	Suburban (B)	Rural (C)	Total
Beyond rehabilitation	75.0	87.5	75.0	77.3
Protect society	21.7	25.0	50.0	26.1
Certain crimes	21.7	50.0	16.7	26.1
Conserve resources	31.7	0.0	8.3	22.7
Deterrence	18.3	12.5	33.3	19.3

to a judge, by a preponderance of evidence, that youths were not amenable to juvenile court treatment before transfer could transpire. In addition, prosecutors had direct certification power over all defendants charged with murder, whereas juveniles over the age of 14 could certify themselves to criminal court.

Members of the sample were asked if they supported these provisions. The vast majority of them opted to keep 18 as the cutoff age from criminal court jurisdiction, whereas another two people believed that the age should be raised. A majority of the respondents also argued that there should be no change in the minimum age of 14 that was required for transfer; another 31% of the participants maintained that the age should actually be raised to between 15 and 17 years old. Whereas slightly more than one-half of the workers thought that the "felonies only" policy was appropriate, an additional 21 persons argued that only first- and second-degree felonies should be transferable to criminal court. The vast majority of respondents elected to continue placing the amenability burden on the prosecutor; nearly two-thirds of the workers wanted to raise the level of proof from a preponderance to clear and convincing or beyond a reasonable doubt (see Table 4).

There was very little support for a "get tough" approach in deciding who to waive to adult court. Nevertheless, nearly three-fourths of the workers endorsed the notion that first offenders should be eligible for certification, and more than two-thirds supported the youth's right of self-certification. Then, again, there was only lukewarm backing of the prosecutor's power to directly transfer defendants charged with murder (see Table 4).

Appropriate Method of Certification

Finally, members of the sample were asked which was the best method of transfer and what were the strengths and weaknesses of each method. Judicial waiver was selected by more than four-fifths of the respondents and by all defense personnel in this study. Limited and pure prosecutorial transfers were identified by only 15 (13 prosecutors) and 2 (both prosecutors) workers, respectively. Two urban court probation officers declared that a reduction in the juvenile court's jurisdictional age was most desirable and was the fairest way to bring juveniles before the criminal court.

Judicial waiver elicited positive descriptions from all but five respondents from Court A. The workers felt that the most valuable feature of judicial transfer was in promoting due process and protection of the youths' rights by providing a formal and neutral forum in which opposing counsel can be heard, on the record, before an impartial fact finder. Judicial certification was also credited with allowing for better analysis of the transfer criteria and the juveniles' records, ensuring less abuse by placing this power in the hands of a judge rather than a prosecutor (which also resulted in greater trust in the process), and reducing the numbers of waivers due to the restraint typically exercised by the judge.

However, a majority of the participants also had negative things to say about

Table 3: What Certification Represented to Percentage of Juvenile Court
Workers

| | Court | | | |
Representations	Urban (A)	Suburban (B)	Rural (C)	Total
Failure in philosophy	31.4	17.6	7.7	26
Societal retribution	30.0	11.8	15.4	25
Safety valve	38.6	29.4	15.4	34
Lack of resources	74.3	88.2	84.6	78
Irresolvable problems	80.0	82.4	76.9	80

Table 4: Percentage of Court Workers Who Supported Current Transfer
Policies

| | Court | | | |
Policies	Urban (A)	Suburban (B)	Rural (C)	Total
Jurisdictional age	85.7	100.0	92.3	89
Certification age	90.0	88.2	100.0	91
Felonies only	75.7	76.5	69.2	75
Prosecutor burden	87.1	100.0	69.2	87
Raise burden of proof	67.1	52.9	69.2	65
First offenders	64.3	94.1	92.3	73
Self-certification	68.6	82.4	46.2	68
Prosecutorial transfers	38.6	29.4	53.8	39

judicial waiver. Court workers observed that it was too subjective and inconsistent. Prosecutors objected to judges refusing to certify appropriate candidates. Finally, judicial transfer was criticized because it was used by judges and prosecutors to plea bargain with the defendant and because judges were often improperly influenced in their decisions by prosecutors, publicity, or probation officers.

Nearly two-fifths of the respondents said something positive about limited prosecutorial waiver; most of these individuals (58.9%) were prosecutors. This form of transfer was seen as particularly appropriate for some offenses (i.e., homicide). Here, the public interest was perceived as having a direct input into processing serious juvenile offenders. In addition, limited prosecutorial waiver was praised for its deterrent effect, equitability, and cheapness. Only 15 individuals had nothing negative to offer about this type of certification, however, and 13 of them were prosecutors. The two major problems were a fear of prosecutorial abuse of power and a lack of individualization in determining which youths should be sent to criminal court. A lack of impartiality and political manipulation by prosecutors were other negative factors cited by the workers.

The reduction of the juvenile court's maximum jurisdictional age (or legislative transfer) was given favorable review by slightly more than one-fourth of the study participants. These individuals observed that it might be time to lower the age of juvenile court or that it was the legislature's prerogative to do so. Legislative certification was also seen as nonsubjective and nondiscriminatory, and as providing for public input into deciding who belonged in which court. Nevertheless, only nine workers had no negative comments to add. Most of the respondents criticized legislative waiver as too automatic, as sending to adult court many youths who did not belong there; many others opposed any notion of lowering juvenile court's maximum age. A few people argued that legislative transfer would make the waiver decision too political and would undermine the philosophy of juvenile court.

Pure prosecutorial transfer was perceived as the least desirable and most problematic type of certification; it was defended by only 14 individuals, all of whom were from the urban court and all but 2 of whom were prosecutors. Supporters usually observed that this arrangement of waiver authority placed transfer power where it belonged; a few others noted that it would bring about deterrence and would be cheaper to employ. Only 2 prosecutors had no negative statements about pure prosecutorial transfer. Nearly everyone in the study envisioned this certification mechanism as ripe for prosecutorial abuse. Like legislative waiver, pure prosecutorial waiver was seen as too political and damaging to juvenile court philosophy; the latter was also perceived as too one-sided by a few court workers.

Discussion of the Findings

The data challenges how certification has recently been represented in the literature. The respondents did not perceive a need for waiver based on its protecting society. Instead, certification was defended by most individuals because it prevented juvenile courts having to address youths who had problems that were beyond the rehabilitative capacities of the system and who threatened to contaminate others' chances of rehabilitation. The workers considered transfer as simply the inability of juvenile court to service all youths, rather than as acting like a safety valve or a form of societal retribution. Most respondents rejected numerous opportunities to adopt get tough measures in certification policies; even prosecutors advised against expanding their waiver powers.

Finally, certification was not a monolithic entity that was basically the same in all juvenile courts. Rather, there were differences in what transfer represented to the three courts. Whereas the granting and denial of waiver was a critical and frequent decision in the urban court, it was virtually irrelevant to the rural court; drug trafficking was making certification more prevalent in the suburban court. Moreover, urban prosecutors were struggling to increase their control over transfer while other Court A workers argued that certification power had to be kept away from prosecutors at all costs. The struggle for power, then, marked many aspects of transfer in Court A. Urban court workers had a more negative view of waiver; they tended to perceive vindictive prosecutors and inconsistent judges who let subjective impressions guide the transfer decision.

The picture was different in the suburban and rural courts, however, where probation officers dominated waiver decisions. There, transfer was seen more as a consequence of the youths' problems than as a result of power-hungry prosecutors. Workers from Courts B and C opposed changes in transfer policies, not because prosecutors would abuse powers, but rather because the criteria for waiver would then be inappropriate. Certification in these courts had not degenerated into a power struggle.

Conclusions and Implications of the Study

Hopefully, this critical examination has put to rest most of the confusion surrounding certification and has produced a clearer understanding as to what waiver is and is not. It seems obvious that persons in the field need to exercise greater care and integrity in defining terms related to transfer.

Second, although the empirical research here was limited to ascertaining the perspectives of 100 workers from three juvenile courts, it sends up some red flags. To date, the certification area has been inundated with literature and data that seem to reflect more the views and agenda of the authors than the two-sided analyses that can be offered by juvenile court employees.

It would seem time for observers to become more realistic, as well. For example, it is useless to point to certification as a violation of juvenile justice philosophy. Few would assert today that everything inconsistent with juvenile justice philosophy is necessarily wrong. It is also implausible to conceive of a juvenile system that provides treatment solutions to *all* young criminals. It is naive, as well, to assume that juvenile court will not experience failures, and does not have to answer to the community for the crimes committed by youths. Nevertheless, it is not the fault of juvenile court or the waiver process that adult courts do not give harsh sentences to all youths who are convicted there. Criminal court leniency does not indicate that transfer was unnecessary.

Although they acknowledged the problems inherent in judicial transfer, the respondents pointed out that the other methods of waiver suffered from even greater difficulties. The workers warned that limited and pure prosecutorial transfer merely shifted inconsistency and subjectivity from the judge to the prosecutor, and legislative waiver went to the other extreme by not discriminating whatsoever among offenders and the treatment they require. Policymakers need to be aware that cleaning up judicial transfer may be preferable to adopting alternative measures.

Finally, those who attack certification as being unequal seem to be challenging the essence of juvenile justice: individualization. Rehabilitation often discriminates among apparently legally equal offenders because they are not necessarily equal in treatment needs. If those who object to this lack of equality truly want greater uniformity in the handling of youths, perhaps it is juvenile court itself and not simply certification that warrants abolition.

Footnotes

[1] Many states allow juveniles to certify themselves, but this maneuver does not involve the juvenile system's *forcing* the youth to go to criminal court, which is the focus of this article.

[2] The legislature is the source of all transfer authority. It can delegate the power to itself (by reducing the jurisdictional parameters of the juvenile justice system), to the judge, or to the prosecutor in either sweeping (concurrent jurisdiction) or more narrow terms (by excluding designated offenses/records). In the last example, the legislature has authorized the prosecutor to certify by virtue of the charge, much like it has empowered the judge to transfer because of nonamenability to treatment. The former is surely no more legislative in nature than the latter, and neither should be referred to as legislative waiver.

[3] Age would appear to be the only automatic, nondiscretionary criterion that could be employed in the transfer decision.

[4] Absent sentencing guidelines or mandatory sentences, there is no way to guarantee severe criminal court sentencing for even the most heinous juvenile offenders prosecuted in adult court. Probably the only completely effective way to reduce the punishment gap between the two systems is to factor juvenile court adjudications directly into criminal court sentencing.

[5] The perspectives of the six public defender social workers were virtually identical with those expressed by the attorneys who worked in that office. The responses of both groups were tabulated together and were frequently referred to as having emanated from the defense ranks (along with private counsel).

[6] Two masters regularly conducted adjudicatory hearings in the suburban juvenile court but were not empowered to preside over transfer hearings; they did not participate in the study.

[7] Two masters regularly conducted adjudicatory hearings in the rural juvenile court but were not empowered to preside over transfer hearings; they did not participate in the study. Due to the scarcity of certification in the rural court, I was forced to interview a former assistant district attorney who had recently worked in juvenile court but who had retired by the latter part of 1987. Similarly, instead of using random selection, I purposely chose the five probation officers with the longest service in the rural court so as to guarantee their having experience in certification matters. Finally, I was able to locate only five private counsel who had had any exposure to transfer proceedings in Court C.

References

Babbie, Earl. 1989. *The Practice of Social Research*, 5th ed. Belmont, CA: Wadsworth.

Barnes, Carole and Randall Franz. 1989. "Questionably Adult: Determinants and Effects of the Juvenile Waiver Decision." *Justice Quarterly* 6:117-35.

Bishop, Donna M. and Charles E. Frazier. 1991. "Transfer of Juveniles to Criminal Court: A Case Study and Analysis of Prosecutorial Waiver." *Note Dame Journal of Law, Ethics and Public Policy* 5:281-302.

Bishop, Donna M., Charles E. Frazier, and John C. Henretta. 1989. "Prosecutorial Waiver: A Case Study of a Questionable Reform." *Crime & Delinquency* 35:179-201.

Bortner, M. A. 1986. "Traditional Rhetoric: Organizational Realities: Remand of Juveniles to Adult Court." *Crime Delinquency* 32:53-73.

Braithwaite, Lloyd and Allen Shore. 1981. "Treatment Rhetoric Versus Waiver Decisions." *Journal of Criminal Law and Criminology* 72:1867-91.

Browne, Elizabeth W. 1977. "Guidelines for Statutes for Transfer of Juveniles to Criminal Court." *Pepperdine Law Review* 4:479-95.

Champion, Dean J. 1989. "Teenage Felons and Waiver Hearings: Some Recent Trends 1980-1988." *Crime & Delinquency* 35:577-85.

Champion, Dean J. and G. Larry Mays. 1991. *Trasferring Juveniles to Criminal Courts: Trends and Implications for Criminal Justice*. New York: Praeger.

Comments. 1966. "Criminal Offenders in Juvenile Court: More Brickbats and Another Proposal." *University of Pennsylvania Law Review* 114:1171-1220.

————. 1968a. "Representing the Juvenile Defendant in Waiver Proceedings." *St. Louis University Law Journal* 12:424-65.

————. 1968b. "Waiver of Jurisdiction in Wisconsin Juvenile Courts." *Wisconsin Law Review* 1968:551-55.

————. 1969. "Waiver of Jurisdiction in Juvenile Courts." *Ohio State Law Journal* 30:132-43.

————. 1976. "Juveniles in the Criminal Courts: A Substantive View of the Fitness Decision." *U.C.L.A. Law Review* 23:988-1016.

————. 1981. "Relinquishment of Jurisdiction for Purposes of Criminal Prosecution of Juveniles." *Northern Kentucky Law Review* 8:377-93.

————. 1987. "Youth on Death Row: Waiver of Juvenile Court Jurisdiction and Imposition of the Death Penalty on Juvenile Offenders." *Northern Kentucky Law Review* 13:495-517.

————. 1991. "The Child-Adult: Michigan Waiver Law." *Detroit College of Law Review* 1991:1071-96.

————. 1992. "Trying Juveniles as Adults: Is The Short Term Gain of Retribution Outweighed by the Long Term Effects on Society?" *Mississippi Law Journal* 62:95-131.

Dawson, Robert O. 1992. "An Empirical Study of *Kent* Style Juvenile Transfers to Criminal Court." *St. Mary's Law Journal* 23:975-1054.

Edwards, Leonard, 1977. "The Case for Abolishing Fitness Hearings in Juvenile Court." *Santa Clara Law Review* 17:595-630.

Eigen, Joel P. 1981a. "The Determinants and Impact of Jurisdictional Transfer in Philadelphia." Pp. 333-50 in *Major Issues in Juvenile Justice Information and Training: Readings in Public Policy*, edited by J. C. Hall, D. M. Hamparian, J. M. Pettibone, and J. White. Columbus, OH: Academy for Contemporary Problems.

————1981b. "Punishing Youth Homicide Offenders in Philadelphia." *Journal of Criminal Law and Criminology* 72:1072-93.

Fagan, Jeffrey and Elizabeth P. Deschenes. 1990. "Determinants of Juvenile Waiver Decisions for Violent Juvenile Offenders." *Journal of Criminal Law and Criminology* 81:314-47.

Fagan, Jeffrey, Martin Forst, and T. Scott Vivona. 1987. "Racial Determinants of the Judicial Transfer Decision: Prosecuting Violent Youth in Criminal Court." *Crime & Delinquency* 33:259-86.

Fagan, Jeffrey, E. Piper, and Martin Forst. 1986. *The Juvenile Court and Violent Youth: Determinants of the Transfer Decision*. San Francisco: Center For Law and Social Policy.

Feld, Barry C. 1978. "Reference of Juvenile Offenders for Adult Prosecution: The Legislative Alternative to Asking Unanswerable Questions." *Minnesota Law Review* 62:515-618.

————. 1981a "Juvenile Court Legislative Reform and the Serious Young Offender: Dismantling the 'Rehabilitative Ideal.'" *Minnesota Law Review* 65:167-242.

————. 1981b. "Legislative Policies Toward the Serious Juvenile Offender: On The Virtues of Automatic Adulthood." *Crime & Delinquency* 27:497-521.

————. 1983. "Delinquent Careers and Criminal Policy: Just Deserts and the Waiver Decision." *Criminology* 21:195-212.

————. 1984. "The Decision to Seek Criminal Charges: Just Deserts and the Waiver Decision." *Criminal Justice Ethics* 3:27-41.

————. 1987. "The Juvenile Court Meets the Principle of the Offense: Legislative Changes in Juvenile Waiver Statutes." *Journal of Criminal Law and Criminology* 78:471-533.

Feld, Barry C. 1989. "Bad Law Makes Hard Cases: Reflections on Teen-Aged Axe-Murderers, Judicial Activism, and Legislative Default." *Law and Inequality* 8:1-101.

Fisher, Wayne S. and Lori Teichman. 1986. "Juvenile Waivers to Adult Court: A Report to the New Jersey State Legislature." *Criminal Justice Quarterly* 9:68-103.

Fitzgerald, Jack D. and Steven M. Cox. 1987. *Research Methods in Criminal Justice: An Introduction.* Chicago: Nelson-Hall.

Flicker, Barbara 1981. "Prosecuting Juveniles as Adults: A Symptom of a Crisis in the Juvenile Courts." Pp. 351-77 in *Major Issues in Juvenile Justice Information and Training: Readings in Public Policy*, edited by J. C. Hall, D. M. Hamparian, J. M. Pettibone, and J. L. White. Columbus, OH: Academy for Contemporary Problems.

————. 1983. *Transferring Juveniles to Adult Court for Trial.* Washington, DC: Institute of Judicial Administration.

Forst, Manin L. and Martha-Elin Blomquist. 1991. "Cracking Down on Juveniles: The Changing Ideology of Youth Corrections." *Notre Dame Journal of Law, Ethics, and Public Policy* 5:323-75.

Gasper, John and Daniel Katkin. 1980. "A Rationale for the Abolition of the Juvenile Court's Power to Waive Jurisdiction." *Pepperdine Law Review* 7:937-51.

Gillespie, L. Kay and Michael D. Norman. 1984. "Does Certification Mean Prison: Some Preliminary Findings From Utah." *Juvenile and Family Court Journal* 35:23-34.

Greenwood, Peter W., Joan Petersilia, and Franklin E. Zimring. 1980. *Age, Crime, and Sanctions: The Transition From Juvenile to Adult Court.* Santa Monica, CA: RAND.

Greenwood, Peter W., A. Abrahamse, and Franklin E. Zimring. 1984. *Factors Affecting Sentence Severity for Young Adult Offenders.* Washington, DC: National Institute of Justice.

Grisso, Thomas, Alan Tomkins, and Pamela Casey. 1988. "Psychosocial Concepts in Juvenile Law." *Law and Human Behavior* 12:403-37.

Grundfest, Andrea R., Anne C. Paskow, Helen E. Szabo, and Richard J. Williams. 1981. "Trial of Juveniles in Adult Court: The Prosecutor's Perspective." Pp. 321-32 in *Major Issues in Juvenile Justice Information and Training: Readings in Public Policy*, edited by J. C. Hall, D. M. Hamparian, J. M. Pettibone, and J. L. White. Columbus, OH: Academy For Contemporary Problems.

Hamparian, Donna M. 1981. "Introduction." Pp. 169-77 in *Major Issues in Juvenile Justice Information and Training: Readings in Public Policy*, edited by J. C. Hall, D. M. Hamparian, J. M. Pettibone, and J. L. White. Columbus, OH: Academy For Contemporary Problems.

Hamparian, Donna M., Linda K. Estep, Susan M. Muntean, Ramon R. Priestino, Robert G. Swisher, Paul L. Wallace, and Joseph L. White. 1982. *Major Issues in Juvenile Justice Information and Training—Youth in Adult Courts: Between Two Worlds.* Columbus, OH: Academy For Contemporary Problems.

Hays, J. Ray and Kenneth S. Solway. 1972. "The Role of Psychological Evaluation in Certification of Juveniles for Trial as Adults." *Houston Law Review* 9:709-15.

Houghtalin, Marilyn and G. Larry Mays. 1991. "Criminal Dispositions of New Mexico Juveniles Transferred to Adult Court." *Crime & Delinquency* 37:393-407.

Institute of Judicial Administration/American Bar Association (IJA/ABA). 1980. *Standards Relating to Transfer Between Courts.* Cambridge, MA: Ballinger. Juvenile Justice Standards Project.

Keiter, Robert B. 1973. "Criminal or Delinquency? A Study of Juvenile Cases Transferred to the Criminal Court." *Crime & Delinquency* 19:528-38.

Lou, Herbert 1927. *Juvenile Courts in the United States.* Chapel Hill: University of North Carolina Press.

Mack, Julian W. 1909. "The Juvenile Court." *Harvard Law Review* 23:104-22.

Mays, G. Larry and Marilyn Houghtalin. 1992. "Trying Juveniles as Adults: A Note on New Mexico's Recent Experience." *Justice System Journal* 15:814-23.

Mountford, Helen and Harvey S. Berenson. 1969. "Waiver of Jurisdiction: The Last Resort of the Juvenile Court." *University of Kansas Law Review* 18:55-70.

Mylniec, Wallace J. 1976. "Juvenile Delinquent or Adult Convict—The Prosecutor's Choice." *American Criminal Law Review* 14:29-57.

National Advisory Committee on Criminal Justice Standards and Goals (NAC). 1976. *Juvenile Justice and Delinquency Prevention*. Washington, DC: Author.

Nimick, Ellen, Linda Szymanski, and Howard Snyder. 1986. *Juvenile Court Waiver: A Study of Juvenile Court Cases Transferred to Criminal Court*. Pittsburgh, PA: National Center For Juvenile Justice.

Notes. 1966a. "Juvenile Delinquents: The Police, State Courts, and Individualized Justice." *Harvard Law Review* 79:775-810.

_____. 1966b. "Problems of Age and Jurisdiction in the Juvenile Court." *Vanderbilt Law Review* 19:833-64.

_____. 1972. "Double Jeopardy and the Waiver of Jurisdiction in California's Juvenile Courts." *Stanford Law Review* 24:874-902.

_____. 1975. "Waiver of Juvenile Jurisdiction and the Hardcore Youth." *North Dakota Law Review* 51:655-77.

_____. 1983. "The Youth Offender: Transfer to Adult Court and Subsequent Sentencing." *Criminal Justice Journal* 6:281-313.

_____. 1986. "The Transfer of Juvenile Offenders to Adult Courts in Massachusetts: Reevaluating the Rehabilitative Ideal." *Suffolk University Law Review* 20:989-1028.

_____. 1992. "State ex. rel. v. E.G.T.: Waiving Childhood Goodbye." *Journal of Contemporary Law* 18:159-76.

Notes and Comments. 1967. "Separating the Criminal from the Delinquent: Due Process in Certification Procedure." *Southern California Law Review* 40: 158-64.

_____. 1980. "A Model for the Transfer of Juvenile Felony Offenders to Adult Court Jurisdiction." *Journal of Juvenile Law* 4:170-86.

Osbun, Lee Ann and Peter A. Rode. 1984. "Prosecuting Juveniles As Adults: The Quest for 'Objective' Decisions." *Criminology* 22:187-202.

Reid, Brad. 1974. "Juvenile Waiver: The Inconsistent Standard." *American Journal of Criminal Law* 2:331-47.

Rogers, Joseph W.and G. Larry Mays, 1987. *Juvenile Delinquency and Juvenile Justice*. New York: Wiley.

Rudman, Cary, Eliot Hartstone, Jeffrey Fagan, and Melinda Moore. 1986. "Violent Youth in Adult Court: Process and Punishment." *Crime & Delinquency* 32:75-96.

Sagatun, Inger, Loretta L. McCollum, and Leonard P. Edwards. 1985. "The Effect of Transfers from Juvenile to Criminal Courts: A Loglinear Analysis." *Crime and Justice* 8:65-92.

Sargent, Douglas A. and Donald H. Gordon. 1963. "Waiver of Jurisdiction: An Evaluation of the Process in the Juvenile Court." *Crime & Delinquency* 9:121-28.

Schornhorst, F. Thomas. 1968. "The Waiver of Juvenile Court Jurisdiction: Kent Revisited." *Indiana Law Journal*43:583-613.

Significant Developments. 1973. "Juvenile Justice—Statutory Exclusion from the Juvenile Process of Certain Alleged Felons." *Boston University Law Review* 53:212-25.

Sorrentino, Joseph N. and Gary K. Olsen. 1977. "Certification of Juveniles to Adult Court." *Pepperdine Law Review* 4:497-522.

Stamm, Mortimer J. 1973. "Transfer of Jurisdiction: An Analysis of the Proceedings, Its Role in the Administration of Justice, and a Proposal for the Reform of Kentucky Law." *Kentucky Law Journal* 62:122-99.

Stapleton, Vaughan, David Aday, and Jeanne A. Ito. 1982. "An Empirical Typology of American Metropolitan Juvenile Courts." *American Sociological Review* 88:549-62.

Thomas, Charles W.and Shay Bilchik. 1985. "Prosecuting Juveniles in Criminal Courts: A Legal and Empirical Analysis." *Journal of Criminal Law and Criminology* 76:439-79.

Twentieth Century Fund (Task Force on Sentencing Policy Toward Young Offenders). 1978. *Confronting Youth Crime*. New York: Holmes and Meier.

Vitello, Michael. 1976. "Constitutional Safeguards for Juvenile Transfer Procedure: The Ten Years Since *Kent v. U.S.*" *DePaul Law Review* 26:23-53.

Whitebread, Charles H. and Robert Batey. 1977. "Transfer Between Courts: Proposals of the Juvenile Justice Standards Project." *Virginia Law Review* 63:221-43.

————. 1981. "The Role of Waiver in the Juvenile Court: Questions of Philosophy and Function." Pp. 207-26 in *Major Issues in Juvenile Justice Information and Training: Reading in Public Policy*, edited by J. C. Hall, D. M. Hamparian, J. M. Pettibone, and J. L. White. Columbus, OH: Academy for Contemporary Problems.

Wizner, Stephen. 1984. "Discretionary Waiver of Juvenile Court Jurisdiction: An Invitation to Procedural Arbitrariness." *Criminal Justice Ethics* 3:41-50.

Young, Marshall. 1981. "Waiver from a Judge's Standpoint." Pp. 309-20 in *Major Issues in Juvenile Justice Information and Training: Readings in Public Policy*, edited by J. C. Hall, D. M. Hamparian, J. M. Pettibone, and J. L. White. Columbus, OH: Academy For Contemporary Problems.

Zimring, Franklin E. 1981. "Notes Toward a Jurisprudence of Waiver." Pp. 193-205 in *Major Issues in Juvenile Justice Information and Training: Readings in Public Policy*, edited by J. C. Hall, D. M. Hamparian, J. M. Pettibone, and J. L. White. Columbus, OH: Academy For Contemporary Problems.

————. 1991. "The Treatment of Hard Cases in American Juvenile Justice: In Defense of Discretionary Waiver." *Notre Dame Journal of Law, Ethics, and Public Policy* 5:267-80.

9

Screwing the System and Making It Work

Juvenile Justice in the No-Fault Society

Mark D. Jacobs

Larry: "Screwing the System and Making It Work"

Dear members of the diagnostic team,

The young man I am sending you today is in great need of help. At the age of thirteen years, Larry has spent four of his last five years in a penal institution. The conduct of the authorities in this case has been incredibly inept.

There is perhaps no way that we at this point can reverse the failures of the past. Larry is hurt, confused, and hard to manage. His educational and emotional needs are enormous. Shortly, his hurt will turn to bitterness, his confusion to violence, and we will have a very dangerous adult felon in our community.

Whatever plan you develop for Larry will be restricted by the following parameters: (1) I will not send Larry to the Department of Corrections; (2) I will be hostile to any institutional setting.

In short, I am asking you to do the impossible. I am confident that if over the next five years we can turn Larry into a functioning adult, we all will have done a service of inestimable value for the community.

I dare you to do your best.

To all appearances, Larry had been treated most unjustly by juvenile authorities in the nearby state he had just left. He seemed primarily neglected rather than delinquent, yet those authorities had warehoused him in various residential institutions for the four years since age nine, when his street cop father was caught in the act of robbing a bank, and his overwhelmed mother, keeping just two of her children, abandoned Larry and two others without support.

His offenses in the nearby state had consisted of running away, breaking and entering, vandalism, and a number of auto thefts and unauthorized uses of automobiles; but these offenses all occurred after his family's disintegration, and many of the offenses were associated with attempts to escape the succession of foster homes, group homes, and state institutions in which he was placed. (Of all these placements, only a Jesuit group home offered Larry a sense of belonging and stability. But even from there he ran within a year, taking the Jesuit father's car after he was disciplined for breach of the home's strict rules.) For his various offenses, so easily understandable, Larry had spent one and a half years in the largest juvenile institution operated by that state's Department of Social Services and had twice been committed to the juvenile training school operated by that state's Department of Corrections.

When Larry's probation officer learned of this treatment, it offended his sense of decency. Here was Larry, still only thirteen, with a record of prior institution-alization longer than any the counselor had ever encountered, except for that of a brutal and deliberate murderer. Larry had just moved in with his father, who had been released early from the penitentiary because of a nervous breakdown and had been living in the court's venue. After supervising Larry for five years, the other state's juvenile authorities had released him directly to the custody of his father without arranging for courtesy supervision as provided by an interstate compact; despite Larry's previously diagnosed severe educational deficiencies, he was enrolled in regular public school classes. When the first set of new complaints were brought against Larry for incorrigibility and unauthorized use of his stepmother's car, a probation officer had been working with Larry's older brother, whom he had already sent to a harsh state training school.

Larry's treatment history so outraged this probation officer, as well as the judge and other staff members who became involved in the case, that the court mobilized an extraordinary degree of commitment to help Larry. The probation officer brought Larry's records to a judge who had been on the bench less than a year and was determined to make the system work. After reviewing the case overnight, the judge decided on the course of noncorrectional treatment for Larry. To demonstrate his intense interest in Larry's case, the judge also made the unprecedented gesture of communicating this decision in a handwritten letter to the director of the court's diagnostic team, an interagency coordinating group that explores all possible dispositional alternatives for youth who have frustrated previous treatment efforts or who seem headed for commitment to the state. The judge called together the probation officer and the director of the diagnostic team into his chambers, personally delivering the challenge of doing "the impossible" and pledging himself to secure any special resources they might need in their efforts. The judge followed their progress with weekly meetings in chambers and frequent meetings over lunch.

"To Make a Difference"

It is neither accidental nor arbitrary that Larry's case received such an extraordinary level of attention from the juvenile court; a combination of mutually reinforcing factors qualified it for special treatment. Larry's prior treatment seemingly exemplified a commonly perceived model of juvenile justice at its worst, in which the system had itself compounded Larry's vulnerability. And Larry was personally an especially appealing boy, able to elicit most intensely the court's normative commitment to care for and protect children in need. The staff's sense of injustice intensified this normative commitment, while Larry's personal appeal intensified the sense of injustice. As the probation officer described his attraction to Larry:

> I responded emotionally to this case because I thought we could make a difference. Larry has a very appealing manner about him when you meet him. It's because there's something very redeeming there, and I can't put my finger on it—something very childlike, something that never grew up, something that is four or five years old, just like our children, that makes you say, "what he needs is someone to really care for and love him—and by golly, I'm the one!"

Although determined to "make a difference" and armed with the judge's full support, Larry's probation officer and the head of the diagnostic team found it exceedingly difficult to arrange a suitable disposition within the scope of the judge's instructions. They considered it necessary to find a small homelike residential placement for Larry because of both the father's character and his desire to be rid of Larry. Yet those very reasons made Larry a poor candidate for community placement, since those placements were trying to recruit children whose families were "workable." Some placements were inappropriate because they did not offer specialized-enough services; Larry required special education for severe language and reading problems, emotional disturbance, and borderline mental retardation. Other placements were inappropriate because the services they offered were too specialized; at least one placement, for example, rejected Larry on the grounds that his behavior disorder was not "organic." Of course the determination of these clinical diagnoses is flexible; underlying these various grounds for rejecting Larry was a sense that someone with Larry's extensive history of institutionalization was too "hard-core."

It was difficult even to complete the application materials for these various placements because the other state's juvenile agency withheld its extensive diagnostic and treatment reports about Larry. In response to a letter from Larry's probation officer requesting those reports, the agency sent only scanty information. They had sent a much fuller set of reports to the schools, which Larry's probation officer was able to obtain from school authorities with the consent of Larry and his father. Still, to obtain such routine information as Larry's exact offense history, dates of institutional stay, and reasons for release, the director of the court's diagnostic team had to make a special trip to inspect the other state's court records, after the judge had interceded to gain permission for him to do so. (The authority of a juvenile court to subpoena records does not extend across state lines.)

Despite all these efforts, it was not until three years later that Larry's probation officer or anyone else on the court staff learned the other half of Larry's story, because the other state had segregated its correctional from its social services records. As it turned out, Larry had suffered years of neglect and physical abuse even before his father's arrest. His parents neither fed nor clothed him properly nor saw him to school regularly, and when he did attend school he often exhibited massive bruises from his father's drunken beatings. His mother often failed to return home at night. Larry's records at the other state's court did not state that at the time of his first court contact there, his family was already under active investigation by a protective services worker.

For six weeks, Larry's probation officer devoted half of every day exclusively to Larry's case: making phone calls, consulting with the head of the diagnostic team, meeting with the judge, seeing Larry at the detention home and Larry's father in his office, visiting possible placements, and trying to gain release of Larry's full records. The diagnostic team coordinator also devoted considerable time to this case. After six weeks, all they had to show for their efforts were dozens of rejections from placements. It was not possible to place Larry anywhere within the state.

Inspiration and Triumph

Finally, the probation officer and diagnostic team coordinator hit on the inspired idea of placing Larry at Boys Town in Nebraska, which not only offered the ideal residential setting they were seeking for Larry, but—uniquely among private agencies—was well enough endowed financially so that funding was not an issue. At first, Boys Town too rejected Larry's application, on the familiar grounds that Larry was too disturbed and too educationally deficient. However the probation officer and diagnostic team coordinator refused to accept this rejection. They had a new educational evaluation performed which found Larry not quite as far below normal achievement levels as had previous testing. Larry's probation officer brought his own personal camera to the detention home and took pictures that highlighted the boy's cheerful demeanor even there. The diagnostic team coordinator wrote back to Boys Town, reporting the new educational test results, enclosing the photographs, stressing again the judge's personal interest in Larry, and requesting that the admissions committee interview Larry in person before reaching a final decision. The diagnostic team coordinator tracked down Larry's father, who had since moved to an adjoining county, to procure Larry's air fare to Nebraska for the interview. The court director had to have an exception made to established financial regulations in order to arrange air fare for Larry's probation officer to accompany Larry. Larry was charming as ever in his appearance before the admissions committee at Boys Town; they accepted him.

It was, reports Larry's probation officer, one of the great emotional moments in his career at the court. The probation officer, the diagnostic team coordinator, and the judge went out to lunch together in celebration. "We really did it—we made the system do something it heretofore had never done—we really screwed the system and made it work, for one impossible kid."

Even after Boys Town's decision, the diagnostic team coordinator had to negotiate a maze of bureaucratic review before concluding arrangements for the out-of-state placement. Because of the judge's concern to decriminalize Larry's case and to ensure the delivery of the services Larry needed, the judge was unwilling to transfer correctional supervision of the case to Nebraska to monitor the placement at Boys Town. For its part, Boys Town required compliance with the Interstate Compact on the Placement of Children, administered by the state Departments of Welfare. The diagnostic team coordinator persuaded Larry's father to pay transportation and medical expenses and a token monthly tuition fee to Boys Town. This obviated the need to secure state funding, since Boys Town was willing to assume the remaining costs. Yet even so, the process of securing approval for Larry's placement took a solid week.

From the county's Department of Social Services, the diagnostic team coordinator had to arrange certification that local or in-state placements were either inappropriate or unavailable. The diagnostic team coordinator also obtained from this department names of the state officials whose approval was required for the Interstate Compact. When the diagnostic team coordinator had finally traced through the welfare chain of command, the response came down that approval was dependent on the recommendation of the state's commissioner of corrections. The diagnostic team coordinator had to start all over again, identifying and satisfying every step in an extended chain of command, this time within the state Department of Corrections. Final approval for Larry's placement at Boys Town required not only document production at every level of review, but personal phone calls from the judge to the directors of the state departments of Welfare and of Corrections.

Aftermath and Hindsight

Larry went off to Boys Town with hope and enthusiasm. However the triumphant climax to his case was quickly overtaken by a tragic denouement: just two weeks after his admission to Boys Town, while the regular houseparents of his cottage were away on leave, Larry left campus without permission and acted as an accomplice to armed robbery, abduction, and attempted rape. Larry's probation officer was shocked to hear a probation officer from Nebraska level the very accusation against him that he had earlier addressed to a probation officer in the state where Larry's case originated: "You dumped on us and didn't even bother to notify us." When he heard the news, the diagnostic team coordinator wept.

Larry was committed to a juvenile correctional facility in Nebraska. Despite running away several times, he finally finished serving his sentence and hitchhiked back to his father's house. In short order, he faced new complaints in several jurisdictions for grand larceny, auto theft, and driving while intoxicated and without a license. Larry's probation officer, now seeing the case as hopeless, wanted to recommend that the juvenile court certify Larry to stand trial as an adult in the circuit court. Anticipating resistance to this plan, however, he instead recommended that Larry be sentenced to the adult jail for one year—the longest term the juvenile court could impose. Larry's case went in before a different judge, who rejected even this recommendation since Larry was still only sixteen and instead committed Larry to yet another state training school.

While awaiting transfer to the training school, Larry and a companion escaped from the juvenile detention home by beating a guard senseless with a baseball bat. The two escapees drove a stolen car across three states before wrecking it in a drunken crash; Larry was in a coma for several days but survived. Returning from the scene of the crash, he escaped yet once again at the airport, but was recaptured to face charges of attempted murder.

Although hindsight obviously changes the assessment of this case, subsequent events do not detract from the dedicated and resourceful casework demonstrated by Larry's placement at Boys Town, which at the time represented the last best hope for a most troubled and troubling youth. "I started out thinking the system ruined this kid," reflected Larry's probation officer. "That's not true; this kid was destroyed by age eight. We could not have saved him, if save is the word. There is probably no institutional program that could have helped him. . . . My impression now is that it's always been hopeless, that we were fooling ourselves, that we acted—consciously—not with the facts in front of us, but from our hearts. Still, what the judge did then was noble."

. . .

What Makes Some Cases Special?

Larry's case, though accorded special attention by court staff, epitomizes the challenges, meanings, triumphs, and disappointments common to more routine cases. These cases reveal the profound disorganization of the court's task environment: the failure of such community institutions as family and school to provide adequate informal controls or help foster the development of adequate personal controls in adolescents, on the one hand, and the failure of such formal institutions as health, welfare, and correctional agencies to provide adequate habilitation or punishment, on the other. Caseworkers resort to inspirational strategies of decision making because the organization's technology is incomplete and even its objectives are uncertain. The very resourcefulness caseworkers must exercise as individuals to secure needed support from clients and colleagues testifies to the scarcity of resources on the systems level; the very density of bureaucratic regulation governing interagency, interjurisdictional, and intergovernmental cooperation indicates as well the absence of domain consensus and the sparseness of administrative coordination. These cases test the definition and relevance of the court's institutional ethos while straining the limits of its organizational competence, with judges and probation officers encountering institutional gaps and cross-purposes as dilemmas of individualized casework and justice.

As the formal agency of last resort in maintaining control over adolescents in the community, the juvenile court confronts most profoundly the dilemma that adolescent behavior is essentially uncontrollable through direct, external means. Social control depends primarily on the indirect, informal controls created by the integration of individual personalities in the social and economic institutions that embody central values and the prevailing technology; as Talcott Parsons puts it, "the most fundamental mechanisms of social control are to be found in the normal processes of interaction in an institutionally integrated social system (1951: 301). Adolescents develop moral judgment, as Jean Piaget describes that process, not from the exercise of adult authority, but rather in the natural course of interacting with their peers:

> the sense of justice, though naturally capable of being reinforced by the precepts and the practical example of the adult, is largely independent of these influences, and requires nothing more for its development than the mutual respect and solidarity which holds among the children themselves. It is often at the expense of the adult and not because of him that the notions of just and unjust find their way into the youthful mind. (1965:198)

The means of legitimate coercion that the court commands are limited in their extent as well as their effectiveness. Due to the inordinate public expense of confining large numbers of individuals to correctional institutions, and the resulting scarcity of prison capacity relative to the criminal population, even chronic offenders often escape incarceration for their crimes. Conversely, not only are means of legitimate coercion scarce, so is the wisdom to know when to refrain from intervention.

Larry's and these other cases indicate how intricate are problems of working with troubled adolescents. Adolescence is the most marginal status within the age structure—a treacherous passage between youth and adulthood when, for both psychodynamic and psychosocial reasons, personal and social controls are weakest. . . .

In psychosocial terms, Erik Erikson describes adolescence as a "moratorium" before the assumption of adult family and work responsibilities, a period of provocative playfulness on the part of youth and of selective permissiveness on the part of society. The maturational task of the adolescent is to develop a sense of inner identity: "The young person, in order to experience wholeness, must feel a progressive continuity between that which he has come to be during the long years of childhood and that which he promises to become in the anticipated future: between that which he conceives himself to be and that which he perceives others to see in him and to expect of him" (1968:87).

Discovering an identity depends then in large part on institutional support. School curricula, for example, must be "relevant" in the sense of instilling technological skills that will equip children to participate in productive adult life: "the configurations of culture and the manipulations basic to the prevailing technology must reach meaningfully into school life, supporting in every child a feeling of competence" (Erikson 1968: 126). "Adolescence . . . is least 'stormy' in that segment of youth which is gifted and well trained in pursuit of expanding technological trends, and thus able to identify with new roles of competency and invention" (129-30). . . .

Larry's case suggests the usefulness of Albert Reiss's conception (1951) that delinquency is a failure of social as well as personal controls. The failure of social controls extends far beyond ineffective rule enforcement by criminal justice agencies, to problems stemming from community disorganization. In Erikson's psychosocial terms, an adolescent's drift into delinquency is the embrace—most likely only temporary—of a negative identity in an attempt to escape from identity confusion. In institutional terms, delinquent drift results largely from the disarticulation between schooling, on the one hand, and the structure of employment opportunities on the other. Lacking are such "linking institutions" as apprentice-ship, work-study, or community service programs to ease the transition from school to employment. Lacking too are linking institutions for strengthening the family in its role of preparing children for school. In disorganized communities, both primary groups and secondary institutions are unstable, isolated, and inadequate in resources. Community disorganization helps cause delinquency directly by weakening the "stakes in conformity" that constitute the most effective social controls and indirectly through a more crescive process of contributing to the formation of weakened personal controls. . . .

As individuals, their problems are multiple, diffuse, and ambiguous. Was Larry, for example, predominantly a hurting child or a hardened predatory criminal, and when? Larry was abused, neglected, emotionally disturbed, borderline mentally retarded, deficient in language and reading skills, alcoholic, and violent. These sorts of problems are not just multiple and diffuse, but synergistic. Low intelligence compounds the effects of emotional disturbance, and vice versa. Larry's outbreaks of violent behavior repeatedly frustrated attempts to provide the nurturance he needed. For another boy, a worsening physical disability helped create and perpetuate severe emotional instability, while the emotional instability prevented him from receiving the preferred treatment for his physical deterioration. In yet another case, a violent and self-destructive heroin addict contracted a serious case of hepatitis, with each aspect of her condition rendering inaccessible required emergency treatment for the other. As intractable as these types of problems are singly in their own right, in combination they defy ministration.

Larry's case and these others illustrate the displacement of child welfare functions assumed by court staff. Judges and probation officers find themselves increasingly responsible to procure, for especially hard-to-serve children who are without adequate parental support, basic nurturance, shelter, health, and educational services that more directly qualified agencies are either unwilling or unable to provide. This responsibility is increasing in part because of statutory revisions inspired by federal delinquency and child welfare legislation, expanding the court's formal authority over other agencies to enforce both the "right to treatment" and the civil liberties of children. The interorganizational role of the juvenile court within the network of child welfare agencies has become more central even as the partly conflicting formal rights and liberties of children have been simultaneously expanding. These recent trends are perhaps best exemplified by probation officers' involvement in obtaining educational services for handicapped students. The same trends also surface in other cases, in which probation officers seek either to secure foster care for their clients from the Department of Social Services or to arrange such foster care on their own in anticipation of rejection by that department; these trends reappear in still other cases, in which probation officers must deal with hospitals, mental hospitals, and other organizations for treatment.

The effective authority of the court is inadequate to fulfill its expanding formal responsibility for child welfare. Not only are the clients it treats marginal in the age and stratification systems, but in practice the court is itself marginal, relegated to the "borderland of criminal justice" (Allen 1964), mediating between the system of law and coercion on the one hand and the welfare system on the other, peripheral to both. Delinquency results in large measure from the institutional disarticulation between schooling and the structure of work opportunities; the juvenile justice system is disarticulated as well. The network of correctional and welfare agencies that appears to children and parents as remote, fragmented, and overspecialized affronts its workers with goal confusion, inadequacy of resources, and lack of administrative coordination. The agencies loosely linked in this network defend their organizational boundaries by harboring information, enforcing red tape, establishing waiting lists, and arguing legal proceedings against each other. These agency boundaries are semipermeable, through the medium of specialized diagnosis, only to casework strategies of "problemization"—strategies that as Margaret Rosenheim argues, "counter . . . the wisdom of 'normalizing' as much delinquent conduct as we possibly can" (1976:52).

. . .

Probation Officers' Tragic Narratives

. . . In Francis Allen's definition, "the rehabilitative ideal is the notion that a primary purpose of penal treatment is to effect changes in the characters, attitudes, and the behavior of convicted offenders, so as to strengthen the social defense against unwanted behavior, but also to contribute to the welfare and satisfaction of offenders" (1981: 2). As Allen's definition makes clear, this ideal embodies the assumption that society's interests are congruent with those of the delinquent, so that it is possible to serve both sets of interests at once. Conceiving penal treatment as a contribution to the delinquent's welfare eliminates ethical concerns about punishment. As long as it remained credible, the rehabilitative ideal provided a satisfying ideological foundation for juvenile justice.

The prominent reformers of the Progressive Era wedded a spirit of evangelical mission to respect for "scientific" principles of philanthropy in seeking to ameliorate social conditions through public policy. By introducing techniques of modern administration, leaders of the charity organization movement sought to improve the efficiency and effectiveness of the "friendly visitors" they sent out as Christian missionaries to the homes of the urban poor. They also sought to apply the laws of biology and economics to problems of individual, family, and social disorganization (Lubove 1965). Progressive reformers were confident that with scientific enlightenment and God's help, the public will would prevail.

Today practitioners of juvenile justice enjoy no such confidence of success. Those who work at juvenile justice are all too aware of the ambiguity of their mission, the scarcity of resources—cultural as well as organizational—they command, the intractability of the problems they face, and the institutional gaps and cross-purposes that impede their efforts. The rehabilitative ideal has lost credibility, creating a profound cultural void which leaves unanswered fundamental questions of meaning. In an age of skepticism—of declining religious faith, declining faith in public authority, and declining faith in the ability of science to solve human problems— what provides meaning and motivation to those who work at juvenile justice, if those were the very faiths that inspired the birth of the juvenile court movement in the last century? In particular, what justifies punishing individuals for behavior in which the entire society is implicated as well?

. . . Evidence abounds that judges and probation officers resist the temptations of organizational expedience in the conduct of their official duties, demonstrating instead genuine commitment to their casework. Consider the heroic efforts devoted to the "special cases" described in part 1, or the remarkable ingenuity for brokering services displayed even in the course of "normal" casework. Probation officers are often visibly disconcerted when their efforts to help children fail. What could inspire this commitment in the current religious, intellectual, and political climate?

Reports that probation officers make about their casework are revealing on this issue. Offered as accounts of casework decisions proposed or already taken, these reports take such official form as written social investigations, statements made in court, and regular case conferences with probation supervisors. Especially informative are the reports departing probation officers bequeath to their successors as they prepare to leave the job. Probation officers attempt to achieve resolution to their own careers as well as those of their probationers. Upon leaving, they "clean up" their caseloads, reducing them to "manageable" size and making them "presentable" to their successors. They "prune" their caseloads of especially trouble-free or especially troublesome probationers, either closing the cases or placing them out-of-home earlier than they might have otherwise; they provide their successors with a descriptive "handle" for each of the cases remaining to be passed on. Typically, they assure their successors that everything is under control, even though the new worker soon learns otherwise. As a probation supervisor notes, "Workers have a tremendous tendency to want to leave things in order, to gloss over problems when they leave . . . all cases resolved, no loose ends."

Casework reports also take such unofficial form as "shop talk" bantered during lunches, happy hours, and parties. Even as banter, these reports are most "serious," not only reflecting judgments about delinquents by probation officers, but also providing the bases of judgments by peers and superiors about the probation officers themselves. Probation officers can learn to abide all sorts of casework frustrations, but they cannot abide challenges to their cultural authority. Probation officers' infrequent displays of open anger or frustration are usually occasioned by judges, lawyers, psychologists, or other professionals who impugn their underlying interpretation of a case. Whatever the success of their case outcomes, probation officers are expected to achieve *understanding* of children's biographies and prospects.

These reports are serious too because they address the moral issues not only of individual transgression but also of societal injustice. Whether or not parents are considered "deserving," it is a tenet of the civil religion that all children are entitled to at least equal opportunity for attaining respectable social standing. In constructing biographies for contemporary delinquents, probation officers inevitably discover unfair handicaps these children have had to suffer, many attesting to what Bellah (1975) calls "the broken covenant." This evidence continues to obligate probation officers to make every effort to help children, despite their awareness of how formidable are the difficulties involved.

Reports of delinquents' pasts and prospects, then, not only express but also help constitute the meaning and motivation of probation work. . . . No longer, however, do they embody confidence in the rehabilitative ideal—belief in the ability of government to enlist social science and Christian charity for preserving the public safety by improving delinquents' private welfare. To explore how that ideal has been transformed and which beliefs have taken its place, this section examines the poetics and dramaturgy of casework narratives.

The Spirit of Modern Tragedy in Probation Work

As expressed in probation officers' narratives, it is the spirit of modern tragedy which fills the cultural void created by the decline of the rehabilitative ideal. Employing the classic themes of tragic flaw, fate, reversal, recognition, and suffering, these narratives dramatize delinquents' adventures as moral struggles illustrating the interaction of character and destiny. They interpret the delinquent act as a combined product of fate and hubris, creating the possibility for redemptive rebirth through recognition (evidenced through adherence to a prescribed form of treatment) and heroic commitment to the painful quest for self-knowledge.

Probation officers generally empathize with the children they work with. One probation officer explains that the most attractive children are "the ones who are going through the same things you went through," but probation officers train themselves to find the good in children. A comment from a set of informal case notes a probation officer drew up for her successor exemplifies this attitude: "likeable kid—a loser who may make it." There are children whom court workers do find unredeemable. A judge profiles "life-style" (as opposed to "episodic") of offenders as children without remorse, sensitive to their own pain but insensitive to that of others, living only for the moment. But as a probation officer claims, "When I start working with kids I can see where they have qualities, that they could, in fact, change their lives. I'd say a majority of the kids I've worked with are that way." Reinforcing this expectation are unexpected discoveries about even the least appealing types.

> This kid verbally intimidated a night watchman into surrendering his money and the keys to his car. He claims he didn't use any force, but when I met him I was totally repulsed by him—I didn't see anything in him redeeming or vulnerable. . . . The teacher at the detention home is getting kids to put their feelings down on paper, and it's showing me things I didn't know about my kids before. This kid writes that his grandmother tells him each day how to act in detention. He has a picture of his grandmother holding him when he was a baby, and he thinks she is the only person who ever loved him.

The empathy court workers feel for most children derives in large part from the cruel role they attribute to fate in helping to cause delinquency. In the most frustrating cases, according to one probation officer, "You feel that if you were in the child's shoes you wouldn't make it either." Another probation officer expresses similar sentiments about a boy in serious trouble. "Having that knowledge of what the background was like—was there any way possible for him to be successful in life, with those surroundings?" Probation officers commonly distinguish children who commit offenses "just because they like to . . . for personal gain or whatever," from those who commit offenses "because of all the crap going on in their lives and all their family problems." Similarly, probation officers feel that "the ones who are real disturbed, you can't hold them accountable." Challenging the description of a child as an arsonist, a probation officer argued, "It would be one thing if he had drunk wine, taken drugs, and gone out and burned down a building. But it's not his fault that he's missing something upstairs. He's like an underdog. . . . You have to give a kid like that a chance."

The probation officer's empathy may accord the child a chance, but only to seek the painful recognition considered a prerequisite for developing the motivation necessary to reshape his or her own fate.

> Easiest to help are the bright ones who are really desperately saying, "I want some help. I don't like the way I am. I don't like what I'm doing to my family; I don't like what my family is doing to me. I don't know what to do, but I want things different." And then I tell them, "It means you change too." And most of them say, "okay." Especially if they're bright enough to look in and see the part they play, really there's a lot you can do there.

Or, in the words of another probation officer, "I would always want these kids to try to understand, the assumption was that they had done something wrong or something was going on." Still another probation officer stresses the therapeutic benefits of "confession" as a first step toward recognition: "I wonder what the recidivism is for kids who plead guilty in court as opposed to those who plead innocent. It would be good feedback for members of the Bar Association. I think it's a good experience for a kid to come in and make a confession, confessing that he did something wrong and accepting society's consequences." This probation officer conditioned an offer to recommend private residential placement for a child instead of commitment to a state training school on the child's recognition of the need for placement: "If you can't admit you're a crook, you're not ready for residential [placement]."

Recognition is seen as the first step in choosing to be responsible for oneself. In one probation officer's description, her aim is to inspire "the moment of decision" when a young person resolves to adopt a standard of mature conduct. Recounting a boy's triumph over alcoholism and family turmoil, a probation officer suggests, "It was lucky that early in the case he had the automobile accident which was clearly caused by his drinking, got scared that he almost died, and got scared enough to reverse how things were going." That recognition motivated the boy "to become an adult . . . being able to set goals for himself and figure out how to meet those goals, how to solve problems, how to see in what kinds of circumstances he created problems for himself." Probation officers learn that though they do not have the power to impose change on children, they can sometimes influence children to change themselves, by demonstrating to them how it is in their own interest to do so. Judges, who command greater power to impose change, seek in the words of one "to hold children accountable for choice." A different judge even discerns some benefit in committing children to state training schools, if that prods children to recognition.

> I think with kids you have somehow or other to get across to them that they are the architects of their own destiny, that it isn't somebody else who's constantly getting into trouble, it isn't somebody else who's doing this. Often I say to them, "You can improve yourself. We'll help you but it has to be your decision. When you come before me and I have to send you to a learning center, it's a choice you've made, not me," and I'd say a very high proportion

> of the kids will say, "well, you told me." That's the first step I think to
> understanding . . . getting them to see that they have an individual responsibility.
> . . . At least they're going to the learning center with the thought that . . .
> as easily as they went downhill they can go uphill, and a lot of them do.

Since the probation officer helps prescribe the terms of a child's recognition, the child's acts of heroic will are hardly as autonomous as the probation officer pretends. However by agreeing to those terms, the child gains not only the opportunity to expiate past sins but also a certain degree of immunity from punishment for future ones. Subsequent troubles only serve to confirm the court's own analysis of the child's unpropitious situation, and the court must recognize the especially formidable difficulty of reconstructing an ignoble protagonist's tragic fate. Like any agency of social control, the court is reluctant to invoke "last resorts" (Emerson 1981) without having exhausted all other alternatives. The child can renew entitlement to the court's understanding tolerance through regular displays of commitment to the tragic scenario legitimated by the court. By convincing demonstrations of constructive resolve, the child can earn official respites from new troubles. At a weekly staff meeting, the members of a probation unit agree that probationers qualify for counseling, as opposed to mere surveillance, by presenting definable problems which they are motivated to work on. Members of other probation units echo this view. One probation officer describes the satisfaction of learning that an alcoholic is finally starting to take medication to counter the physical craving of addiction. "There's a glimmer of hope. It will be really hard, and he'll probably fail, but at least he's trying." Comments made independently by various other probation officers indicate that they share similar personal criteria for extending tolerance to probationers. "I expect kids to try. That's all I expect from them. If not, they need sanctions." "I take kids back to court on violations when I'm working harder than they are to keep them out of trouble." "While working with kids, when you see their potential you develop expectations. The only thing I really expect is to give an honest effort for themselves, to be interested in what happens to them. When a kid sits in front of me and says, 'I don't care,' I go crazy. Those are the ones you give up on. You wind up locking them up."

Court workers' casework narratives conform to the rhythm of tragedy. A judge observes that some children can only begin to pull their lives together "after hitting rock bottom, like alcoholics or drug addicts." This judge tailors his courtroom dramaturgy and dispositional strategies to the different phases of the tragic cycle.

> You see cases at various stages. There are kids who are on their way down
> to the bottom, there are kids who are making progress, falling back from time
> to time but it's generally an upward trend. I think you have to make that
> evaluation first. Looking at this kid overall, there are some successes that
> he's beginning to have. If there are, you try and support those and at the same
> time try and do something about the bad things that he's doing. If things have

now gone sour, experiencing difficulty at home, at school, or jobs, you don't let him now wait until he hits flat bottom. Then it's time to be very assertive and take action. It may be early in the case, but if you see those indicators it's time to pull him out of the home and get him out of the tailspin and have him do something else. There are cases you don't know, don't have enough information at this point, and what you're trying to do is maintain the status quo and put off the final decision because inevitably those other stages will come up—he'll either start to do better or start to do worse.

A probation officer, just returned from devoting his summer vacation to conducting a church youth group on the theme of "death and resurrection," notes that he tells his probationers, "probation is a time of loss—but it can also be a time of growth." Another probation officer describes the decision to place a child out-of-home as the culmination of a progression of events triggered by further trouble and the child's failure to make any progress at home. Similarly, she sees some benefit in the fact that commitment "is the following through of a process."

. . .

Larry's Case Revisited

The themes of mutual exculpation and immunity from evaluation pervade the narratives related by court workers at various stages in Larry's case, starting with the judge's eloquent referral note to the diagnostic team cited in the opening passage. This note embodies a poetics of tragedy. It assumes that although there is hope for redemption, both Larry and the probation staff will need to summon heroic efforts of will to alter the troubled course of his destiny. ("The young man I am sending you today is in great need of help. . . . His educational and emotional needs are enormous. Shortly, his hurt will turn to bitterness, his confusion to violence and we will have a very dangerous adult felon in our community.") It exculpates Larry by attributing the cause of his delinquency to abuse and neglect suffered first at the hands of his own family, then at the hands of public officials from a neighboring state. ("The conduct of the authorities in this case has been incredibly inept.") In consideration of these circumstances, the narrative commits the court to Larry's assistance and grants him immediate relief from further punishment. ("I will not send Larry to the Department of Corrections. . . . I dare you to do your best.") However this commitment and relief are conditioned on the good faith of Larry's struggle for self-reform. Larry will have to learn to recognize his character flaws and adhere to a treatment regimen designed to help him overcome them. Thus the ultimate responsibility is Larry's; the tragic nature of these circumstances exonerate the court in advance from probable failure. ("There is perhaps no way that we at this point can reverse the failures of the past. . . . In short, I am asking you to do the impossible.") Nevertheless, it is the court which stands to gain the credit in the unlikely case of success. ("I am confident that if over the next five years we can turn Larry into a functioning adult we all will have done a service for the community of inestimable value.")

This explains the triumphant pride with which Larry's probation officer, the director of the diagnostic team, and the judge celebrated the most promising imaginable disposition of Larry's case, placement at Boys' Town. ("We really did it—we made the system do something it heretofore had never done—we really screwed the system and made it work, for one impossible kid.") It also explains the mood of fatalism with which Larry's probation officer reflected upon the ultimate devolution of the case into a series of increasingly violent new offenses:

> I started out thinking the system ruined this kid. That's not true; this kid was destroyed by age eight. We could not have saved him, if save is the word. There is probably no institutional program that could have helped him. . . My impression now is that it's always been hopeless, that we were fooling ourselves, that we acted—consciously—not with the facts in front of us, but from our hearts. Still, what the judge did then was noble.

While acknowledging "fooling ourselves," this narrative denies accountability for misjudging the severity of Larry's case or for shifting liability to a private institution. While the court freely blamed Larry's troubles on the authorities from whom they had inherited the case, this narrative denies the reciprocal verdict brought against them by the probation officer in Nebraska who inherited the case in turn: "You dumped on us, and didn't even bother to notify us."

Confronting the contentious evasions of delinquents on the one hand and related public officials on the other, court workers too must seek to obscure the bases of their accountability; in the no-fault society, evasions of mutual obligation feed each other. Continually thrown back on their own personal resources in managing systemic casework dilemmas, probation officers resort to manipulative strategies of artifice and special pleading in attempting to enforce civic obligations and entitlements. . . . Despite the unmistakably resourceful dedication of probation officers to helping children—efforts that belie stereotypes of probation officers as "street-level bureaucrats"—the juvenile court is severely constrained by the more general weakness of social control in which it operates.

Juvenile delinquency can only be treated effectively by families, schools, communities, and workplaces supporting each other in authoritatively coordinated ways to integrate growing children into the emergent social order. Constrictive individualism, the blurred delineation of public and private responsibilities, and laxity in the rule of law impede such interinstitutional cooperation in the no-fault society. Synchronizing community institutions will require a formidable program of political reform, community organization, and institution building, at once impelling and impelled by an associated set of cultural changes: expanding civic consciousness, clarifying the increasingly complex division of public and private responsibilities, and strengthening the rule of law. It is unclear how such a reform program could ever develop in the no-fault society, but there is no alternative path to effective delinquency treatment. However inspired, the manipulations of isolated individuals cannot compensate for the absence of authoritative institutional means for achieving valued collective goals. Like vain struggles for a foothold in a steeply banked sand dune, attempts to out-manipulate the no-fault society produce only a deeper rut. In the no-fault society, as Larry's court workers sorrowfully learned, merely screwing the system cannot make it work.

References

Allen, Francis A. 1964. *The Borderland of Criminal Justice*. Chicago: University of Chicago Press.
_____. 1981. *The Decline of the Rehabilitative Ideal*. New Haven: Yale University Press.
Bellah, Robert. 1975. *The Broken Covenant*. New York: Seabury.
Emerson, Robert. 1981. "On Last Resorts." *American Journal of Sociology* 89:1-22.
Erikson, Erik. 1968. *Identity: Youth and Crisis*. New York: Norton.
Lubove, Roy. 1969. *The Professional Altruist*. Cambridge: Harvard University Press.
Parsons, Talcott. 1951. *The Social System*. New York: Free Press.
Piaget, Jean. 1965. *The Moral Judgment of the Child*. Trans. Marjorie Gabain. New York: Free Press.
Reiss, Albert. 1951. "Delinquency as a Failure of Personal and Social Controls." *American Sociological Review* 16:196-208.
Rosenheim, Margaret. 1976. "Notes on Helping Juvenile Nuisances." In Margaret Rosenheim, ed., *Pursuing Justice for the Child*. Chicago: University of Chicago Press.

10

Restorative Justice
What's "New" about the Balanced Approach?

Gordon Bazemore

In 1988 the National Council of Juvenile and Family Court Judges (NCJFCJ) broke new ground by publishing a monograph outlining a "Balanced Approach" mission for juvenile probation (Maloney, Romig and Armstrong, 1988). Since that time, interest in the Balanced Approach as a mission not only for probation, but also for the juvenile justice system as a whole, has increased exponentially. Some fourteen states, including most recently California and Pennsylvania, have adopted Balanced Approach language in their juvenile justice codes (Klien, 1996). Other states, such as Florida, and a much larger number of local juvenile courts, probation departments and residential programs, have issued policy statements that specifically require probation staff to use Balanced Approach objectives when developing dispositional recommendations and supervision plans.[1]

Meanwhile, a worldwide movement based on *restorative justice,* now recognized by many as the underlying value or philosophical framework for the Balanced Approach (Zehr, 1990; Van Ness, 1993; Bazemore and Umbreit, 1995), has had rather dramatic practical impact on juvenile justice policy and practice in some nations. Several European countries, as well as Canada and Australia, have made significant policy changes directly influenced by restorative justice practices and values. Since 1989, New Zealand has required that all juvenile offenders over 14 (with the exception of

Bazemore, Gordon. 1997. Restorative Justice: What's "New" about the Balanced Approach? *Juvenile & Family Court Journal,* 48:1:1–19.

offenders involved in serious violent crimes and child welfare cases) be referred to a conference in which restorative goals are addressed in community meetings including victims, offenders, their respective support groups and/or families, and other citizens (McElrae, 1993; Morris and Maxwell, 1993).

As interest has grown, and as the amount of commentary and published literature on the Balanced Approach and restorative justice has increased, the practical meaning of the new mission and philosophical framework for the juvenile court and the juvenile justice system has been a source of some controversy and confusion. Some have viewed Balanced Approach proponents as apologists for the current system and have implied that the new mission is "nothing new." These observers seem to view the Balanced Approach as simply another effort to reaffirm the juvenile court's individual treatment mission or even to resurrect and obfuscate *parens patriae* abuses (Feld, 1995).[2] In contrast, others have argued that "balance" is effectively impossible and have implied that the new mission's advocates are simply apologists for the new retributive, just deserts, approaches to juvenile justice reform (Forst and Blomquist, 1992). Some policymakers and professionals have added to the confusion by adopting the new mission's language as "window dressing" for public relations purposes to create support for current practices that often have little to do with balanced intervention (Bazemore, 1992).

A premise of this chapter is that the Balanced Approach mission has often been misunderstood and trivialized. Superficial criticisms and misinterpretations notwithstanding, however, important practical and conceptual questions and concerns about the Balanced Approach have yet to be addressed. This paper attempts to answer what is now the most frequently asked question about the new mission: "How is it different?" To do so, I will argue that the Balanced Approach can be distinguished from both the individual treatment mission and the new retributive, or just deserts, mission for juvenile justice based on six related dimensions.

What Is It? Balancing Community Needs, Achieving New Goals

- In inner-city Pittsburgh, young offenders in an intensive day treatment program solicit input from community organizations about service projects the organizations would like to see completed in the neighborhood. The offenders then work with community residents on projects that include home repair and gardening for the elderly, voter registration drives, painting homes and public buildings, and planting and cultivating community gardens.
- In cities and towns in Pennsylvania, Montana and Minnesota—as well as in

Australia and New Zealand—family members and other citizens acquainted with an offender or victim of a juvenile crime gather to determine what should be done in response to the offense. Often held in schools, churches or other community-based facilities, these *Family Group Conferences* are facilitated by a Community Justice Coordinator or Police Officer, and are aimed at ensuring that offenders are made to hear community disapproval of their behavior, and at developing an agreement for repairing the damage to victim and community and a plan for reintegrating the offender.

• In more than 150 cities and towns throughout North America victims and offenders meet with volunteer mediators in victim-offender mediation sessions or other victim-offender meetings to allow victims to express their feelings about the crime to the offender, gain information about the offense, and develop a restitution agreement with the offender.

• In several Montana cities, college students and other young adult "corps members" in the Montana Conservation Corps supervise juvenile offenders on environmental restoration, trail building and other community service projects and also serve as mentors to one or more of the young offenders.

As juvenile justice systems around the country are being dismantled or dismembered (e.g., Lemov, 1993), many professionals have become demoralized. Others appear to view the current juvenile justice crisis as an opportunity for creative thought and action. Many of these professionals view the Balanced Approach as a "third alternative" for juvenile justice aimed at preserving a juvenile court with a distinctive youth justice mandate that is neither punitive nor lenient in focus (Bazemore, 1996; cf., Rosenberg, 1993; Bazemore and Umbreit, 1995).

The Balanced Approach mission is a "back-to-basics" (some say "forward to basics") attempt to reorient juvenile justice systems to respond more effectively to community expectations. Essentially, most citizens expect that any "justice" system will support fundamental community needs to sanction youth crime; to rehabilitate and reintegrate offenders; and to enhance public safety by assisting the community in preventing and controlling crime. Increasingly, justice systems have also been expected to address a fourth need, to attempt to restore victim loss.

To meet these needs the Balanced Approach authors advanced three overall purposes for juvenile justice intervention (Maloney, Romig and Armstrong, 1988). These purposes define three macro goals for the juvenile justice system and micro goals to be addressed in the response to each case (see Figure 1). Contrary to the assumptions of some critics of the new mission, "balance" does not mean simply attempting to provide equal or appropriate doses of punishment and treatment.[3] Rather, "balance" is achieved at a system level when administrators ensure that resources are allocated equally among efforts to ensure accountability to crime victims, to increase competency in offenders, and to enhance community safety.

Balance is achieved in each case by giving equal attention to broader needs which underlie new sanctioning, safety and rehabilitative goals as depicted in Figure 1.

What do these goals mean and how do they address these broader needs? The authors of the Balanced Approach have designated the three goals of the juvenile justice system using common terms—accountability," "competency," and "community protection"—in a somewhat uncommon way. Defining these goals is an important first step in distinguishing what are in fact unique approaches to sanctioning, rehabilitation, and public safety enhancement under the Balanced Approach mission.

Accountability

Sanctioning needs are best met (1) when offenders assume responsibility for the crime and the harm caused to victims, (2) when they take action to make amends by restoring the loss, and (3) when communities and victims play active roles in sanctioning and feel satisfied with the process. Because an offense incurs a primary obligation to crime victims, accountability cannot be equated simply with being responsible to the court or to juvenile justice professionals such as by merely obeying curfew, complying with drug screening, or writing an essay. Nor can accountability be equated with punishment. If the sanctioning process is to allow communities to set tolerance limits, express disapproval of juvenile crime, and provide appropriate consequences for harmful behavior, the process works best when it allows crime victims and other citizens maximum involvement and input.

Competency

Rehabilitation needs are best met when young offenders make measurable and demonstrated improvements in educational, vocational, social, civic, and other competencies that improve their ability to function as capable, productive adults. When competency is defined as the capacity to do something well that others value, the standard for achieving success in competency development is ultimately measured in the community. Competency cannot be equated with the absence of bad behavior (e.g., being drug free does not provide young offenders with the support and bonds to law abiding adults they need to avoid further delinquency). Nor can it be attained simply by completing a treatment program. While treatment and remedial services provide critical support for competency development, competencies are most likely to be increased when youth assume active rather than passive roles in service and work projects involving community members. Hence, competency development must also involve increasing the capacity of adults and community groups to allow troublesome youths opportunities to practice competent behavior.

Community Protection

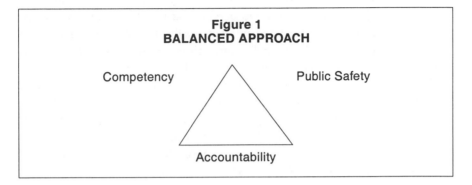

Figure 1
BALANCED APPROACH

Competency   Public Safety

Accountability

Public safety needs are best met when community groups increase their ability to prevent crime, resolve conflict, and reduce community fear and when known offenders are adequately monitored and develop internal controls. Locked facilities are an important part of any public safety approach. But they are the least cost-effective component of a balanced strategy which invests heavily in citizen involvement in monitoring offenders and developing new ways to prevent youth crime. A complete strategy to decrease risk to citizens and reduce fear must be "problem-oriented" as well as case-driven. In practice, such a strategy would first ensure that the time of offenders under supervision in the community is structured around work, education, community service, victim awareness and other activities during waking hours, and that community adults, including but not limited to parents, are assigned clear roles in monitoring offenders. Finally, such a strategy would begin to cultivate and promote new partnerships with community police officers and new roles for juvenile justice professionals as resources to schools, employers, and other community groups in prevention and positive youth development (e.g., as advisors to schools in mediation and conflict resolution).

Representing jurisdictions and communities as diverse as inner-city Pittsburgh, rural Oregon, suburban Minnesota, and urban South Florida (Bazemore and Umbreit, 1995), professionals attempting to develop a balanced focus on these three goals share a commitment to "reinvent" a new juvenile justice system based on a new vision. The vision is one of a *community-oriented* response to youth crime based on the restorative justice philosophical framework (Zehr, 1990; Van Ness, 1993; Bazemore and Umbreit, 1995). Through the restorative "lens" (Zehr, 1990), crime is viewed as important because of the harm it causes victims, communities, and offenders (Van Ness, et al., 1989). Hence, rather than focus solely on treating or punishing the offender, the "justice" process and any justice system should be concerned first with repairing this harm and preventing its reoccurrence. From a restorative perspective true "balance" in juvenile justice must ultimately be gauged in terms of the system's effectiveness in meeting the needs of victims and communities, as well as offenders, and involving each as clients or coparticipants in the justice process.

Core elements of this restorative vision, and much of the difference between the new system envisioned and current alternatives, are encompassed in the community-building interventions described at the beginning of this section. Juvenile justice professionals making the most significant changes consistent with the Balanced Approach mission are building on new partnerships with youth and victim advocates and with concerned citizens and civic groups, while using these interventions as small demonstrations which can point the way to more holistic changes in the organizational culture and structure of their agencies (Carey and Umbreit, 1995). In doing so, they are using the new mission as a concrete "roadmap" to guide them toward this restorative vision for changing the relationship between the juvenile justice system and the community (Bazemore and Day, 1996).

How *Is* It Different?
Systemic v. Programmatic Reform

What they're saying about the Balanced Approach:

"This is what we've always done. What's new? Where's the Beef?"

"We do that competency development, but we just call it treatment. Accountability? Oh yeah, that's our detention center and our jail tours."

"My caseload is 53 and I'm stuck in court 20 hours a week. Don't talk to me about working with the community."

"Now I know what my job is really about!"

"As a manager, I have a better sense of how to allocate, or reallocate, our resources. And my staff are getting a better sense of what their role is and how this fits with my vision of what the community's role should be. We know we're really 'out of balance' but now we have a strategic plan to move forward without chasing every fad and new program that comes along."

"We can also talk to the community about what we're doing in a way that they understand and want to help; our judges and prosecutors are also starting to find some common ground with us in probation. The biggest surprise is that I never expected crime victims could be our allies!"

(A Community Member) "I'm glad to see somebody is finally trying to instill some responsibility in these kids. I'm happy to help when it's obvious that we're trying to make taxpayers out of these kids, rather than tax liabilities."

(A Victim) "In the mediation session I learned that the offender was just a little kid and not the threat I thought he was. I also learned he had some needs that weren't being met but for the first time (I've been a victim before), it seemed like someone was responding to my needs and listening to me."

(An Offender) "When I first walked into the conferencing meeting and saw the victim and her friends and then saw my grandfather there, I wished I could have gone to jail instead. But once everybody had talked about the crime, I began to realize that Mrs. B was really hurt and scared by what I had done. I had to work hard to earn the money to pay her back and to do the community service hours (but the work on the crew was pretty fun) and I thought it was fair after all."

Few juvenile justice professionals claim to support an "unbalanced approach"; similarly, few favor incompetent offenders or oppose public safety and accountability. Many, if not most, initially support the model but believe, as reflected in the first comment above, that the Balanced Approach is "nothing new." Others, as reflected in the last comment in the top half, remind us that staff are unlikely to refocus their efforts toward achieving balanced approach objectives unless significant changes are made in current role expectations and the current juvenile justice process.

In one sense, most components of the Balanced Approach are not new. Restorative justice is based on ancient values and practices that have been at the core of many religious and ethical traditions (Van Ness, 1993; Zehr, 1990). In addition, the balanced mission was developed based on programs and practices such as restitution, community service, work experience, and victim offender mediation that have been proved effective over two decades of field experience and research.[4] But, while almost all juvenile courts and juvenile justice systems have used these practices at least sporadically, in most systems they receive low priority relative to other requirements.

Any justice system or agency can add new programs and many jurisdictions have adopted a wide array of specialized units. Certainly programs are available in many jurisdictions to support interventions consistent with the balanced mission. However, if only 10% of offenders are referred to a court's restitution program, and similar proportions complete meaningful community service, or meet with their victims, the jurisdiction can hardly be said to be "balanced" or "restorative." While useful, programmatic change alone does not change the focus of intervention in the system as a whole. In jurisdictions working to implement the Balanced Approach, however, managers view it as a framework for integrating and institutionalizing these practices as core, rather than secondary or tertiary, interventions and as a tool to help them plan, execute, and monitor change (Bazemore and Washington, 1995).

Currently, decisions about staff roles—what it is that juvenile justice professionals "do" in the response to youth crime—as well as resource allocation and management approaches, are based primarily on tradition and the needs of juvenile justice bureaucracies (e.g., for case workers, service providers). Too often, these decisions seem to be based on the need to be in step with the "program trend of the month." Seldom are staff roles and management imperatives reexamined to ensure that they are driven by essential community needs and expectations.

What is most "new" and different about the Balanced Approach mission, therefore, is its agenda for systemic restructuring to make juvenile justice value and client-driven and outcome-oriented. Such reform at the level of mission, seeks to alter both the content and process of intervention, and by changing the role of victims, other citizens, offenders, and staff, to also change the context of intervention. In so doing, reform based on the balanced mission is aimed at reordering the priorities of staff and the relationship between juvenile justice agencies and their clients. As Figure 2 suggests, in juvenile justice systems and agencies using the Balanced Approach mission, managers and staff are being challenged to base decisions and actions on a different set of values or guiding principles, which in turn demand a commitment to three clients rather than one. New decision-making processes, which involve victims, citizens, and offenders actively in the justice process and which are sensitive to their needs, determine what will be done in response to the crime. In turn, new performance outcomes gauge the success of an intervention based on the extent to which measurable changes are brought about in the status of each client. Finally, these outcomes are used to establish intervention priorities and initiate new programs (or discontinue old ones) based on their ability to accomplish competency, accountability, and public safety objectives, rather than simply to punish offenders or deliver treatment in the traditional sense.

How Do We Know It When We See It?
Six Ways the Balanced Approach Is Different

As the remainder of this paper will illustrate, the six differences shown in Figure 2 underscore the limits of both the treatment and retributive justice missions and distinguish the Balanced Approach mission as a strategy for systemic juvenile justice reform

Different Values: Restorative Justice

As implied earlier, several practices and programs commonly associated with the Balanced Approach such as community service and restitution are currently used with some regularity in many juvenile courts. Unfortunately, however, such sanctions may be included in a dispositional order simply to fulfill statutory requirements or to accomplish punishment, diversion or

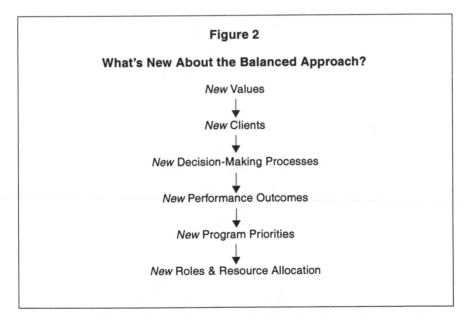

Figure 2

What's New About the Balanced Approach?

New Values

↓

New Clients

↓

New Decision-Making Processes

↓

New Performance Outcomes

↓

New Program Priorities

↓

New Roles & Resource Allocation

other objectives that have little to do with the goals of the new mission (e.g., Bazemore and Maloney 1994). In the absence of restorative values or principles, and a commitment to address the needs of victims, offenders, and communities, such practices will do little to increase "balance" in the juvenile justice response to crime and may even further alienate these primary clients of a balanced justice system (Bazemore and Umbreit, 1995; Umbreit, 1994).

If crime is important because it damages real people and communities, the "justice" process should focus primarily on repairing this harm. The most important question to be answered in a restorative response to crime is not "what do we do to punish or treat the offender." Rather, as Howard Zehr (1990) suggests, the justice process must begin with three primary questions: (1) what is the harm? (2) what needs to be done to make it right? (3) and who is responsible?

Questions one and two are best answered with input from victims, offender(s), and other citizens in decision-making processes that maximize their input into the disposition of the case. These questions are addressed in the sections which follow. Restorative values are also unique in their designation of responsibility. First, offenders are responsible for making it right with their victims, and a restorative juvenile justice system would ensure that offenders are, to the greatest extent possible, held accountable for the damage and suffering caused to victims and victimized communities. However, the system cannot assume sole responsibility. Rather, restorative justice affirms that not only government (i.e., the juvenile justice system), but victims, offenders, and communities (especially families) must be actively involved in the justice process (e.g., Zehr, 1990; Van Ness, 1993). As in any relationship, a community's general health is directly related to the extent to which members participate in decisions governing the community. One of the most important things a justice system can do is work to strengthen the capacity of communities to respond to crime and empower them to do so. As Canadian Judge Barry Stuart observes:

> When citizens fail to assume responsibility for decisions affecting the community, community life will be characterized by the absence of a collective sense of caring, a lack of respect for diverse values, and ultimately a lack of any sense of belonging. Conflict, if resolved through a process that constructively engages the parties involved, can be a fundamental building ingredient of any relationship. (Stuart, 1995)

From a restorative justice perspective, crime is often a symptom of community conflict and disharmony (e.g., Van Ness et al., 1989). If this is true, neither community "justice" nor community safety can be achieved by a government "war on crime." Justice and safety also cannot be achieved simply by punishing or treating individual offenders, but will instead require peacemaking efforts aimed at building, or rebuilding, "right relationships" (Pepinsky & Quinney, 1990; Van Ness, 1993). As community members learn to resolve disputes creatively, their capacity to do so also increases, as does the ability of the collective to sanction crime, habilitate and reintegrate offenders, and enhance public safety. When they facilitate or contribute to these processes, juvenile justice professionals are more likely to address the root causes of crime. They are also less likely to take on too much responsibility (Stuart, 1995).

What is perhaps most unique about the restorative justice value base, and most difficult for some juvenile justice professionals to accept, is its elevation of the role of crime victims in the justice process. While "victims' rights" has become a popular buzzword, victims' needs are addressed in the current system only after the needs of judges, prosecutors, probation, treatment providers and even offenders are considered. Restorative justice does not focus only on victims, nor does it define victim rights as the absence of offender rights. To bring balance to an offender driven system, however, it is necessary to give immediate priority to victims' needs for physical and material reparation and for emotional healing.

For the most part, restorative justice values can exist side-by-side with most traditional goals of juvenile justice intervention such as rehabilitation, and even deterrence and incapacitation. Proponents of restorative justice, for example, recognize the need for attempts to deter and incapacitate some offenders, as secondary reinforcements when they willfully and repeatedly disregard restorative obligations, or to protect citizens from offenders who continually victimize others (e.g., Braithwaite and Mugford, 1994; Young, 1995). But restorative justice would give lowest priority to punishment for its own sake, and would in practice challenge current "easy" solutions that simply reinforce and devote additional resources to traditional punishment, treatment and unimaginative approaches to enhancing public safety. From a restorative perspective, it is easy to get offenders to "take the punishment" (Wright, 1990), but it is much more difficult—and more important—to get them to take responsibility. It is equally easy to get many offenders to submit passively to the requirements of treatment programs, but it is much more difficult—and more important—to get them to actively earn their way back into the community and involve themselves in meaningful, productive roles that can potentially change their image from liability to community asset. It is easy to routinely lock up offenders in the name of public safety. But it is more difficult and more important to promote genuine public safety by building community capacity to control and prevent crime (e.g., Barajas, 1995).[4]

The basic principle behind restorative justice is that justice is best served when victims, offenders and communities receive equal attention as clients of the justice system. Ultimately then, restorative justice requires a "three-dimensional" focus which guides the search for solutions and just responses to crime to mutual concern for the needs of each client, and toward efforts to ensure that each is actively involved in the justice process. Crime breaks social and civil bonds between victims, offenders, and communities; it injures relationships of mutual respect, understanding and support. Achieving "justice" will involve "restoring" victims, offenders and communities.

In this way, the values of restorative justice allow managers using the balanced mission to effectively integrate efforts to meet sanctioning, safety and rehabilitative needs, restore victim losses, and ultimately serve and involve the three clients. As will become clear in the discussion which follows, restorative values underlie each of the other five differences between the Balanced Approach and current mission alternatives.

Different Clients

Based on restorative values, the Balanced Approach offers a new vision for how three primary clients or co-participants will be involved in the juvenile justice process. As Table 1 suggests, this "community justice" vision (Barajas, 1995; Young, 1995; Bazemore & Day, 1996) is perhaps best understood by first examining what the model "looks like" for these co-participants.

By these standards of victim, offender and community participation, the new mission is a "work in progress"; no juvenile justice system today is completely "balanced" or fully restorative. But if most juvenile justice systems, including those most committed to the model, seem far away from the level of community and client involvement indicated in the table, it is not, as the practical examples in the previous section illustrate, because the model is utopian. Rather, it is because these systems are driven by insular, conceptually and practically incomplete, "closed system" paradigms (Byrne, 1988; Reiss, 1986).

Both the traditional individual treatment and the new retributive/punitive models are incomplete because they are exclusively offender-focused. Neither treatment nor punishment models address victims and other citizens as co-participants or "customers" in the juvenile justice process.

What does it mean to view someone as a client or customer? In the Total Quality Management (TQM) movement (e.g., Deming, 1986; Martin, 1993), the idea of a client or "customer" has three components: a recipient of service, a target of intervention and change, and a co-participant who must have input into the process and be involved to the greatest extent possible. Although it may seem unusual to view offenders and their families, victims, and community members as customers, some jurisdictions are beginning to provide services to each of these clients and are attempting through various interventions to improve the disempowered, damaged, and fearful status of crime victims, as well as the preventative capacity of community groups (e.g. Bazemore and Schiff, 1996, Young, 1995). Moreover, some juvenile justice professionals are finding the input and active involvement of each of the client groups to be most critical for effectiveness (e.g., Umbreit and Carey, 1995).

While some degree of participation from each client group of the type depicted in Table 1 is essential to achieve the goals of the Balanced

**Table 1: What Does it Look Like?
Balanced and Restorative Justice**

In a Balanced And Restorative Juvenile Justice System:

Crime Victims:
❏ Receive support, assistance, compensation, information and services.
❏ Receive restitution and/or other reparation from the offender.
❏ Are involved and are encouraged to give input at all points in the system and direct input into how the offender will repair the harm done.
❏ Have the opportunity to face the offenders and tell their story to offenders and others if they so desire.
❏ Feel satisfied with the justice process.
❏ Provide guidance and consultation to JJ professionals on planning and advisory groups.

Offenders:
❏ Complete restitution to their victims.
❏ Provide meaningful service to repay the debt to their communities.
❏ Must face the personal harm caused by their crimes by participating in victim offender mediation, if the victim is willing or through other victim awareness process.
❏ Complete work experience and active and productive tasks which increase skills and improve the community.
❏ Are monitored by community adults as well as juvenile justice providers and are supervised to the greatest extent possible in the community.
❏ Improve decision-making skills and have opportunities to help others.

Citizens, Families, and Community Groups:
❏ Are involved to the greatest extent possible in holding offenders accountable, rehabilitation, and community safety initiatives.
❏ Work with offenders on local community service projects.
❏ Provide support to victims.
❏ Provide support to offenders as mentors, employers, and advocates.
❏ Provide work for offenders to pay restitution to victims and service opportunities which provide skills and also allow offenders to make meaningful contributions to the quality of community life.
❏ Community groups assist families to support the offender in the obligation to repair the harm and increase competencies.
❏ Play an advisory role to courts and corrections and/or play an active role in disposition through one or more neighborhood sanctioning processes.

Approach, currently few nonprofessionals are meaningfully involved in juvenile justice intervention. First, although some juvenile justice professionals work hard at "service brokerage," such efforts at collaboration seldom move beyond the usual network of professional social service "experts" to include employers, civic leaders, ministers, and other neighborhood residents. Unfortunately, even when "nonexperts" are recruited to work with the system, the experts may be given little time to nurture and support them.

Second, because juvenile justice has been unable to identify meaningful and appropriate roles that engage citizens in activities associated with tangible offender and victim outcomes, involvement is often short term and unsatisfying. Even programs aimed at establishing more lasting and significant bonds between community members and offenders, such as mentoring, often fail to provide a context (e.g., mutual involvement in a community service project) in which such bonds are likely to form (Bazemore & Day, 1996).

Finally, what citizen participants have been asked to do frequently seems to appeal to a more abstract obligation to participate out of civic duty rather than personal commitment. As Braithwaite and Mugford (1994) have observed, citizens are generally more willing to become involved if they have a personal interest in the offender, victim, and/or the family of either. Hence, although "community" may be difficult to identify in areas where it seems that there is disorganization and/or little sense of caring or mutual support, almost every crime involves small, personal "communities of concern" for the victim, the offender, and their families, and those citizens directly impacted by the crime (Stuart, 1995). These personal communities can become a critical resource as a support network in a response to youth crime that meets the needs of victim, offender and the neighborhood, and it is around them that much citizen participation in an emerging community justice is being built (Braithwaite & Mugford, 1994).[5]

Precisely because they do not focus simply on punishing or providing expert treatment to offenders, the programs and practices given priority in the Balanced Approach assume and invite a high level of citizen participation. While mobilizing community involvement is by no means easy, it may be more meaningful and personally satisfying, for example, for citizens to support an offender who needs a job to make victim restitution, provide support for a victim, or provide a useful community service opportunity than to assist with paper work or aid to a traditional counseling program.

The basic assumption, or theory, behind restorative justice is that harm to one community member is harm to everyone. Therefore, the needs of one client (e.g., the victim's needs for healing; the offender's needs to be held accountable and then reintegrated) cannot be met unless the needs of the other clients are also addressed. Moreover, public safety, rehabilitation, and sanctioning goals need not conflict. In a restorative system, practices, policies and processes aimed at repairing the harm to victims should therefore reinforce or "resonate" with those which are aimed at rehabilitative and public safety objectives. Specifically, a sanctioning process that holds offenders accountable to victims and the community is a first step in the rehabilitative process. Developing capacities for competent behavior in offenders increases community safety by increasing offender connectedness, skills, and ability to work with others. Strengthening community safety makes it possible to carry out meaningful sanctioning and effective reintegration of offenders into the community, while also supporting and restoring victims. And, finally, increasing citizens' ability to resolve conflict ultimately makes communities safer.[6]

Different Decision-Making Processes

Recently, in a large city a 32-year-old man entered the home of a neighbor, and walked upstairs into the bedroom of her 14-year-old daughter. For almost an hour, the man made lewd and offensive comments while sitting on the girl's bed. After the man had been arrested and charged, the young woman and her mother were asked by the court to complete a victim impact statement. Except for a brief moment when the man had lightly stroked her hair, she had not been physically molested by the intruder. Yet, the young girl had felt traumatized and "dirtied" by the fact that the man had sat on her bed. After talking at length with her mother, the two decided that what the girl most needed was a new bed. The victim impact statement submitted asked for $500 in restitution from the offender to cover the cost of the bed, an apology, and a recommendation for a year of therapy and other assistance for the offender. The judge ordered 12 months' jail time and a $500 fine, but payable to the court.

In a small town in the same state, a 14-year-old male, after pointing a loaded gun (which was actually a BB rifle) at a neighbor, was arrested, charged with second degree assault with a deadly weapon, and eventually sent to juvenile court intake in the small town where he resided. The neighbor, an adult male of about 35 who had been so frightened and upset by the incident that he insisted the case be fully prosecuted, was reluctantly persuaded to participate with the offender in a victim offender mediation session. At the session, after venting his anger and frustration at being startled with the loaded weapon, the victim learned that the boy liked to hunt. When he asked in the mediation session whom the boy hunted with and learned that it was his grandfather, an idea emerged that he would later propose when it was time to discuss an appropriate sanction. The outcome of the mediation was that, at the victim's request, the boy would be required to tell his grandfather what he had done. After several days of reluctant hesitation, the boy told his grandfather and so informed the victim.

The experiences in each case were dramatically different for the offender, the victim, and even the community. Most who have heard the young man's story believe that he learned an important lesson (and did not get off easy) and that the victim was satisfied. Moreover, some have observed that the small community may have witnessed an important example of how disputes that might otherwise have created a serious offense record for the youth, wasted court time, provided little relief to the victim, and created fear in the community of "armed and dangerous" juveniles could be effectively resolved. In the first case, most agree that the victim was ignored and again victimized, that the offender got no treatment and might even have been more dangerous at the completion of his jail time, and that the community paid the cost of the jail term while receiving little in return.

Most are also upset with the judge in the first case for ignoring the victim's request. But while the conversion of the victim's request for restitution into a court fine seems especially insensitive, the judge was merely operating on the basis of the assumptions of the current system of justice decision making. Referred to by some as a retributive justice paradigm (Zehr, 1990; Bazemore and Umbreit, 1995), these assumptions result in the exclusion and disempowerment of victims, offenders and other citizens and, in part, are responsible for the general absence in most juvenile justice systems of the co-participant involvement depicted earlier in Table 1. Although these cases are not necessarily typical, the contrast between them provides a useful illustration of how victim, community and offender needs are not addressed effectively by an approach to dispositional decision-making that is limited by rigid, legalistic processes (see Table 2).

In contrast, restorative processes, whose potential benefits to each co-participant are illustrated by the first case, are premised on the active participation of these clients and demand opportunities for such participation that are sensitive to and supportive of client needs. Crime victim needs are especially likely to be overlooked unless victims are given a direct voice in decision making. When actively engaged, victims will often have unique concerns and interests which are often unrelated to offender punishment, or even the need for material reparation:

> . . . I can tell you that what most victims want most is quite unrelated to the law. It amounts more than anything else to three things: victims need to have people recognize how much trauma they've been through . . . they need to express that, and have it expressed to them; they want to find out what kind of person could have done such a thing, and why to them; and it really helps to hear that the offender is sorry—or that someone is sorry on his or her behalf. (Elaine Berzins, quoted in Stuart, 1995a, pg. 12)

Most formal juvenile court proceedings with some flexible discretion by judges and other court decision makers could accommodate some of the changes needed to increase the active involvement of victims, offenders, and citizens in dispositions and thus make sanctions and court requirements more meaningful. But if critics of formal, legalistic processes are correct, minor changes in the court process will be insufficient to alter the current image of these insular systems that have proved themselves inadequate to the task. As Judge Stuart insists:

> Crime (control and prevention) should never be the sole, or even pri-mary business of the State if *real differences* are sought in the well being of individuals, families and communities. The structure, procedures, and evidentiary rules of the formal criminal justice process coupled with most justice officials' lack of knowledge and connection to (the parties) effected by crime, preclude the state from acting alone to achieve trans-formative changes. (Stuart, 1995b, p. 1, emphasis in original)

Table 2: Paradigms of Justice—OLD and NEW*

Victims and Community

Retributive Justice	Restorative Justice
Victims are peripheral to the process	Victims are central to the process
Community on sideline, represented abstractly by state	Community as facilitator in restorative process
Imposition of pain to punish and deter/pre-vent	Restitution as a means of restoring both parties; goal of reconciliation/restoration

Crime and Reaction

Retributive Justice	Restorative Justice
Crime is an act against state, a violation of a law, or an abstract idea.	Crime is an act against another person and the community
Punishment is effective 　a. The threat of punishment deters crime 　b. Punishment changes behavior	Punishment alone is not effective in chang-ing behavior and is disruptive to community relationships
The criminal justice system controls crime	Crime control lies primarily in the commu-nity

The Offender

Retributive Justice	Restorative Justice
Offender accountability defined as taking punishment	Accountability defined as taking responsibil-ity and taking action to repair harm
The offender is defined by deficit	The offender is defined by the capacity to make reparation
No encouragement for repentance and for-giveness	Possibilities for forgiveness.

*Adapted from Zehr (1990)

Achieving balanced and restorative goals and the general vision of restorative justice are therefore likely to require that juvenile court judges and other court professionals exercise strong leadership to actively develop and promote expanded use of viable decision-making alternatives that allow for greater and more meaningful involvement of citizens and victims in decisions about the response to juveniles who commit crimes. New Zealand, as mentioned earlier, has gone furthest toward institutionalizing the active involvement of citizens and victims, as well as offenders and their families, in the court dispositional process through its nationwide adoption of the Family Group Conferencing model (McElrae, 1993; Maxwell & Morris, 1993). There are other processes as well which may be more appropriate for certain cases and work best in certain communities. Table 3 suggests some successful existing models for victim and citizen participation in decision making.

These alternative processes assume an offender who has admitted guilt or been found guilty and are concerned with dispositional decision making rather than fact finding. However, in most jurisdictions where cases are routinely plea bargained or resolved by consent decree or other informal negotiation prior to formal disposition, this may in fact account for a majority of cases (cf., McElrae, 1993; Belgrave, 1995). Currently, there are precedents for restorative decision-making models being used around the world at several points in both the juvenile and criminal justice systems including pre-adjudication, pre- and post-disposition, as a requirement or option at institutional commitment, and as a part of aftercare (Belgrave, 1995; Umbreit, 1994; Bazemore & Schiff, 1996; Morris & Maxwell, 1993). While these alternative processes will not be fully developed overnight and will never replace the need for the court in some cases, or the need for a commitment to due process, restorative justice is a holistic model that seeks to maximize crime victim and community input through less formal, less adversarial processes at all possible points in and outside of the system.

Different Performance Objectives

If treatment and punishment are, as suggested earlier, insular in their exclusive focus on the needs and risks presented by the offender, they are also one-dimensional. That is, both the treatment and retributive missions fail to address the various, and multiple, justice needs of communities. While the new punitive approach to juvenile justice may appease some of the public demand for retribution, it does nothing to address expectations that offenders be rehabilitated and reintegrated. In contrast, most citizens view treatment as solely related to the offender's needs. Treatment programs seem to require little of lawbreakers beyond participating in counseling, remedial services, or recreational programs, and they may even be viewed as providing only benefits to offenders, while failing to reinforce conventional values such as the work ethic (Bazemore & Umbreit, 1995b). Ultimately, retributive punishment addresses one small aspect of a community's need to sanction crime, while treatment addresses one small aspect of rehabilitation and reintegration. Neither addresses the community's need for safety and input into the process or the need for more meaningful approaches to sanctioning and rehabilitation that attempt to also involve victims and address their needs.

As models for developing outcomes that could be used to gauge the true effectiveness of juvenile justice agencies and systems and to guide the selection of programs to achieve these objectives, treatment and punishment approaches are flawed in two primary ways. First, while advocates of various treatment interventions remind us that some things do work (e.g., Gendreau & Ross, 1987), what "works" for offenders who happen to make it into treatment programs may make little difference to victims of juvenile crime, to citizens concerned with their neighborhoods' safety and to those who want to see young people held accountable for their actions (Braithwaite & Mugford, 1994). As offender-driven models, punishment and treatment are useful only in developing outcomes for offenders under court jurisdiction. They are of little assistance in articulating goals that address the need for positive changes in crime victims and communities. Second, while the long-range concern of both punishment and treatment is to prevent recidivism and the short-term goal is to gain enough control over the

---

Table 3:   Some Restorative Decision-Making Processes

1. *Victim Offender Mediation*—Trained mediators facilitate face-to-face discussion between offender and victim to allow for expression of feelings, discussion of harm and obligation, and arrive at agreement with offender to repair the harm.

2. *Family Group Conferencing*—Allows for community, victim and family input into the development of a restorative sanction for juvenile offenders in a process initiated by a trained facilitator.

3. *Circle Sentencing*—A sentencing and problem-solving process currently being implemented in Canada facilitated by a judge or community member and attended by victim, offenders and a variety of local citizens who support both and wish to develop a local resolution of the crime.

4. *Community Reparative Boards*—Currently being implemented in Vermont, these citizen sentencing panels develop agreements with nonfelony offenders that focus their probation on victim and community reparation, understanding of harm caused by their crime, avoiding future offending behavior.

5. *Reparative Court Hearings*—Though best implemented in an informal community setting, some judges hold special hearings to determine victim reparation as a separate part of the dispositional process in court.

offender to do this, neither model offers good intermediate performance outcomes for offenders.

Completing a treatment program and ceasing bad behavior while under court supervision does not equip offenders with the capabilities and the desire to do something other than offending. Likewise, simply "taking the punishment" produces few measurable outcomes (other than possible anger and resentment). While many would also argue that juvenile justice should not be held solely responsible for reducing recidivism (and in any case, few juvenile justice agencies systematically track recidivism rates), systems and agencies should, however, be accountable for achieving other objectives that may be associated with reduced recidivism and ultimately with lower crime rates.

One purpose of the Balanced Approach mission is to provide juvenile justice systems with intermediate performance outcomes related to the primary expectations of the communities they serve. In systems applying the Balanced Approach, communities are working with juvenile justice professionals to develop intermediate outcomes to gage success in achieving the sanctioning, rehabilitative and public safety goals put forward in the balanced mission and to assess positive change in the three juvenile justice clients. But the most important outcomes in the Balanced Approach are unlikely to be the same as those that have been given the primary focus in the traditional system. Rather, they are focused on making what Judge Stuart calls "real differences" in relationships that allow victims to heal, offenders to become reconnected, and families and communities to begin to take responsibility for these things to occur:

> . . . communities should not measure the success of any . . . community based initiative upon what happens to the offender . . . (Rather, they should measure) . . . the impact of community based initiatives upon victims, upon the self-esteem of others working (in the community justice process), on strengthening families, building connections within the community, on enforcing community values, on mobilizing community action to reduce factors causing crime, to prevent crime—and ultimately to make the community safer. . . . (Stuart, 1995: 8)

Different Programs

Although there is no one Balanced Approach or restorative intervention or program, it has become clear, based on years of research and program experience, that there are several types of programs and practices that need to receive priority if systems are to achieve the goals of competency development, accountability, and community protection.

In addition to articulating intermediate performance outcomes, juvenile justice agencies and systems will also need to conduct a baseline audit or inventory of current intervention practice. Specifically, to develop a fair evaluation of the extent to which they are accomplishing balanced and restorative goals, a thorough assessment should examine whether certain programs, practices, and processes designed to accomplish key objectives such as victim restoration, offender competency development and so on are available to the jurisdiction and are being used effectively. For example, if a jurisdiction has no systematic procedure or program for determining restitution, monitoring payments, and ensuring that offenders have ways to earn funds to repay victims, it can hardly be expected to achieve its accountability objectives (Schneider, 1985; Bazemore, 1991). Likewise, it may also be important to critically examine the extent to which current assessment and dispositional processes may limit efforts to achieve balanced performance outcomes. If a goal is to maximize the number of young offenders who complete fair restitution obligations to their victims, this goal cannot be accomplished if judges make unreasonable orders without regard to whether the jurisdiction is providing earning opportunities for the offender (Bazemore, 1991). If a goal is to ensure that each offender will be required to complete a meaningful work experience or provide community service that meets real community needs, this goal will not be achieved if the standard practice in many jurisdictions of sending youth with service hours, unsupervised to pick up paper in local parks continues (Bazemore & Maloney, 1994). If a goal is to ensure that each victim who wishes to have a face-to-face meeting with the offender has an opportunity to do so, the goal is unlikely to be achieved in the absence of a victim-offender mediation program or other structured opportunity for victim input and victim-offender dialogue such as family group conferencing (Morris & Maxwell, 1993).

Although I will not elaborate on operational issues of specific programs here, it is important to reiterate that simply adding programs in the absence of change in values and client priorities is unlikely to lead to balanced and restorative outcomes. As juvenile justice systems become "program-driven," managers may develop what Goldstein (1979; 1988) referred to in law enforcement as a means-over-ends focus. Programs are not ends in themselves but simply a means to achieve outcomes that flow from a clear understanding of community and other client needs. Programs and practices are "restorative" to the extent that they are consistent with the underlying values of restorative justice and responsive to these clients. On the other hand, some programs with apparently restorative objectives are not based on restorative values and may be easily coopted to serve other ends (e.g., mediation and restitution programs used primarily to divert offenders rather than involve victims and offenders in reaching agreements for reparation; community service that is ordered primarily as punishment rather than community restoration).

Moreover, from a "community justice" perspective (Barajas, 1995; Bazemore and Schiff, 1996), the value of a program and quality of its implementation must also be gauged primarily in terms of the extent to which it involves community members at all levels of planning, implementation, and monitoring. For example, one may ask of a community service or victim-offender-mediation program which uses only paid staff and does not consult neighborhood residents on their priorities (e.g., for work service projects) whether such programs are simply *in* rather than *of* the community.

Different Roles for Juvenile Justice Professionals

The new, active roles for the three juvenile justice clients, or coparticipants, discussed earlier (and depicted in Table 1) have obvious implications for the roles of juvenile justice professionals. Hence, perhaps the most important, and also most difficult, change in moving toward Balanced and Restorative Justice will be to begin to alter the job descriptions and professional role orientations of juvenile justice staff. For probation professionals accustomed to casework with individual offenders or residential treatment providers trained in institution-based treatment protocols, the role change implied by the need to engage victims and communities in the process may be a dramatic and difficult one. For many of these professionals, the idea of working with victims and community members, when time and resources to meet the needs of offenders alone appear inadequate, seems counterintuitive.

But making significant differences in the lives of offenders, the kind of differences that help to reintegrate them into conventional communities, is ultimately unlikely without the active involvement of victims and nonprofessional citizens (e.g., Stuart, 1995a & b).

Making amends to victims and then gaining the sponsorship of community adults (e.g., employers, ministers, family members) are the steps that open the doors to community acceptance for offenders. Hence, achieving rehabilitative objectives will require that juvenile justice no longer treat the offender in isolation. To make the shift toward viewing victim and community intervention as part of the juvenile justice role, probation and treatment staff will need to understand this restorative justice principle and ultimately also witness the transformative changes that can occur when community members and victims are involved in the response to youth crime (e.g., Braithwaite and Mugford 1994; Stuart, 1995).

The specifics of this role change are beyond the scope of this paper and need to be worked out locally with staff, managers, and citizen advisers. Still, it is clear that the role of probation and other intervention staff in jurisdictions implementing a Balanced Approach mission will gradually be transformed from direct service provider, or even "service broker," to "community justice facilitator." As Table 4 suggests, this transformation will require that juvenile justice professionals begin to define their new roles and functions in relation to and in support of the new more active role of each of the three co-participants. They will, for example, work with each of the three clients in activities focused on capacity-building for crime prevention, in ensuring that community adults provide opportunities for competency development and assist with monitoring offenders, in engaging employers and civic groups to provide meaningful work for offenders, and in meeting with victims and victim advocacy groups.

Judges, prosecutors, and other court decision makers will also be challenged by the Balanced Approach mission to reassess their current roles. There will, as previously noted, always be cases that require use of formal

---

Table 4   New Roles in the Balanced and Restorative Justice Model

The Co-Participants

Victim	Active participation in defining the harm of the crime and shaping the obligations placed on the offender.
Community	Responsible for supporting and assisting victims, holding offenders accountable, and ensuring opportunities for offenders to make amends.
Offender	Active participation in reparation and competency development.

Juvenile Justice Professionals

Sanctioning	Facilitate mediation; ensure that restoration occurs (by providing ways for offenders to earn funds for restitution); develop creative and/or restorative community service options; engage community members in the process; educate community on its role.
Rehabilitation	Develop new roles for young offenders which allow them to practice and demonstrate competency; assess and build on youth and community strengths; develop partnerships.
Public Safety	Develop range of incentives and consequences to ensure offender compliance with supervision objectives; assist school and family in their efforts to control and maintain offenders in the community; develop prevention capacity of local organizations.

---

legal processes and determination of guilt through formal due process. However, judges in particular can play vital leadership roles in encouraging communities and citizens to resolve conflict creatively and informally and to begin to take more responsibility in the response to, and prevention of, youth crime (Stuart, 1995). If they are to empower victims and community members as co-participants, they must take on this challenge and take risks to expand the variety of alternative decision-making processes such as mediation, family group conferencing, and similar forums and allow greater numbers of cases to be heard in these settings.

The Limits of Current Paradigms:
Toward Community Juvenile Justice

For the most part the decade-long debate about the future of the juvenile court and the justice system has been stale and unimaginative. Often couched in legalistic and procedural terms focused on which young offenders should receive juvenile and which should receive adult dispositions and how this should be decided, this debate has typically had little to do with the content and focus of juvenile court intervention—or with how those offenders who remain in the juvenile justice system, their communities, or their victims will benefit from this intervention. As a result, it has been of little interest to the public, a growing number of whom seem to sense that the important issues of community safety, juvenile crime, and youth development cannot be reduced to issues of the relative efficacy of juvenile and adult court.

Many citizens and a growing number of juvenile justice professionals also seem to be growing tired of the even older debate about the relative efficacy of treatment vs. punishment. For these observers, there is a suspicion that something is missing in an endless discussion about what feel like, as one judge put it, "bad choices between sending kids to jail or sending them to the beach." While recent research suggests that much of the public continues to support rehabilitation (e.g., Doble, 1996; Schwartz, 1992), many appear to doubt the capacity of juvenile justice systems to accomplish this objective and seem to suspect that neither "jail" nor "the beach" provides much of an answer.

Meanwhile, the system continues to expand and increase expenditures with relatively little to show in improved outcomes for offenders, families, and communities. At the same time, staff feel that they are working harder and doing more with less.[7] While advocates of reaffirming the individual treatment model may be right in arguing that the system has never been given adequate support, critics, as well as many defenders of juvenile justice, now argue that juvenile justice leaders have also failed to articulate a vision of success. If juvenile justice is underfunded, it is also underconceptualized. Increasingly reliant on professional experts, more facilities, and more programs, many, if not most, juvenile justice agencies and programs today have lost the critical ingredient needed to develop a meaningful response to juvenile crime: community support and meaningful citizen involvement in the justice process.

I have suggested here that debate about the future of juvenile justice has been limited by closed-system, offender-driven, and one-dimensional punishment and treatment paradigms. The individual treatment and the retributive/punitive models are not, however, the only options for juvenile justice. Treatment and punishment remain important components of many juvenile court dispositions, but it is possible to envision a more empowering, more holistic and more marketable, restorative community justice agenda for a future response to youth crime (Young, 1995; Bazemore and Day, 1996). Such an agenda would put victims' needs for information, reparation, validation, healing, and input at its core and would promote development of strong, crime-resistant neighborhoods where residents feel safe. It would emphasize the need for rehabilitative/reintegrative relationship building between young people and adults and for active, experiential involvement of young offenders in work, service learning and other productive roles that provide more structured pathways to bonding with community members. Perhaps most important, a community juvenile justice would articulate new and more meaningful roles for crime victims, employers, civic groups, religious communities, teachers, families and other citizens in offender habilitation/rehabilitation; in a more meaningful, more effective and more educational nonretributive approach to sanctioning; and in carrying out a more effective public safety enhancement agenda (see earlier Table 1).

Conclusion: Moving Toward Balance

The Balanced Approach mission was originally proposed not to reaffirm the individualized treatment agenda of the juvenile court, but rather to restructure juvenile justice to move it closer to the community and its needs. A primary danger in the Balanced Approach's new popularity is that it will be misunderstood and inappropriately applied. Thus, supporters, as well as critics, should continue to raise questions about the use of this new mission, while also questioning the utility of current approaches. In the current political climate, it is especially important to remain alert to efforts to simply use the rhetoric of balance or restoration to disguise retributive policies that merely respond to what Dennis Maloney has referred to as policymaker "urges" to get tough.

The failure of current paradigms has moved many policymakers toward more desperate attempts to "improve" the response to juvenile crime by abolishing the juvenile justice system. A growing number who want to preserve a separate and effective juvenile justice system, and see Balanced Approach mission and the restorative justice framework as providing hope for doing so, realize that any new system must be crafted not with the needs of professionals, but with the community in mind.

Notes

[1]There is substantial variation in the way in which the balanced mission is presented in this legislation and policy. While some statutes refer specifically to the Balanced Approach, others simply articulate the three goals of the mission—public safety, competency, and accountability. A grow-

ing number of juvenile justice managers, policymakers and funding agency administrators in states such as California, Montana, Pennsylvania, and Minnesota now speak of a Balanced and Restorative Justice model (Bazemore & Umbreit, 1994; Umbreit & Carey, 1995; Pennsylvania Council on Crime and Delinquency, 1996; Montana Board of Crime Control, 1996).

[2] In part because the authors of the NCJFCJ monograph came down squarely on the side of preserving the juvenile court, it has perhaps been easy for some critics of the Balanced Approach to simply equate the new mission with a defense of the individual treatment mission. Misunderstanding is also no doubt due to the fact that to date only a few jurisdictions have begun to make the systemic changes in policy and practice consistent with the vision of Maloney, Romig and Armstrong (1988) and to the fact that the restorative justice philosophy has only been sporadically discussed in most juvenile justice circles.

[3] For reasons that will be discussed later, treatment and punishment are actually viewed as secondary goals in the balanced approach mission. The critique of the individual treatment model presented here is not premised on the largely discredited "nothing works" perspective, nor is the need for an effective rehabilitative model for juvenile justice questioned.

[4] Restorative justice would essentially give new priority to goals such as victim and community involvement that have been neglected in the current system. Though punishment is likely to remain a central component of any juvenile justice model, it is perhaps the least effective and most expensive approach to sanctioning crime. For empirical evidence that criminal justice decision makers typically overestimate the perceived punitive effects of incarceration and commentary on other more educative and expressive approaches to setting tolerance limits for crime, providing consequences for offenders, and allowing for the expression of public disapproval of offending in ways that promote community solidarity and peaceful dispute resolution; see Braithwaite (1989), Wilkins (1995), Bazemore & Umbreit (1995), Crouch (1993) and Bishop, et al., 1996). A growing body of research and an emerging theoretical base is supportive of the view that the experience of making amends for harm done to victims and the community through monetary restitution and unpaid service may have positive rehabilitative as well as reparative effects (Eglash, 1975; Schneider, 1986; 1990; Butts and Snyder, 1991; Wright, 1991).

[5] For more detailed description of the New Zealand and Australian models of family group conferencing and related models such as Circle Sentencing, including research findings and critical concerns about implementation in some jurisdictions, see Maxwell and Morris (1993), Alder and Wundersitz (1994), Umbreit and Stacy (1995) and Stuart (1995).

[6] This concept of "resonance" in the Balanced Approach was first articulated by Troy Armstrong (see, Armstrong, Maloney and Romig, 1990). Some have also argued that it is possible to think and speak of a restorative approach to rehabilitation and a restorative approach to public safety (Van Ness, 1993; Bazemore, 1996).

[7] Indeed the critique of current policy and practice presented in this paper is in no way a criticism of juvenile justice professionals. Rather, it is a critique of the bureaucratic systems which limit their effort to implement meaningful reform.

References

Alder, C. & J. Wundersitz, 1994, *Family Group Conferencing and Juvenile Justice: The Way Forward of Misplaced,* Conberra, ACT: Australian Institute of Criminology.

Armstrong, T., D. Maloney, & D. Romig., 1990, "The Balanced Approach to Juvenile Probation: Principles, Issues, and Application." *Perspectives,* Winter 8–13.

Barajas, Jr., E., 1995, "Moving Toward Community Justice," Topics in *Community Corrections,* National Institute of Corrections Community Division, Annual Issue 1995.

Bazemore, G., 1991, "New Concepts and Alternative Practice in Community Supervision of Juvenile Offenders: Rediscovering Work Experience and Competency Development," *Journal of Crime and Justice*, 14 (2), 27–52.

Bazemore, G., 1992, "On Mission Statements and Reform in Juvenile Justice: The Case of the 'Balanced Approach,'" *Federal Probation*, 56(3).

Bazemore, G., 1996, "Three Paradigms for Juvenile Justice," Chapter 2 in Joe Hudson and Burt Galaway (eds.), *The Practice of Restorative Justice*. Monsey, New York: Criminal Justice Press, forthcoming.

Bazemore, G. & S. Day, 1996, "Restoring The Balance: Juvenile Justice and Community Justice," *Juvenile Justice*. Volume III, No. 1 (3–14) December.

Bazemore, G. & S. Senjo, 1996, "Cops, Kids and Police Reform: An Exploratory Study of Themes and Styles in Police/Juvenile Interaction in Community Policing," paper presented at the American Society of Criminology Meetings, Boston, November.

Bazemore, G. & P. Cruise, 1994, "Reinventing Rehabilitation: Exploring a Competency Development Model for Juvenile Justice Intervention," *Perspectives*, Fall, 12–21.

Bazemore, G., & D. Maloney, 1994, "Rehabilitating Community Service: Toward Restorative Service in a Balanced Justice System," *Federal Probation*, 58(l), 24–34.

Bazemore, G. & C. Terry, 1997, "Developing Delinquent Youth: A Reintegrative Model for Rehabilitation and a New Role for the Juvenile Justice System," *Child Welfare* (forthcoming).

Bazemore, G. & M. Schiff, 1996, "Community Justice/Restorative Justice: Prospects for a New Social Ecology for Community Corrections," *International Journal of Comparative and Applied Criminal Justice*, 20(1), Fall (311–335).

Bazemore, G. & A. Umbreit, 1995a, *Balanced and Restorative Justice for Juveniles*. Office of Juvenile Justice and Delinquency Prevention. U.S. Department of Justice, Washington, D.C.

Bazemore, G. & M. Umbreit, 1995b, "Rethinking the Sanctioning Function in Juvenile Court: Retributive or Restorative Responses to Youth Crime," *Crime and Delinquency*, 41(3), 296–316.

Bazemore, G. & C. Washington, 1995, "Charting the Future of the Juvenile Justice System: Reinventing Mission and Management," *Spectrum: The Journal of State Government*, 68(2), 51–66.

Belgrave, J., 1995, *Restorative Justice: A Discussion Paper*. New Zealand Ministry of Justice. Wellington, New Zealand.

Bishop, D., C. Frazier, L. Lanza-Kuduce, & L. Wimmer, 1996, "The Transfer of Juveniles to Criminal Court: Does It Make a Difference?," *Crime & Delinquency*, 42(2), 171–191.

Braithwaite, J., 1989, *Crime, Shaming, and Reintegration*. New York: Cambridge University Press.

Braithwaite, J. & S. Mugford, 1994, "Conditions of Successful Reintegration Ceremonies," *British Journal of Criminology*, 34(2), 139–171. (Australia)

Byrne, J. M., 1989, "Reintegrating the Concept of Community into Community-Based Corrections," *Crime & Delinquency*, 35(3), 471–499.

Butts, J. and S. Howard, 1991, *Restitution and Juvenile Recidivism*. Monograph, National Center for Juvenile Justice, Pittsburgh, PA.

Crouch, J., 1989, "Is Incarceration Really Worse? Analysis of Offenders' Preferences for Prison Over Probation," *Justice Quarterly* 10:67, 88.

Deming, W. E., 1986, *Out of Crisis*. Cambridge, Mass. MIT Center for Advanced Engineering.

Dickey, W., 1995, "Why Neighborhood Supervision?" Pages 42–46 in E. Barajas (ed.), *Community Justice: Topics in Community Corrections*, National Institute of Corrections, U.S. Department of Justice, Washington, D.C.

Eglash, A., 1975, "Beyond Restitution: Creative Restitution," pages 91–101 in J. Hudson & B. Galaway (eds.), *Restitution in Criminal Justice*. Lexington, PA: Lexington Books.

Feld, B., 1991, "The Punitive Juvenile Court and the Quality of Procedural Justice: Distinctions Between Rhetoric and Reality," *Crime & Delinquency* 36, 443–64.

Feld, B., 1995, "Violent Youth and Public Policy: A Case Study in Dismantling Juvenile Justice Law Reform," *Minnesota Law Review* 79, 965–992.

Forst, M. L., & M. Blomquist, 1992, "Punishment, Accountability, and the New Juvenile Justice,"

Juvenile & Family Court Journal. 23(2), 1–9.

Gendreau, P. & R. Ross, 1994, "Correctional Treatment: Some Recommendations for Successful Intervention," *Juvenile and Family Court Journal,* 34, 31–40.

Goldstein, H., 1978, "Improving Policing: A Problem-Oriented Approach," *Crime & Delinquency* 25, 236–258.

Guarino-Ghezzi, S. & A. Klein, 1997, "A Public Safety Role for Juvenile Justice," in G. Bazemore & L. Walgrave (eds.), *Restoring Juvenile Justice.* Amsterdam: Kugler International, forthcoming.

Klien, A., 1996, *Balanced Approach Legislation in the States.* Monograph, Balanced and Restorative Justice Project, Florida Atlantic University, Ft. Lauderdale, Florida.

Lemov, P., 1994, "The Assault on Juvenile on Juvenile Justice," *Governing,* December, 26–31.

Maloney, D., D. Romig, & T. Armstrong, 1988, *Juvenile Probation: The Balanced Approach.* Reno, NV: National Council of Juvenile and Family Court Judges.

Martin, L., 1993, *Total Quality Management in Organizations.* Newbury Park: Sage.

McAllair, D., 1993, "Reaffirming Rehabilitation in Juvenile Justice," *Youth and Society,* 25(1), 104–125.

McElrae, F. W. M., 1993, "A New Model of Justice," pages 1–14 in *The Youth Court in New Zealand. A New Model of Justice.* Legal Research Foundation, Pub. 34.

Moore D. & T. O'Connell, 1994, "Family Conferencing in Wagga Wagga: A Communitarian Model of Justice," pp. 96–110 in C. Adler & J. Wundersitz (eds.), *Family Group Conferencing: The Way Forward or Misplaced Optimism?* Canberra, ACT: Australian Institute of Criminology.

Morris, A. & G. M. Maxwell, 1993, "Juvenile Justice in New Zealand: A New Paradigm," *Australia & New Zealand Journal of Criminology* 26 March, 72–90. (New Zealand)

Montana Board of Crime Control, 1996, Request for Proposals. Helena, Montana.

Pennsylvania Council on Crime and Delinquency, 1996, Request for Proposals, Harrisburg, Pennsylvania.

Palindt, T, 1994, *The Re-Emergence of Correctional Intervention.* Beverly Hills: Sage.

Pepinsky, H.E. & R. Quinney, 1991, *Criminology as Peacemaking.* Bloomington: Indiana University Press.

Reiss, A., 1986, "Why Are Communities Important in Understanding Crime?" pps. 1–33 in *Communities and Crime,* A. J. Reiss and M. Tonry (eds.). Chicago: University of Chicago Press.

Regnery, A., 1985, "Getting Away with Murder: Why the Juvenile Justice System Needs an Overhaul," *Policy Review* 34:65–8.

Rosenberg, I., 1993, "Leaving Bad Enough Alone: A Response to the Juvenile Court Abolitionists," *Wisconsin Law Review,* 1993, 163–185.

Schneider, A., 1985, (ed.) *Guide to Juvenile Restitution.* Washington, DC: Office of Juvenile Justice and Delinquency Prevention.

Schneider, A., 1986, "Restitution and Recidivism Rates of Juvenile Offenders: Results From Four Experimental Studies," *Criminology,* 24 (3), 533–552.

Schneider, A., 1990, *Deterrence and Juvenile Crime: Results From a National Policy Experiment.* New York: Springer-Verlag.

Schwartz, I. M., 1992, "Public Attitudes Toward Juvenile Crime and Juvenile Justice: Implications for Public Policy," pp. 225–250 in I. Schwartz, *Juvenile Justice Policy.* Lexington, MA: Lexington Books.

Sparrow, M., M. Moore, & D. Kennedy, 1990, *Beyond 911.* New York: Basic Books.

Stuart, B., 1995a, "Circle Sentencing: Mediation and Consensus—Turning Swords into Ploughshares," unpublished paper. Territorial Court of the Yukon.

Stuart, B., 1995b, "Sentencing Circles: Making Real Differences," unpublished paper. Territorial Court of the Yukon.

Umbreit, M., 1994, *Victim Meets Offender. The Impact of Restorative Justice in Mediation.* New York: Criminal Justice Press.

Umbreit, M. and S. Stacy, 1996, "Family Group Conferencing Comes to the U.S.: A Comparison with Victim Offender Mediation," *Juvenile and Family Court Journal,* 29–39.

Van Ness, D., 1993, "Now Wine and Old Wineskins: Four Challenges of Restorative Justice," *Criminal Law Forum,* 4(2), 251–276.

Van Ness, D., D. Carlson, T. Crawford & R. Strong, 1989, *Restorative Justice Practice.* Monograph. Justice Fellowship, Washington, D.C.

Wachtel, T., 1995, "Family Group Conferencing: Restorative Justice in Practice," *Juvenile Justice Update* 1(4).

Walgrave, L., 1993, "Beyond Retribution and Rehabilitation: Restoration as the Dominant Paradigm in Judicial Interpretation in Juvenile Crime," paper presented at International Congress on Criminology, Budapest, Hungary.

Wilkins, L., 1995, *Punishment, Crime and Market Forces.* Brookfield, VT: Dartmouth Publishing Co.

Wright, M., 1991, *Justice for Victims and Offenders.* Buckingham, Open University.

Young, M., 1995, *Restorative Community Justice: A Call to Action.* Washington D.C.: Report for National Organization for Victim Assistance.

Zehr, H., 1990, *Changing Lenses: A New Focus for Crime and Justice.* Scottsdale, PA: Herald Press.

11

Teen Court
A Therapeutic Jurisprudence Perspective

Allison R. Schiff and David B. Wexler

Youths under 18 currently account for more than 16 percent of all arrests in this country.[1] Since 1989, referrals to Tucson, Arizona's juvenile court have increased by 53 percent;[2] in Raleigh, North Carolina, more than twice as many juveniles were transferred to adult superior court in 1994 as in 1993.[3] Such devastating statistics reveal the continued allure of drugs, guns, and fast money to the modern American teen. Since the typical offender embarks on his criminal career at age 14 and continues into his early 20s, early intervention is imperative.[4]

To combat this epidemic, teen courts offer an alternative to juvenile courts for teens who commit their first misdemeanors. These courts are intended to serve as effective intervention and prevention programs, with both social and economic objectives: to turn troubled kids around before they become hardened criminals and to reduce the number of criminals, imprisoned at costs approaching $50,000 a year each.[5] The original teen court, the model for more than 70 cities throughout the country, originated in 1983 in Odessa, Texas.[6] There are now approximately 30 courts in Texas and 150 nationwide.[7] While costs of the programs range from $30,000 a year in Odessa, Texas, to over $87,000 a year in Tucson, Arizona, these figures are still substantially less than the cost of processing the same youths through the juvenile court system.

Shiff, Allison R. and David B. Wexler. 1996. Teen Court: A Therapeutic Jurisprudence Perspective. *Criminal Law Bulletin*, 32 (4), 342–357.

Teen courts employ positive peer pressure in an attempt to divert these first-time offenders from becoming career criminals. Teen jurors demand a high level of responsibility from their peers; because jurors know the pressures teens face, they also know that these pressures can be resisted. Judge Pro Tem Karen S. Adam agrees that in Tucson's teen court, "[t]he kids tend to be harder on each other than adults would be. . . . They really want their peers to be held accountable."[8] This hands-on participation in the legal process can benefit teens by socializing them and aiding in the adaptation of appropriate behaviors.[9]

Teen courts have implemented these goals through a variety of formats. The two most common formats employed are: (1) the typical court format, with a teen prosecutor and a teen defense attorney presenting the case to a teen jury, and (2) the grand jury format, in which a teen presents his own case and is questioned by the jury, typically composed of six or twelve teens.[10] In either scenario the only adult present, besides the defendant's parent, is the volunteer judge facilitating the proceedings. A suggested variation, discussed later in this article, might build on these formats by providing a teen attorney to represent the victim.

Teen court's allure is that it teaches juveniles the consequences of breaking the law while keeping their records clear of criminal violations. To prevent abuse of the system, most teen courts are limited to first-time offenses that involve relatively mild transgressions. Typical referrals to the courts include misdemeanors such as vandalism, shoplifting, assault, disorderly conduct, graffiti, and possession and consumption of alcohol.

In addition to limiting participation to first-time offenders, most teen courts require that the offender first admit guilt and agree to accept the judgment. Sentences usually involve community service but may also require long essays, formal apologies to victims, restitution for damages, traffic survival school, after-school tutoring programs, self-esteem workshops, drug and alcohol counseling, and conflict mediation programs.

Tucson's teen court imposes three mandatory sentences on all offenders: a basic training class (a parent-child program that focuses on self-esteem, communication skills, and decision making); at least one jury duty service; and at least one letter of apology. The jury determines who receives such letters, but more than one letter is typically required as part of a sentence (i.e., shoplifting may require apology letters to both the store and the defendant's parents). An offender typically has sixty days to complete his sentence.[12] Once completed, the charges are expunged from his record.

The Process, the Participants, and Preliminary Results

Teen courts focus on changing future behavior of the primary player, the defendant. The teen jurors and the teen attorneys, however, are equally crucial to the teen court concept.

Defendants

An Illinois court illustrates the typical process for defendants who participate in teen courts: A youth who commits a crime is given the opportunity to attend teen court by the state's attorneys, police, probation, or school officials; the youth must admit guilt prior to attending teen court; the youth appears in front of teen jurors and lawyers with a parent/guardian; jurors hand down a sentence under the supervision of an adult judge; the defendant apologizes to the victim and serves his sentence; after completing the sentence, the youth returns to teen court as a juror; if the defendant rejects or fails to complete the sentence, the case reverts to juvenile court.[13]

Before the teen may participate in the teen court process, a parent must sign an agreement to comply with the rules (such as attendance at parenting classes and, for teens found in possession, attendance at drug and alcohol classes). If the parent fails to follow through with any aspect of the contract, the case is sent back to juvenile court.

Jurors

Juries are composed of both former defendants and teen volunteers, but no specific ratio between the two is required. Certain courts do, however, impose some restrictions. For example, one Los Angeles court requires that jurors not attend the same school as defendants or know the youth they are sentencing.[14]

Former defendants whose sentences include jury duty must select their trial dates at their exit interviews. The rest of the jury slots are then filled with volunteers. Prior to service, jurors must complete a training session, which includes a mock trial observation. Volunteers are attracted through the media, presentations at local schools.

Attorneys

Students participate in training sessions to become attorneys, learning the basic philosophies and duties of their roles. The judicial system's professionals who run these sessions emphasize the importance of fairness and confidentiality.[15] In addition to these overriding concepts, teens are advised as to practical matters: They are taught to project their voices, bring notebooks and pens, spend time preparing prior to court, and to maintain eye contact with the jurors. Practicing attorneys also assist teens in analyzing cases by helping identify aggravating and mitigating circumstances.

Results

While juvenile courts have been in operation for years, teen courts are asserted to be a more effective means of deterring and rehabilitating youths who commit minor crimes. Teen courts boast a long list of benefits over the current juvenile justice system for teens charged with minor offenses: They lighten the juvenile justice system's load, provide community service volunteers, process cases more quickly and cheaply, result in very low rates of recidivism, discourage juvenile delinquency, reduce street crime, and educate teens about the legal system.

Further, the passion exhibited by teens representing other teens cannot be duplicated by adults who have worked in the system for years. One of teen court's primary benefits is that participants take their work seriously; cases that might be overlooked in the regular court system are given thorough attention by teens. A teen lawyer remarked, "I take it very seriously. I pay attention to every single case because there's a kid's life at stake here."[16] The program coordinator added, "They do a lot of research, a lot of calling—school police, Highway Patrol, mothers, sisters, teachers and anybody else—to find out the true story."[17]

Statistics reveal that rates of recidivism from teen courts are impressively low: Las Vegas has not had a single repeat offender from a teen court participant;[18] a teen court in Gila County, Arizona, noted a drop in teen recidivism from 45 percent to 12 percent;[19] only 17 out of 107 defendants in Denver have re-offended, mostly involving minor violations;[20] only 3 percent of juveniles who appeared before teen court in Los Angeles County have been re-arrested;[21] and finally, 30 teen courts in Texas show a recidivism rate below 5 percent, versus the 30–50 percent rate in the state's juvenile courts.[22]

The Lens of Therapeutic Jurisprudence

Therapeutic jurisprudence is a discipline that looks at the therapeutic impact of the law on the various participants involved. This section proposes to use therapeutic jurisprudence to look at teen courts through a somewhat different lens. Legal rules, legal procedures, and the roles of legal actors constitute social forces that often produce therapeutic or antitherapeutic consequences; therapeutic jurisprudence challenges us to reduce antitherapeutic consequences, and to enhance therapeutic consequences, without subordinating due process and other justice values.[23] Examining teen court through a therapeutic jurisprudence lens may help us to analyze and further develop the use of this decision-making body.

In teen courts, the principal player targeted by the process is clearly the defendant. The jurors, teen attorneys, and victims are, however, also likely to be affected by the process.

Defendants and Defense Attorneys

Defendants who participate in teen courts may be influenced, and perhaps in part rehabilitated, by such peer review. Confronting defendants with a jury of their peers helps promote the acceptance of responsibility; this positive peer pressure seems to work. Fall River, Massachusetts City Council President Steven Camara explains, "When I was young . . . if an authority figure rendered a punishment, I always felt resentful. But when my peers caused me discomfort, I felt, 'What can I do to make them accept me?' As a teen, you want to be accepted by your group."[24]

Teen defendants seem more likely to take responsibility for their actions when they feel that the triers of fact understand them. Peer review in this forum provides defense attorneys with the unique opportunity to confront their clients with possible juror perceptions of the facts.[25] In addition, this socially aware jury is better able to question a teen's motives. Teen juror Claire Skipper, 16, of Saugus, California, commented that teen court has jurors who "can smell a lie . . . a teen-ager can sense when another teen-ager is lying . . . [t]hey know how real teens are."[26] Therefore, teen courts encourage defendants to put themselves in jurors' shoes, take responsibility for their actions, and understand how society views their crimes.

Teen courts engage in individualized sentencing, with rehabilitation as an important objective. Further, including jury duty in an offender's sentence helps emphasize the former offender's membership in law-abiding society, allowing him to view the system from the other side. Teen courts can therefore be effective in preventing the negative effects of a "delinquent" label from channeling a teen toward a criminal career;[27] sentences provide a two-way street, which allows offenders to turn back once they have repaid the community.

The role of the defense attorney may also be therapeutic for the defense attorneys themselves. In defending their peers, defense attorneys may gain a better understanding of some of the underlying reasons teens may be driven to crime. Many teen defense attorneys incorporate these underlying influences into their oral arguments as mitigating factors.[28] By illustrating the way society views offenders, this interaction may be therapeutic in "inoculating" the attorneys from their own future entanglement with the law and in rehabilitating former defendants who serve as defense attorneys. But the defendant/defense attorney interaction also poses potential problems. Teen defense attorneys may misconstrue their role as one in which they must re-characterize the crime to try to achieve the least possible sentence. A defense attorney's effort to minimize the offense, in an attempt to minimize the penalty, may impede a defendant's acceptance of responsibility.

When a defense attorney focuses solely on striving for the least possible sentence—by accepting a defendant's story at face value, by mischaracterizing the crime, or by portraying the defendant as the victim—this approach may conflict with the court's general goal of rehabilitating defendants (and of propelling the teen attorney along a responsible, law-abiding and law-respecting path). In seeking to minimize the defendant's sentence, defense attorneys may forego the opportunity to confront their clients with their crimes. Accepting a defendant's statements at face value, without further questioning, may add to the defendant's resistance and inhibit the courts' effectiveness in deterring future criminal behavior.[29] Mischaracterization is also a problem in the courts. One teen defense attorney instructed her client, "You have to look like a perfect angel," emphasizing the importance of appearing innocent, rather than taking responsibility for her actions.

A related problem results when defense attorneys characterize the perpetrators as victims, overemphasizing mitigating circumstances or a less-than-perfect home life. This coincides with the popular trend in today's society of shirking responsibility for one's actions by claiming to be a victim, rather than seeking out solutions to problems.[30]

One possible way to avoid the defendant's denial of responsibility is to begin the trial by having the judge and jury ask the defendant to reaffirm his admission of guilt. Such an admission, after all, is a prerequisite to participation in teen court. If the defendant refuses to take full responsibility for his actions in front of the jury, the case may then be sent back to juvenile court.

An additional way to avoid such antitherapeutic results is to modify the role of teen defense attorneys, changing the role of the attorneys to one of affirmatively proposing and justifying acceptable sentences. Having the defendant assist his attorney in proposing an appropriate sentence is an additional method of confronting the defendant with his acts and giving him a sense of voice in designing the appropriate penalty.

People regard the decision-making process as being fairer when they are allowed to participate. Thus, this modified role for attorneys, and for attorney-client interaction, should not only help the defendant take responsibility for his actions but should also provide him with a more positive view of the system as a whole.[31] Adherence to such sentences should then be heightened by the defendant's active involvement in designing and negotiating his or her own sentence.[32]

The Jury

Teens pass barbecue chips and Goobers around the table while debating the appropriate sentence for a defendant. Having teens as jurors in this setting brings both law-abiding and former law-breaking teens face-to-face with some of the toughest issues in the juvenile crime debate. How much punishment is appropriate for a teen? How can a teen be turned away from crime?

Participation as a teen juror may benefit both the court and the teen juror.

Teen juries, like adult juries, serve several important functions: (1) by placing the verdict in the hands of a group of impartial individuals, the jury system works to enhance accuracy in developing an appropriate sentence;[33] (2) by including community members who are independent of the formal judicial structure, the jury system legitimizes the process and strives to increase offender compliance;[34] and (3) by educating jurors, the jury system informs teens as to the inner-workings of the judicial system and enhances jurors' attitudes of the system's fairness.[35]

Just as allowing defendants input in proposing their own sentences should increase their satisfaction with and respect for the process, allowing teens to participate as jurors may also give them a greater sense of respect for the judicial system.[36] Granting impartial teens a "voice" in teen justice may then increase their perceived fairness of such a system and encourage them to obey the law in the future. The process may therefore operate to rehabilitate former defendants serving as jurors and may, at the same time, "inoculate" others on the jury from committing similar crimes.

Further, allowing teens to serve as jurors instills in them a sense of confidence. In an age when teens constantly feel criticized, positive statements from adults increase teens' self-respect and self-esteem. Teen courts provide positive attention adolescents need. Nik Stanworth, 17, of Santa Ana, California, enjoys serving on juries, explaining, "When you are up there you feel older, more mature."[37]

The courts' impact on teen jurors—by discouraging them from committing similar offenses and by educating them about the court system—may be substantial.[38] Educating teens about the legal system can be significant in legal socialization. Citizen's rights mean more to those who understand, experience, and appreciate the entitlement of such freedoms;[39] legal socialization theorists emphasize the impact of experiential variables over didactic instruction of legal concepts.[40] One such theorist has hypothesized that legal-socializing effects result from participation in legal decision making, especially if a conflict of ideas is involved and if constructs are linked to everyday decisions.[41] Teen courts can teach legal socialization in a practical and useful context. Therefore, teen courts can help teens to better understand their role as future legal decision makers and as law-abiding citizens.

Allowing juries to be composed of both teen volunteers and former defendants (serving as part of their sentences) poses potential problems; these former defendants may be excessively tough on new offenders.[42] However, having the opportunity to be tough on new offenders may, in turn, make teens tougher on themselves when confronted with future challenges. Although some courts require a unanimous verdict, the judge may determine the appropriate sentence if the teens are unable to come to an agreement.

While having such control over a peer's future may be positive in empowering teens, jurors often catch a slight case of megalomania. This suggests that, in addition to providing for a more defined composition of former defendants to volunteers, limits should be set on how many times a juror may be allowed to serve.[43]

Prosecuting Attorneys

The role of the prosecuting attorney, in emphasizing that teens should be held accountable for their actions regardless of a bad background or other extenuating circumstances, may be therapeutic for both the defendant and the attorney. One student prefers the role of the prosecuting attorney, stating, "I've learned a lot of respect for the system."[44]

The role may inoculate at-risk teen attorneys from committing the same crimes and may be particularly effective in rehabilitating former defendants who serve as prosecuting attorneys. Representing the state in such an area should make these participants more law-abiding and break through teens' possible inclination to minimize the effects of committing criminal acts.

The downside of the role of the prosecuting attorney is that teen attorneys often think they are required to mischaracterize defendants or their crimes. Such a perception may breed a sense of disrespect for the judicial system. It is in this role, especially, that the danger of courtroom dramatics may lead to defendant-badgering in a teen's effort to emulate his television counterparts.[45] To combat this, the importance of truthful representation and "doing justice" must be key points emphasized in legal training.[46]

Victims

Because teen courts are limited to minor crimes, the cases do not typically involve traumatized victims. Nonetheless, the courts currently involve victims in the process through the commonly used penalties of apologies and restitution to the victim. Such involvement is likely to help defendants and jurors develop empathy for crime victims, and it is likely to have a beneficial effect on victims' mental health.[47]

Victims' Rights and Empathy Training Through Law

Teen court coordinators might consider introducing into teen court some elements of the adult arena's growing victim rights movement. Such reforms basically fall into three areas: victim compensation, victim satisfaction, and victim impact.[48]

Victim compensation reforms are typically designed to provide victims restitution for their harm. This component has already been integrated into the courts by sentences involving monetary restitution and penalties aimed at compensating the harm caused by the defendant. Victim satisfaction reforms typically enable victims to be more comfortable in their interactions with the criminal justice system. Since victims of teen-court crimes are not typically traumatically affected by these misdemeanors, this component need not play as great a role in teen courts. Allowing the victims to participate in the process may nonetheless help victims by indicating to them that the criminal justice system takes care of their needs.

Victim impact reforms, those which allow victims to have a voice in criminal proceedings, can beneficially be introduced into teen courts. An example of such a reform would give victims the right to provide the court with victim impact statements. These statements could include victim testimony regarding the economic, psychological, or social effects the crime has had on the victim. The very preparation and presentation of such statements should be therapeutically beneficial for the victims: a substantial body of psychological research suggests that positive healing effects (in terms of mental and physical health) are derived from writing and speaking about negative emotional events.[49] The victim impact statement should, of course, then be used as a factor in the sentence imposed by the jurors. Moreover, by considering the crime from the vantage point of the victim, which would be part-and-parcel of proposing and setting an appropriate sentence, the defendant, the teen attorneys, and the teen jurors should all learn better to empathize with crime victims—and the conventional wisdom holds that empathy is a crucial component in law-abiding behavior.[50]

An important role for empathy training in teen courts is suggested by recent victim-empathy work relating to "relapse prevention" treatment.[51] William Pithers, a prison psychologist who developed a "perspective-taking" therapy in the context of working with child molesters, explains, "[E]mpathy with the victim shifts perception so that the denial of pain, even in one's fantasies, is difficult."[52] Teaching a former offender empathy for his victim helps combat his distorted thinking about his crime and its effect on the victim, motivating him to resist the temptation to repeat his crime.

The psychologist attempts to convey victim empathy through a variety of processes:

> The offenders read heart-wrenching accounts of crimes like their own, told from the victim's perspective. They also watch videotapes of victims tearfully telling what it was like to be molested. The offenders then write about their own offense from the victim's point of view, imagining what the victim felt. They read this account to a therapy group and try to answer questions about the assault from the victim's perspective. Finally, the offender goes through a simulated reenactment of the crime, this time playing the role of the victim.[53]

While some courts currently focus on developing victim empathy by use of mandatory apology letters and restitution tailored to the crime, we believe the emphasis on empathy can perhaps best be expanded by the appointment of a third teen attorney in the process—a *victim's* attorney. A teen attorney could represent the victim, help prepare a victim impact statement, brief the victim for testifying, or help prepare a videotaped interview and impact statement.

The role of victim's attorney could itself be particularly therapeutic for at-risk teens—and for former *defendants* (who, in addition to being sentenced to serve on a teen jury, might also be sentenced to serve as victim's attorney in the future). Serving in the real-life role of victim's attorney would force the teen to identify with the crime victim's perspective— seemingly accomplishing, through the operation of the legal system itself, something closely akin to the "perspective-taking" empathy therapy proposed by the prison psychologist. Since lack of empathy appears to be a major factor in the development of criminal behavior, the use of the legal system to teach empathy to youths may be a particularly fruitful enterprise—perhaps even more fruitful than teaching empathy to adult offenders who lack it.

Conclusion

The teen court concept is interesting and important. Although preliminary recidivism statistics must be read cautiously, teen court may well prove to be a highly therapeutic tool, especially if fine-tuned to increase victim participation and if honed to exploit its potential for teaching empathy.

In fact, the concept is so intriguing that jurisdictions ought to explore the possibility of increasing teen involvement—and extensive victim participation—in ordinary juvenile court. To be sure, teens could not be the principal participants or decision makers in such courts, but that does not prevent the use of teens (including former defendants participating as part of a sentence) as "advisory juries" on adjudication or disposition, or as legal assistants to attorneys representing the state, the defense, or victims.

The teen court model described here seems to share some important features with the Continental criminal justice system, where a decision-making body, composed of a judge and "lay assessors," actively interacts with and questions the defendant; where the defendant is encouraged to accept responsibility; where the victim, as well as the state and the defendant, is represented by an attorney; and where the sentencing structure permits the judge and lay assessors to impose a sentence geared at least in part toward rehabilitation.[54] As therapeutic jurisprudence increases its comparative law focus,[55] American scholars and reformers should explore other legal models and consider whether the rehabilitative yield of the legal system might be increased, without sacrificing justice-related objectives,[56] by importing certain features of other systems. (Indeed, such a comparative law focus may result also in other nations' considering the feasibility of modifying their own systems to incorporate certain features of American law, such as teen court.) In any event, perhaps we should think creatively about "rejuvenating" juvenile court instead of, as some are proposing, simply throwing in the towel and abolishing it.[57]

Notes

[1] CBS Evening News: Las Vegas Teen Crime Being Tried in Teen Courts (CBS television broadcast, Dec. 27, 1994).

[2] Edward L. Cook, "Volunteers Needed for Teen Court Work," Ariz. Daily Star, Jan. 1, 1995, at B2.

[3] Jaleh Hagigh, "Record Number of Juveniles Tried as Adults in '94," The News & Observer, Jan. 13, 1995, at B1.

[4] Roger Tatarian, "In This Court, Teens Truly Face Jury of Peers," Fresno Bee, Feb. 19, 1995, at B5.

[5] Tatarian, supra note 4.

[6] CBS This Morning: Recap of CBS This Morning's News (CBS television broadcast, Dec. 28, 1994).

[7] Carol Masciola, "Teen Courts Taking Off on Success in L.A.," Texas, The Orange County Register, June 1, 1995; Donnette Dunbar, "Kids Face Peers in Teen Court," The Omaha World-Herald 1, Mar. 18, 1996.

[8] Cook, supra note 2. Brent Trinacty, "Teen Court Convenes," Tucson Citizen, Jan. 28, 1995, at A1.

[9] Gary B. Melton, "Children as Legal Actors," in D. K. Kagehiro & W. S. Laufer, Handbook of Psychology and Law 275–291 (1992).

[10] Nancy Weil, "Teenagers' Court Does Justice to Education," St. Petersburg Times, Feb. 7, 1995, at 5. There are several variations on these models. In Fresno's teen court, the defendant presents his own case and the probation officer presents the state's. Peer jurors then question the defendant and his parents. Tartarian, supra note 4.

[11] Mary Doclar, "Teen Court Teaches Lessons Early," Ft. Worth Star-Telegram, Jan. 2, 1995, at 11.

[12] Failure to complete the sentence results in the case's referral back to the juvenile court system.

[13] 'Good' Peer Pressure Sought in Proceedings of Teen Court," State Journal Register (Springfield, IL), Jan. 23, 1995, at 18.

[14] Andrea Gerlin, "Teenage Defendants Get Juries of Their Peers," Wall St. J., June 3, 1994, at B1.

[15] Trinacty, supra note 8.

[16] CBS This Morning: Recap of CBS This Morning's News, supra note 6.

[17] Id.

[18] Id.

[19] Trinacty, supra note 8.

[20] David J. Chaffee, "Teen Court: Empowering Teens to Judge Teens," 22 Colo. Law. 2521 (1993).

[21] "Teen Court Getting Tough About Crime," Orange County Register, Dec. 27, 1994, at A16.

[22] Recidivism statistics touting teen courts must, however, be read with some caution. Teen courts do not get into hard-core cases where correction is less likely. Teen court is limited to defendants who have committed their first minor crimes; these defendants usually participate because they desire to clear their records. This self-selection may be a reason that teen courts have resulted in lower rates of recidivism. Therefore, it is not surprising that these teens who commit their first minor offenses are less likely than juvenile court defendants to re-offend in the future. Comparing rates of recidivism from the two courts may actually be comparing rates for conscientious juve-

niles committing their first-time misdemeanors with teens embarking on their criminal careers.

[23] David B. Wexler & Bruce J. Winick, Essays in Therapeutic Jurisprudence (Carolina Academic Press, 1991). David B. Wexler & Bruce J. Winick, "Therapeutic Jurisprudence as a New Approach to Mental Heath Law Policy Analysis and Research," 45 U. Miami L. Rev. 979, 981 (1991).

[24] Linda Borg, "Teen Court Program Proposed," Providence J. Bull., July 7, 1995, at DO1.

[25] If regularly employed by defense attorneys, this form of cognitive restructuring by confrontation may help to promote a defendant's acceptance of responsibility.

[26] Laurence Darmiento, "Teen Court to Start in Newhall," L.A. Daily News, July 31, 1995.

[27] Bruce J. Winick, "The Side Effects of Incompetency Labeling and the Implications for Mental Health Law," 1 Psychol., Pub. Pol'y & L. (1995); Chris Patterson, "Bay County Bar Forwards Teens Court as Juvenile Sanction Alternative," 69 Oct. Fla. BJ 95 (1995).

[28] In one case, while prosecutors claimed that a teen "should have known better than to succumb to peer pressure," defense attorneys responded that the teen is "a good student with no previous alcohol problems," and is both "ashamed and sorry for her actions." Carmen Duarte, "Teen Court Staff Tests Its Judgment, Meting Out Punishment to 'Defendant,'" Ariz. Daily Star, Jan. 22, 1995, at B1.

[29] David B. Wexler & Robert F. Schopp, "Therapeutic Jurisprudence: A New Approach to Mental Health Law," in D. K. Kagehiro & W. S. Laufer, Handbook of Psychology and Law 361–378 (1992).

[30] Martha Minow, "Surviving Victim Talk," 40 UCLA L. Rev. 1411 (1993).

[31] Tom R. Tyler, Why People Obey the Law (1990).

[32] David B. Wexler, "Therapeutic Jurisprudence and the Criminal Courts," 35 Wm. & Mary L. Rev. 279, 292 (1993). See also David B. Wexler, "Some Therapeutic Jurisprudence Implications of the Outpatient Civil Commitment of Pregnant Substance Abusers," Politics & Life Sci. 24 (Feb. 1996) (in press). Tom R. Tyler, "The Psychological Consequences of Judicial Procedures: Implications for Civil Commitment Hearings," 46 SMU L. Rev. 433 (1992).

[33] Glenn Newman, Note, "The Summary Jury Trial as a Method of Dispute Resolution in the Federal Courts," 1990 U. Ill. L. Rev. 177, 182 (1990).

[34] Herbert Jacob, Justice in America: Courts, Lawyers and the Judicial Process 125–136 (1978). Daniel W. Shuman, et al., "The Health Effects of Jury Service," 18 Law & Psychol. Rev. 267, 280 (1994).

[35] Daniel W. Shuman, et al., "Jury Service—It May Change Your Mind: Perceptions of Fairness of Jurors and Nonjurors," 46 SMU L. Rev. 449, 468 (1992).

[36] Tyler, supra note 31.

[37] Leslie Berkman, "A Jury of Their Peers," L.A. Times, June 1, 1995, at 1.

[38] Jury service promotes positive behavior by allowing teens to understand how society views the perpetrators of crime. Orange County, California Superior Court Judge James P. Gray expressed that, "We know full well some of the jurors have probably done the same things as the perpetrator, so we are showing them as well that it isn't appropriate." Berkman, supra note 37.

[39] Gary B. Melton, "The Significance of Law in the Everyday Lives of Children and Families," 22 Ga. L. Rev. 851, 889–890 (1988).

[40] Melton, supra note 9 at 285.

[41] Melton, supra note 9 at 286.

[42] To avoid this possibility, any sentence must be approved by the judge overseeing the proceedings.

[43] For instance, volunteers might be permitted to serve once, former defendants, twice. If teens desire future involvement in the courts, these veteran jurors could serve as victims' attorneys in the proposed structure, discussed later, which includes representation of victims.

[44] Angel Hernandez, "The Young Arm of the Law," Rocky Mtn. News, Dec. 28, 1994, at A30.

[45] One teen stated that, "We have to bring out the worst in them, as terrible as it seems." Another teen added, "We are supposed to make them look like a loathsome criminal." Doclar, supra note 11.

[46] See Brady v. Maryland, 373 US 83 (1963).

[47] See Richard P. Wiebe, The Mental Health Implications of Crime Victims' Rights, in Law, Mental Health, and Mental Disorder 414 (B. Sales & D. Shuman, eds.) (1996). For more on apology, see Bruce Feldthusen, "The Civil Action for Sexual Battery: Therapeutic Jurisprudence?" 25 Ottawa L. Rev. 203 (1993). Daniel W. Shuman, "The Psychology of Compensation in Tort Law," 43 U. Kansas L. Rev. 39 (1994).

[48] See Wiebe, supra note 47.

[49] James W. Pennebaker, Opening Up: The Healing Power of Confiding in Others (1990).

[50] In addition to impact statements, other ways to incorporate this empathy component are to: (1) videotape all victims affected by the defendant's behavior, play these videotapes for the court, and have the defendant's letter of apology include a summary of the crime from the victim's perspective; (2) have victims testify as part of the trial and ask the defendant to address this testimony in his letter of apology; (3) have the victim testify and the defendant explain how and why a crime was committed, along with the defendant's apology; and (4) have defendants examine the list of possible sentences and suggest and justify an appropriate sentence for the crime.

For more on empathy, and on its relation to relapse prevention in sex offenders, see W. L. Marshall, "Assessment, Treatment, and Theorizing About Sex Offenders: Developments During the Past Twenty Years and Further Directions," 23 Crim. Just. & Behav. 162, 173–174, 183, 185–186 (1996). Much more work needs to be performed on the development of empathy in adolescents and on its role in turning teens away from delinquent behavior. For a recent review of the rehabilitation literature in general, see Paul Gendreau, "Offender Rehabilitation: What We Know and What Needs to be Done," 23 Crim. Just. & Behav. 144 (1996).

[51] Daniel Goleman, "Therapies Offer Hope for Sex Offenders," NY Times, Apr. 14, 1992, at C1. Used with child molesters, such treatment has proved promising, resulting in half as many of its participants reoffending when compared with those not treated with empathy therapy.

[52] Daniel Goleman, Emotional Intelligence 107 (1995).

[53] Id.

[54] Myron Moskovitz, "The O.J. Inquisition: A United States Encounter with Continental Criminal Justice," 28 Vand. J. Transnational L. 973 (1995).

[55] E.g. , David Carson, "Therapeutic Jurisprudence for the United Kingdom?" 6 J. Forensic Psychiatry 463 (1995).

[56] David B. Wexler, "Justice, Mental Health, and Therapeutic Jurisprudence," 40 Cleveland State L. Rev. 517 (1992). See generally "Symposium: Comparative Criminal Justice Issues in the United States, West Germany, England, and France," 42 Maryland L. Rev. 1 (1983). For a summary of the empirical research regarding accuracy and perceived fairness in adversary, inquisitorial, and hybrid decision-making methods, see Mark R. Fondacaro, "Toward a Synthesis of Law and Social Science: Due Process and Procedural Justice in the Context of National Health Care Reform," 72 Denver Univ. L. Rev. 303, 325–337 (1995). American behavioral science, as well as American law, needs to transcend its national boundaries. See Gendreau, supra note 50, at 152 ("More blatant examples of ethnocentrism are the fact that American reviews on treatment effectiveness almost never reference the literature from foreign countries where different approaches to the 'crime problem' exist (e.g., less incarceration).").

[57] See Martha Minow, "What Ever Happened to Children's Rights?" 80 Minn. L. Rev. 267, 291 & n. 138 (1995).

Section IV

The Juvenile in Confinement

The incarceration of juvenile offenders is a difficult issue. While it is important to protect society from some offenders, for juveniles the decision to incarcerate has serious long-term implications, because most incarcerated juveniles will eventually be released into the community. The nature of their confinement may have a major impact on their ability to re-enter society without further criminal offending. Thus, decisions about who is incarcerated, the conditions of their confinement, and the availability of treatment are of importance both to the offender and to society as a whole.

Many juvenile facilities are facing serious shortages of space, and even when space is available it is often physically distant from family or friends who might provide emotional support to the juvenile—further weakening his or her ties to the community. In their search for creative, affordable solutions to this problem, some jurisdictions have utilized a policy of house arrest. Richard Ball, C. Ronald Huff and J. Robert Lilly discuss these issues in "House Arrest and Juvenile Justice." They describe the use of house arrest, the conditions of house arrest, and the process by which young people are chosen for the house arrest alternative. Finally, they discuss the problem of deciding what constitutes a successful house arrest program. They conclude that while some house arrest programs do seem more effective than others, the reasons for this success are not clear. While research on the topic continues, it seems likely that the use of house arrest will continue as long as the system is strapped for resources.

Although house arrest is an attractive option in many jurisdictions, there are still a large number of juveniles held in detention centers. These facilities raise issues about the special needs of juveniles and the corresponding programs required to meet those needs. David W. Roush considers these issues in "Juvenile Detention Programming" and makes it clear that good programming in juvenile detention centers must meet a variety of needs and requires considerable planning. Roush suggests that good programming is not only the humanitarian thing to do, but that it has many practical advantages for the juvenile.

In the last article in this section, "Incarcerated Juvenile Offenders: Integrating Trauma-Oriented Treatment with State-of-the-Art Delinquency Interventions," Evvie Becker and Annette U. Rickel argue that many institutionalized juvenile offenders have a long history of exposure to violence and trauma. These early experiences may not only explain some of their offending behavior, but also must be taken into account as part of any treatment program for these offenders. The authors argue that much of what has been learned about treating people with traumatic life experiences can be applied to treating violent juvenile offenders. In particular, they emphasize the importance of treatment interventions occurring at multiple levels, including the family, the school, and the community.

12

House Arrest and Juvenile Justice

Richard A. Ball, C. Ronald Huff
and J. Robert Lilly

Placing juveniles on house arrest, as an alternative to the use of secure detention facilities, has evolved in response to concerns about (1) the harmful effects of confining juveniles in adult jails, (2) the dysfunctional aspects of isolating youths from their families and from the communities in which they live, (3) the overcrowding that exists in many adult jails and juvenile detention centers, and (4) the absence of suitable facilities in many areas of the nation. The history of juvenile justice in America is filled with policy debates—even social movements— concerning the confinement of juveniles in jails and other secure detention facilities. The preadjudicatory detention of juveniles in a secure facility, analogous to holding an adult in jail prior to trial, has been the subject of numerous task forces and commissions, which have concluded that tight restrictions should be placed on juvenile detention practices.

Jailing Juveniles: A Suicidal Policy?

The most severely criticized practice has been the use of adult jails to detain youths. A federal initiative to reduce this practice has won support, not only from child advocates, but from the National Association of Counties, the National League

of Cities, and the National Sheriffs Association, among others (Rubin, 1985: 128).
In addition to being concerned about the welfare of children locked up in such
jails, these professional associations are also keenly aware of the problems involved
in jailing juveniles — including inefficient use of jail space and the expanded
personal liability they may face if a juvenile is victimized or commits suicide while
in jail.

Nonetheless, approximately 500,000 youths are held in adult jails each year,
about 60 of whom die before leaving jail (Rubin, 1985: 128). A recent national
study found that the suicide rate for juveniles in adult jails is nearly five times
greater than it is for juveniles in the general population, and nearly eight times
greater than it is for juveniles held in separate juvenile detention centers (Community Research Center, 1980). This high suicide rate is a good illustration of
how a well-intentioned policy can have unintended consequences. Federal policy
mandating the separation of juveniles from adults "by sight and by sound" was
intended to eliminate the assaults, rapes, and other abuses that had occurred as
a result of the "commingling" of adults and juveniles in confinement. However,
as is so often the case, the implementation of such policy reform often presents
its own set of problems.

One of the authors has visited many adult jails, built in the late 1800s, where
compliance with this federal policy means that when a juvenile is being held, he
or she will be placed either in the basement of the jail or its top floor. This isolation,
intended to separate and protect the youth from older, perhaps more "hardened,"
inmates, also makes it almost impossible to supervise these isolated youths in
understaffed jails.[1] Since youths held in jail following their arrest may be filled
with feelings of guilt, remorse, or even self-hatred, it is not difficult to appreciate
why the risk of suicide is dramatically elevated. The isolated location of these
youths within the jail precludes both effective supervision and any meaningful
opportunity to discuss their problems. Also, such facilities typically offer little
or no programming for either youths or adult inmates. For example, when asked
what the juveniles do for recreation, a jailer told one of the authors, "Oh, we
take them out to the [country] fairgrounds and let 'em run once in awhile" (Huff,
1980).

The Deinstitutionalization Movement

Although many areas of the nation still do not have separate detention facilities
for juveniles (and many of those that *do* exist are inadequate), the focus of more
recent reformers has shifted to advocacy for community-based *alternatives* to
detention centers and jails. In the juvenile justice arena, this movement gained
considerable momentum as a result of two pieces of federal legislation — the
Omnibus Crime Control and Safe Streets Act of 1968[2] and the Juvenile Justice
and Delinquency Prevention Act of 1974[3] (as amended in 1977) — both of which
mandated the deinstitutionalization of status offenders. This means, in effect, that

youths who are charged with, or who are found to have committed, "offenses" that would not be illegal acts if committed by an adult, shall not be confined in a secure detention or correctional facility (except, under certain conditions, for a period not to exceed 24 hours, or for having violated a valid court order).

The rationale for community-based alternatives to institutional confinement has at least some of its roots in a theoretical perspective commonly known as "labeling theory,"[4] which holds that the juvenile and adult justice systems, especially their correctional facilities, are themselves "criminogenic," or cause additional criminality and delinquency, by treating their "clients" as abnormal. According to this perspective, the stigma associated with these systems "marks" an individual in our society, thus reducing his or her chances of being accepted and leading a normal, noncriminal life.

Although the general validity of the labeling perspective has not been effectively demonstrated, it has great intuitive appeal and "face validity." Furthermore, the implications of labeling theory overlap significantly with the emphasis of those promoting the development of a "least restrictive alternatives" policy in the administration of juvenile justice. From the latter point of view, the least restrictive alternative should be used in each case, and secure detention should be reserved almost exclusively for those charged with or convicted of serious crimes, especially crimes against persons.

Consider, for example, the juvenile detention policy guidelines advocated by a joint task force of the Institute of Judicial Administration and the American Bar Association. Detention, the task force said in Standard 6.6, should be limited to juveniles who are fugitives from justice or who are charged with violent felonies where commitment to a secure institution is likely if the offense is proven, and where one of the following additional factors is present:

(1) the crime charged is a class one juvenile offense;

(2) the juvenile is an escape from an institution or other placement facility where he was sentenced following adjudication for criminal conduct; or

(3) there is a recent record of willful failure to appear at juvenile proceedings, and no measure short of detention will reasonably ensure his appearance at court (Institute for Judicial Administration—American Bar Association, 1980).

These IJA-ABA *Standards*, as well as those promulgated by the National Advisory Committee for Juvenile Justice and Delinquency Prevention (1980), reflect a "least restrictive alternatives" policy preference, developed in response to the over-crowding, neglect, and abuse in many of the nation's detention facilities and jails.

House Arrest: The Least Restrictive Alternative?

Just a few years after the catalytic Omnibus Crime Control Act of 1968, the nation's first house arrest program for juveniles was implemented in St. Louis.

Since that beginning, in 1971, many additional programs — known variously as house arrest, home detention, or home supervision — have evolved, and most have been patterned after the programmatic model developed in St. Louis.

How do these programs work? Who staffs them? How are they structured? What are the major goals of these programs? What policy issues do they address? How successful are they? What does *success* really mean? What is their comparative cost? Who is referred to them and what criteria do they use to screen potential candidates for house arrests? Do they threaten public safety by keeping in the community juveniles who belong behind bars? Do they represent a true alternative to secure detention or do they merely expand the "net" of social control by focusing on youths who normally would have been placed on regular probation with less intensive supervision? All of these questions, and others, must be addressed if we are to make responsible policy choices in the controversial area of juvenile correction. Fortunately, some valuable descriptive and evaluative information on such programs is available (see, for example, Keve and Zanick, 1972; Young and Pappenfort, 1977; Swank, 1979; Rubin, 1979, 1985). In the remainder of this chapter, we shall review what is known about house arrest programs for juveniles in the United States.

How do These Programs Operate and What are the Rules?

In Jefferson County (Louisville), Kentucky, house arrest is imposed on the youth and his or her parents or guardian. The probation officer is expected to discuss with the youth and family all conditions imposed by the court prior to their leaving court, to ensure that the youth and family have a contact at the agency 24 hours a day, and to check for compliance, "If the probation officer suspects for any reason that these conditions are not being adhered to" and "to inform the Court of any noncompliance" (Jefferson County Juvenile Probation Services, 1983).

The court order imposing house arrest specifies the conditions and exceptions concerning the youth's activities during the house arrest sanction, and makes clear that the youth is considered to be in detention status, just as if he or she were detained in the Youth Center, and that any violation of the order will result in a return to the Youth Center. The parents or guardian are expected to enforce the rules of house arrest; if they fail to do so and fail to notify the court concerning violations, they may be prosecuted for contempt of court or for contributing to the delinquency of a minor (Jefferson County Juvenile Probation Services, 1983).

The Jefferson County Juvenile Court may also impose home supervision, if a juvenile and his or her family are thought to be in need of additional support services during the adjudicatory process. Workers supervising youths placed in home supervision status have a maximum caseload of five and are expected to (1) execute a contract with the youth and the parent or guardian prior to their leaving court, (2) have at least one face-to-face *and* one telephone contact with the youth, and (3) have at least one face-to-face *or* one telephone contact with the parent or guardian each week. These contacts are intended to enable staff to identify problems, monitor the youth's adjustment, and provide needed services. If a youth violates the provisions of the agreement, a conference is held to determine whether to return the youth to court for noncompliance.

According to Swank (1979), the San Diego Home Supervision Program began in 1976 with a grant from the State Office of Criminal Justice Planning to the San Diego County Probation Department. Prior to the implementation of this program, whenever Juvenile Hall was overcrowded, minors had been released at detention hearings under house arrest and advised to stay at home until their next hearing. There was one major problem with this arrangement: The youths were not monitored to see if they were complying with the court's order. This situation changed dramatically on March 14, 1977, when the first two juveniles were referred to the Home Supervision Program, which assured judges that youths referred to the Program would either stay at home as required or be taken into custody.

Despite the warnings given to these first two youths, less than a week passed before one of them was arrested for smoking dope in his bedroom with his buddies. While being returned to Juvenile Hall, the youth reportedly commented, "I didn't think you'd be coming. I've never seen a probation officer so much" (Swank, 1979: 50). The staff was apprehensive that this initial program failure might cause the referring judge to lose confidence in the program. Actually, just the reverse occurred. The judge was impressed that the probation officers were enforcing the court's orders. That incident stimulated judicial confidence in the program's accountability and helped fuel its subsequent growth.

Rapid growth of these programs can, in fact, present significant problems, and the San Diego program is a good example. Consider the fact that San Diego County is approximately the size of the State of Connecticut. Then contemplate the fact that in the early days of the program, two probation officers were responsible for supervising youths throughout the County and that officers often carried caseloads of 30 or so at any one time (Swank, 1979)! Nonetheless, with the assistance of volunteers, the program was able to provide random monitoring 24 hours a day and 7 days a week.

On January 1, 1977, the Dixon Bill,[5] having been enacted by the California Assembly, officially became law. This law encouraged increased community treatment and the separation of status offenders from delinquents. It also required that all counties operate home supervision programs as one type of community alternative to the use of detention facilities. Further, the California Welfare and Institutions Code (Section 628.1) required the probation officer to release a minor from the detention center and place him or her on home supervision if the probation officer "believes 24-hour secure detention is not necessary in order to protect the minor or the person or property of another, or to ensure that the minor does not flee the jurisdiction of the court" (San Diego County Probation Department, 1986). Two goals are mandated for such home supervision programs in California: (1) to assure appearance at interviews and court hearings and (2) to assure that the

the minor obeys the conditions of release and commits no offenses pending disposition of the case.

Workers' salaries are essentially subsidized by the state and caseloads may not exceed 10. When possible, supervising officers are assigned to monitor youths in the same geographic area in which the officers reside. San Diego County's commitments, in return for these funds, are: (1) to maintain at least 80% of the minors in the community without returning them to custody, (2) to personally contact each minor at least once a day, and (3) to provide supervision for at least 800 minors who would otherwise be detained. Minors who do not comply with the terms of home supervision may be arrested by probation officers and returned to juvenile court for review and possible placement in secure detention.

All seven of the early house arrest programs evaluated by Young and Pappenfort (1977) were administered by juvenile court probation departments. In general, these programs were staffed by paraprofessionals known as "outreach workers," "community youth leaders," or "community release counselors." Each staff member typically had a caseload of five youths at any one time. All seven programs expected their youth workers to exercise daily supervision and to keep their charges "trouble free and available to the court" for their hearings.

Surveillance in these programs was accomplished primarily by daily personal contacts (at least one per day) with each youth, and daily telephone or personal contacts with the youths' parents, teachers, and (where applicable) employers. The youth workers who staffed these programs typically worked out of their automobiles and their own homes rather than at probation offices or court facilities. There was an effort to keep paperwork requirements to a minimum so the youth workers would have more time to be actively engaged in the supervision of their assigned cases. In fact, travel vouchers and handwritten daily activity logs often constituted the only significant paperwork required of these workers.

The youths placed in such programs typically had the program's rules of participation explained to them in the presence of their parents. These rules usually included:

(1) attending school;

(2) observing a specified curfew;

(3) notifying parents or work as to whereabouts at all times when not at home, school, or work;

(4) abstaining from drugs; and

(5) avoiding companions or places that "might lead to trouble."

In addition to these general guidelines, additional rules or conditions could usually be added as agreed upon by the parties involved. Written contracts setting forth these conditions were frequently used in these programs.

All seven programs were based on the rationale that close supervision would generally keep juveniles "trouble free and available to the court." Six of the seven programs also rested on another assumption: that this type of program would enable youth workers to provide needed services to youths and their families, thus increasing the probability of success. Some programs emphasized counseling and services more than others did, however, even going so far as to expect youth workers to try to achieve a "big brother" type of relationship with each youth supervised, sometimes combined with advocacy and involvement with the youths' parents. Youth workers in three of the seven programs organized weekly recreational or cultural activities for all youths placed in their respective programs.

Youth workers in these programs often coordinated their efforts to provide better services (for example, one worker "covering" or taking responsibility for another when necessary). In all seven programs, youths who did not adhere fully to program requirements could be taken to secure detention by program youth workers.

Who is Referred to House Arrest Programs and What Screening Criteria are Used?

It is interesting that not one of the seven programs evaluated by Young and Pappenfort (1977) was designed exclusively for status offenders. Two programs accepted only alleged delinquents, while the other five included both alleged delinquents and status offenders. Most (5) of the programs served 200-300 youths per year, while the other two accepted just over 1,000 youths in the fiscal year preceding the evaluation.

A recent study by one of the authors found that in the State of Ohio, juvenile court judges responding to a statewide survey reported that they consider three factors to be the most important in screening candidates for house arrest:

(1) the seriousness of the alleged offense;

(2) the youth's previous record; and

(3) the home environment.

A second "cluster" of factors, though less important, are also taken into consideration. These factors include protection of the child, protection of others, population or crowding in the detention facility, school adjustment, and time of day when the alleged offense occurred. Judges reported that the recommendations of court staff, especially probation officers, are very important in the decision to use house arrest (Huff, 1986).

In the seven programs assessed by Young and Pappenfort (1977), burglary was the most frequent delinquency charge filed against program participants. When charges filed against program participants were compared with those filed against youths in secure detention facilities, the two populations were similar, except for homicide, aggravated assault, and rape (relatively infrequent and rarely released to such alternative programs). Most delinquency charges filed against program participants were judged to be moderately serious.

What Does *Success* Mean in Such Programs and How Successful are They?

In attempting to assess program success, the key question is one of definition. What constitutes success? Should one consider it a success if a youth, while in home detention status, is not charged with any new *offenses* prior to adjudication? Or does success require that he or she complete the period of home detention without any violations of the home detention agreement? Or without having been returned to secure detention? Bear in mind that even if a youth violates the rules and is returned to secure detention, he or she is still available to the court, just as would have been the case had the youth been in the detention center the entire time. This question is somewhat similar to the distinction made between parole revocation for an alleged criminal *offense* versus revocation for a *technical violation* of parole conditions.

Depending on one's operational definition of success, the data reported by Young and Pappenfort (1977) indicate that home detention programs' "success rates" ranged from 71% to 98%. That is, if one defines success as having completed home detention *without incident* (the most restrictive possible definition of success), Young and Pappenfort's data indicate that the *least* successful programs in their sample were 71% successful. If, on the other hand, one adopts a more liberal definition of success (having completed home detention without any new alleged offenses), the *best* programs they evaluated attained a success rate of 98%. In addition, the San Diego program reports that it monitored 910 minors in Fiscal Year 1984 and had a "97%+" success rate (San Diego County Probation Department, 1986).

In all seven of the programs selected for Young and Pappenfort's (1977) national evaluation, the percentages of youths returned to secure detention for rules violations exceeded those returned for either alleged new offenses or for running away. This suggests that the quality of supervision in these programs was quite high. Also, because all of the youths returned to secure detention for rules violations did subsequently appear in court, one might argue that the preventive measures of returning them to detention should be viewed as a success (it may have prevented serious delinquency and the youth was still available to the court), rather than as a program failure. Indeed, return to secure detention is a planned option in all such programs.

It is noteworthy that those programs, designed exclusively for alleged delinquents, were as effective as those that accepted status offenders as well as delinquents (Young and Pappenfort, 1977), underscoring once more the fact that "offense categories" are often a poor proxy, for either past behavior or future risk. Indeed, the researchers concluded that additional youths could have been handled in home detention programs and other alternative programs, and that some courts were "unnecessarily timid" in referring youths to such programs (Young and Pappenfort, 1977: 31).

A recent Ohio study found that a sample of 2,708 youths released on house arrest in 1984, a total of 2,470, or 91%, successfully complied with the conditions imposed upon them during the period of conditional release and subsequently appeared for adjudication. In this study, technical violations again accounted for far more "failures" than did new allegations of offenses (Huff, 1986). Furthermore, 85% of the juvenile courts responding to the survey indicated that their experience with house arrest was either "good" or "very good," with none rating the results worse than "fair" (Huff, 1986).

Of course, not all youths placed on house arrest succeed. One who did not is described in an anecdote involving one of the most memorable (and humorous) apprehensions in the history of house arrest programs:

> A home supervision officer was chasing a violator who scaled a wall. When the officer also went over the wall, he realized he had stumbled into a nude swimming party. The quick thinking youth apparently shed his clothes and disguised himself as one of the guests. He was apprehended the following day (fully clothed and grinning ear-to-ear) [Swank, 1979: 51].

What is the Comparative Cost of these Programs?

According to Keve and Zanick (1972), the cost per child per day in the original (St. Louis) home detention program was $4.85, compared to $17.54 per child per day in the juvenile detention center. This approximate one-to-four cost advantage also characterized another early home detention program begun in Louisville, Kentucky, in 1975 (Rubin, 1979: 101). Huff's (1986) Ohio study of house arrest indicated that secure detention costs averaged $42.57 per day; nonsecure detention and other nonsecure placements cost an average of $280.07 per day; and that house arrest was the least expensive of these three categories at just $14.94 per day (about one-third the cost of secure detention).

Conclusion

In this chapter, we have considered the nature and evolution of house arrest programs for juveniles in the context of historical reform movements and the policy debates surrounding juvenile detention. The smoke from these fiery debates over what to do with "juvenile delinquents" has not yet cleared, with articulate proponents of "locking them up" squaring off against equally eloquent adversaries favoring policies that promote the use of "the least restrictive alternatives" and "community based corrections."

We have also presented an overview of what is known about house arrest programs nationally, based on available research findings. The corpus of this research, while encouraging the proponents of house arrest as a viable alternative to secure detention, leaves unanswered many questions that must be resolved if we are to develop sound public policy. Like much of the program evaluation literature, what we have reviewed tends to concentrate on *aggregate* findings and general descriptions. We are left with a blurry picture of generally successful programs, but we don't come away knowing *why* they work, fail to work, or work for some and not others. Very little of what has been published helps us understand the *differential* effects of these programs on different subgroups of participants, the political contexts in which house arrest programs operate, the views of the judiciary who refer youths and the workers who supervise them, and other important matters.

Editor's Note: Many of the issues raised in the conclusion of this chapter are subsequently addressed in the larger work from which this chapter was drawn.

Footnotes

[1] Such jails, many of them in rural counties, typically have neither sufficient staffing nor the equipment required for effective electronic monitoring inside the jail.
[2] Omnibus Crime Control and Safe Streets Act of 1968, Public Law No. 90-351, 82 Stat. 204 (codified as amended at 42 U.S.C. Section 3701, *et seq.*).
[3] Juvenile Justice and Delinquency Prevention Act of 1974, Public Law No. 93-415, 88 Stat. 1109 (1974).
[4] Although typically referred to as "labeling theory," this is really a theoretical *perspective*, rather than a systematic theory, since it does not incorporate any explanation of the subject's illegal behavior *prior* to his or her involvement in the justice system (the behavior that led to the arrest). If "labeling effects" explain subsequent law violations, what explains the original law violations? Labeling "theory" is essentially silent on this point.
[5] California Assembly Bill 3121, effective January 1, 1977.

References

American Bar Association/Institute of Judicial Administration Standards. 1980. New York: American Bar Association.
Community Research Center. 1980. An Assessment of the National Incidence of Juvenile Suicide in Adult Jails, Lockups, and Juvenile Detention Centers. Champaign, IL: Community Research Center.
Huff, C. Ronald. 1980. Field notes (interview in a rural jail), July.
Huff, C. Ronald. 1986. "Home detention as a policy alternative for Ohio's juvenile courts: A final report to the governor's office of criminal justice services." (unpublished)
Jefferson County, Kentucky. 1983. Juvenile Probation Services Policy and Procedures Manual, Sections 803.11 and 803.12.
Keve, Paul C. and Casimir S. Zanick. 1972. Final Report and Evaluation of the Home Detention Program, St. Louis, Missouri, September 30 (1971) to July 1 (1972). McLean, VA: Research Analysis Corp.
National Advisory Committee for Juvenile Justice and Delinquency Prevention Standards for the Administration of Juvenile Justice. 1980. Washington, DC: Government Printing Office.
Rubin, H. Ted. 1985. Juvenile Justice: Policy, Practice, and Law (2nd ed.). New York: Random House.
Rubin, H. Ted. 1979. Juvenile Justice: Policy, Practice, and Law. Santa Monica, CA: Goodyear.
San Diego County, California Probation Department. 1986. Personal correspondence (February).
Swank, William G. 1979. "Home supervision: Probation really works." *Federal Probation* (December): 50-52.
Young, Thomas M. and Donnell M. Pappenfort. 1977. Secure detention of juveniles and alternatives to its use. National Evaluation Program, Summary Report, Phase I. National Institute of Law Enforcement and Criminal Justice, LEAA. Washington, DC: Government Printing Office.

13

Juvenile Detention Programming

David W. Roush

Introduction

Juvenile detention is an often overlooked, often maligned, and often misunderstood component of the juvenile justice system. However, current juvenile justice policy issues are bringing increased attention to juvenile detention (Schwartz, 1992). Detention is seen as an important component of various reform strategies, even though many practitioners have mixed reactions to the national limelight. While any attention to the concerns of juvenile detention is significant to the overall improvement of the profession, juvenile justice policy analysts also identify, reveal, scrutinize, and condemn many of the shortcomings and negative aspects of detention with little regard for the origin of the problems or constructive solutions (Frazier, 1989). Practitioners are quick to acknowledge the inadequacies of juvenile detention, but the intensity of the criticisms levied by reformers frequently generates defensive responses by practitioners, aggravated by the commonplace absence of any practitioner input into the understanding of detention by the majority of policy analysts. . . .

The problems associated with juvenile detention and the old policy research and reform efforts are twofold. In addition to the lack of constructive ideas about

From *Federal Probation*, Vol. 57, no. 3 (September), pp. 20-33.

This article is based on an earlier work by the author which was funded by a grant from the Probation Training Division of the Center for Legal Studies at Sangamon State University, Springfield, Illlinois.

how to remediate the problems of detention, the traditions of knowledge about detention were also overlooked in policy efforts and foundation projects. . . . This article represents one attempt to organize detention knowledge around one important topic and to find an appropriate form of dissemination so that future policy and reform efforts will be fully able to consider the traditions contained herein.

Detention Programming

A critical issue in successful detention is programming. The principles of effective programming were first discussed by Healey and Bronner (1926) and Warner (1933), but the emergence of a body of programming knowledge is associated with Sherwood Norman (1961). As a former detention practitioner and as the juvenile detention consultant to the National Council on Crime and Delinquency (NCCD), Norman conducted a national study of juvenile detention centers in 1946 and elaborated the tradition of helpful programs as derived from his national assessment of effective detention practices. The culmination of his works in the NCCD *Standards and Guides to the Detention of Children and Youth*, published in 1958 and updated for a second edition in 1961. Other works have superseded it regarding contemporary issues and current perspectives on institutional management, standards compliance, and liability, but even after three decades, it remains the seminal piece for understanding juvenile detention, having generated a series of works that explore and expand the helpful programs concept.

The approach taken in this review of daily programming is based on the perspectives of a wide range of practitioners. Specifically, discussions about daily programming are built upon the essential program elements outlined in the ACA *Standards for Juvenile Detention Facilities* (2nd edition) and elaborated by recent efforts of the ACA Juvenile Detention Committee (Smith, Roush, & Kelley, 1990). . . .

Definitions

Jurvenile Detention

There are numerous definitions of juvenile detention, but until recently no single definition had achieved consensus. Without such a definition, juvenile detention had become all things to all segments of the juvenile justice system (Hammergren, 1984). On October 31, 1989, the board of directors of NJDA (National Juvenile Detention Association) unanimously adopted the following definition of juvenile detention:

> Juvenile detention is the temporary and safe custody of juveniles who are accused of conduct subject to the jurisdiction of the court who require a restricted environment for their own or the community's protection while pending legal action.

Further, juvenile detention provides a wide range of helpful services that support the juvenile's physical, emotional, and social development.

Helpful services minimally include: education; visitation; communication; counseling; continuous supervision; medical and health care services; nutrition; recreation, and reading.

Juvenile detention includes or provides for a system of clinical observation and assessment that complements the helpful services and reports findings.

. . .

Programming

There are two constructs that guide our understanding of detention programs. First, a clear definition is needed of the word "program," and second, the process of programming requires some further explanation.

Program represents a plan or procedure for dealing with something. As described above, a program would be required to implement each of the nine helpful services identified in the NJDA definition of a juvenile detention. . . . Each plan would define the range of services offered and would contain a logical sequence of the operations to be performed as spelled out in policies and procedures. . . .

Detention programs become fragmented and disjointed if there is no overall plan or strategy that unifies them. Edwards (1975) described this phenomenon accordingly:

> It is a seeming paradox that many institutions have fine programs, but no program. There may be a modern school building with excellent facilities, a good social services staff with great organization, a cottage-life department with regular inservice training, but no overall, coordinating set of objectives that comprise a program. (p. 52)

For this reason, programs imply a program philosophy. It is the function of the philosophy to set mutually acceptable goals for all programs. These goals can be translated into performance objectives that serve to increase consistency between programs. The philosophy also sets the tone for how all programs will be implemented. It is the combination of a specific plan and an overall philosophy that defines a program.

Programming is the process of building programs. As a process, programming is an ongoing characteristic of the successful detention facility. Programming is contingent upon the ability to acquire reliable information about programs. Effective programming must take into consideration the nature of the environment, the juvenile offenders, the staff, the resources, and the facility history. . . .

Next, programming calls for feedback data on all programs. The requirement for such data presumes a system to measure and collect outcomes. Evaluative feedback then becomes new information about the nature of programs, and it changes and reinforces the decisions about those programs. These decisions are ongoing, and they concern basic program modifications that will increase outcome effectiveness. Programming is the essence of good detention. Successful programming is not an event or an accomplishment, rather it is a process that virtually occurs all the time.

Why Programs?

Four reasons are given in response to the question of why have programs. First, the empowering statute or legislation that creates juvenile detention usually includes an expectation or requirement for programs and services. Many state statutes are becoming more explicit, and an increasing number of states has created licensing standards or administrative rules that define the nature and scope of detention programs. Second, and expanding on the notion that programs are required by law, Bell (1992) notes that programs are required by the U.S. Supreme Court as a method of meeting the constitutional rights of detained juveniles. Third, the traditions of juvenile justice (Taylor, 1992) and its professional associations, such as ACA and NJDA, identify a wide range of programs as one of the essential distinctions between adult and juvenile detention. Fourth, and finally, practitioners report that programs make the job easier, more effective, and more enjoyable. When taken together, these rationales present a very compelling argument for programming, so compelling that the most direct and simple answer to the question of "why programs" is because "you have to provide programs."

Since the concepts of programs and programming are a key part of juvenile detention, it is important for line workers to understand why these concepts are of such significance. It is easier for staff to support and implement detention programming when they understand the rationales for its existence. . . .

Rationales

Four general categories of rationales are discussed in the helpful services literature:

1. **Systems Rationale.** This category includes a set of four general rationales that are linked to the goals of the juvenile justice system. First, one of the primary purposes of the juvenile justice system is the protection of society. Since it is impossible to keep a juvenile offender locked up for his/her entire lifetime, the one way to fulfill an obligation to the protection of society is by changing the juvenile. This change process implies goals, objectives, resources, and systems for intervention. In other words, change implies action, action implies a plan, and plans imply helpful programs.

Second, changing the juvenile offender is also a pragmatic or rational strategy for protecting the child from himself. Educational and therapeutic programs can provide the necessary skills to enable a youngster to stop those self-defeating behaviors that have precipitated juvenile court intervention.

Third, the juvenile justice system was developed to help solve the problems of children and families. Juvenile delinquency is often viewed as proof of either family problems, social problems, or educational problems. In each instance, the ability of the juvenile justice system to solve these problems is contingent upon the development of effective programs. Programs help the juvenile justice system to achieve its mission.

Fourth, within the juvenile justice system there is the pervasive and inherent notion that helpful programs are the ultimate goal of an effective system. Both juvenile court officers and detention workers agree that as the juvenile justice system moves toward an ideal definition, it includes a greater number of helpful and therapeutic programs (Mulvey & Reppucci, 1984).

2. **Restoration Rationale.** The NJDA definition of detention of detention stresses the importance of restoring the juvenile to a productive role in the community. No other concept more directly evokes a call for programs than does restoration. The fundamental mission of the juvenile justice system is the restoration of the juvenile offender to a successful life upon returning home (Norman, 1951, p. 339). This is commonly translated by juvenile detention to mean assisting a youth's growth in personal responsibility and self-esteem.

Restoration implies change. This perspective requires programming. As opposed to providing individual programs, restoration is associated with an overriding positive philosophy that unifies each program component. This philosophy targets the successful reintegration of a juvenile to the home community. Care is taken here to avoid the notion of equating restoration with rehabilitation. Many in the human services are quick to ask, "How can we rehabilitate someone who has never been habilitated?" The issue for detention programming is not the process of habilitating again (re-habilitating). Instead, the purpose of helpful programs is derived from one of the dictionary definitions of "rehabilitate" which is "to restore." Hence, the central question of the restoration rationale is: What is to be restored? The answer is simple and defines the essence of all helpful programs. It is human worth and self-esteem that are restored.

3. **First-Aid Rationale.** In 1951, Sherwood Norman introduced the "New Concept of Detention" that incorporated such therapeutic program components as individual and group counseling. The reluctance of both the juvenile court and detention administrators to make detention more conducive to therapeutic programs is what Norman (1957) called a "national disgrace." While the debate continues around the competing paradigms of detention as therapeutic or preventive, Norman's first-aid rationale is a central concept of helpful programs.

First-aid programs create an image of a large and complex hospital, fully equipped to handle a wide range of health problems. Let the hospital itself represent the juvenile justice system. Within this context, various specialists and generalists work in harmony to return the patient to a healthy lifestyle. The majority of patients enter through the main entrance, referred or diagnosed for some specific intervention. Others enter through the emergency room. Their problems are such that they require immediate attention. The purpose of this type of intervention is to repair minor damage or serve as the first step in a longer and more complex healing process.

Juvenile detention is the emergency room. First-aid programs imply that detention is the place where restoration begins. Like the emergency room, juvenile detention is not meant to be an end in itself, rather it is a means to an end (Brown, 1983). Stepanik (1986) expressed the first-aid rationale as follows:

> Progressive detention professionals have no desire to completely habilitate or rehabilitate youth. Rather, they understand the need to begin the process as comprehensively and as soon as possible, and thus serve a more meaningful role as part of the system at large. (p. 2)

There is, also, a larger issue that employs the logic of the first-aid rationale. As a secure institution, it must be assumed that incarceration in a juvenile detention facility is punishment. Furthermore, detention has been described as a negative and potentially harmful experience (Frazier, 1989). Within the first 25 years of its existence, detention was characterized as possessing inherent dangers for youth (Healey & Bronner, 1926). Many of these dangers stem from the trauma induced through the loss of freedom, the separation from home and family, the involuntary exposure to new people and procedures, and the complete uncertainty of the detention experience. Although these factors apply to all correctional institutions, the impact is greatly amplified when applied to children. A further intensification of this effect results from the preadjudicatory status of youth where stress and anxiety increase prior to a youth's court hearing. Many youths characterize daily detention life as a condition of constant waiting and uncertainty. When combined with the unfamiliar circumstances inherent in this new and unusual environment, tension and anxiety often become manifest through hostile passivity or hostile aggression. Juvenile detention is the time of greatest need for helpful programs. . . .

4. **Inevitability Rationale.** Norman (1951, p. 344) maintained that each and every staff-resident interaction has the potential for therapeutic change. Thus, behavior change within this context becomes inevitable and is a "given" in every juvenile detention facility. While some interactions between staff and residents are characterized as punishing, most detention practitioners describe each interaction with youth as an opportunity for positive change.

The inevitability rationale is taken one step further when applied to the institutional concepts of discipline and social climate (Roush, 1984). The nature of juvenile detention guarantees that these two factors will be ever present. First, some strategy will be employed jointly or individually by staff to control behavior. This strategy is commonly referred to as a system of discipline. Second, detention constitutes a total institution and reflects its own social climate. The nature of helpful programming rests upon the use of a program philosophy that coordinates discipline and the social climate. The value that a detention facility or juvenile justice system places on the dignity of juveniles is expressed most directly by the manner in which program development shapes or affects discipline and the social climate. When discipline becomes punitive and the social climate reinforces the predominance of control, program development is stifled. In most instances, the relationship between helpful programs and punishment is inversely proportional. That is, as helpful program development expands, the emphasis on and the need for punishment decreases.

The inevitability rationale is very important. This argument implies that change is inevitable through the interactions of staff and residents. However, the direction of that change is a function of the programming philosophy of the detention facility. Without a strong helpful programs orientation, juvenile detention facilities run the risk that the inherent punishers within the system will expand to the point that discipline and the social climate will exert a negative influence on youth.

Some specific effects of punitive programs are prevalent among correctional officers and are relevant to direct care staff in juvenile detention (Cressey, 1982). First, without a strong rationale for helpful programs, direct care workers often ignore residents and assume that there is no obligation to be helpful. Second, a punitive philosophy fosters an atmosphere where staff members may be tempted to look away when one resident is being physically punished by another or other residents. Since staff members cannot legally administer corporal punishment, they can refuse to intervene when residents take disciplinary measures into their own hands. Third, resident conflicts create divisiveness and tensions between youths that reduce the threat of a significant loss of staff control. That is, when groups of residents expend their energies in conflicts with each other, they are less likely to plan and execute staff assaults or escape attempts. Fourth, direct care workers have an incentive to retreat to the control room and allow residents to run their own system.

While many veteran staff members may disavow the existence of these issues, new staff members facing the problems of surviving the shift may be more inclined to use one or more of these strategies. The ongoing criticism of inadequate staff training creates a situation where detention staff members are frequently placed in a position of responsibility without adequate skills and resources. Two solutions to these problems involve the creation and implementation of a positive program philosophy and a competent staff training program.

Program Objectives

After detailing the rationales for helpful detention programs, it is equally important to explain in general terms the objectives of these programs. Listed below are six common objectives that are based on the helpful programming experiences of Vince Carbone (1984) while at the Polk County (Iowa) Detention Center.

1. **Social Order.** Every institution has a social order. The social order is the set of formal and informal rules and relations that govern social interaction. . . .

The relationship between detention programming and the social order can be explained in simple terms. An unstructured environment leads to high levels of uncertainty among detention residents. Uncertainty also produces anxiety that is tied to acting-out behaviors in juveniles. These situations threaten the psychological and physical safety within the detention facility. Because of the wide range of problems associated with detained youth, a juvenile detention facility can easily become a chaotic social environment. Under these conditions, disruptive behaviors commonly occur. Typical reactions by staff are to increase punishment and surveillance methods. It is not unusual to find high levels of inconsistency between staff practices during periods when the social environment is chaotic. Conversely, strong program development creates structure that reduces uncertainty and anxiety. Structure helps to create a safe and secure environment.

Experience in numerous detention facilities indicates that the gradual implementation of systematic and helpful programs creates a more appropriate social order. Staff members become more positive in their interactions with youth while residents demonstrate an increased amount of socially appropriate behavior. It is the structure of helpful programs that provides and maintains a sense of control within the institutional setting. Without this control, psychological and physical safety and security are difficult to attain.

2. **Behavior Change.** This objective calls to mind the familiar training adage, "When you're up to your elbows in alligators, it's difficult to remember that your primary objective was to drain the swamp." Without the ability to establish minimally acceptable levels of appropriate behavior, behavior change efforts will receive an inadequate amount of attention. Too much time will be spent resolving petty misbehaviors, and behavior change programs will become the first fatality. Programs provide both the structure and opportunities for personal choice (Norman, 1951) which help youth change specific misbehaviors. . . .

From a social learning perspective, behavior change is associated with the development of social skills (Goldstein & Glick, 1987). In particular, social skills programs have been widely used in postdispositional settings or training schools. These social skills reeducation programs have resulted in the successful development of alternative appropriate behaviors that substitute for verbal and physical aggression, drug abuse, and criminal behavior (LeCroy, 1983). Improved social skills also result in enhanced interpersonal relationships with family members, probation officers, school personnel, and peers. Beyond the limited focus of specific behavior change strategies, Rubenstein (1991) used a social skills approach as the basis for an integrated strategy to improve program and staff effectiveness at a large state training school. A study designed to measure results revealed significant positive behavior changes in the students, increased staff competence and confidence, and an increase in morale and feelings of teamwork among staff. Rubenstein's experience serves as an excellent example of how a positive program philosophy can change all elements of the institutional environment. . . .

3. **Staff Training.** The goals and objectives of a systematic and helpful set of programs also define the goals and objectives of staff training. All direct care workers in juvenile detention need to be taught the requisite skills to implement a program successfully. A commitment to programming implies a commitment to staff training. Numerous benefits are derived from a staff training program based on systematic and helpful programs. For example, training programs will address a complete and comprehensive description of adolescent behavior, juvenile delinquency, and abnormal behavior. Program skills can be objectifiable, observable, and measurable. Therefore, training becomes clearer to direct care staff.

Clarity in programs also permits the delineation of appropriate juvenile behaviors in observable and measurable terms for a variety of settings. Well written and easily understandable training manuals and program manuals can be developed which include these behavioral components. Most importantly, clear program goals provide a procedure for gathering data to evaluate resident performance, staff performance, and institutional performance.

4. **Reduction of Punishment.** Both Sherwood Norman and Vince Carbone make two important observations about the relationship between helpful programs and punishment. Norman addresses the theoretical incompatibility between helpful programs and the use of punishment. When helpful programs incorporate clinical diagnosis and observation, competent information can be supplied to the court regarding an appropriate course of action to return the juvenile to a productive role in the community. When this information comes from trained professionals in a helpful program, the information going to the court will emphasize alternatives to punishment. From Norman's perspective, the most effective way to reduce the use of punishment in a detention facility is to control the diagnostic and clinical information that goes to the court.

In an evaluation of a juvenile detention facility, Carbone and Lynch (1983) discovered an inordinately high frequency of punishing consequences (room confinements and reprimands) which were directly linked to aggressive misbehaviors by youth. Further investigation into this situation revealed that the staff members were increasing the frequency and magnitude of punishments. In the absence of a positive program philosophy, staff members chose to ignore appropriate behavior and to punish misbehavior harshly. This produced a highly volatile situation and contributed to the high frequency of behavioral disturbances within the detention facility. In effect, punishment produces changes, but not necessarily positive ones.

In addition to the immediate problems caused by a reliance upon punishment, Carbone raised other legal and ethical issues. Because detention facilities are especially susceptible to the abuses of punishment, advocates for the legal and ethical rights of children have shown a particular interest in monitoring the punishment procedures in juvenile institutions. Cases alleging child abuse and violations of constitutional rights are especially strong when there are no systematic and helpful programs intended to reduce the need for punishment. Consequently, a good faith effort to develop helpful programs within a positive program philosophy may be one of the best alternatives available to detention administrators to reduce the risk of liability. This is particularly relevant to the use of isolation, a form of institutional punishment most vulnerable to abuse and litigation (Mitchell & Varley, 1991).

5. **Evaluation.** When you don't know where you're going, any road will get you there. No matter where you go, there you are. These aphorisms describe succinctly the importance of a plan for program implementation. The plan implies a beginning, based on the diagnostic and assessment components of a helpful program. Next, the plan includes an intervention based on the information supplied by the initial assessment. Finally, the program has a definite end, a point where target or end behaviors can be identified. By specifying, objectifying, and measuring these constructs, feedback is incorporated into each component of the program to aid in its effectiveness. The most important part of successful programs is an evaluation component.

Effective juvenile detention facilities use evaluation information that guides decisions regarding program outcomes, staff effectiveness, and institutional effectiveness. In the absence of a systematic program, an evaluation component is not possible. When detention practices are not clearly defined and are not consistently applied, it is difficult to make statements regarding the effectiveness of one approach versus another. Under these circumstances, changes in the daily program are typically prompted by a significant behavioral disruption or by administrative whim. In these situations, many effective practices may go undetected.

6. **Accountability.** Information generated by an evaluation plan must be applied to a system of accountability for staff, residents, and the institution. It should be noted, however, that accountability carries with it the notion of both positive and negative sanctions. It is equally as important to reinforce appropriate behavior as it is to correct inappropriate behavior. This applies to individual staff behavior, resident behaviors, and institutional program philosophy. Without reliable outcome information, staff, residents, and programs may drift aimlessly.

Successful programs set high but reasonable and attainable goals for staff. These goals and their behavioral performance objectives create a benchmark against which staff performance can be evaluated. When staff behavior is clearly inadequate, successful programs provide a vehicle for employee assistance. If these remedial efforts are unsuccessful, marginal and inadequate job performance leads to termination. Just as successful programs attract and develop good people, they also get rid of those individuals who present a threat to residents and programs. Program integrity is a function of positive program philosophy that is actually implemented by staff. Accountability implies that when staff performance deviates to the extent that residents and programs are in jeopardy, decisive action is taken to rid the institution of that particular staff member.

What Is a Good Detention Program?

The rationales and objectives for detention programming serve as methods to explain the programming process to line workers. . . . However, this information does not explain or describe the key elements of an effective detention program.

Three elements of successful programs are important. First, there is a commitment to programs by administration. When programs are endorsed as valuable and important, all staff members are oriented toward seeking programming alternatives. Second, successful programs consistently exhibit six identifiable characteristics. Third, the list of program components named in the NJDA definition statement serves as an important checklist for minimally acceptable programming.

Necessary Program Characteristics

1. **Primacy of Staff.** Good programs adhere to a staff primacy concept (Brendtro & Ness, 1983). This means that there are adequate numbers of staff with proper qualifications. As opposed to some institutional emphases on hardware, security equipment, and physical plant, the staff primacy characteristic places the relationship between the juvenile and the staff member at a very high level of importance. Lenz (1942) first described the relationship between staff and disruptive behaviors by maintaining that:

> If we do not wish to depend on bars and locks, we must build up a staff on whose skills we can rely to prevent more than occasional incidents of this sort. (p. 22)

John Sheridan stresses the importance of staff when he claims that with an adequate number of properly trained staff, he could operate a training school using only tents. Although staffing ratios are of critical importance, the key component of a good program is a good staff.

Staff primacy requires good staff training programs. When in-service training pinpoints the critical knowledge, skills, and abilities required for helpful programs, consistency improves. As one of the most revealing indicators of an effective program, consistency is a mark of a good detention staff. This long-standing element of successful detention practice promotes increased communications among staff. Information exchange is vitally important in fulfilling the diagnostic functions of juvenile detention. . . . In addition to these benefits, a team approach can increase job satisfaction and perceptions of professional skill development (Roush & Steelman, 1981).

2. **Safety.** A second characteristic of a good program is its concern for safety. In addition to the more obvious factors of physical safety, helpful programs pay

particular attention to the psychological safety of detained juveniles. Emphasis on psychological safety very simply stresses the reduction, removal, or control of those persons or factors that create fear and anxiety. As was earlier discussed, secure programs frequently assume responsibility for these issues. In juvenile detention facilities, the risk of a resident suicide creates an environment that is extremely security conscious. When taken to its logical conclusion, security can mean elaborate auditory and visual surveillance devices for monitoring youth. However, the hardware and procedures are only part of the solution. A critical variable again looks at staff. Norman (1951) summarized this situation when he said, "Whatever the physical setting, the fundamental basis for security lies in the relationship between the child and his supervisors" (p. 343). Norman's observation applies equally to both physical and psychological security.

3. **Activities.** The range of activities constitutes the third characteristic of successful programs. The functions of activities are many. In addition to providing a diversion from the monotony inherent in institutional life, activities represent ways of teaching social skills and problem-solving skills. When these learning components are tied to a positive program philosophy, activities acquire a therapeutic value.

In addition, a full activities program requires a schedule. In the institution, a schedule of daily activities and events provides structure. The use of structure constitutes a very important part of teaching responsibility. Beyond the creation of rules for behavior, a systematic schedule provides a sense of control in the lives of adolescents who sometimes wonder if they are ever in control of themselves. At a very minimum, activities extend beyond ping-pong, basketball, and television.

4. **Leadership.** Successful and helpful institutional programs are traditionally associated with one or more strong leaders. Within the area of programming, leaders provide direction and guidance regarding program implementation issues. . . .

Leaders must be knowledgeable about programs, institutions, and juvenile offenders. Knowledge and expertise combine to provide direct care staff with the confidence and certainty that the program is effective. Knowledgeable leadership is not inherited. With regard to juvenile detention, leaders are developed through experience in institutional settings with juvenile offenders.

5. **Education.** Successful program development is not a function of trial and error. Successful program leaders do not "shoot-from-the-hip" or make up the program as they go along. Unfortunately, too many judges and corrections experts believe that almost anyone can develop programs for juvenile detention. Ironically, if this were the case, there would be a greater number of successful, helpful, and exemplary programs for juvenile detention.

To build a successful program, staff must be educated about detention programs. The juvenile justice literature contains an adequate amount of information to enable detention staff to make wise and educated decisions about program development.

All that is needed to find this valuable information is a little research and reading. . . .

Successful programs are smart programs. A wealth of programming information is available to detention personnel.

6. **Evaluation.** The final characteristic of successful programs is a strong evaluation component. The evaluation process was described above, but it is worth reiterating that successful programs are continuously in search of and responsive to feedback and information about program outcomes.

Necessary Program Components

Various opinions exist on what specific program components should be included within the helpful services provided by the detention facility. Others agree on the range of program components, but they disagree about which component should take the highest priority. Therefore, the following represents a list of program components traditionally associated with successful programs. Only basic descriptions are presented.

The best resources for understanding the range of program components are the ACA standards and the NJDA definition statement:

1. **Education.** A successful detention program contains a strong education component (Roush, 1983). Staffed by fully and appropriately certified teachers, the education component is the core of the programming strategy. Education should include instruction in math, reading, GED preparation and information, vocational awareness and training, survival skills, general academic programming, physical education, and arts and crafts. Class sizes should be kept at a minimum to promote individualized instruction. And education should increase self-esteem and should serve to motivate youth to continue their education upon release. Finally, teacher salaries should be competitive with those of local public schools. Without financial parity, juvenile detention education programs will be unable to attract quality personnel.

2. **Visiting.** Successful programs recognize and exploit the juvenile's link to the community since most youth in detention facilities soon return to their home environment. It is important to provide ample and ongoing opportunities for juveniles to visit with family members and appropriate persons from the community to assist the reintegration process.

3. **Communication.** Successful programs recognize and promote the legal rights of juveniles. Nowhere is this more evident than in the area of private communications, particularly mail. Case law is very clear in this area. Correspondence may be opened in the presence of the juvenile and inspected for contraband, but it should not be read unless convincing reasons exist. When staff members treat a juvenile's rights with respect and dignity, a positive relationship builds between the resident and the institutional staff. There are numerous small ways to build

trust and confidence in detention programs. One very effective method is to respect the legal rights of juveniles.

4. **Counseling.** More than just active listening, counseling is a process where a trained counselor forms a therapeutic relationship with a juvenile offender for the purposes of helping the juvenile to solve personal, social, and educational problems. Counseling also includes the teaching of personal problem-solving techniques and normally takes the form of individual or group sessions that should be made available to all detention residents. Detention represents a highly unsettling time in the life of a juvenile. Competent and professional helping services are a characteristic component of successful programs.

5. **Continuous supervision.** Successful programs have policies, procedures, and training programs that underscore the importance of continuous supervision. This means that staff members are always present during waking or program hours. During nonwaking hours, staff members continually supervise juveniles through periodic visual observations and continuous auditory monitoring. Continuous supervision provides valuable information about juveniles while simultaneously increasing safety and security.

6. **Medical and health care.** As an area of extremely high liability, the ACA standards emphasize medical and health care services for incarcerated juveniles as the section with the highest concentration of mandatory standards. The best guidelines and standards for medical and health care services have been developed by the National Commission on Correctional Health Care (NCCHC). These standards are quite comprehensive and call for a significant commitment of resources on the part of the parent agency.

While a successful program conveys its concern for the best interest of juveniles through a variety of methods, the emphasis on medical and health care services is a direct result of recent prisoners' rights litigation. Applied equally to juvenile offenders, these decisions establish medical and health care services as a basic constitutional right and create a target for litigation for all of juvenile corrections. . . .

7. **Nutrition.** A well-balanced and nutritious diet is an important factor in maintaining good health. Because of the high concentration of people in a confined space, health concerns become a central part of successful programs.

Attractive and tasteful meals are essential. Food is a universal symbol of love, and it is a mistake to underestimate the positive effects derived from it. For example, meals should offer a nutritious variety of food selections in generous quantities. Detention is not a time when juveniles should be hungry, and positive programs do not use food as a negative sanction. Great meals have positive impacts on juveniles.

8. **Recreation.** Well-organized and well-supervised recreational activities are a key component to successful programs. As mentioned earlier, these events and

activities have the potential for program learning. Staff members are presented with an ongoing opportunity to model appropriate behaviors. Additionally, juveniles are placed in a reinforcing situation that addresses those types of social interactions that will be present when the juveniles return to the community.

Recreation also provides for an opportunity to learn teamwork. Most successful programs that emphasize the teaching of responsibility will address the concept of mutual cooperation. From this perspective, recreation can be a powerful learning tool.

Recreation and vigorous physical activity provide a release for physical and emotional tension. Because the detention environment is associated with an increase in tension, recreation becomes even that much more important. When combined with good food in abundant quantities, recreation also provides a means of burning off calories. Both food and activity combine to reduce the tendency toward acting-out behaviors.

9. **Reading.** Successful programs contain a special emphasis on reading. This reading component takes two forms. First, reading materials are available to residents in all areas of the detention facility. These materials are age-appropriate and of high interest. Detention staff members are fortunate to have available an incredibly wide array of books and magazines that are oriented toward teenagers. Reading materials must be everywhere.

Second, reading must be incorporated into special programs. Many successful programs have a Chapter I remedial reading program that operates as a part of the detention education program. This type of program specifically addresses reading deficits and stresses skill development. As more and more detainees qualify for special education programs, the importance of special reading programs continues to increase.

The combination of materials and programs serves to communicate directly to juveniles that reading is fundamentally important. Once this message becomes a part of the program or social order, efforts to improve reading skills, regardless of one's status, become an acceptable task and responsibility. In one detention center, residents and staff take a 30-minute rest period following the evening meal. Residents may be in their rooms or in the day room. Everyone, residents and staff alike, must make some form of reading material the source of their attention for that 30- minute period. If a juvenile wishes to work on instructional material from a reading class, this is appropriate. If a juvenile wishes to read a newspaper or magazine, this is appropriate. If a juvenile wishes to look at a book of pictures, this, too, is appropriate. Successful programs elevate reading to a priority status.

Obstacles to Successful Programming

Even with a thorough understanding of program rationales, objectives, characteristics, and components, there are no guarantees that a successful detention program will be accomplished. The creation and maintenance of helpful programs are a function of these factors occurring in conjunction with a favorable political climate. Philosophies of juvenile justice may change to such an extent that programs and services are no longer supported by the public, legislative bodies, funding sources, or juvenile court judges. When this occurs, financial resources may become scarce, and programs and staff are put to the test. Changes in philosophy may also represent changes in attitudes. In these situations, decision-making groups and public officials must be persuaded that programs are an important part of juvenile detention. Public education about the importance of programs remains a serious failing of most juvenile detention facilities and underscores the fragile nature of programming effort in politically volatile jurisdictions.

In light of this general warning about the fragile relationship between programs and politics, Carbone (1984) identified eight general barriers to effective detention programming.

Detention Criteria

Even the most well conceived detention programs are frequently under tremendous pressure to accept juveniles who vary widely in terms of age, referring problems, histories of previous treatments, and social maturity. It is the responsibility of juvenile detention to participate in the creation of admission criteria so as to limit detention to only those juveniles who are truly in need of incarceration and for whom no other appropriate services exist (Norman, 1951). Juvenile court judges should consider the Institute of Justice Administration/American Bar Association (IJA/ABA) standards for detention admission or the detention criteria set forth by the National Advisory Council. Within these limited definitions for appropriate detention, programming can be developed for a specific population of juvenile offenders. In the absence of detention criteria, detention runs a greater risk of fulfilling Hammergren's warning about detention becoming all things to all segments of the juvenile justice system.

Overcrowding

When a detention facility accepts juveniles beyond its rated capacity, overcrowding becomes one of the most powerfully negative forces within the institution, capable of negating the positive effects associated with such effective program strategies as ACA accreditation. In addition to the problems associated with limited physical space and resources, the social environment dramatically suffers under crowded conditions (Roush, 1989). Staff supervision and general behavior management practices are typically affected adversely. Consequently, even the well-trained staff with effective behavior management skills will begin changing policy and procedure to find shortcuts when the detention center is overcrowded (Cosgrove, 1985). These shortcuts invariably include an increased amount of punishment, for even the uninformed soon realize the power of effective punishment to suppress even the most irritating forms of inappropriate behavior. Increased uses of punishment usually mean increased frequencies of restrictions, confinements, and restraints with the concomitant increased risks of abuse and litigation. It is the responsibility of the juvenile court judge in court-operated detention facilities or the detention administrator in county or state-operated facilities to ensure that overcrowding does not occur.

Detention as a Disposition

Even when clear and precise criteria for detention exist, there is still a temptation on the part of the juvenile court to use detention as an additional dispositional alternative. This practice has been around for many years and has taken various forms. As examples, juveniles on probation may be detained for only a few days (generally on the weekend) for a relatively minor offense or a probation violation, and the probation officer has no intention of pursuing the infraction to adjudication since the purpose of the short stay is that the youth takes probation seriously. This has become more popular as a practice in rural jurisdictions as a result of misguided applications of the "Scared Straight" approach. Moreover, many youths are released from detention at the dispositional hearing, effectively imposing an informal detention disposition for the period of time between the adjudicatory and dispositional hearings. Detention practitioners understand this informal use of detention as a disposition.

Several state legislatures have boldly formalized detention as a disposition by placing postdispositional sentencing options in the juvenile code, permitting the postdispositional placement of youth in traditionally (and in some cases statutorily defined) preadjudicatory detention facilities for periods of confinement of up to 180 days. Despite the excessive burdens placed on staff and programs under this arrangement, the sentencing option may be seen by the juvenile court as the only feasible alternative. Most jurisdictions do not have a range of detention alternatives at their disposal. Rather than make a costly commitment to the state for more appropriate services, juvenile court officials choose the less costly alternative (detention as a disposition), reasoning that (a) detention does provide some help and treatment and (b) a sentence to secure detention is viewed as "one last shot" at getting a youth's attention before lowering the boom, i.e., training school or waiver to adult court. According to the Annie E. Casey Foundation, this practice reflects the belief that juvenile offenders can be shocked into better behavior and that a stay in detention will give them "a taste of the system" (Flintrop, 1991). This action also presents a "get tough" image by the court, an important consideration in any reelection strategy for most juvenile court judges.

Both of these strategies create chaos for detention programs and staff due to the increases in offense seriousness, lengths of stay, and age of offenders (Cosgrove, 1985). Detention programs are typically not designed for a population of juvenile offenders that is older and more aggressively disruptive. In addition to a wholesale change in the characteristics of the detention population, detention as a disposition challenges the temporary element in the definition of detention by increasing the length of stay. For these and many other reasons, the National Juvenile Detention Association and the American Correctional Association have formally voiced their opposition to the use of juvenile detention as a disposition.

Length of Stay

According to the NJDA definition, juvenile detention should be a temporary phenomenon. Of all the methods of incarceration within the criminal justice system, only juvenile detention stresses this temporary nature: it is a hallmark characteristic of juvenile detention. Nowhere is this more evident than in Cook County, Illinois. Located in Chicago, the Audey Home for Children is the Nation's first public detention facility, established in 1907. In 1971 the county-administered juvenile detention operations were moved into a new and spacious facility designed to detain just under 500 juveniles. Due to the leadership and perseverance of superintendent James Jordan, the name was changed to the Cook County *Temporary* Juvenile Detention Center (emphasis added). In his explanation for the name change, Jordan forthrightly admitted that he wanted to stress the temporary nature of juvenile detention. The best strategy was to have the word "temporary" officially placed in the name, on the letterhead, and carved above the entrances. In essence, detention should be a short as possible.

Jordan (1985) also warned that when lengths of stay exceed this definition, all programs feel the strain, and it becomes increasingly difficult to meet the needs of troubled youth when they are forced to spend prolonged periods of time in a locked facility that is designed and programmed for temporary care. Ironically, overcrowding due largely to the detention of "automatic transfers" (youth held in juvenile detention while awaiting trial in adult court) has placed tremendous burdens on the operation of the Cook County Temporary Juvenile Detention Center, where the average length of stay for 1992 exceeded 100 days care. Most juvenile justice experts agree that the majority of juvenile offenders have limited social repertoires, require some form of special attention, and probably could benefit from a short stay in a good detention facility. However, as the stay in detention lengthens, the risks of overcrowding increase, and most of the helpful services (education, counseling, and clinical services) are quickly exhausted. A comprehensive range of in-depth and sustainable helpful services is simply unavailable within the current system of juvenile detention. Consequently, juveniles may well end a lengthy detention with an even greater need for services.

Staff Training

It is imperative that detention workers receive extensive and well-planned staff training. Because successful programs are defined in terms of the interactions between and among the staff and residents, comprehensive training that includes performance feedback is required to ensure that interactions are of a helpful nature. As the problems facing youth continue to become more complex, greater skills are needed on the part of detention workers. It can no longer be assumed that anyone who can walk and chew gum is qualified to work with troubled youth. Acceptable training programs, as defined in ACA standards, begin with a requirement of a minimum of 40 hours of preservice orientation, 80 hours of specialized training during the first year of employment, and an additional 40 hours of planned training each year thereafter. In every assessment of why juvenile detention succeeds or fails, staff training is a top priority.

Security

While security is a necessary condition of any detention program, an overemphasis on the physical security of the detention facility can become a barrier to effective programming. There appears to be an inverse relationship between security hardware and the development of a positive social climate. In other words, as the mechanical and electronic methods to control behavior become more comprehensive and effective, the staff may retreat to the control room, and the perception is reinforced that there is no longer a need to create a social environment or program that enhances appropriate and desirable behavior. While control is the objective of both approaches, only a well-designed program based on interpersonal relationships between residents and staff can generate the type of social climate that will be able to help juveniles. Detention administrators should be warned that physical security is a means to an end, not an end in itself. The best way to achieve a detention environment that is physically and psychologically safe and secure requires a greater emphasis on "staff secure" versus "hardware secure."

Understaffing

Although most states have set standards that define an acceptable staffing ratio, understaffing continues to be a problem in juvenile detention. Staff absences, resignations, and overcrowding frequently cause a detention program to be understaffed. Without entering into the definitional debate about staff sufficiency, it is important to note that once an effective staffing pattern has been established, problems will occur when this pattern is reduced by a level of only one direct care worker per shift. The result of this reduction in staff is an immediate increase in the use of punishment to control resident behavior. Other studies demonstrate that reduced staffing levels contribute to direct care staff burnout and to a shift in program philosophy from helpful programming to custodial programming.

Punishment-Oriented Legal Systems

It is unlikely that a juvenile detention program will be successful if the underlying philosophy of the juvenile court within that jurisdiction is punishment-oriented. When the general attitude of the court emphasizes the notion that juvenile detention is a form of punishment, the result is an ineffectual program plagued with misbehavior. It is incumbent upon detention programmers to use positive information, outcome data, anecdotal incidents, and case histories to persuade the juvenile court that helpful programs are in the best interest of juveniles, the court, and the public.

Summary

Helpful programming reflects two important concerns for juvenile detention. These concerns are ideological and pragmatic. When helpful programs incorporate both concerns, the best interest of juveniles is safeguarded.

Programs make an ideological statement. First, the nature and quality of those programs described above reinforce the idea that children are different from adults. Helpful programs maintain a clear distinction between adult and juvenile offenders and are the logical outcomes of a comprehensive program or strategy for working with troubled youth (Edwards, 1975). This is an underlying rationale for the establishment of the juvenile justice system.

Also, as a part of a human services network, the goal of juvenile detention is to help young people. The most effective and efficient way of protecting society is to solve or resolve the problems of troubled youth before the youth return home (Richards, 1968). Helpful programs are the best vehicle to reach these goals. A 1973 membership recruitment poster from the Michigan Juvenile Detention Association still adorns the office of Kirk Blackwood. The poster contains Sherwood Norman's quote about the importance of helpful programs, "When detention lowers a juvenile delinquent's self-esteem, it destroys the basis for his rehabilitation." While the statement is an excellent summary of helpful programs, it has a foreboding element. Norman predicted that when the very first of the powerful and restrictive interventions in the juvenile justice process (juvenile detention) lowers a juvenile's self-esteem, then the *entire* process is tainted.

Helpful programs are also pragmatic. As they become systematic and objective, programs help institutional staff members to increase their effectiveness through an increase in consistency. A pragmatic approach also uses programming to create an institutional resistance to liability. Finally, pragmatic programming systematically reduces the reliance upon restrictive consequences, such as punishment.

There are many reasons why some juvenile detention programs are successful and others are not. The key elements of a successful program have been outlined above. For the most part, these successful programs are ideological, systematic, and pragmatic. But above all else, they are helpful, and, as Sherwood Norman clearly understood, programs that express a genuine concern for the best interest of juveniles are remarkably successful.

References

Brendtro, L. K., & Ness, A. E. (1983). *Re-educating troubled youth: Environments for teaching and treatment.* New York: Aldine Publishing.

Bell, J. R. (1992). Rights and responsibilities of juveniles. In *Juvenile careworker resource guide.* Laurel, MD: American Correctional Association.

Brown, M., Jr. (1983). *Juvenile detention* (Professional Development Program Series Monograph). Austin: Texas Juvenile Probation Commission.

Carbone, V. J. (1984). Programming in juvenile detention facilities. *The Rader Papers: A Journal of Juvenile Detention Services, 1,* 3-8.

Carbone, V. J. & Lynch, R. (1983). The functional analysis of behavior in a juvenile detention facility. *Journal of Offender Counseling, Services & Rehabilitation, 6,* 21-41.

Cosgrove, J. P. (1985). Behavioral adjustment of juveniles committed to detention centers, *The Rader Papers: A Journal of Juvenile Detention Services, 2,* 14-17.

Cressey, D. R. (1982). Foreword. In F. T. Cullen & K. E. Gilbert, *Reaffirming rehabilitation.* Cincinnati: Anderson Publishing.

Edwards, D. (1975). Specific objectives for the institutional treatment of juveniles. In R. E. Hardy & J. G. Cull (Eds.), *Introduction to correctional rehabilitation.* Springfield, IL: Charles C. Thomas.

Flintrop, R. (1991, Winter). Voiceless children: Juvenile detention in the U.S. *Focus: A Quarterly Report from the Annie E. Casey Foundation,* pp. 2-6.

Frazier, C. E. (1989). Preadjudicatory detention. In A. R. Roberts, *Juvenile justice policies, programs, and services.* Chicago: Dorsey Press.

Goldstein, A. P., & Glick, B. (1987). *Aggression replacement training: A comprehensive intervention for aggressive youth.* Champaign, IL: Research Press.

Hammergren, D. R. (1984). Juvenile detention: Becoming all things to all segments of the juvenile justice system. *The Rader Papers: A Journal of Juvenile Detention Services, 1,* 1-3.

Healey, W., & Bronner, A. F. (1926). *Delinquents and criminals: Their making and unmaking.* New York: Macmillan.

Jordan, J. M. (1985). How serious offenders are impacting the system: The juvenile detention viewpoint. *The Rader Papers: A Journal of Juvenile Detention Services, 2,* 13-14.

LeCroy, C. W. (Ed.). (1983). *Social skills training for children and youth.* New York: Haworth Press.

Lenz, M. W. (1942). A yardstick for measuring detention homes. *Federal Probation, 6,* 20-23.

Mitchell, J., & Varley, C. (1991, Fall). Isolation and restraint in juvenile correctional facilities. *Journal for Juvenile Justice and Detention Services, 6,* 31-37.

Mulvey, E., & Reppucci, N. D. (1984). Perceptions of appropriate services for juvenile offenders. *Criminal Justice and Behavior, 11,* 401-422.

Norman, S. (1951). New goals for juvenile detention. In P. Tappan (Ed.), *Contemporary corrections.* New York: McGraw-Hill.

Norman, S. (1957). Juvenile detention. *NPPA Journal, 3,* 392-403.

Norman, S. (Ed.). (1961). *Standards and guides for the detention of children and youth* (2nd edition). New York: National Council on Crime and Delinquency.

Richards, A. (1968). Clinician's views on correctional education. In Federal Bureau of Prisons, *Supplement to re-educating confined delinquents.* Washington, DC: U.S. Government Printing Office.

Roush, D. W. (1983). Content and process of detention education. In S. Chaneles, *(Ed.), Current trends in correctional education: Theory and practice.* New York: Haworth.

Roush, D. W. (1984). Contributions to the therapeutic milieu: Integrating key theoretical constructs. *Child Care Quarterly, 13,* 233-250.

Roush, D. W. (1989). Far from the maddening crowd: The relationship between crowding and safety in juvenile institutions. In *The state of corrections.* Laurel, MD: American Correctional Association.

Roush, D. W., & Steelman, B. T. (1981, November). A team approach to detention staff development. *Juvenile & Family Court Journal, 32*, 33-43.

Rubenstein, F. D. (1991, June). A facility-wide approach to social skills training. *Journal of Correctional Education, 42*, 88-93.

Schwartz, I. M. (Ed.). (1992). *Juvenile justice and public policy: Toward a national agenda.* New York: Lexington Books.

Smith, J. S., Roush, D. W., & Kelley, R. (1990, January 14). *Public correctional policy on juvenile services: Juvenile detention.* Unpublished manuscript, Juvenile Detention Committee, American Correctional Association, Laurel, MD.

Stepanik, R. L. (1986, August 25). A perspective for change in the field of juvenile detention. *Juvenile Justice Digest, 14*, 1-3.

Taylor, W. (1992). Overview of the juvenile justice system. In *Juvenile careworker resource guide.* Laurel, MD: American Correctional Association.

Warner, F. M. (1933). *Juvenile detention in the United States.* Chicago: University of Chicago Press.

14

Incarcerated Juvenile Offenders
Integrating Trauma-Oriented Treatment with
State-of-the-Art Delinquency Interventions

Evvie Becker
Annette U. Rickel

"There is very little reverence for children in Chicago," wrote British journalist William T. Stead in 1894 in *If Christ Came to Chicago* (quoted in Hawes, 1991, p. 32). Stead's work documented what he considered to be appalling conditions for children at the turn of the century, chronicling examples of young boys who carried messages in and out of jails and sold newspapers in the bordellos.

What would Stead say today about children in Chicago? One hundred years later, James Garbarino and others have documented conditions in Chicago (and elsewhere) that rival and, indeed, surpass those that shocked Stead. For example, in interviews in Chicago housing projects, Garbarino (1995) found "virtually all the children have firsthand experience with shooting by the time they are five years old" (p. 75). Also in Chicago, a wider survey of 1,035 African American children aged 10 to 19 found 75% of boys and 10% of girls had witnessed the shooting, stabbing, robbing, or killing of another person (Shakoor & Chalmers, 1991). Others have documented high levels of family violence in the lives of children and adoles-

Becker, Evvie and Annette U. Rickel. 1998. Incarcerated Juvenile Offenders: Integrating Trauma-Oriented Treatment with State-of-the-Art Delinquency Interventions. Pp. 230–255 in Thomas P. Gullotta, Gerald R. Adams, and Raymond Montemayor (Eds.). *Delinquent Violent Youth: Theory and Interventions*. Thousand Oaks, CA: Sage Publications.

cents, particularly in areas of poverty, where violence in the home co-occurs with violence in the streets (American Psychological Association, 1996; Osofsky, Wewers, Hann, & Fick, 1993).

Beginning with a historical perspective, the chapter that follows outlines the ways in which violent conditions inflicted upon youth interact with other societal and individual factors to perpetuate adolescent involvement in crime, and the implications of those interactions for treatment of youthful offenders. New findings regarding treatment for the most recalcitrant offenders are described, with suggestions for integration with other emerging treatment modalities. The message herein is one of hope despite the pessimistic times in which we find ourselves. As the American Psychological Association Commission on Violence and Youth (1993) concluded:

> Many factors, both individual and social, contribute to an individual's propensity to use violence, and many of these factors are within our power to change. Although we acknowledge that the problem of violence involving youth is staggering and that there are complex macrosocial, biomedical, and other considerations that must be addressed in a comprehensive response to the problem, there is overwhelming evidence that we can intervene effectively in the lives of young people to reduce or prevent their involvement in violence. (p. 14)

The "Correctional" System: Where Has All The "Correction" Gone?

Shortly after the publication of Stead's tract, described above, on the plight of Chicago's children, social workers and club women in Chicago advocated successfully for a separate trial court for juveniles in that city (Hawes, 1991). The legislature passed the Illinois Juvenile Court Act of 1899, the first in the United States, creating a separate court for youth under age 16 who had violated a law or ordinance and guaranteeing a right to request and receive a jury trial. Furthermore, this legislation allowed individuals to complain to the court regarding any child who was delinquent, but also any who were believed to be neglected, and the court was granted broad power to remove children from their homes and place them in a variety of settings, from institutions to foster care. In 1901, in an attempt to broaden the reach of the court to help children further, the law was expanded to include children who associated with questionable companions, frequented dangerous or immoral establishments, or who exhibited other behavior that today might be termed "high risk." The legality of a separate juvenile court was upheld by the Pennsylvania Supreme Court in 1906.

Early in the 20th century, the idea that delinquency was a psychiatric problem to be treated, rather than punished, gathered strength and momentum. William A. Healy's first youth guidance clinic, the Juvenile Psychopathic Institute, was established in Chicago in 1909 to treat youthful offenders. The system developed at the beginning of the century included training, reform schools, and other institutional settings, and also community rehabilitation efforts through probation and suspended sentences (National Research Council, 1993).

Throughout the first half of the century, the trend continued, and in the flurry of change that characterized the decades of the 1960s and 1970s, the move toward deinstitutionalization of psychiatric patients and the developmentally delayed affected the juvenile population as well (Zigler, Thussig, & Black, 1992). The Juvenile Justice and Delinquency Prevention Act of 1974 required that juvenile-status offenders be provided alternatives to institutionalization (status offenses for juveniles are crimes resulting from the age of the perpetrator; e.g., truancy, violations of liquor or driving laws, running away). Consequently, the number of juveniles held in public facilities dropped by 60% by the end of the 1970s, and juveniles detained in adult facilities dropped by more than 80,000 youth.

Simultaneously, however, other forces worked to move juveniles away from their own facilities and back toward processes similar to those of adults in the justice system. The U.S. Supreme Court's 1967 Gault decision extended the Fifth and Sixth Amendment protections to juveniles, increasing the similarity of juvenile court proceedings to the adult process. Meanwhile, many states were engaged in a movement toward punishment and deterrence in juvenile cases and away from rehabilitation and treatment. States became increasingly willing to allow adolescents to be tried in adult courts. The concentration of racial minorities in poverty areas has confounded the problem, with inequality and discrimination prevalent in the criminal justice system for youth and for adults (American Bar Association, 1993; National Research Council, 1993).

Gradually, this movement has grown, so that, after the initial decrease at the end of the 1970s, noted above, the population of juveniles in public facilities began to increase again. By 1989, the population of juveniles in public facilities was 19% greater than it was in 1975 (National Research Council, 1993). Increasing violence among youth and escalating severity of violence have contributed to the public's fear of juvenile offenders. Treatment and rehabilitation have given way to punishment and retribution as the focus has shifted to community protection (Tate, Reppucci, & Mulvey, 1995).

Lack of solid evidence of the effectiveness of interventions with juvenile offenders has been cited as one reason for this trend (Tate et al., 1995; Zigler et al., 1992). Yet the rejection of treatment and rehabilitation by the public is also due in part to politicians who play upon the public's fears, calling for more jails and tougher sentencing as a means of political gain.

"The United States has been engaged in an unprecedented imprisonment binge," wrote Irwin and Austin (1994, p.1), who suggested that politicians choose to focus on crime because it is a safe political issue when compared to root problems of greater complexity (e.g., economic issues such as unemployment and spiraling costs of living).

Calls for adjudicating youthful offenders as adults have come from legislators but also from the courts, where judges have shown a willingness to try juveniles as adults and to consider homicide by juveniles as a capital offense. All of these trends, together with stiffer punishments for adult offenders, have led to large increases in the number of inmates in state and federal prisons. This population tripled from 1980 to 1994, from 329,821 to more than a million (Kupers, 1996). In the federal penal system, rehabilitation is no longer even a goal.

Deteriorating conditions resulting from this overcrowding not only fail to rehabilitate, they may actually increase the rage, psychiatric symptomatology, and resultant violence of the incarcerated offender. Frequent fighting, racial strife, fear of violence (including assault and rape), staff brutality, anonymity, and boredom are among the factors that may lead a criminal to a greater propensity for violence after imprisonment than before incarceration, particularly if he or she has significant psychiatric problems and/or a traumatic history (Kupers, 1996).

Juveniles who are placed within the adult criminal justice system are exposed to all of these conditions, as well as to experienced offenders as role models, and they are particularly vulnerable to victimization in prison. Yet at no other time in our history have the effects of violence and victimization on children and youth been better articulated. The effects of violence at home, in the media, or in the streets, as well as the effects of poverty on children, have been documented extensively (American Psychological Association, 1993, 1996). Among the problems associated with exposure to violence for children include difficulties with emotional regulation, an increase in aggressive behaviors, a negative self-image, symptoms of posttraumatic stress disorder, and difficulties in interpersonal relationships (Osofsky, 1995).

White House conferences on children and youth have been held periodically since the beginning of this century, with the debate shifting from a focus on families as the source of answers to the belief that experts had the solutions (Rickel & Allen, 1987). The 1960 fifth White House conference focused on increasing violence in the United States, specifically for adolescent individuals and youth gangs, and in 1970 and 1971, a conference for youth was held separately from that for children's issues.

Yet ever since the 1930 White House Conference on Children asserted that a child had a right to a "secure and loving home," children and youth have been subjected to family violence, street violence, multiple foster placements, abusive foster homes, drawn-out termination-of-parental-rights proceedings, latchkey situations, and lack of adequate food and housing, all contributing to the failure to fulfill on this historic promise to our children.

Nevertheless, most American youth are better off today than they were in 1641, when Massachusetts adopted a law that provided that any offspring 16 or older who cursed or struck a parent would be put to death, and 5 years later added that the death penalty could be applied to those 16 or older who failed to obey their parents (Hawes, 1991). Just 200 years ago, infanticide was not only permitted but accepted as the right of a father to manage his property (Zigler & Gordon, 1982), and only in 1938 was the first permanent child labor law finally enacted as part of the Fair Labor Standards Act.

The historical perspective suggests that solutions may lie in the convergence of multiple approaches to serving children and families. Multilevel solutions are suggested by history, and, as will be shown, are supported by research evaluations of effective treatment approaches.

Violent Histories, Violent Youth

> A six-year-old girl once told me that her job was to find her two-year-old sister whenever the shooting started and get her to safety in the bathtub of their apartment. "The bathroom is the safest place," she told me. Being responsible for the safety of another, younger child is a big responsibility for a six-year-old girl. Too big, I think. (Garbarino, 1995, p. 64)

As this anecdote illustrates, many children in the United States today have good reason to feel unsafe when their lives are threatened daily by the violence around them. But as Garbarino (1995) further observes, children living in more benign settings also report feeling unsafe: A Harris poll found that 35% of youth worried about being shot; another survey found that 12% of children felt unsafe, and the majority reported feeling only "somewhat" safe. Kidnapping and family dissolution are also worries for a large number of children.

These fears reflect the increasingly violent society in which we live. The United States continues to be a world leader—but not for our educational system, nor for our thriving economy. Rather, America leads the world for our rates of violence. The United States has the highest homicide rate of any industrialized country, a rate far above the country with the next highest rate (American Psychological Association, 1993). Only countries that are "profoundly distressed," such as Colombia, have similar homicide rates, according to Garbarino (1995), who computed the odds for children living in Northern Ireland before the 1994 IRA cease-fire and found that children in the United States are 15 times more likely to be killed than are children in Northern Ireland.

The psychological costs of this threat are tremendous. A recent study of 96 low-income, multiethnic youth in alternative high schools in Miami found that more than 93% had witnessed at least one violent event in their community, 44% had been victims of at least one of these violent events, and 41.6% had witnessed a murder (Berman, Kurtines, Silverman, & Serafini, 1996). Posttraumatic stress disorder (PTSD) symptoms were common among these students. For the large majority who had witnessed violence, an average number of 10 PTSD symptoms were reported. Examining the PTSD symptom reports for their clinical significance, 34.5% met the full criteria for a PTSD diagnosis, and 48.8% were symptomatic without meeting the full criteria; 16.7% were without symptoms. Similar findings have been reported for low-income, African American youth aged 7 to 18: Both victimization and witnessing violence were significantly related to reported PTSD symptoms, which were moderately high in this sample (Fitzpatrick & Boldizar, 1993).

As testimony in a 1993 hearing on youth and violence before the U.S. Senate Labor Subcommittee on Children indicated (Keeping Every Child Safe, 1993), victims may be inner-city youth in Bridgeport, as reported by a 16-year-old honor student in a magnet school who had lost several friends to shootings, or they may be adolescents in suburbia, such as the son of a suburban Virginia woman who was taken into the woods and shot by a friend, an Eagle Scout, just before he went off to college.

Victims may be visitors from other countries, such as German tourists murdered in Florida or the Japanese exchange student killed in Louisiana. Or they may be federal workers and children in day care, such as those killed in the Oklahoma City bombing. Yet race and ethnicity, primarily because of the concentration of ethnic minorities in poverty areas, are factors in the risk of death: A young African American female is four times more likely to be a victim of homicide than a young, non-African American female; a young African American male has a likelihood of being a homicide victim that is 11 times greater than that for young non-African American males. For young African Americans of both genders, homicide is the leading cause of death (American Psychological Association, 1993).

Guns are readily available to children in many communities. The rate of penetrating trauma in the emergency room at Children's National Medical Center in Washington, DC, increased by 1,740% from 1986 to 1989 (American Psychological Association, 1993). In Los Angeles County, military surgeons had to be brought in to teach medical residents at Martin Luther

King Hospital how to deal with the overwhelming numbers of gunshot wounds and other traumatic injuries resulting from violence.

Consequent to this culture heavily laden with violent images, children are themselves becoming ever more violent, and at younger ages. We hear the horrifying stories, such as the teenager who opened fire on a public swimming pool filled with children, or those cited by Coudroglou (1996): a 13-year-old who shoots a friend in an argument over a girlfriend, dumping the body in a garbage can; a 6-year-old and twin 8-year-olds who beat and kick a 4-week-old infant within inches of its life because it cried while they were burglarizing the home; three preteens who throw a 5-year-old down 14 stories, killing him because he refused to steal for them; a 10-year-old who shoots and kills his 5-year-old sister when she refuses to go to her room; a group of 10- to 15-year-olds who gang rape a 13-year-old girl.

Statistics support the conclusion that youth violence is increasing: Between 1984 and 1991, homicides committed by youth during the commission of another crime increased by 200%, and homicides resulting from interpersonal conflict increased by 83% (Cornell, 1993). Adolescent homicide perpetrators are far more likely to use a handgun than are adults who kill, and juveniles are more likely to have an accomplice.

As Coudroglou (1996) concludes, however, these incidents "ought to spark an agonizing inquiry into why otherwise ordinary people do bad things; why children and adolescents replace the joy of play with the horror of violence" (p. 324).

Violence and Victimization in the Lives of Youthful Offenders

"Does violence beget violence?" Widom (1989a, 1989b) asked in her landmark work examining the relationship between a documented history of child maltreatment and records of criminal activity as juveniles and as adults. She found a strong relationship between a history of either physical abuse or neglect and later violent behavior. Other studies have reported a relationship between a history of sexual abuse and sexual offending by youth, although neglect, physical abuse, and witnessing family violence were more prevalent among adolescent sexual offenders than was sexual victimization (Kaplan, Becker, & Cunningham-Rathner, 1988; Pierce & Pierce, 1987).

Subsequent findings have indicated that while the link is not inevitable between maltreatment as a child and later violent or abusive behavior, the greater the violence and victimization in the home, the more likely a child will engage in violent or abusive behavior (American Psychological Association, 1996). Osofsky (1995) notes the importance of including measures of family violence when studies are conducted of children and youth exposed to community violence. She cites her own and other researchers' findings that indicate considerable co-occurrence of family and neighborhood violence.

Family patterns in the homes of delinquent juveniles have been studied for a number of years. Duncan, Kennedy, and Patrick (1995) summarize long-standing findings in this area that suggest that families of delinquents, compared to those of nondelinquents, are "cold and conflictual," and "rigid and less cohesive" (p. 250).

Studies have continued to document relationships among violence exposure, victimization, and delinquency (Rickel & Becker-Lausen, 1995). For example, one study of 50 abused women and 80 of their children, aged 11 to 12 years, revealed that among youth exposed to family violence, the earlier the abuse began in the lives of the children, the more frequent and severe was the youth's own participation in offending behavior (Kruttschnitt & Dornfeld, 1993).

Likewise, studies of 225 African American adolescents aged 11 to 19 (44% male), living in or near public housing projects, have documented the relationship between exposure to violence and youth violence (DuRant, Cadenhead, Pendergrast, Slavens, & Linder, 1994; DuRant, Pendergrast, & Cadenhead, 1994). Results indicated that 16.2% of the variance in frequency of fighting by the teen in the past year was explained by exposure to violence and victimization, school grades, and number of sexual partners. Exposure to violence and victimization, hopelessness, and the anticipation of future socioeconomic status accounted for 15% of variability in the frequency of gang fighting. Results overall were strongest for relationships among the youth's self-reported use of violence and exposure to violence (particularly victimization), family conflict, and severity of punishment or discipline. Researchers also found a relationship between depression and use of violence that was independent of violence exposure.

Similar findings were reported by Bell and Jenkins (1991, 1993) in studies of inner-city children and African American youth in Chicago. Among 536 inner-city children (in Grades 2 through 8), those who witnessed a shooting or a stabbing, as well as those exposed to family fighting, were more likely to report their own involvement in fighting. Among another sample of 1,035 youth aged 10 to 19, those who had perpetrated violence had also been witnesses and victims of violence.

Bell and Jenkins (1994) further note the resulting posttraumatic stress symptoms, lowered self-esteem, and decline in cognitive performance that are likely to occur in these children, and the anger, despair, and psychic numbing related to exposure to chronic and repeated trauma. They suggest that victims of family and community violence will have difficulty benefiting from interventions unless the symptoms of trauma are addressed.

Research with a sample of 1,140 incarcerated adult male felons (most of whom had not experienced combat-related trauma) found a relationship between PTSD and arrest and incarceration for expressive violence, when demographic variables, antisocial personality, and problem drinking were controlled (Collins & Bailey, 1990). Among subjects with at least one PTSD symptom and expressive violence arrest, PTSD symptoms occurred in the same year as the arrest or earlier, supporting the directionality necessary for ultimately establishing a causal link.

However, studies of child maltreatment history and delinquency have failed to consistently document a clear-cut relationship between the two (Leiter, Myers, & Zingraff, 1994; Schwartz, Rendon, & Hsieh, 1994). For example, Zingraff, Leiter, Myers, and Johnsen (1993) found that although maltreated children had higher rates of delinquency than nonmaltreated children, the effects decreased substantially when demographic variables and family structure were controlled. Specific types of maltreatment failed to predict any type of offending behavior.

The latter finding is consistent with maltreatment researchers' recent recommendations that investigators move away from studies of specific forms of abuse (e.g., sexual abuse) in favor of investigating broader maltreatment as an aggregate variable (Elliott, Briere, McNeil, Cox, & Bauman, 1995; Finkelhor & Dziuba-Leatherman, 1994; Sanders & Becker-Lausen, 1995).

The Trauma Perspective

The still broader formulation of psychological trauma, which has emerged from a combination of studies on child maltreatment, combat veterans, natural disasters and other phenomena, provides a more comprehensive framework in which to consider the concept of juvenile offending behavior. From this perspective, it is possible to examine the accumulation of risk factors for children and youth from the various elements, including poverty, racism, and community violence, in addition to family violence and victimization (Garbarino, 1993).

Pynoos, Steinberg, and Goenjian (1996) note that the trend in trauma research and treatment has been a movement from broad categories of trauma to more narrow formulations, as specific features of traumatic experiences become more clearly delineated. Although this would seem to contradict the recommendations of maltreatment researchers noted above, in fact it does not. The narrowing of the field described by Pynoos et al. differs from the simple naming of types of abuse (i.e., physical abuse, sexual abuse, or neglect) criticized by others in the field. Examples listed by the authors make clear the distinction between the differentiation of traumatic experiences and simplistic categories of abuse: "Exposure to direct life threat . . . Being trapped or without assistance . . . Proximity to violent threat . . . Number and nature of threats during a violent episode . . . Witnessing of atrocities . . . Degree of brutality and malevolence" (pp. 336–337). These examples and others of this nature have been found to be associated with symptoms of PTSD. Trauma research and treatment are discussed in greater detail in the next section.

Traumatic Life Experiences: Research and Treatment

"Experiencing trauma is an essential part of being human; history is written in blood," van der Kolk and McFarlane (1996, p. 3) state at the beginning of their edited volume, *Traumatic Stress*, one of several recent comprehensive works on trauma research and treatment. Trauma may be defined simply as any life event or experience that overwhelms one's ability to cope. Traumatic experiences in childhood may cause changes in cognitive, affective, behavioral, and physiological systems.

As suggested by the quote above, it may be virtually impossible to get through life without experiencing some type of trauma—yet there are major differences in the levels of traumatic experiences; the age at which the trauma occurs and the subsequent impact on individual development; and the resources available to the traumatized person, both psychic and social (Becker-Lausen, Sanders, & Chinsky, 1995; Briere, 1992; Finkelhor & Dziuba-Leatherman, 1994; Herman, 1992).

Only in the latter part of this century has trauma become the focus of widespread scientific inquiry. Since the recognition by psychiatry in 1980 of PTSD as a diagnosis, research has supported the assertion that traumatic experience is a relatively common occurrence. Surveys reveal about one-fourth of American adolescents to about three-fourths of U.S. adults report extremely stressful experiences; full PTSD for these individuals was estimated to occur in about 10% of adults and about 20% of the youth experiencing trauma (van der Kolk & McFarlane, 1996).

Yet as indicated in the earlier discussion, many youth living with violence are responding to a complicated interplay of victimization, exposure to violence between adult caretakers, and street violence. Furthermore, as Pynoos et al. (1996) point out, earlier investigations of family factors, such as parental psychopathology or substance abuse, have failed to consider the traumatic experiences inherent within these situations, such as finding a depressed parent attempting suicide or cleaning up the vomit of an unconscious, drunken parent. These complex interactions affect measurement and may be one of the reasons child maltreatment and delinquency have failed to be consistently related in research studies.

Key issues related to the traumatic stress response affect how individuals perceive and process the world around them (van der Kolk & McFarlane,

1996): (a) the persistent intrusion of traumatic memories that distract from incoming stimuli in the present; (b) the compulsive exposure to situations similar to the traumatic experience; (c) the avoidance of environmental cues related to trauma-based emotional reactions, with accompanying numbing of emotional responses; (d) loss of ability to modulate responses to general physiological stress; (e) a generalized difficulty with attention and concentration; and (f) shifting defenses and identity diffusion.

Knowledge of the effects of trauma has gradually accumulated through-out this century, ever since Freud first uncovered his patients' memories of incest and then rejected the incest interpretation in favor of the explanation that these were fantasized sexual wishes of the young child toward the parent (Herman, 1992). Clinical work with combat veterans, first from World War I and then from World War II as well as with concentration camp survivors from World War II added to the understanding of effects of the experience of extreme circumstances on human beings, and studies of Vietnam War veterans substantially increased awareness of posttraumatic stress symptoms (van der Kolk, Weisaeth, & van der Hart, 1996). Finally, studies of women and children experiencing trauma such as rape, incest, child maltreatment, and kidnapping further broadened the awareness of traumatic experiences.

A framework for treatment of traumatic stress has evolved gradually. A phase-oriented approach to the treatment of traumatized individuals has been described and endorsed by many in the trauma field. Herman (1992) has proposed that recovery moves through three stages: (a) establishing a sense of safety; (b) remembering the trauma and grieving over it ("remembrance and mourning," p. 155); and finally, (c) reconnecting with everyday life. Furthermore, the greater the trauma, the more the individual is expected to move back and forth between stages (e.g., returning to the establishment of safety again and again as traumatic experiences are worked through).

Others have delineated the stages further, yet the three-stage model provides a useful overlay for the more detailed formulations, outlined briefly here based on those proposed by Brown and Fromm (1986) and van der Kolk, McFarlane, and van der Hart (1996). The first phase, often termed stabilization, includes the establishment of a therapeutic alliance, education of the patient regarding the effects of trauma, identification of feelings, and the teaching of coping strategies. During the period of remembering and mourning, traumatic memories and responses are deconditioned, and the cognitive schemes connected with the trauma are restructured. This is the period of integration, which should begin only after stabilization is established, when supportive therapy can provide the client a safe place to gradually uncover and integrate the past experiences into his or her present self-concept. This period provides the foundation for the final stage, that of reconnecting with everyday life. Self-development includes distinguishing appropriate boundaries between self and others, values clarification, exploration of identity issues, and interest in new and previously untried activities to expand the limits and possibilities available to the newly integrated self. Work on establishing secure social relationships, which may include interventions such as assertiveness training and sex therapy, assists the client in a successful passage into this final stage of treatment.

Throughout these phases, and particularly at the beginning of therapy, psychopharmacology may be appropriate to help the client manage symptomatology (Brown & Fromm, 1986). Intense emotionality, including grief, anger, and withdrawal, is an expected reaction to the process of working through and integrating traumatic experiences (van der Kolk, McFarlane, & van der Hart, 1996).

Although the framework for these interventions initially came from work with adults, the interventions subsequently have been found to be useful structures for work with children and adolescents as well (Gil, 1991; James, 1989; Johnson, 1989; Straus, 1994). Use of play and other techniques specific to children and youth substitute for adult methods, but the approach still follows the pattern of safety and stabilization; remembering, grieving, and integrating the experience; and ultimately, moving back into ordinary life. However, treatment of children must take into account the child's developmental level and the resources available to the child at the time of treatment, so that, for example, the entire focus of psychotherapy may be on stabilization only.

Thorough diagnosis and assessment also have been stressed as essential at the beginning of therapy. Numerous assessment devices for diagnosing PTSD are described by Newman, Kaloupek, and Keane (1996), including self-report measures, interviews, and psychophysiological assessments. Although most of these measures were designed for adults, some may be applicable to adolescents. Checklists, such as the Trauma Symptom Inventory (Briere, Elliott, Harris, & Cotman, 1995) and the Trauma Symptom Checklist for Children (Elliott & Briere, 1994), are useful with youth, particularly adolescents in the justice system who may have severe deficits in reading ability. In some cases, interviews and behavioral ratings by others (e.g., parents, teachers) may be the primary source of information about these youth, because of widespread difficulties with reading in this population.

Treatment Programs for Juvenile Offenders

For youth who have committed only minor offenses, some form of diversion program to prevent the development of more serious delinquent behavior is preferable to incarceration, particularly where adolescents who have committed more severe infractions are housed. Preventive approaches are critical, particularly given how ubiquitous violence has become in today's society. Community-based, comprehensive prevention programs that include thorough assessment of local problems, identification of target issues, and selection of a range of interventions for employment by the community, as well as encouraging collaboration among civic groups, juvenile justice, local leaders, and youth themselves, have the best possibility of success (Howell, 1995).

Although preventive approaches are always preferred, by the time youth are incarcerated, severely dysfunctional behavior has become pervasive throughout their lives. As discussed above in regard to juveniles placed in adult facilities, exposing younger or less experienced offenders to older, more violent, or more established perpetrators makes them highly vulnerable to victimization, as well as more likely to adopt behaviors similar to those around them (American Psychological Association, 1993).

Unfortunately, studies have indicated that about 15% of high-risk youth are responsible for 75% of the violent juvenile offenses committed. These chronic, violent offenders are considered the least receptive to preventive efforts, primarily because they have such a high degree of cumulative risk factors. Early interventions with firm sanctions are considered the best strategy for this group; however, this is not typically what has occurred: Although violent youth behavior tends to peak between ages 16 and 17, arrests peak at ages 18 to 19 (Howell, 1995).

Encouragingly, studies of institutional treatment programs have, in general, shown positive results with regard to recidivism. Behavioral treatment programs appear to be more effective than psychodynamic approaches or life skills programs. Andrews et al. (1990) delineated the essential appropriate correctional services necessary for an institutional program to be the most effective. These services included targeted delivery to those with higher risk factors, behaviorally oriented programs, and matching of treatment to individual needs. Programs not using behavioral interventions were also found to be appropriate when they were designed for a particular crime and were highly structured. Least effective strategies included traditional, nondirective counseling or group counseling where the focus is on communication only, without other interventions, as well as other approaches that were unstructured, loosely structured, or based on ineffective assessment of need. Deterrence programs that attempt to shake up the youth by exposing them to information about criminal penalties or to adults who have experienced them (such as a Scared Straight approach) have also been shown to be ineffective.

Many states have adopted an approach that allows for a graduated program of increasingly severe sanctions, depending on the nature of the offense, the individual's criminal history, and other risk factors relevant to escalating delinquency behavior. The array of services may include any or all of the following, from the least restrictive to the most secure:

1. Mentoring programs are for early intervention with teens in high-risk groups or for low-level juvenile offenses (e.g., truancy).

2. Community *supervision* may be carried out by volunteers trained to work with juveniles at low levels of delinquency, who in turn are monitored by professionals. Community *service* provides short-term, supervised work that may be for the purpose of restitution to victims or on projects for the betterment of the community. Either of these sanctions is designed for minor offenses and allows juveniles to remain at home and within the community.

3. Intermediate sanctions are targeted for violent offenders with the lowest risk factors: juveniles committing serious crimes such as robbery or arson, regardless of risk factors, and those committing less serious crimes, such as vandalism, auto theft, or larceny, who have high levels of risk factors. Intermediate sanctions programs include:

   a. Intensive supervision programs, the least restrictive of intermediate sanctions. The range of these services includes day treatment programs, where youth remain at home but attend special educational, counseling, and recreational services; specialized group homes, where adolescents live in a small residential facility but attend school and pursue other activities within the community; and programs that combine secure residential treatment with day treatment and aftercare services.
   b. Family preservation programs, with intensive, individualized treatment plans addressing systemic issues within the home. Multisystemic therapy, described below, may be a part of these programs.
   c. "Boot camps," wilderness camps, and job training programs that provide discipline, physical challenges, and work training in short-term, residential settings. These programs typically last about 90 days and are followed by aftercare in the community. They may be designed for nonviolent offenders only, such as the About Face program in Memphis, Tennessee, or in some cases, for more serious offenders, such as VisionQuest, a nationwide wilderness program. VisionQuest, which lasts 12 to 15 months, has been shown to reduce recidivism rates for serious juvenile offenders. However, research on the effectiveness of the boot camp approach has been mixed. Strictly punitive programs stressing control have been found to be generally ineffective, whereas those mixing control with treatment produce inconclusive results (Howell, 1995). Recidivism has not been shown to decline after the boot camp experience; however, educational and

employment gains have been documented for some programs (Peterson, 1996).

d. Community-based residential programs, which generally provide 6 months or more of intensive intervention in a restricted setting. Individual, group, and family therapy, combined with behavior modification programs, are usually part of this treatment approach.

4. Programs for the most violent offenders are typically secure, locked facilities where the average stay is about a year. The best of these programs limit the number of residents, provide anger management and conflict resolution, and work to disengage youth from gangs. Initial aftercare may consist of referral to an intermediate sanctions program for continued intervention.

Based on a thorough review of research and assessments of all types of youth programs on a continuum of care, including those representing prevention, diversion, residential, and aftercare services, the OJJDP (Howell, 1995) concluded that the principles associated with effective programs are essentially the same regardless of the stage in which they occur. It is, they suggest, not the stage in which intervention takes place that matters, but rather the program's quality, the intensity of the intervention, the appropriateness of fit with the stage it addresses, and its direction. What successful programs appear to have in common are the ability to address risk factors effectively for individual youth, strengthen those factors that provide protection and enhance resiliency, provide sufficient support and effective supervision, and increase prosocial attitudes by providing youth with a sense of having an increased stake in society.

Because of the multiplicity of risk factors associated with serious, violent offending by youth, multimodal, well-coordinated efforts must be mounted to counteract this behavior pattern. Interventions must address issues within the educational system, family system, peer group, and neighborhood if they are to be effective (American Psychological Association, 1993).

State-of-the-Art Offender Treatment: Multisystemic Therapy

A program of multisystemic therapy (MST) has been developed that provides the sustained, multilevel interventions necessary for effective intervention with young offenders. So far, it is the only treatment that has shown short- and long-term success in reducing antisocial and violent behavior in youth. MST is child-focused and family-centered. By addressing issues multisystemically, MST meets the criteria for intervention at multiple levels that has long been recognized as needed for effective treatment of youthful offenders, and it also provides flexible, individualized, comprehensive services that empower families and communities (Henggeler, 1994).

Based on a social-ecological approach, MST reflects the perspective that family members behave in a context of multiple connections with systems both outside the family and within. Delivery of services within the natural environment of home, school, or community is essential to the effectiveness of interventions, which are designed in collaboration with family members (Henggeler, Schoenwald, & Pickrel, 1995). Interventions are present-centered, targeting factors that have been identified as related to adolescent delinquent behavior, particularly those that are intrapersonal and systemic (Borduin et al., 1995). Sessions are action-oriented and usually occur in the family home or in a community setting. (For a detailed account of the multisystemic approach, its rationale, and the various applications, see Henggelier & Borduin, 1990.)

Borduin et al. (1995) studied 176 juvenile offenders at high risk of recidivism (average prior arrests = 4.2; mean severity of most recent arrest = 8.8 on a scale of increasing severity from 1 to 17, where 8 = assault /battery, 11 = grand larceny, 17 = murder). The group receiving MST was compared to a group that received individual therapy only, using multimethod assessment batteries from multiple sources before and after the intervention. Those receiving MST were more likely to show improvement in key family factors related to antisocial behavior and to show better adjustment among individual family members. A 4-year follow-up analysis of subsequent arrests indicated that those who received MST, compared to those who received only individual therapy, were less likely to be re-arrested and less likely to commit violent offenses. Other studies with this modality have shown equally promising results (Henggeler et al., 1995).

Henggeler et al. (1995) credit the success of MST to four key elements: (a) Factors determined through empirical research to be related to dysfunctional behavior are addressed comprehensively, yet tailored to the individual client; (b) services are delivered to youth and families in their natural settings; (c) therapists are well-trained, well-supported, and monitored for adherence to the treatment approach; and (d) considerable effort is invested to develop, nurture, and maintain positive relationships among the various agencies involved.

Integration of Multisystemic and Phase-Oriented Treatment Approaches

Both MST and phase-oriented therapy for trauma are relatively new and exciting breakthroughs in treatment with a great deal to offer the clinician attempting to intervene with an adolescent during the incarceration period.

MST findings suggest the importance of collaborative efforts among systems so that follow-up community treatment may continue after incarceration. Working to bring family members into the setting for systemic work, to the degree that it is possible, also appears to be an extremely important element. Where parents are not available to the youth because of substance abuse, their own incarceration, or because they have simply disappeared from the scene, the clinician should attempt to locate other family members, such as aunts, uncles, cousins, or older siblings, and try to interest them in taking a role in the youth's care.

Although MST has been used with families where child maltreatment and other family violence is occurring (Brunk, Henggeler, & Whelan, 1987; Henggeler & Borduin, 1990), the focus of the MST approach has not been the reduction of traumatic symptoms. We suggest that phase-oriented treatment of trauma should inform any individual work with these youth, who are likely to have experienced traumatic events in their history, particularly those who are from neighborhoods with high levels of community violence. Especially during incarceration, providing a safe space for youth within the therapeutic relationship may help them contain symptoms and also may allow further work to occur once the adolescent is back in the community.

Both treatment approaches stress the importance of thorough assessment at the outset, and this cannot be overemphasized. MST approaches, by including assessment of exposure to violence and other traumatic experiences in the family, as well as in the individual youth, may improve the design of individualized treatment plans. Treatment of traumatic symptoms, particularly dissociation, depression, rage, and psychic numbing, in youth and in family members, may further increase the efficacy of the multisystemic intervention. Likewise, trauma-oriented clinicians may increase the potency of individual treatment of adolescents by working systemically with schools and families.

Policy Implications

According to a report by the American Bar Association (1993),

> Once sentenced, a growing number of young people are detained in unhealthy and dangerous conditions, and denied necessary services. . . . Today, almost one-half of all incarcerated juveniles are held in overcrowded facilities. . . . Overcrowding is unhealthy and often generates violence among residents and between residents and guards. (pp. 63–64)

The report goes on to note that in addition to overcrowding, juvenile facilities often lack compliance with basic standards for safety, education, health care, and the monitoring of suicidal behavior. In some states, juveniles in need of mental health care are "dumped in correctional facilities" (p. 67) because there are too few psychiatric treatment facilities for adolescents.

Clearly, in this atmosphere, where there is any attempt at treatment, the clinician faces an uphill battle. Consequently, reform of facilities and of the juvenile justice system itself must be a high priority for all who are concerned about the well-being of youth in this country. Task forces from the National Research Council (1993), the American Bar Association (1993), and the American Psychological Association (1993), among others, all conclude that prevention at an earlier age, and short of that, treatment interventions demonstrated to be effective, are far preferable to our current attempt to lock up problem youth. To encourage the public, legislators, and policy makers to invest in prevention and treatment efforts will require all professionals with an interest in children and youth to join efforts, to speak with one voice.

The American Psychological Association and the American Bar Association have begun such a collaboration for children's issues. Although at the present it is focused on divorce and custody issues, the intention of the collaboration is to build a broader coalition for children and families. The two associations cosponsored a conference in April 1997 in Los Angeles that was titled "Children, Divorce and Custody: Lawyers and Psychologists Working Together." An APA task force on APA–ABA relations is actively involved in building a longer term relationship encompassing common concerns.

Convincing the public and policymakers that prevention is cost-effective will be one important place to begin. Tate et al. (1995) note that in 1992, keeping an adolescent in a correctional facility cost about $105.27 per day, compared to the $31.43 per day for multisystemic therapy (about $3,300 per client for 15 weeks of treatment). Likewise, the American Bar Association (1993) pointed out that incarcerating a juvenile costs about $30,000 a year, and foster care to age 18 costs $123,000, which is "more than it costs to attend a first-class boarding school, private college or to support a slot in the Job Corps" (p. vi).

We can make a difference with youth. We have tools that are proven to be effective in reducing recidivism, and we are more knowledgeable about the root causes of delinquency than ever before in our history. But until we work together to change the structure of the juvenile justice system, our treatment of offenders is likely to fall far short of our vision of what is possible.

References

American Bar Association. (1993). *America's children at risk: A national agenda for legal action.* A report of the American Bar Association Presidential Working Group on the Unmet Legal Needs of Children and Their Families. Chicago: Author.

American Psychological Association. (1993). *Violence and youth: Psychology's response: Volume I. Summary report of the American Psychological Association Commission on Violence and Youth.* Washington, DC: Author.

American Psychological Association. (1996). *Violence and the family: Report of the American Psychological Association Presidential Task Force on Violence and the Family.* Washington, DC:

Author.

Andrews, D. A., Zinger, I., Hoge, R., Bonta, J., Gendrew, P., & Cullen, F. (1990). Does correctional treatment work? A clinically relevant and psychologically informed meta-analysis. *Criminology, 28,* 369–404.

Becker-Lausen, E., Sanders, B., & Chinsky, J. M. (1995). Mediation of abusive childhood experiences: Depression, dissociation, and negative life outcomes. *American Journal of Orthopsychiatry, 65,* 560–573.

Bell, C. C., & Jenkins, E. J. (1991). Traumatic stress and children. *Journal of Health Care for the Poor and Underserved, 2,* 175–185.

Bell, C. C., & Jenkins, E. J. (1993). Community violence and children on Chicago's southside. *Psychiatry Interpersonal and Biological Processes, 56(1),* 46–54.

Bell, C. C., & Jenkins, E. J. (1994). Effects of child abuse and race. *Journal of the National Medical Association, 86,* 165, 232.

Berman, S. L., Kurtines, W. M., Silverman, W. K., & Serafini, L. T. (1996). The impact of exposure to crime and violence on urban youth. *American Journal of Orthopsychiatry, 66,* 329–336.

Borduin, C. M., Mann, B. J., Cone, L., Henggeler, S. W., Fucci, B. R., Blaske, D. M., & Williams, R. A. (1995). Multisystemic treatment of serious juvenile offenders: Long-term prevention of criminality and violence. *Journal of Consulting and Clinical Psychology, 63,* 569–578.

Briere, J. N. (1992). *Child abuse trauma: Theory and treatment of lasting effects.* Newbury Park, CA: Sage.

Briere, J., Elliott, D. M., Harris, K., & Cotman, A. (1995). Trauma Symptom Inventory: Psychometrics and association with childhood and adult victimization in clinical samples. *Journal of Interpersonal Violence, 10,* 387–401.

Brown, D. P., & Fromm, E. (1986). *Hypnotherapy and hypnoanalysis.* London: Lawrence Erlbaum.

Brunk, M., Henggeler, S. W., & Whelan, J. P. (1987). A comparison of multisystemic therapy and parent training in the brief treatment of child abuse and neglect. *Journal of Consulting and Clinical Psychology, 55,* 311–318.

Collins, J. J., & Bailey, S. L. (1990). Traumatic stress disorder and violent behavior. *Journal of Traumatic Stress, 3,* 203–220.

Cornell, D. G. (1993). Juvenile homicide: A growing national problem. *Behavioral Sciences and the Law, 11,* 389–396.

Coudroglou, A. (1996). Violence as a social mutation. *American Journal of Orthopsychiatry, 66,* 323–328.

Duncan, R. D., Kennedy, W. A., & Patrick, C. J. (1995). Four-factor model of recidivism in male juvenile offenders. *Journal of Clinical Child Psychology, 24,* 250–257.

DuRant, R. H., Cadenhead, C., Pendergrast, R. A., Slavens, G., & Linder, C. W. (1994). Factors associated with the use of violence among urban Black adolescents. *American Journal of Public Health, 84,* 612–617.

DuRant, R. H., Pendergrast, R. A., & Cadenhead, C. (1994). Exposure to violence and victimization and fighting behavior by urban Black adolescents. *Journal of Adolescent Health, 15,* 311–318.

Elliott, D. M., & Briere, J. (1994). Forensic sexual abuse evaluations of older children: Disclosures and symptomatology. *Behavioral Sciences and the Law, 12,* 261–277.

Elliott, D. M., Briere, J., McNeil, D., Cox, J., & Bauman, D. (1995, July). *Multivariate impact of sexual molestation, physical abuse and neglect in a forensic sample.* Paper presented at the Fourth International Family Violence Research Conference, Durham, NH.

Finkelhor, D., & Dziuba-Leatherman, J. (1994). Victimization of children. *American Psychologist, 49,* 173–183.

Fitzpatrick, K. M., & Boldizar, J. P. (1993). The prevalence and consequences of exposure to violence among African American youth. *Journal of the American Academy of Child and Adolescent Psychiatry, 32,* 424–430.

Garbarino, J. (1993). Children's response to community violence: What do we know? *Infant Mental Health Journal, 14*(2), 103–115.

Garbarino, J. (1995). *Raising children in a socially toxic environment.* San Francisco: Jossey-Bass.

Gil, E. (1991). *The healing power of play.* New York: Guilford.

Hawes, J. M. (1991). *The children's rights movement: A history of advocacy and protection.* Boston: Twayne.

Henggeler, S. W. (1994). A consensus: Conclusions of the APA task force report on innovative models of mental health services for children, adolescents, and their families. *Journal of Clinical Child Psychology, 23*(Suppl.), 3-6.

Henggeler, S. W., & Borduin, C. M. (1990). *Family therapy and beyond: A multisystemic approach to treating the behavior problems of children and adolescents.* Pacific Grove, CA: Brooks/Cole.

Henggeler, S. W., Schoenwald, S. K., & Pickrel, S. G. (1995). Multisystemic therapy: Bridging the gap between university- and community-based treatment. *Journal of Consulting and Clinical Psychology, 63,* 709–717.

Herman, J. L.(1992). *Trauma and recovery.* New York: Basic Books.

Howell, J. C. (Ed.). (1995). *Guide for implementing the comprehensive strategy for serious, violent, and chronic juvenile offenders.* Washington, DC: U.S. Department of Justice, Office of Juvenile Justice and Delinquency Prevention.

Irwin, J., & Austin, J. (1994). *It's about time: America's imprisonment binge.* Belmont, CA: Wadsworth.

James, B. (1989). *Treating traumatized children.* Lexington, MA: Lexington Books.

Johnson, K. (1989). *Trauma in the lives of children.* Claremont, CA: Hunter House.

Kaplan, M. S., Becker, J. V., & Cunningham-Rathner, J. (1988). Characteristics of parents of adolescent incest perpetrators: Preliminary findings. *Journal of Family Violence, 3,* 183–191.

Keeping every child safe: Curbing the epidemic of violence: joint hearings before the Subcommittee on Children, Family, Drugs and Alcoholism, of the Committee on Labor and Human Resources, United States Senate, and the Select Committee on Children, Youth, and Families, House of Representatives, 103rd Cong., 1st Sess. 33 (1993).

Kruttschnitt, C., & Dornfeld, M. (1993). Exposure to family violence: A partial explanation for initial and subsequent levels of delinquency? *Criminal Behaviour and Mental Health, 3*(2), 61–75.

Kupers, T. A. (1996). Trauma and its sequelae in male prisoners: Effects of confinement, overcrowding, and diminished services. *American Journal of Orthopsychiatry, 66,* 189–196.

Leiter, J., Myers, K. A., & Zingraff, M. T. (1994). Substantiated and unsubstantiated cases of child maltreatment: Do their consequences differ? *Social Work Research, 18*(2), 67–82.

National Research Council. (1993). *Losing generations: Adolescents in high-risk settings.* Panel on High-Risk Youth, Commission on Behavioral and Social Sciences and Education. Washington, DC: National Academy Press.

Newman, E., Kaloupek, D. G., & Keane, T. M. (1996). Assessment of posttraumatic stress disorder in clinical and research settings. In B. A. van der Kolk, A. C. McFarlane, & L. Weisaeth (Eds.), *Traumatic stress: The effects of overwhelming experience on mind, body, and society* (pp. 242–275). New York: Guilford.

Osofsky, J. D. (1995). The effects of exposure to violence on young children. *American Psychologist, 50,* 782–788.

Osofsky, J. D., Wewers, S., Hann, D. M., & Fick, A. C. (1993). Chronic community violence: What is happening to our children? *Psychiatry Interpersonal and Biological Processes, 56*(1), 36–45.

Peterson E. (1996, June). *Juvenile boot camps: Lessons learned.* Fact Sheet #36. Washington, DC: U.S. Department of Justice, Office of Juvenile Justice and Delinquency Prevention.

Pierce, L. H., & Pierce, R. L. (1987). Incestuous victimization by juvenile sex offenders. *Journal of Family Violence, 2,* 351–364.

Pynoos, R. S., Steinberg, A. M., & Goenjian, A. (1996). Traumatic stress in childhood and adolescence: Recent developments and current controversies. In B. A. van der Kolk, A. C. McFarlane, & L. Weisaeth (Eds.), *Traumatic stress: The effects of overwhelming experience on mind, body, and society* (pp. 331–358). New York: Guilford.

Rickel, A. U., & Allen, L. (1987). *Preventing maladjustment from infancy through adolescence.* Newbury Park, CA: Sage.

Rickel, A. U., & Becker-Lausen, E. (1995). Intergenerational influences on child outcomes: Implications for prevention and intervention. In B. A. Ryan, G. R. Adams, T. P. Gullotta, R. P. Weissberg, & R. L. Hampton (Eds.), *The family-school connection: Theory, research, and practice.* Thousand Oaks, CA: Sage.

Sanders, B., & Becker-Lausen, E. (1995). The measurement of psychological maltreatment: Early data on the Child Abuse and Trauma scale. *Child Abuse & Neglect, 19,* 315–323.

Schwartz, I. M., Rendon, J. A., & Hsieh, C. M. (1994). Is child maltreatment a leading cause of delinquency? *Child Welfare, 73,* 639–655.

Shakoor, B. H., & Chalmers, D. (1991). Co-victimization of African-American children who witness violence: Effects on cognitive, emotional, and behavioral development. *Journal of the National Medical Association, 83,* 233–238.

Straus, M. (1994). *Violence in the lives of adolescents.* New York: Norton.

Tate, D. C., Reppucci, N. D., & Mulvey, E. P. (1995). Violent juvenile delinquents: Treatment effectiveness and implications for future action. *American Psychologist, 50,* 777–781.

van der Kolk, B. A., & McFarlane, A. C. (1996). The black hole of trauma. In B. A. van der Kolk, A. C. McFarlane, & L. Weisaeth (Eds.), *Traumatic stress: The effects of overwhelming experience on mind, body, and society* (pp. 3–23). New York: Guilford.

van der Kolk, B. A., McFarlane, A. C., & van der Hart, O. (1996). A general approach to treatment of posttraumatic stress disorder. In B. A. van der Kolk, A. C. McFarlane, & L. Weisaeth (Eds.), *Traumatic stress: The effects of overwhelming experience on mind, body, and society* (pp. 417–440). New York: Guilford.

van der Kolk, B. A., McFarlane, A. C., & Weisaeth, L. (1996). History of trauma in psychiatry. In B. A. van der Kolk, A. C. McFarlane, & L. Weisaeth (Eds.), *Traumatic stress: The effects of overwhelming experience on mind, body, and society* (pp. 47–74). New York: Guilford.

Widom, C. (1989a). Does violence beget violence? A critical examination of the literature. *Psychological Bulletin, 106,* 3–28.

Widom, C. (1989b). The cycle of violence. *Science, 244,* 160–166.

Zigler, E., & Gordon, E. W. (Eds.). (1982). *Day care: Scientific and social policy issues.* Boston: Auburn House.

Zigler, E., Taussig, C., & Black, K. (1992). Early childhood intervention: A promising preventative for juvenile delinquency. *American Psychologist, 47,* 997–1006.

Zingraff, M. T., Leiter, J., Myers, K. A., & Johnsen, M. C. (1993). Child maltreatment and youthful problem behavior. *Criminology, 31,* 173–202.

Section V

Policy Considerations

The last section of the reader addresses several important policy issues for the future. The most serious problem for juvenile justice is the absence of careful policy development. Despite a much-improved body of knowledge about juvenile crime and what works and what does not work in juvenile justice, our policies still too often are driven by the rare sensational case that makes the headlines. The school shooting and the reckless murder of a small child are tragedies that must be addressed, but too often our policies are formed as though such cases were typical. For most cases we continue to find ourselves torn between the demands for punishment and the demands for treatment and rehabilitation.

In "Juvenile (In)Justice and the Criminal Court Alternative" Barry C. Feld outlines how the Supreme Court has been torn between these conflicting demands on the juvenile justice system. He also outlines some of the major changes in the handling of juvenile offenders and shows how these changes also reflect contradictory images of the juvenile and contradictory expectations of the juvenile court. These many competing images also mean that the juvenile court's future can follow one of several paths. Feld presents three possible policy trends regarding juvenile justice that might emerge from these contradictory images. It is clear that the juvenile court of tomorrow may look very different from the juvenile court of today.

James Hacker's "The Need to Do Something" echoes the earlier arguments raised by Frank Tannenbaum who argued that in the process of officially labeling someone a criminal and publicly branding them with that title, we may actually encourage the very activities we are trying to stop. Branding someone a delinquent can become a self-fulfilling prophecy. Hackler notes that the demands to do something are always there, and once we conclude that our intentions are good, there is virtually no limit to the harm that we can accomplish. Persons of goodwill often attempt to impose their own views in the policy development process; concurrently, they resist new knowledge which might point them in different directions. However, his discussion of the resistance to accept new knowledge provides some clues to the future of juvenile justice, and to the barriers to the development of realistic and successful policies.

This section concludes with the insight of the Honorable Lindsay G. Arthur, who asks if we should "Abolish the Juvenile Court?" Judge Arthur makes clear that abolishing the juvenile court and substituting the adult process would be a mistake. He carefully outlines the reasons why some would abolish the juvenile court, and then systematically demonstrates why this would be a step away from justice and away from building a safer society. In fact, he boldly concludes that "The public might be safer if the adult system were abolished!"

15

Juvenile (In)Justice and the Criminal Court Alternative

Barry C. Feld

The Supreme Court's decision in *In re Gault* (1967) began transforming the juvenile court into a very different institution than the Progressives contemplated. Progressive reformers envisioned an informal court whose dispositions reflected the "best interests" of the child. The Supreme Court engrafted formal procedures at trial onto juvenile courts' individualized treatment sentencing schema. Although the Court's decisions were not intended to alter the juvenile courts' therapeutic mission, legislative, judicial, and administrative responses to *Gault* have modified the courts' jurisdiction, purpose, and procedures (Feld 1984, 1988b). The substantive and procedural convergence between juvenile and criminal courts eliminates most of the conceptual and operational differences between social control strategies for youths and adults. With its transformation from an informal, rehabilitative agency into a scaled-down, second-class criminal court, is there any reason to maintain a separate punitive juvenile court whose only distinction is its persisting procedural deficiencies?

Three types of reforms—jurisdictional, jurisprudential, and procedural—reveal the transformation of the contemporary juvenile court (Feld 1991b). Recognizing that juvenile courts often failed to realize their benevolent purposes has led to two jurisdictional changes. Status offenses are misconduct by juveniles, such as truancy or incorrigibility, that would not be a crime if committed by an adult. Recent

From *Crime & Delinquency* (Vol. 39, No. 4, October 1993), pp. 403-424, copyright © 1993 by Sage Publications, Inc. Reprinted by permission of Sage Publications, Inc.

reforms limit the dispositions that noncriminal offenders may receive or even remove status offenses from juvenile court jurisdiction. A second jurisdictional change is the criminalizing of serious juvenile offenders. Increasingly, courts and legislatures transfer some youths from juvenile courts to criminal courts for prosecution as adults (Feld 1987). As jurisdiction contracts with the removal of serious offenders and noncriminal status offenders, the sentences received by delinquents charged with crimes are based on the idea of just deserts rather than their "real needs." Proportional and determinate sentences based on the present offense and prior record, rather than the best interests of the child, dictate the length, location, and intensity of intervention (Feld 1988b). Increased emphasis on formal procedures at trial has accompanied the enhanced role of punishment in sentencing juveniles (Feld 1984). Although, theoretically, juvenile courts' procedures closely resemble those of criminal courts, in reality, the justice routinely afforded juveniles is lower than the minimum insisted upon for adults.

The Progressive Juvenile Court

Prior to the creation of the juvenile court, the only special protections received by youths charged with crimes were those afforded by the common law's infancy *mens rea* defense, which conclusively presumed that children less than 7 years old lacked criminal capacity, those 14 years old or older were responsible, and those between 7 years old and 14 years old were rebuttably irresponsible (Fox 1970b). Changes in the cultural conception of children and in strategies of social control during the 19th century led to the creation of the juvenile court (Fox 1970a; Feld 1991b). By the end of the century, children increasingly were seen as vulnerable, innocent, passive, and dependent beings who needed extended preparation for life (Ainsworth 1991; Sutton 1988). The ideology of crime causation changed, as positivistic criminology, which regarded crime as determined rather than chosen, superseded classical explanations that attributed crime to free-willed actors (Allen 1981). Attributing criminal behavior to antecedent causes reduced offenders' moral responsibility, focused efforts on reforming rather than punishing them, and fostered the "rehabilitative ideal." At the dawn of the 20th century, Progressive reformers used the new theories of social control and the new ideas about childhood to create a social welfare alternative to criminal courts to treat criminal and noncriminal misconduct by youths.

By redefining social control, Progressive reformers removed children from the adult criminal system and achieved greater flexibility and supervision of children (Platt 1977; Sutton 1988). Progressives envisioned the juvenile court as a welfare agency in which an expert judge, assisted by social workers and probation officers, made individualized dispositions in a child's best interests (Rothman 1980). The inquiry into the "whole" child accorded minor significance to crime because the specific offense indicated little about a child's real needs. They maximized discretion to provide flexibility in diagnosis and treatment and focused on the child's character and lifestyle. Because juvenile courts separated children from adults and provided an alternative to punishment, they rejected procedural safeguards of criminal law such as juries and lawyers. Informal procedures, euphemistic vocabularies, confidential and private hearings, limited access to court records, and findings of "delinquency" eliminated any stigma or implication of a criminal proceeding. Indeterminate, nonproportional dispositions continued for the duration of the minority, because each child's "treatment" needs differed and no limits could be defined in advance.

The Constitutional Domestication of the Juvenile Court

The Supreme Court's *Gault* (1967) decision mandated procedural safeguards in delinquency proceedings and focused judicial attention initially on whether the child committed an offense as prerequisite to sentencing (Feld 1984, 1988b). In shifting the focus of juvenile courts from real needs to legal guilt, *Gault* emphasized two crucial gaps between juvenile justice rhetoric and reality: the theory versus practice of rehabilitation, and the differences between the procedural safeguards afforded adults and those available to juveniles (Feld 1990b). The *Gault* Court emphasized that juveniles charged with crimes who faced institutional confinement required elementary procedural safeguards, including notice of charges, a hearing, assistance of counsel, an opportunity to confront and cross-examine witnesses, and a privilege against self-incrimination.

In *In re Winship* (1970), the Court concluded that the risks of erroneous convictions required delinquency to be proven by the criminal standard "beyond a reasonable doubt" rather than by a lower civil standard of proof. In *Breed v. Jones* (1975), the Court posited a functional equivalence between criminal trials and delinquency proceedings and applied the ban on double jeopardy to delinquency convictions.

In *McKeiver v. Pennsylvania* (1970), however, the Court denied juveniles the constitutional right to jury trials and halted the extension of full procedural parity with adult criminal prosecutions. Although *Gault* and *Winship* recognized the need for procedural safeguards against governmental oppression, *McKeiver* denied the need for such protections, invoked the mythology of benevolent juvenile court judges, and justified the procedural differences of juvenile courts by their treatment rationale (*McKeiver* 1970, pp. 550-51; Feld 1988b).

Transformation of the Juvenile Court
Reformed but Not Rehabilitated

Gault (1967), *Winship* (1970), and *McKeiver* (1970) precipitated a procedural and substantive revolution in juvenile justice that unintentionally but inevitably transformed its Progressive conception. By emphasizing criminal procedural regularity in determining delinquency and formalizing the connection between crime and sentence, the Court made explicit a relationship previously implicit and unacknowledged. Legislative and judicial responses to those decisions—decriminalizing status offenders, waiving serious offenders, punitively sentencing delinquents, and formalizing procedures—further the convergence between criminal and juvenile courts.

Noncriminal Status Offenders

The definition and administration of status jurisdiction has been criticized extensively in the post-*Gault* decades. The President's Crime Commission (President's Commission on Law Enforcement and Administration of Justice 1967) recommended narrowing the grounds for juvenile court intervention, and many professional organizations subsequently have advocated reform or elimination of status jurisdiction (American Bar Association [ABA] 1982). Some critics focused on its adverse impact on children because, traditionally, status offenses were a form of delinquency and status offenders were detained and incarcerated in the same institutions as criminal delinquents (Handler and Zatz 1982). Others noted its disabling effects on families and other sources of referral, as parents overloaded juvenile courts with intractable family disputes and schools and social agencies used the court as a "dumping ground" to coercively impose solutions (Andrews and Cohn 1974). Legal critics contended that it was "void for vagueness," denied equal protection and procedural justice, and had a disproportionate impact on poor, minority, and female juveniles (Rubin 1985).

Diversion

Disillusionment with juvenile courts' coercive treatment of noncriminal youths led to efforts to divert, deinstitutionalize, and decriminalize them. The Federal Juvenile Justice and Delinquency Prevention Act (1974) required states to begin a process of removing noncriminal offenders from secure detention and correctional facilities and provided an impetus to divert status offenders from juvenile court and decarcerate those remaining in the system (Handler and Zatz 1982).

Progressives created the juvenile court to divert youths from criminal courts and deliver services; now diversion exists to shift otherwise eligible youths away from juvenile court to provide services on an informal basis. Many question whether diversion programs have been implemented coherently or effectively (Klein 1979). Rather than reducing the court's client population, diversion may have had a "net widening" effect, as juveniles who previously would have been released now are subject to informal intervention (Klein 1979).

Deinstitutionalization

Although the numbers of status offenders in secure facilities declined by the mid-1980s, those efforts were frustrated by amendments to the Federal Juvenile

Justice Act (1974) in 1980, which weakened the restrictions on secure confinement and allowed youths who ran away from nonsecure placements or violated court orders to be charged with contempt of court and incarcerated (Schwartz 1989). Although subsequent probation violations may result in confinement, juveniles adjudicated for status offenses often receive fewer procedural rights than do youths charged with delinquency (Smith 1992).

Decriminalization

Almost every state "decriminalized" conduct that is illegal only for children by creating nondelinquency classifications such as Persons or Children in Need of Supervision (PINS or CHINS) (Rubin 1985). Such label changes simply shift youths from one jurisdictional category to another without significantly limiting courts' dispositional authority. Using labels of convenience, officials may relabel former status offenders downward as dependent or neglected youths, upward as delinquent offenders, or laterally into a "hidden system" of control in chemical dependency facilities and mental hospitals (Weithorn 1988).

Sentencing Juveniles

Historically, juvenile courts imposed indeterminate and nonproportional sentences to achieve the delinquent offender's best interests. In the post-*Gault* era, a fundamental change in the jurisprudence of sentencing occurred as the offense rather than the offender began to dominate the decision (Von Hirsch 1976). A shift in sentencing philosophy from rehabilitation to retribution is evident in the response to serious juvenile offenders and in routine sentencing of delinquent offenders.

Waiver of Juvenile Offenders to Criminal Court

Whether to sentence persistent or violent young offenders as juveniles or adults poses difficult theoretical and practical problems and implicates the relationship between juvenile and adult court sentencing practices. Virtually every state has a mechanism for prosecuting some juveniles as adults (Feld 1987). Two types of statutes—judicial waiver and legislative offense exclusion—illustrate the alternative mechanisms and changes in juvenile sentencing philosophies. With judicial waiver, a judge may transfer jurisdiction on a discretionary basis after a hearing to determine whether a youth is "amenable to treatment" or a "threat to public safety" (Feld 1987). With legislative offense exclusion, by statutory definition, youths charged with certain offenses simply are not within juvenile court jurisdiction.

Judicial Waiver

Judicial waiver embodies the juvenile court's approach to individual sentencing. In *Kent v. United States* (1966), the Court mandated procedural due process at a waiver hearing where a judge assesses a youth's amenability to treatment or dangerousness. But, if there are no effective treatment programs for serious juvenile offenders, no valid or reliable clinical tests with which to diagnose youths' treatment potential, and no scientific bases by which accurately to predict future dangerousness, then judicial waiver statutes are simply broad grants of standardless discretion (Feld 1978, 1987; Zimring 1991). The inherent subjectivity of discretionary waiver results in racial disparities (Fagan, Forst, and Vivona 1987), and "justice by geography" as different courts within a single state interpret and apply the law inconsistently (Feld 1990a).

Treatment as a juvenile or punishment as an adult is based on an arbitrary line that has no criminological significance other than its legal consequences. There is a relationship between age and crime, and crime rates for many offenses peak in mid- to late adolescence. Rational sentencing requires a coordinated response to active young offenders on both sides of the juvenile/adult line. Because offenders are not irresponsible children one day and responsible adults the next, except as a matter of law, juvenile and criminal courts may work at cross-purposes when juveniles make the transition to criminal courts. Most juveniles judicially waived are charged with property crimes like burglary, rather than with serious offenses against the person; when they appear in criminal courts as adult first offenders, typically they are not imprisoned (Feld 1987; Hamparian et al. 1982).

Legislative Exclusion of Offenses

Legislative waiver simply excludes from juvenile court jurisdiction youths charged with certain offenses (Feld 1987). Because legislatures create juvenile courts, they may modify their jurisdiction as they please. Increasingly, legislatures use offense criteria either as dispositional guidelines to limit judicial discretion or to automatically exclude certain youths (Feld 1987). Some states amended their judicial waiver statutes to use offense criteria to structure discretion, to reduce inconsistency, and to improve the fit between juvenile waiver and adult sentencing practices. More states reject the juvenile court's individualized sentencing philosophy, at least in part, emphasize retributive policies, and exclude some youths from juvenile court. Exclusion statutes remove judicial sentencing discretion entirely and base the decision to try a youth as an adult on the offense. These statutes emphasizing offenses provide one indicator of the "get-tough" mentality and the shift from a treatment philosophy to a more retributive one. Punishing serious young offenders as adults exposes some youths to the death penalty for the crimes they commit as juveniles (*Stanford v. Kentucky* 1989).

Punishment in Juvenile Courts

McKeiver denied jury trials and justified a juvenile system separate from the adult one by invoking distinctions between punishment and treatment (Feld 1988b). Whether juvenile courts punish or treat may be determined by examining (a) legislative-purpose clauses and court opinions, (b) juvenile court sentencing statutes and practices, and (c) conditions of confinement and evaluations of treatment effectiveness (Feld 1990b). Despite rehabilitative rhetoric, treating juveniles closely resembles punishing adult criminals.

Purpose of Juvenile Court

Although 42 states' juvenile codes contain statements of legislative purpose, within the past decade, about one quarter of them have redefined their juvenile codes to de-emphasize rehabilitation and the child's best interest and to assert the importance of public safety and punishing youths for their offenses (Feld 1988b, 1990b). Courts considering these changes in purpose clauses recognize that they signal a basic philosophical reorientation in juvenile justice, even as they endorse punishment as an appropriate juvenile disposition (Feld 1990b).

Juvenile Court Sentencing Statutes

Sentencing statutes provide another indicator of whether juvenile courts punish or treat. Whereas most states' sentencing statutes are indeterminate and nonproportional to achieve a child's best interests, about one third of the states use present offense and/or prior record to regulate some sentencing decisions through determinate or mandatory minimum-sentencing statutes (Feld 1988b, 1990b). Washington state created a juvenile sentencing guidelines commission and based presumptive "just deserts" sentences on a youth's age, present offense, and prior record (Feld 1988b; Walkover 1984). In other states, juvenile court judges consider offense, criminal history, and statutory "aggravating and mitigating" factors when imposing determinate sentences on juveniles (Feld 1988b, 1990b). Some states' mandatory minimum sentences for serious offenses impose terms of confinement ranging from 12 to 18 months up to the age of 21 or to the adult limit for the same offense (Feld 1990b).

Juvenile Court Sentencing Practices

Juvenile court judges enjoy great discretion because of paternalistic assumptions about children and the need to look beyond the offense to their best interests. The exercise of judicial discretion raises concerns about its discriminatory impact, however, because poor and minority youths are disproportionately overrepresented in juvenile correctional institutions (Pope and Feyerherm 1990a, 1990b; Krisberg et al. 1987).

Although evaluations of juvenile court sentencing practices are contradictory, two general findings emerge. First, present offense and prior record account for most of the variance in sentencing that can be explained (McCarthy and Smith 1986; Fagan, Slaughter, and Hartstone 1987; Feld 1989). Second, after controlling for present offense and prior record, individualized discretion is often synonymous with racial disparities in sentencing juveniles (Pope and Feyerherm 1990a, 1990b;

Krisberg et al. 1987; Fagan, Slaughter, and Hartstone 1987). A comprehensive review of the influence of race on juvenile sentencing concluded that "race effects may occur at various decision points, they may be direct or indirect, and they may accumulate as youths are processed through the system" (Pope and Feyerherm 1990a, p. 331). Although offense variables exhibit a stronger relationship with dispositions than do social variables, most of the variance in sentencing juveniles remains unexplained. The recent changes in juvenile court sentencing statutes may reflect disquiet with individualized justice, idiosyncratic exercises of discretion, and the inequalities that result (Feld 1988b).

Conditions of Juvenile Confinement

Gault (1967) belatedly recognized the longstanding contradictions between rehabilitative rhetoric and punitive reality; conditions of confinement motivated the Court to insist upon minimal procedural safeguards for juveniles. Contemporary evaluations of juvenile institutions reveal a continuing gap between rehabilitative rhetoric and punitive reality (Feld 1977, 1981). Simultaneously, lawsuits challenged conditions of confinement, alleged that they violated inmates' "right to treatment," inflicted "cruel and unusual punishment," and provided another outside view of juvenile corrections. A number of courts found inmates beaten by staff, injected with drugs for social control purposes, deprived of minimally adequate care and individualized treatment, routinely locked in solitary confinement, forced to do repetitive and degrading make-work, and provided minimal clinical services (Feld 1990b). The reality for juveniles confined in many treatment facilities is one of violence and punishment.

Effectiveness of Treatment

Evaluations of juvenile treatment programs provide scant support for their effectiveness (Whitehead and Lab 1989; Lab and Whitehead 1988). Empirical evaluations question both the efficacy of treatment programs and the scientific underpinnings of those who administer the enterprise. Although the general conclusion that "nothing works" in juvenile corrections has not been persuasively refuted (Melton 1989), it has been strenuously resisted by those who contend that some types of programs may have positive effects on selected clients under certain conditions (Palmer 1991).

The critique of the juvenile court does not rest on the premise that nothing works or ever can work. Even if some demonstration model programs produce positive changes for some youths under some conditions, after a century of unfulfilled promises, a continuing societal unwillingness to commit scarce resources to rehabilitative endeavors, and treatment strategies of dubious efficacy, the possibility of effective treatment is inadequate to justify an entire separate justice system.

Procedural Convergence between
Juvenile and Criminal Courts

A strong nationwide movement, both in theory and in practice, away from therapeutic, individualized dispositions and toward punitive, offense-based sentences eliminates many of the differences between juvenile and adult sentencing practices (Feld 1988b, 1990b). These changes repudiate juvenile courts' original assumptions that youths should be treated differently than adults, that they operate in a youth's best interest, and that rehabilitation is indeterminate and cannot be limited by fixed-time punishment.

The emphasis on punishment contradicts *McKeiver*'s (1970) premise that juveniles require fewer safeguards than do adult defendants and raises questions about the quality of procedural justice (Feld 1990b). Under *Gault*'s (1967) impetus, the formal procedures of juvenile and criminal courts increasingly converge (Feld 1984). There remains, however, a substantial gulf between theory and reality, between the law on the books and the law in action. Theoretically, delinquents are entitled to formal trials and the assistance of counsel. In actuality, juvenile justice is far different. Nearly 3 decades ago, the Supreme Court observed that "the child receives the worst of both worlds: he gets neither the protections accorded to adults nor the solicitous care and regenerative treatment postulated for children" (*Kent v. United States* 1966, p. 556). Despite criminalizing juvenile courts, most states provide neither special procedures to protect juveniles from their own immaturity nor the full panoply of adult procedural safeguards. Instead, states treat juveniles like adult defendants when equality redounds to their disadvantage and use less adequate juvenile court safeguards when those deficient procedures provide an advantage to the state (Feld 1984).

Jury Trials in Juvenile Court

Procedural safeguards are critical when sentences are punitive rather than therapeutic. In denying juries to juveniles, *McKeiver* (1970) posited virtual parity between the accuracy of judges and juries when finding facts. But juries provide special protections to assure factual accuracy, use a higher evidentiary threshold when they apply *Winship*'s (1970) "proof beyond a reasonable doubt" standard, and acquit more readily than do judges (Feld 1984; Ainsworth 1991).

Moreover, *McKeiver* (1970) simply ignored that juries prevent governmental oppression by protecting against weak or biased judges, injecting the community's values into law, and increasing the visibility and accountability of justice administration (Feld 1984; *Duncan v. Louisiana* 1968). Such protections are even more crucial in juvenile courts, which labor behind closed doors immune from public scrutiny.

The Right to Counsel in Juvenile Court

Gault (1967) established a constitutional right to an attorney in delinquency proceedings. Despite formal legal changes, the actual delivery of legal services in juvenile courts lags behind; it appears that in many states, half or less of all juveniles receive the assistance of counsel (Feld 1988a, 1989). One study (Feld 1988a) reported that in three of the six states surveyed, only 37.5%, 47.7%, and 52.7% of juveniles charged with delinquency and status offenses were represented. Research in Minnesota (Feld 1989, 1991a) indicates that most juveniles are unrepresented and that many youths removed from their homes or confined in correctional institutions lacked counsel.

The most common explanation for why so many juveniles are unrepresented is that they waive their right to counsel. Courts use the adult standard—"knowing, intelligent, and voluntary" under the "totality of the circumstances"—to assess the validity of juveniles' waivers of constitutional rights (*Fare v. Michael C.* 1979). The crucial issue for juveniles, as for adults, is whether waiver of counsel can be knowing, intelligent, and voluntary when it is made by a child alone without consulting with an attorney. Because juveniles are not as competent as adults, commentators criticize the "totality" approach to waivers as an instance of treating juveniles like adults when equality puts them at a disadvantage (Grisso 1980, 1981).

The Future of the Juvenile Court
Three Scenarios

For several decades, juvenile courts have deflected, co-opted, ignored, or accommodated constitutional and legislative reforms with minimal institutional change. The juvenile court remains essentially unreformed despite its transformation from a welfare agency into a scaled-down, second-class criminal court. Public and political concerns about drugs and youth crime encourage repressing rather than rehabilitating young offenders. Fiscal constraints, budget deficits, and competition from other interest groups reduce the likelihood that treatment services for delinquents will expand. Coupling these punitive policies with societal unwillingness to provide for the welfare of children in general, much less those who commit crimes, is there any reason to believe the juvenile court can be rehabilitated?

What is the justification for maintaining a separate court system whose only distinction is that it uses procedures under which no adult would consent to be tried (Feld 1988b; Ainsworth 1991)? Whereas most commentators acknowledge the emergence of a punitive juvenile court, they recoil at the prospect of its outright abolition, emphasize that children are different, and strive to maintain separation between delinquents and criminals (Melton 1989; Rosenberg 1993). Most conclude, however, that juvenile courts need a new rationale that melds punishment with reduced culpability and procedural justice.

There are three plausible responses to a juvenile court that punishes in the name of treatment and simultaneously denies young offenders elementary procedural justice: (a) juvenile courts could be "restructured to fit their original [therapeutic] purpose" (*McKeiver* 1970, p. 557); (b) punishment could be accepted as appropriate in delinquency proceedings but coupled with all criminal procedural safeguards (Melton 1989; ABA 1980c); or (c) juvenile courts could be abolished and young offenders tried in criminal courts with certain substantive and procedural modifications (Feld 1984, 1988b; Ainsworth 1991).

Return to Informal, Rehabilitative Juvenile Justice

Proponents of informal, therapeutic juvenile courts contend that the experiment should not be declared a failure because it has never been implemented effectively (Ferdinand 1989, 1991). From its inception, juvenile courts and correctional facilities have had more in common with penal facilities than welfare agencies (Rothman 1980). Despite its long-standing and readily apparent failures of implementation, proposals persist to reinvigorate the juvenile court as an informal, welfare agency (Edwards 1992).

Even if a flood of resources and a coterie of clinicians suddenly inundated a juvenile court, it would be a dubious policy to recreate it as originally conceived. Despite formal statutes and procedural rules, the "individualized justice" of juvenile courts is substantively and procedurally lawless. To the extent that judges individualize decisions in offenders' best interests, judicial discretion is formally unrestricted. But without practical scientific or clinical bases by which to classify or treat, the exercise of sound discretion is simply a euphemism for judicial subjectivity. Individualization treats similarly situated offenders differently on the basis of personal characteristics and imposes unequal sanctions on invidious bases.

Procedural informality is the concomitant of substantive discretion. If clinical decision making is unconstrained substantively, then it cannot be limited procedurally either, because every case is unique. Although lawyers manipulate legal rules for their clients' advantage, a court without objective laws or formal procedures is unfavorable terrain. But without lawyers to invoke laws, no mechanisms exist to make juvenile courts conform to legal mandates. Closed, informal, confidential proceedings reduce visibility and accountability and preclude external checks on coercive intervention.

Subordinating Social Welfare to Social Control

Focusing simply on failures of implementation, inadequate social services or welfare resources, abuses of discretion, and persisting procedural deficiencies, however, systematically misleads both proponents and critics of the juvenile court and prevents either from envisioning alternatives. The fundamental shortcoming of the juvenile court is not just its failures of implementation, but a deeper flaw in its basic concept. The original juvenile court was conceived of as a social service agency operating in a judicial setting, a fusion of welfare and coercion. But providing for the social welfare of young people is ultimately a societal responsibility rather than a judicial one. It is simply unrealistic to expect juvenile courts, or any other legal institution, either to alleviate the social ills afflicting young people or to have a significant impact on youth crime.

Despite claims of being a child-centered nation, we care less about other people's children than we do our own, especially when they are children of other colors or cultures (National Commission on Children 1991). Without a societal commitment to adequately meet the minimum family, medical, housing, nutritional, and educational needs of all young people on a voluntary basis, the juvenile court provides a mechanism for imposing involuntary controls on some youths, regardless of how ineffective it may be in delivering services or rehabilitating offenders.

Juvenile Courts' Penal Emphasis

When social services and social control are combined in one setting, as in juvenile court, custodial considerations quickly subordinate social welfare concerns. Historically, juvenile courts purported to resolve the tension between social welfare and social control by asserting that dispositions in a child's best interests achieved individual and public welfare simultaneously. In reality, some youths who commit crimes do not need social services, whereas others cannot be meaningfully rehabilitated. And, many more children with social service needs do not commit crimes.

Juvenile courts' subordination of individual welfare to custody and control stems from its fundamentally penal focus. Delinquency jurisdiction is not based on characteristics of children for which they are not responsible and for whom intervention could mean an improvement in their lives—their lack of decent education, their lack of adequate housing, their unmet medical needs, or their family or social circumstances (National Commission on Children 1991). Rather, delinquency jurisdiction is based on criminal law violations that are the youths' fault and for which the youths are responsible (Fox 1970b). As long as juvenile courts emphasize criminal characteristics of children least likely to elicit sympathy and ignore social conditions most likely to engender a desire to nurture and help, they reinforce punitive rather than rehabilitative impulses. Operating in a societal context that does not provide adequately for children in general, intervention in the lives of those who commit crimes inevitably serves purposes of penal social control, regardless of the court's ability to deliver social welfare.

Due Process and Punishment in Juvenile Court

Acknowledging that juvenile courts punish imposes an obligation to provide all criminal procedural safeguards because "the condition of being a boy does not justify a kangaroo court" (*Gault* 1967, p. 28). Although procedural parity with adults may end the juvenile court experiment, to fail to do so perpetuates injustice.

Punishing juveniles in the name of treatment and denying them basic safeguards fosters injustice that thwarts any reform efforts.

Developing rationales to respond to young offenders requires reconciling contradictory impulses engendered when the child is a criminal and the criminal is a child. If juvenile courts provide neither therapy nor justice, then the alternatives are either (a) to make juvenile courts more like criminal courts, or (b) to make criminal courts more like juvenile courts. Whether young offenders ultimately are tried in a separate juvenile court or in a criminal court raises basic issues of substance and procedure. Issues of substantive justice include developing and implementing a doctrinal rationale to sentence young offenders differently, and more leniently, than older defendants (Feld 1988b). Issues of procedural justice include providing youths with *all* of the procedural safeguards adults receive *and* additional protections that recognize their immaturity (Rosenberg 1980; Feld 1984).

Most commentators who recoil from abolishing juvenile court instead propose to transform it into an explicitly penal one, albeit one that limits punishment based on reduced culpability and provides enhanced procedural justice (Melton 1989; ABA 1980a). The paradigm of the "new juvenile court" is the American Bar Association's Juvenile Justice Standards. The Juvenile Justice Standards recommend repeal of jurisdiction over status offenders, use of proportional and determinate sentences to sanction delinquent offenders, use of offense criteria to regularize pretrial detention and judicial transfer decisions, and provision of all criminal procedural safeguards, including nonwaivable counsel and jury trials (Flicker 1983; Wizner and Keller 1977). Although the ABA's "criminal juvenile court" combines reduced culpability sentencing and greater procedural justice, it fails to explain why these principles should be implemented in a separate juvenile court rather than in a criminal court (Melton 1989; Gardner 1989). The ABA's Juvenile Justice Standards assert that "removal of the treatment rationale does not destroy the rationale for a separate system or for utilization of an ameliorative approach; it does, however, require a different rationale" (ABA 1980b, p. 19, note 5). Unfortunately, although the ABA standards virtually replicate the adult criminal process, they provide no rationale for a separate juvenile system.

Some commentators contend that maintaining a separate punishment system for juveniles may avoid some stigmatic effects of a "criminal" label (Gardner 1989). Others speculate that because some specialized juvenile procedures and dispositional facilities will remain, it is more practical and less risky to retain than to abolish juvenile courts (Rubin 1979). Some emphasize criminal courts' deficiencies—overcrowding, ineffective counsel, insufficient sentencing alternatives—as a justification for retaining juvenile courts, even while acknowledging that these are characteristics of juvenile courts as well (Dawson 1990). Given institutional and bureaucratic inertia, however, it might be that only a clean break with the personnel and practices of the past would permit the implementation of procedural justice and sentencing reforms.

The only real difference between the ABA's criminal juvenile court and adult criminal courts is that the former would impose shorter sentences (ABA 1980c; Wizner and Keller 1977). Particularly for serious young offenders, the sanctions imposed in juvenile court are less than those of criminal courts, and a separate court might be the only way to achieve those shorter sentences and insulate youths from criminal courts.

But, recent research suggests that there might be a relationship between increased procedural formality and sentencing severity in juvenile courts. Despite statutes and rules of statewide applicability, juvenile courts are highly variable. Urban courts, which typically are the most formal, also detain and sentence more severely than do their more traditional, rural counterparts (Feld 1991a). If procedural formality increases substantive severity, could a separate criminal juvenile court continue to afford leniency? Will juvenile courts' procedural convergence with criminal courts increase repressiveness and erode present sentencing differences? Can juvenile courts only be lenient because discretion is hidden behind closed doors? Would imposing the rule of law prevent them from affording leniency to most youths? The ABA Standards do not even recognize, much less answer, these questions.

Young Offenders in Criminal Court

If the primary reason a child is in court is because he or she committed a crime, then the child could be tried in criminal courts alongside adult counterparts. Before returning young offenders to criminal courts, however, a legislature must address issues of substance and procedure in order to create a juvenile criminal court. Substantively, a legislature must develop a rationale to sentence young offenders differently and more leniently than older defendants. Procedurally, it must afford youths full parity with adults and additional safeguards.

Substantive Justice—Juveniles' Criminal Responsibility

The primary virtue of the contemporary juvenile court is that young serious offenders typically receive shorter sentences than do adults convicted of comparable crimes. One premise of juvenile justice is that youths should survive the mistakes of adolescence with their life chances intact, and this goal would be threatened by the draconian sentences frequently inflicted on 18-year-old "adults." However, even juvenile courts' seeming virtue of shorter sentences for serious offenders is offset by the far more numerous minor offenders who receive longer sentences as juveniles than they would as adults.

Shorter sentences for young people do not require that they be tried in separate juvenile courts. Criminal law doctrines and policies provide rationales to sentence youths less severely than adults in criminal courts (Feld 1988b; Melton 1989). Juvenile courts simply extended upward by a few years the common law's infancy presumptions that immature young people lack criminal capacity (Fox 1970b). "Diminished responsibility" doctrines provide additional rationale for shorter sentences for youths, because within framework of "deserved" punishments, it would be unjust to sentence youths and adults alike (ABA 1980c). Although an offender's age is of little relevance when assessing harm, youthfulness is highly pertinent when assessing culpability.

Developmental psychological research confirms that young people move through developmental stages with respect to legal reasoning and ethical decision making akin to the common law's infancy defense. Even youths 14 years of age or older, who abstractly may know "right from wrong," might still not be as blameworthy and deserving of comparable punishment as adult offenders. Families, schools, and communities socialize young people and share some responsibility for their offenses (Twentieth Century Fund 1978). To the extent that the ability to make responsible choices is learned behavior, the dependent status of youths systematically deprives them of opportunities to learn to be responsible (Zimring 1982).

The Supreme Court in *Thompson v. Oklahoma* (1988) provided additional support for lesser sentences for reduced culpability even for youths above the common-law infancy threshold of 14 years of age. In vacating Thompson's capital sentence, the Court noted that even though he was criminally responsible, he should not be punished as severely. Despite a late decision upholding the death penalty for 16-year-old or 17-year-old youths (*Stanford* 1989), the Court has repeatedly emphasized that youthfulness is an important mitigating factor at sentencing. The argument for shorter sentences for reduced culpability is not a constitutional claim because the Supreme Court consistently has resisted developing a criminal law *mens rea* jurisprudence (Rosenberg 1993). Rather, like the juvenile court itself, it is a matter of state legislative sentencing policy.

"Youth Discount"

Shorter sentences for reduced culpability is a more modest rationale to treat young people differently from adults than the juvenile court's rehabilitative claims. Criminal courts can provide shorter sentences for reduced culpability with fractional reductions of adult sentences in the form of an explicit "youth discount." For example, a 14-year-old might receive 33% of the adult penalty, a 16-year-old 66%, and an 18-year old the adult penalty, as is presently the case (Feld 1988b). Of course, explicit fractional youth discount sentence reductions can only be calculated against a backdrop of realistic, humane, and determinate adult sentencing practices. For youths younger than 14 years old, the common-law *mens rea* infancy defense acquires a new vitality for shorter sentences or even noncriminal alternative dispositions (Fox 1970b).

A graduated age-culpability sentencing scheme avoids the inconsistency and injustice played out in binary either/or juvenile versus adult judicial waiver determinations (Feld 1987). Sentences that young people receive might differ by orders of magnitude, depending upon whether or not transfer is ordered. Because of the profound consequences, waiver hearings consume a disproportionate amount of juvenile court time and resources. Abolishing juvenile court eliminates waiver hearings, saves resources that are ultimately expended to no purpose, reduces the "punishment gap" when youths cross from one system to the other, and assures similar consequences for similar offenders.

Trying young people in criminal courts with full procedural safeguards would not appreciably diminish judges' sentencing expertise. Although Progressives envisioned a specialist juvenile court judge possessing the wisdom of a "kadi" (Matza 1964), judges increasingly handle juvenile matters as part of the general docket or rotate through juvenile court on short-term assignments without acquiring any particular dispositional expertise. In most juvenile courts, social services personnel advise judges and possess the information necessary for appropriate dispositions.

Punishing youths does not require incarcerating them with adults in jails and prisons. Departments of corrections already classify inmates, and existing juvenile detention facilities and institutions provide options for age-segregated dispositional facilities. Insisting explicitly on humane conditions of confinement could do as much to improve the lives of incarcerated youths as has the "right to treatment" or the "rehabilitative ideal" (Feld 1977, 1981). Recognizing that most young offenders return to society imposes an obligation to provide resources for self-improvement on a voluntary basis.

Procedural Justice for Youth

Since *Gault*, most of the procedures of criminal courts are supposed to be routine aspects of juvenile courts as well. Generally, both courts apply the same laws of arrest, search, identification, and interrogation to adults and juveniles, and increasingly subject juveniles charged with felony offenses to similar fingerprinting and booking processes as adults (Feld 1984; Dawson 1990). The more formal and adversarial nature of juvenile court procedures reflects the attenuation between the court's therapeutic mission and its social control functions. The many instances in which states treat juvenile offenders procedurally like adult criminal defendants is one aspect of this process (Feld 1984). Despite the procedural convergence, it remains nearly as true today as 2 decades ago that "the child receives the worst of both worlds" (*Kent* 1966, p. 556). Most states provide neither special safeguards to protect juveniles from the consequences of their immaturity nor the full panoply of adult procedural safeguards to protect them from punitive state intervention.

Youths' differences in age and competence require them to receive more protections than adults, rather than less. The rationales to sentence youths differently and more leniently than adults also justify providing them with *all* of the procedural safeguards adults receive *and* additional protections that recognize their immaturity. This dual-maximal strategy explicitly provides enhanced protection for children because of their vulnerability and immaturity (Feld 1984; Rosenberg 1980; Melton

1989). As contrasted with current practices, for example, a dual-maximal procedural strategy produces different results with respect to waivers of constitutional rights. Although counsel is the prerequisite to procedural justice for juveniles, many youths do not receive the assistance of counsel because courts use the adult standard and find they waived the right in a "knowing, intelligent, and voluntary" manner under the "totality of the circumstances." The Juvenile Justice Standards recognize youths' limitations in dealing with the law and provide that the right to counsel attaches when a youth is taken into custody, that it is self-invoking and does not require an affirmative request as is the case for adults, and that youths must consult with counsel prior to waiving counsel or at interrogation (ABA 1980a).

Providing youths with full procedural parity in criminal courts and additional substantive and procedural safeguards could afford more protection than does the juvenile court. A youth concerned about adverse publicity could waive the right to public trial. If a youth successfully completes a sentence without recidivating, then expunging criminal records and eliminating collateral disabilities could avoid criminal labels and afford as much relief from an isolated act of folly as does the juvenile court's confidentiality.

The conceptual problems of creating a juvenile criminal court are soluble. The difficulty is political. Even though juvenile courts currently provide uneven leniency, could legislators who want to get tough on crime vote for a youth-discount sentencing provision that explicitly recognizes youthfulness as a mitigating factor in sentencing? Even though young people presently possess some constitutional rights, would politicians be willing to provide a justice system that assures those rights would be realistically and routinely exercised? Or, would they rather maintain a juvenile system that provides neither therapy nor justice, that elevates social control over social welfare, and that abuses children while claiming to protect them?

Abolishing juvenile court forces a long overdue and critical reassessment of the meaning of "childhood" (Ainsworth 1991). A society that regards young people as fundamentally different from adults easily justifies an inferior justice system and conveniently rationalizes it on the grounds that children are entitled only to custody, not liberty (*Schall v. Martin* 1984). The ideology of therapeutic justice and its discretionary apparatus persist because the social control is directed at children. Despite humanitarian claims of being a child-centered nation, cultural and legal conceptions of children support institutional arrangements that deny the personhood of young people. Rethinking the juvenile court requires critically reassessing the meaning of childhood and creating social institutions to assure the welfare of the next generation.

References

Ainsworth, Janet. 1991. "Re-imagining Childhood and Reconstructing the Legal Order: The Case for Abolishing the Juvenile Court." *North Carolina Law Review* 69:1083-1133.

Allen, Francis A. 1981. *The Decline of the Rehabilitative Ideal: Penal Policy and Social Purpose.* New Haven: Yale University Press.

American Bar Association—Institute of Judicial Administration. 1980a. *Juvenile Justice Standards Relating to Counsel for Private Parties*. Cambridge, MA: Ballinger.

———. 1980b. *Juvenile Justice Standards Relating to Dispositions*. Cambridge, MA: Ballinger.

———. 1980c. *Juvenile Justice Standards Relating to Juvenile Delinquency and Sanctions*. Cambridge, MA: Ballinger.

———. 1982. *Juvenile Justice Standards Relating to Noncriminal Misbehavior*. Cambridge, MA: Ballinger.

Andrews, R. Hale and Andrew H. Cohn. 1974. "Ungovernability: The Unjustifiable Jurisdiction." *Yale Law Journal* 83:1383-1409.

Dawson, Robert. 1990. "The Future of Juvenile Justice: Is It Time to Abolish the System?" *Journal of Criminal Law & Criminology* 81:136-55.

Edwards, Leonard P. 1992. "The Juvenile Court and the Role of the Juvenile Court Judge." *Juvenile and Family Court Journal* 43:1-45.

Fagan, Jeffrey, Martin Forst, and Scott Vivona. 1987. "Racial Determinants of the Judicial Transfer Decision: Prosecuting Violent Youth in Criminal Court." *Crime & Delinquency* 33:259-86.

Fagan, Jeffrey, Ellen Slaughter, and Eliot Hartstone. 1987. "Blind Justice? The Impact of Race on the Juvenile Justice Process." *Crime & Delinquency* 33:224-58.

Feld, Barry C. 1977. *Neutralizing Inmate Violence: Juvenile Offenders in Institutions*. Cambridge, MA: Ballinger.

———. 1978. "Reference of Juvenile Offenders for Adult Prosecution: The Legislative Alternative to Asking Unanswerable Questions." *Minnesota Law Review* 62:515-618.

———. 1981. "A Comparative Analysis of Organizational Structure and Inmate Subcultures in Institutions for Juvenile Offenders." *Crime & Delinquency* 27:336-63.

———. 1984. "Criminalizing Juvenile Justice: Rules of Procedure for Juvenile Court." *Minnesota Law Review* 69:141-276.

———. 1987. "Juvenile Court Meets the Principle of Offense: Legislative Changes in Juvenile Waiver Statutes." *Journal of Criminal Law and Criminology* 78:471-533.

———.1988a. "*In re Gault* Revisited: A Cross-State Comparison of the Right to Counsel in Juvenile Court." *Crime & Delinquency* 34:393-424.

———. 1988b. "Juvenile Court Meets the Principle of Offense: Punishment, Treatment, and the Difference it Makes." *Boston University Law Review* 68:821-915.

———. 1989. "The Right to Counsel in Juvenile Court: An Empirical Study of When Lawyers Appear and the Difference They Make." *Journal of Criminal Law and Criminology* 79:1185-1346.

———. 1990a. "Bad Law Makes Hard Cases: Reflections on Teen-Aged Axe-Murderers, Judicial Activism, and Legislative Default." *Journal of Law and Inequality* 8:1-101.

———. 1990b. "The Punitive Juvenile Court and the Quality of Procedural Justice: Disjunctions Between Rhetoric and Reality." *Crime & Delinquency* 36:443-66.

———. 1991a. "Justice by Geography: Urban, Suburban, and Rural Variations in Juvenile Justice Administration." *Journal of Criminal Law and Criminology* 82:156-210.

———. 1991b. "The Transformation of the Juvenile Court." *Minnesota Law Review* 75:691-725.

Ferdinand, Theodore N. 1989. "Juvenile Delinquency or Juvenile Justice: Which Came First?" *Criminology* 27:79-106.

———. 1991. "History Overtakes the Juvenile Justice System." *Crime & Delinquency* 37:204-24.

Flicker, Barbara. 1983. *Standards for Juvenile Justice: A Summary and Analysis*. 2nd ed. Cambridge, MA: Ballinger.

Fox, Sanford J. 1970a. "Juvenile Justice Reform: An Historical Perspective." *Stanford Law Review* 22:1187-1239.

———. 1970b. "Responsibility in the Juvenile Court." *William & Mary Law Review* 11:659-84.

Gardner, Martin. 1989. "The Right of Juvenile Offenders to be Punished: Some Implications of Treating Kids as Persons." *Nebraska Law Review* 68:182-215.

Grisso, Thomas. 1980. "Juveniles' Capacities to Waive Miranda Rights: An Empirical Analysis."
    California Law Review 68:1134-66.
———. 1981. *Juveniles' Waiver of Rights*. New York: Plenum.
Hamparian, Donna, Linda Estep, Susan Muntean, Ramon Priestino, Robert Swisher, Paul Wallace,
    and Joseph White. 1982. *Youth in Adult Courts: Between Two Worlds*. Washington, DC: Office
    of Juvenile Justice and Delinquency Prevention.
Handler, Joel F. and Julie Zatz, eds. 1982. *Neither Angels Nor Thieves: Studies in Deinstitutionalization
    of Status Offenders*. Washington, DC: National Academy Press.
Klein, Malcolm W. 1979. "Deinstitutionalization and Diversion of Juvenile Offenders: A Litany of
    Impediments." Pp. 145-201 in *Crime and Justice: An Annual Review*, edited by M. Tonry and
    N. Morris. Chicago: University of Chicago Press.
Krisberg, Barry, Ira Schwartz, Gideon Fishman, Zvi Eisikovits, Edna Guttman, and Karen Joe. 1987.
    "The Incarceration of Minority Youth." *Crime & Delinquency* 33:173-205.
Lab, Steven P. and John T. Whitehead. 1988. "An Analysis of Juvenile Correctional Treatment." *Crime
    & Delinquency* 34:60-83.
Matza, David. 1964. *Delinquency and Drift*. New York: Wiley.
McCarthy, Belinda and Brent L. Smith. 1986. "The Conceptualization of Discrimination in the Juvenile
    Justice Process: The Impact of Administrative Factors and Screening Decisions on Juvenile Court
    Dispositions." *Criminology* 24:41-64.
Melton, Gary B. 1989. "Taking *Gault* Seriously: Toward a New Juvenile Court." *Nebraska Law Review*
    68:146-81.
National Commission on Children. 1991. *Beyond Rhetoric: A New American Agenda for Children and
    Families*. Washington, DC: U.S. Government Printing Office.
Palmer, Ted. 1991. "The Effectiveness of Intervention: Recent Trends and Current Issues." *Crime
    & Delinquency* 37:330-46.
Platt, Anthony. 1977. *The Child Savers*. 2nd ed. Chicago: University of Chicago Press.
Pope, Carl E. and William H. Feyerherm. 1990a: "Minority Status and Juvenile Justice Processing:
    An Assessment of the Research Literature (Part I)." *Criminal Justice Abstracts* 22:327-35.
———. 1990b. "Minority Status and Juvenile Justice Processing: An Assessment of the Research
    Literature (Part II)." *Criminal Justice Abstracts* 22:527-42.
President's Commission on Law Enforcement and Administration of Justice. 1967. *The Challenge of
    Crime in a Free Society*. Washington, DC: U.S. Government Printing Office.
Rosenberg, Irene M. 1980. "The Constitutional Rights of Children Charged with Crime: Proposal
    for a Return to the Not So Distant Past." *University of California Los Angeles Law Review*
    27:656-721.
———. 1993. "Leaving Bad Enough Alone: A Response to the Juvenile Court Abolitionists." *Wisconsin
    Law Review* 1993:163-85.
Rothman, David J. 1980. *Conscience and Convenience: The Asylum and Its Alternative in Progressive
    America,* Boston: Little Brown.
Rubin, H. Ted. 1979. "Retain the Juvenile Court? Legislative Developments, Reform Directions and
    the Call for Abolition." *Crime & Delinquency* 25:281-98.
———. 1985. *Juvenile Justice: Policy, Practice, and Law*. 2nd ed. New York: Random House.
Schwartz, Ira M. 1989. *(In)Justice for Juveniles: Rethinking the Best Interests of the Child*. Lexington,
    MA: Lexington Books.
Smith, Erin. 1992. "In a Child's Best Interest: Juvenile Status Offenders Deserve Procedural Due
    Process." *Journal of Law & Inequality* 10:253-303.
Sutton, John R. 1988. *Stubborn Children: Controlling Delinquency in the United States*. Berkeley:
    University of California Press.
Twentieth Century Fund Task Force on Sentencing Policy Toward Young Offenders. 1978. *Confronting
    Youth Crime*. New York: Holmes & Meier.
Von Hirsch, Andrew. 1976. *Doing Justice*. New York: Hill and Wang.

Walkover, Andrew. 1984. "The Infancy Defense in New Juvenile Court." *University of California Los Angeles Law Review* 31:503-62.

Weithorn, Lois A. 1988. "Mental Hospitalization of Troublesome Youth: An Analysis of Skyrocketing Admission Rates." *Stanford Law Review* 40:773-838.

Whitehead, John T. and Steven P. Lab. 1989. "A Meta-Analysis of Juvenile Correctional Treatment." *Journal of Research in Crime and Delinquency* 26:267-95.

Wizner, Steven and Mary F. Keller. 1977. "The Penal Model of Juvenile Justice: Is Juvenile Court Delinquency Jurisdiction Obsolete?" *New York University Law Review* 52:1120-35.

Zimring, Franklin. 1982. *The Changing Legal World of Adolescence.* New York: Free Press.

———. 1991. "The Treatment of Hard Cases in American Juvenile Justice: In Defense of Discretionary Waiver." *Notre Dame Journal of Law, Ethics and Public Policy* 5:267-80.

Cases

Breed v. Jones, 421 U.S. 519 (1975).

Duncan v. Louisiana, 391 U.S. 145 (1968).

Fare v. Michael C., 442 U.S. 707 (1979).

In re Gault, 387 U.S. 1 (1967).

Kent v. United States, 383 U.S. 541 (1966).

McKeiver v. Pennsylvania, 403 U.S. 528 (1970).

Schall v. Martin, 467 U.S. 260 (1984).

Stanford v. Kentucky, 109 U.S. 2974 (1989).

16

The Need to Do Something

James C. Hackler

It is time you knew of Tagoona, the Eskimo. Last year one of our white men said to him. "We are glad you have been ordained as the first priest of your people. Now you can help us with their problem." Tagoona asked, "What is a problem?" and the white man said, "Tagoona, if I held you by your heels from a third story window, you would have a problem." Tagoona considered this long and carefully. Then he said, "I do not think so. If you saved me, all would be well. If you dropped me, nothing would matter. It is you who would have the problem."

—Margaret Craven

Responding to Delinquency

It is appropriate to ask how society selects and responds to those features that are seen as troublesome. Social problems change from time to time. Frequently these changes reflect the current concerns of the public as much as the "problem" itself. For example, the Ruhr Valley in Germany has suffered from pollution for many years, but the workers at the Krupp factories and other heavy industries in that area have not complained about the "pollution" problem. Those most concerned with pollution do not

James C. Hackler, "The Need to Do Something," *The Prevention of Youthful Crime: The Great Stumble Forward,* Methuen Press, Toronto, 1978, pp. 8-23. Reprinted by permission of the author.

necessarily live in areas where this problem is the most threatening. Similarly, these concerns change with time. At an earlier period in this century, pollution was viewed as a major concern. Then interest faded. In the 1960's interest was revived. Now it seems that this particular "social concern" is again losing its grip on the public imagination.

Although there is always much public interest in delinquency, different aspects attract attention at different times. In the late 1950's gang wars received much publicity. In the 1960's drug use attracted great attention. In the late 1970's these aspects have been the focus of less public interest, even though these activities have probably continued with only modest changes. In other words, delinquency, or any other social problem, cannot be isolated and studied outside of its social context. Since we cannot study everything at once, we have to focus on different aspects of the delinquency problem, viewing the situation from one perspective and then another. Our first task is to note how society responds to delinquency and distinguish which responses are temporary and which are enduring. This may help us to understand the dynamics of societal responses to juvenile delinquency.

Even though the definition of a social problem varies from time to time and place to place, we should not treat all social ills as simply being "in the eye of the beholder." Rather, social problems are deeply woven into the fabric of society and cannot be understood without taking into account the reaction of the public, the social structure of the society, the relations between various elements in the society, and the social characteristics of human beings. It is difficult to recognize many aspects of this complex pattern and to discern which behaviour patterns are the most important. The actors who "cause" the problems or who initiate action are not always easy to identify. Those who stand at centre stage may actually be less important than those in supporting roles or those who operate the lights, write the scripts, or prepare the make-up. However, we have a tendency to provide simplistic answers to most questions concerning social problems. This is also understandable. The news media want to cover a topic in a few minutes; political leaders need to present issues in clear, unambiguous terms. One characteristic of society which influences social problems is that the public demands straightforward answers to questions concerning topics such as delinquency and crime. Before attempting to recommend some reasonable responses to delinquency and crime, we need to review the dynamics of societal responses and the settings in which these responses take place.

The "We've Got to Do Something" Syndrome

After an outbreak of vandalism, purse snatching, or other malicious behavior by local juveniles, there is usually a public demand for action. Under such circumstances it is unwise for some academic to point out that the harm done to life and limb by juveniles is a tiny fraction of the injuries caused by the automobile or that the economic losses are trivial compared with those resulting from cheating on income tax, and the variety of crimes committed by more affluent members of society. Enduring certain nuisances while concentrating on vital problems has never characterized human society. Down through the ages our literature is filled with comments of how the younger generation is going to hell. While other social problems come and go, attempts to "reform" the young continue. Although juvenile delinquency may be receiving more attention than it deserves, in terms of its danger to society, it is clearly a legitimate social problem. Yet we should keep in mind that this concern is heavily tempered with emotionalism and confusion, which in turn influence the problem itself. Individuals and agencies working in the delinquency field are a product of these factors and their responses are conditioned by them.

Clearly, then, we've got to do something—not because delinquency is objectively a tremendous threat to society, but because the demands for action are always there. Since we must act, it is normal to ask the "experts" to research the problem, analyze the causes, generate reasonable proposals, launch programs based on these proposals, evaluate these programs and rationally select the programs that "cure" delinquency. Many believe that this scientific approach will lead to the "solution" of the problem. Although a scientific perspective on understanding human behaviour is valid to a degree, there is a growing belief that this "rational" approach to problem solving is oversimplified and not as revealing as was initially hoped. Therefore, I will devote considerable attention to such factors as the problems connected with the launching of delinquency prevention programs and their evaluation. Some of these activities, I will argue, are self-defeating.

Hans Mohr, a sociologist at York University who was with the Law Reform Commission of Canada for three years, argues that the logic of social science practices and the logic of social practices are not the same and therefore should not be used interchangeably. The strategy for dealing with a scientific problem is not the same as that directed toward a social concern. The response of a community to delinquency will not be "rational" in terms of "curing delinquency" if we judge it by scientific standards. However, community behaviour makes more sense when one understands that there are many different forces pulling in different directions. Community action will be a compromise response to these pressures. The public response will "make sense" even though it ignores relevant scientific knowledge. Similarly, the activities of those doing research on delinquency, launching programs, conducting evaluations, or drafting legislation will have their own dynamics. It is erroneous to believe that deductions that arise out of social science research will or should automatically be transformed into social policy. Nor should we assume that a supposedly reasonable social policy will automatically influence delinquent behaviour. Many researchers in delinquency continually complain that social policy fails to incorporate social science findings. Actually, social policy does utilize social science research, but how and when this occurs is contingent on a number of other factors.

This does not mean that science research is unimportant. Rather, it might be wiser to see the social scientist as a person who provides a smorgasbord of facts and ideas. The policy maker must choose from this selection to put together a reasonable meal. The scientist may recommend spinach because it has lots of vitamins, but if people hate spinach, they will overlook its benefits. In other words, as a strategy to obtain social action researchers should generate many alternatives. What is finally selected for public policy is based not just on what is "correct" but also on what will be acceptable to a wide portion of the public. It is clear that when the government official expects the scientist to draft legislation or when the scientist expects the public official to enshrine research findings in legislation, both of them will be disappointed.

The Ineffectiveness of Men of Goodwill

The confusion which exists in our attempts to develop a clear social policy regarding delinquency prevention is the product of neither a deliberate strategy nor ignorance. True, these two components may contribute, but the facts of delinquency are difficult to distinguish from plausible hypotheses and myths. One of the major stumbling blocks to effective social policy is the persistent belief that the intentions of "men of good will" surely result in progress.

This faith in the power of good intentions is a common response to the "we've got to do something" syndrome. However, developing courses of action on the basis of good intentions does not automatically lead to effective social policy. Just as the best will in the world, combined with the best existing knowledge, has failed to cure cancer, so the best intentions and the best existing knowledge have failed to rid the world of delinquency.

An appropriate first step, then, to a discussion of policies related to delinquency, may be to examine the various perspectives and orientations which people have toward the problem of correcting or treating people who are considered deviant. Different orientations will naturally advocate different courses of action. These orientations and recommended courses of action are a product of prevalent ideologies and beliefs. Any action program should be viewed within the context of the larger social milieu.

Societal Attitudes Toward Treatment

During the nineteenth century in Italy, public officials were concerned because people kept urinating in the street. Public urination was illegal and people guilty of it were punished. A famous criminologist of that period, Cesare Lombroso, suggested that such criminals be confined for their actions. Reflecting his own conclusions about crime, Lombroso logically argued that people who commit crimes are inherently different from others and there is little that one can do to change these innate characteristics. Therefore, society should simply confine those who commit criminal acts. However, a young student of Lombroso, Enrico Ferri, who was to become a famous criminologist in his own right, suggested an alternative: public urinals.

The point is, it is possible that no action program is needed, at least in terms of correcting deviants. Changes made elsewhere in the social milieu may be more meaningful. The need for action and the nature of both prevention and treatment programs come out of our image of man and society. For Lombroso the problem lay in the make-up of human beings. Ferri saw it as the result of a specific deficiency in society. Regardless of the correctness of any social perspective, its simple existence is a social fact. We must maintain a critical attitude toward our images of man and constantly reevaluate any policy proposals in this light.

The Resistance to the Acceptance of New Knowledge

Let us begin with two questions: does knowledge have any impact on social policy and would we recognize a solution if it was in fact discovered?

The story of Ignaz Semmelweis, a Hungarian physician working in Vienna in the nineteenth century, is revealing. This young doctor noted that women who gave birth to children in hospitals died more frequently than those who gave birth in rural areas or even in the streets next to the hospital. He performed many autopsies on victims of "childbed" fever and observed the practices of his colleagues with the hope of finding an answer to this problem. He noted that doctors examined cadavers, wiped the blood and pus on the lapels of their coats, then without washing their hands, proceeded to probe the vaginas of pregnant women.

It dawned on Semmelweis that doctors were somehow transferring the infection which they contacted in their surgical activities to healthy patients. His conclusion was that it would be wise if the doctors washed their hands before examining pregnant women. It seemed like an obvious solution, but the medical profession at that time showed little inclination to change its habits. It is difficult for us to imagine how a professional mentality could be so obtuse. In spite of remarkable declines in the death rate of pregnant women in Semmelweis' care, other doctors refused to acknowledge the demonstrated connection between dirty hands and infection. They clung to their filthy coats as status symbols in a professional hierarchy, and it was some time before they adopted Semmelweis' suggestions.

Likewise our programs dealing with juvenile delinquents frequently ignore vitally relevant knowledge. Social change takes place for a variety of reasons, and the discovery of new knowledge may be only *one* of the less important contributors. For those who set great store in public education this is an uncomfortable thought. Although we must not abandon our pursuit of knowledge, perhaps we should not be surprised when society does not utilize what we consider relevant knowledge until *other* dynamic processes have come into play.

Just as the customs and status-determining characteristics of medicine were more crucial than knowledge in Vienna in the middle of the nineteenth century, the benefits derived by those who administer the criminal justice system may outweigh academic knowledge. For example, certain ideas about "law and order," although based upon acknowledged ignorance and half truths, may form an enduring psychological base for the majority of the population.

When a policeman is killed in a shootout with a criminal, there is usually increased public demand for the death penalty. However, capital punishment may be irrelevant to the problem of protecting policemen. Most policemen, like the rest of us, risk their lives in auto accidents much more often than they do on the job. Also, intervention in family arguments is more frequently the cause of police injuries than confrontation with criminals. But the public is not always interested in objective knowledge. Justice, revenge and many other concepts may be more important. We must accept the reality that the application of knowledge plays a minor role in influencing social policy when emotions are involved and other social processes are operating.

Our mistake is in assuming that the knowledge *should* be applicable to such policy decisions, or that it should be more relevant than other factors, such as the needs and biases of those who administer a system. For example, the evidence that counseling or psychiatric treatment are irrelevant to the success or failure of delinquent rehabilitation programs is unlikely to influence the behaviour of those who are in charge of delivering the services. Unless those in authority are satisfied that their needs for security, power and prestige can continue to be met under the proposed policy change, they will resist such changes. The actual effectiveness of counseling is but one of many factors that will influence the persistence or change in delinquency prevention practices.

In addition to arguing that knowledge influences social policy only when certain conditions exist, we might well be cautious about applying new knowledge immediately. Let us speculate on the long-term consequences of any obviously sensible recommendation. Let us assume that Semmelweis had been successful early in convincing his colleagues to wash their hands. Let us further assume that the five million or so mothers who died of child-bed fever survived instead. Would Europe have had a population explosion which would have depleted its resources, led to starvation, etc.? Of course, one could speculate in the other direction. The increase in fertility could have led to the discovery of reliable birth control methods sooner and a response to population pressures at an earlier level in our technology. This in turn might have influenced the rest of the world and led to the stabiliza-tion of world population early in the twentieth century. Today's wisdom may be tomorrow's folly.

Is Knowledge Always Useful?

Let us provide another illustration. When juvenile corrections in Alberta were transferred from the Attorney General's Department to the Department of Health and Social Development, changes were made in one of the training institutions. A high wire fence topped by barbed wire which circled the perimeter of the grounds was removed in an attempt to create a new image for the training school as a place conducive to rehabilitation. Soon the rate of escapes soared. The police were annoyed. The staff had to pay more attention to locking outside doors. Conducting activities out in the yard became a problem. After a few years many people wondered whether removing the fence actually restricted the freedom of the juveniles because of the need for compensating measures.

Obviously, hindsight is more accurate than foresight. Applying current knowledge is not always the "wisest" choice. For example, it would now be difficult to rebuild the wire fence around that institution even if new know-ledge suggested that its advantages outweighed its disadvantages. The point is that the conservative manner in which knowledge works its way into policy decisions may have certain positive attributes, even though this delay causes frustration and arouses charges of incompetence.

True, humility should not paralyze us. Many reforms make sense. Un-foreseen negative consequences may occur, but such risks should not be used as a reason for opposing all change. On the other hand, since the con-sequences of reforms may be negative, change should be approached cau-tiously.

We might benefit from looking carefully at research and ideas which try to trace the consequences of programs that have been launched. Instead of asking, "How does one prevent delinquency?", we should be asking, "What have been the unanticipated consequences when carefully reasoned delinquency prevention programs have been introduced?"

Treatment Versus Justice

In the above section I have tried to show that delinquency prevention programs will be influenced by the social milieu. Current beliefs, which may be considered "knowledge" by some but not by others, will play a role, but not necessarily a direct one. A number of factors will influence the way knowledge is used or ignored. Let us now turn to the question of what might happen when certain ideas are polarized. For several decades North America has favoured a philosophy advocating help or treatment rather than punishment as a means for changing delinquent behaviour in juveniles. At the same time counter pressures to the treatment approach have been growing. These criticisms have arisen from disappointment with the effectiveness of treatment programs. Another source of pressure against the treatment approach is generated by some of the questions raised by the neo-Marxists. Some argue that the institutions generated by the "child-saving movement" were created to meet the needs of those who wanted to do the saving rather than those to be saved (Platt, 1969; Dahl, 1974). There is a further suspicion that juveniles may not have benefited from a juvenile court philosophy that pays little attention to legal safeguards in its efforts to help rather than punish the child. Some scholars argue that the child is presently getting the worst of both worlds (Lemert, 1971).

Let us assume, however, that society has resolved some of the issues raised above and government programs are moving forward in a coordinated manner. Are there other pitfalls and unanticipated consequences that require our vigilance?

The Dangers of Doing Something

Improving Illegal Skills

One of the most carefully evaluated programs in Canada was a treatment program at Matsqui Institution, a federal medium-security prison for delinquent drug addicts, located at Abbotsford, British Columbia. The treatment involved a therapeutic community setting, daily group therapy, and an academic upgrading program to grade 10 (Murphy, 1972). Surprisingly, the control group did better than the group receiving the sophisticated treatment. The findings indicate that the treatment made no difference in terms of changing the amount of time legally employed or the dollar value of legal earnings; however, compared with the control group, the treated group spent more time illegally employed, had more illegal earnings, and used more drugs after completion of the program.

It seems that treatment group members learned to express themselves in ways more likely to be pleasant to others. This social ability combined with academic skills learned by the treatment group made little difference in the legal employment sphere but gave them an edge over other delinquent addicts in the competition for scarce illegal opportunities and drug supplies.

Sophisticated Crime Disguised as Success

Another study in British Columbia by Tony Parlett and Eric Linden focused heavily on upgrading education (Parlett, 1974). While it may have been effective in terms of achieving higher levels of educational skills, Parlett notes that there could have been some unanticipated consequences.

> One of our most successful graduates from the programme has now spent more time on the street, i.e., less time in jail, than at any time in his adult life. If we did not know his background quite intimately we would consider him a successful citizen. However, the amount of money which we know he spends is very much greater than he earns. (8 or 9 times greater). Thus we are aware that he is successfully dealing in the heroin trade. He was, before we educated him, a minor, unsuccessful trafficker. Now he is a major, successful dealer. (Parlett, 1975)

This last study is particularly relevant because it illustrates how some subjects would normally be rated "successful" if the researcher did not know the truth of the situation. It is important to realize that we can get into various kinds of trouble when reacting to the demand to "do something." First, the program itself can have a negative impact on the clients; second, skilled researchers can be led astray; and third, attempts to evaluate a program, instead of simply observing it, can create a distorted picture of the program's success.

Ignoring Relevant Knowledge

Do action programs launch activities which are contrary to present knowledge? The desire to do good is often so overwhelming that it is easy to ignore present knowledge. For example, a sociologist was invited to advise a project which was designed to motivate underprivileged students to want to go to college. The consulting sociologist noted that one of the popular theories of deviance emphasized the discrepancy between desire to have certain things and the actual means available to reach these goals. When the gap between the aspirations and the means to achieve those goals is large, it is claimed that there would be an inclination toward deviant behaviour to achieve those goals (Merton, 1938). Therefore, the visiting sociologist asked if the program would also provide the means to achieve the new goals; that is, would it provide scholarships so the increased aspirations would be realized.

No, he was informed that the project was not designed to provide scholarships; it was designed to motivate underprivileged students. The sociologist argued that increasing aspirations without increasing means could lead to a rise in frustration and delinquency. Perhaps it would be better to lower aspirations and decrease frustration. The sociologist was not invited back.

Knowing the cause, of course, will not necessarily provide a cure (Nettler, 1970: 168). Some causes might not be alterable. If low I.Q. led to delinquency, there might be little we could do. If in fact the "causes" of delinquency are largely unalterable, our tendency to "do something" should be examined even more carefully.

In their study of delinquency in a birth cohort, Wolfgang, Figlio and Sellin (1972) have noted that many offenders tend not to repeat their delinquency. In fact, their data suggest that there is little to gain by treating first, second or even third offenders. Those with a fourth offence or more might profitably be the target of intervention. This recommendation differs markedly from the more frequent comment, "We must intervene earlier, so we can help." The same study also notes that offenders who were punished severely had worse subsequent delinquent careers than those who were punished mildly, even after controlling for the category of offences.

True, there may be situations where only dramatic changes can bring about any changes, and this may apply to some aspects of juvenile programs in some parts of North America. It is also possible that loud voices crying for drastic changes will help set the stage for more cautious reforms; but despite the criticsm from the Left that a policy of gradualism will automatically be ineffective, I would argue that none of the advocates of revolutionary changes has demonstrated the superiority of their recommendations. The same judgement applies to law and order advocates on the other end of the political spectrum. There may be times when a situation is considered so serious that we are willing to accept the gamble of an extreme policy, but we should be acutely aware that it is a gamble. An alternative strategy is to see delinquency as a trade-off for other features in our society. How much are we willing to pay for a highly individualistic society?

Delinquency: The Price We Must Pay for Individualism?

That delinquency is a social evil is a point of view most people would accept; that it may be a necessary one is an opinion many would find abhorrent. In this context the analogy of delinquency and disease can prove useful.

I personally find that treating delinquency as if it were a sickness is a dubious strategy, but let us ask if certain sicknesses are not useful to society. In Africa, sickle-cell anemia is common in certain areas. It is inherited through a recessive gene; that is, some people in the population carry the disease in their genes but show no symptoms of the disease themselves. Africans with recessive genes for sickle-cell anemia have a greater resistance to malaria and are, therefore, able to live in areas where that disease is common.

A second category includes those individuals who inherit genes for sickle-cell anemia from both the father and mother. Under these conditions the recessive trait becomes dominant. These people will be anemic and it is likely that they will not live very long.

A third group of individuals will not inherit genes for sickle-cell anemia from either the father or mother and will be incapable of producing offspring who have the disease or passing on the characteristics. However, such individuals will have a relatively low tolerance to malaria and will die more easily in infested areas.

As we can see, this particular disease has certain positive effects. It enables some persons to live in malaria-infested areas. On the other hand, approximately one-quarter of the children born to a population where this gene is widespread will be anemic and will die young. A primitive society without the technology to eliminate malaria might look upon sickle-cell anemia as a "price" paid for protection against malaria.

Can juvenile delinquency be seen in a similar manner? Is it the price we pay for a creative and individualistic society? Those who are treatment-oriented will resist such a philosophy. Perhaps it is necessary to accept that random delinquency is preferable to organizing these deviants for the purpose of social improvement. After all, Hitler was successful in turning hoodlums into soldiers by giving them uniforms and letting them go around assaulting citizens and breaking up printing presses. Drastic and over-simplified cures have failed to work in the past, yet they continue to attract supporters. Even a past president of the Canadian Psychiatric Association, Keith Yonge, has suggested that special work camps be established for young people who use drugs and refuse to take advantage of the educational opportunities in our society (Edmonton *Journal,* November 21, 1969). The possibility that the cure could be worse than the disease is relevant to a balanced perspective on delinquency. A little delinquency may be essential to a healthy society. Thinking of delinquency as a disease that can be eradicated or a war that can be won is nice-sounding rhetoric for politicians; however, it is unlikely that delinquency will be cured, solved, or conquered in battle.

The Great Stumble Forward

Given the debate between those who wish to "treat" and those who wish to return to a more legalistic approach, we can anticipate a greater demand for evidence that a specific program works or does not work. Hence, there will be an increasing demand for the evaluation of programs. Those of us in the research business should welcome this increased interest in evaluation. However, it is possible that some of these efforts could consume vast amounts of scarce resources and have a variety of negative side effects.

Yet stumble forward we must. Society demands it and the reasons for proceeding outweigh those for doing nothing. Our rather trivial accomplishments should make us hesitant, but the momentum is great. Despite loud and seemingly confident voices, the direction is not clear. There is good reason to believe that some of the seemingly promising routes will in fact be long detours. Even if we correctly identify some of the routes which will bring us closer to the goal, the path will probably be bumpy. There may be tremendous forces dragging us down certain roads, and usually it will be difficult to distinguish the cries of those who are wise and courageous from those who are simply frightened and confused. A reasonable strategy suggests that we should study the experiences of those who have stumbled on ahead of us. Therefore, let us look carefully at some of the more sophisticated delinquency prevention programs and their evaluations to see if we can chart a reasonable course.

References

Dahl, Tove Stang, "The Emergence of the Norwegian Child Welfare Law," *Scandinavian Studies in Criminology,* 1974, 5: 83-98.

Lemert, Edwin, M., "Instead of Court: Diversion in Juvenile Justice," 1971, National Institute of Mental Health, Rockville, Maryland.

Merton, Robert K. "Social Structure and Anomie," *American Sociological Review,* 1938 3: 672-682.

Murphy, Brian C., "A Quantitative Test of the Effectiveness of an Experimental Treatment Program for Delinquent Opiate Addicts," Research Centre Report 4, 1972. Ottawa: Solicitor General of Canada.

Nettler, Gwynn, "Explanations," 1970, New York: McGraw-Hill.

Parlett, T.A.A., "The Development of Attitudes and Morality in Adult Offenders," 1974 Unpublished Ph.D. Dissertation, University of Victoria, B.C.

Parlett, T.A.A., Personal correspondence, 1975.

Platt, Anthony M., "The Child Savers," 1969, Chicago: University of Chicago Press.

Wolfgang, Marvin E., Robert M. Figlio and Thorsten Sellin, "Delinquency in a Birth Cohort," 1972, Chicago: University of Chicago Press.

17

Abolish the Juvenile Court?

Judge Lindsay G. Arthur

> The question is not what is the most gratifying way to take revenge on
> criminals, but what are the most effective ways to fight crime.[1]

For at least three decades there have been voices wanting to abolish the
juvenile court and its dedication to rehabilitation.[2] Their voices have grown
louder with the public outcry that something be done about the growing
number of violent crimes. But when the abolition proposals are analyzed,
they don't do much to reduce violent crime. They may provide crueler
punishments. They may provide longer punishments. They may satisfy the
public's demand for revenge for past crime. But they don't reduce future
crime. Tougher sentences may lock people up longer but they don't scare or
deter even the graduates of the prisons very much: two-thirds of them
return within three years.[3] Rather than reduce crime, moving juveniles into
the adult system may even increase the threat to public safety.

> Given the studies which suggest that transferred juveniles are more
> likely to recidivate, transferring nonviolent offenders to criminal court
> may actually undermine public protection.[4]

The Goal is to Reduce Re-offending—
Go back to basics

The primary and maybe the only goal of any criminal justice system,
juvenile or adult, very simply is to reduce future offending, to protect the

Arthur, Lindsay G. 1998. Abolish the Juvenile Court? *Juvenile and Family Court Journal,*
49 (1), 51–58.

public by having less repeat crime. The public demands retribution to satisfy its sense of vengeance but vengeance has no social value. Vengeance doesn't make the recipient any more law abiding; it may make him less law abiding, demanding a revenge of his own. Uniform sentences for all similar offenders may strike a blow against racism but there is uniformity only as to offenses, not as to impact on the offenders; better that offenders were sentenced according to the danger they pose in the future[5] rather than according to whatever plea bargained offense they committed in the past. Proportionality, which provides more serious punishment for more dangerous *offenses*, would be fine if it provided more serious punishment for more dangerous *offenders*. If punishment and prisons, "just deserts," "proportionality," "uniformity,"[6] and "accountability" would reduce recidivism, we should use them for both adults and juveniles, as the adult system does now; but the adult system makes no claim that it reduces recidivism. Its goal is to reduce discrimination, not crime.[7] If considering the reasons for an individual's criminality—his family and environment, his friends and their activities, his school/job record, his respect for others—and providing rehabilitation for these will reduce recidivism, we should use rehabilitation for both juveniles and adults. The juvenile system has been doing this for a hundred years, and more effectively reducing recidivism than the adult system.[8]

> —there is no evidence that young offenders handled in criminal court are less likely to recidivate than those remaining in juvenile court.[9]

Harsher Punishment?

The public demands that every crime must be punished with ever harsher sentences[10] as though locking a violent young person in a cage[11] with violent older criminals[12] and pervasive boredom will somehow persuade him not to be violent. It doesn't work that way and most of the young prisoners will commit a felony when released.[13] Locking a juvenile in a huge, barred room with nothing but felons and with nothing for the unmotivated to do but make license plates[14] will not make him law-abiding when back on the streets, where he will have the same criminal propensities, run with the same gang, live with the same family, have the same lack of marketable skills, face the same dead-end as before. Better to do as the juvenile system tries to do: change his propensity for crime, give him a new gang through such as the Boys Club or the Scouts, work with his family on controlling and listening to the child and giving him a value system.

The adult system emphasizes punishing the *offense,* not the *offender.*[15] But in fact the system seldom punishes the offense that was committed:

plea bargaining dismisses most offenses. If an offender is charged with several offenses, he is allowed to plead to one and have the others dismissed. If he is charged with a serious offense, the charge is reduced to a lesser offense that the offender will plead to. Plea bargaining makes a shambles of the neat "guideline" grids[16] of carefully proportioned punishment for every offense—and teaches offenders they can beat the system. The juvenile court's rehabilitative model looks to the future: it focuses not just on what the offender did but on why he did it, who and what influenced him, and what can be done to improve these influences in the future. The juvenile court's individualized, rehabilitative system looks at each offender and his danger in the future. The adult punitive system looks at each plea bargained offense with the same punishment for every person who commits the offense, regardless of whether one of them may commit a new crime as soon as he's released.[17] The adult system puts control of sentencing in the hands of two over-worked lawyers who bargain the offense and thus the sentence because they don't have time for trials. The juvenile rehabilitative system puts control of sentencing in the hands of judges, most of whom are dedicated and highly trained.[18] The juvenile rehabilitative system produces less recividism.[19]

Longer Time?

Abolishing the juvenile court or merging it with the adult system does not necessarily mean a much longer sentence. Violent offenders in the adult system, whatever their threat to society, are now released after serving an average of only about five years, not much longer than in the juvenile system. Nor will keeping adults or juveniles in prison for longer terms necessarily deter crime.[20]

Exposing a juvenile to living in prison with hundreds of violent men will not teach him to be a good citizen when he is released [21]—and virtually all prisoners in the adult system are released.[22] They are released by the adult system after a fixed term with a third of their sentences reduced if they behaved well in the prison, regardless of how well they will behave in public. They are usually released on parole; but only half of them will successfully complete the parole term.[23] The juvenile system, within statutory limits, keeps each offender until it is safe to release him.

Manage Predators

There are those who say the juvenile courts cannot handle amoral, predatory juveniles who have no concern for the fights or lives of others, vicious juveniles who need to be locked up until it is safe to release them. The critics are right. With the age limits placed on them, the juvenile courts cannot handle them. As a consequence, in every state, the juvenile courts have for years been sending the predatory juveniles to the adult courts. But a judge[24] determines by a due process hearing[25] which are predators, a hearing the reformers would deny both the predators and the less violent. Automatic referrals required by some state legislatures are sending into the adult system too many juveniles who don't need strict controls.[26] They are sent to an adult system which in most states locks them up for only a predetermined, fixed term of months,[27] and then releases them when the term is over, whether still dangerous or not. The public is rightly concerned that in the name of uniformity, no attention is paid to which individual is dangerous and which is safe for release.[28] They are all released!

Manage the Non-Violent

Those who would abolish the juvenile court make little mention of the petty and middle offenders: the shoplifters, fist-fighters, public nuisances, the truants, the runaways, the incorrigibles and car thieves who would automatically be in the full adult criminal system if there were no juvenile court. Presumably they would be run through the maw of the adult system,[29] allowed to plead to some lesser offense because the lawyers don't have time to try the real offenses? Twelve- and thirteen-year-olds would be put in jails and workhouses, mixed with all the adult bums and cheap crooks and in prisons full of some hundreds or thousands of felons?[30] Would this somehow help them? Would they be protected from homosexual rape?[31] Would juvenile staff be moved to adult staff? Would it mean abolishing juvenile intake, which screens out large numbers of first offenders who aren't going to commit another offense, with or without court? Would it mean sending all these children into the mass of the criminal system?

More Due Process?

There are those who say the juvenile courts fail to provide adequate due process, that some offenders face the juvenile courts without lawyers. Just about as many adult offenders in the adult courts have no lawyers. Public defenders are badly overworked in both systems. They fail to show that the adult courts are any better than the juvenile courts.[32] Neither system provides counsel for traffic offenders. No counsel is provided for juvenile status offenders. The public defenders provided for adult minor offenders carry massive caseloads. Waiver of counsel is rife and too easy in both systems. It's as easy to improve one as the other.

—the reality of adult criminal proceedings is crowded courtrooms in which justice is dispensed through waivers and pleas negotiated by defense attorneys who are often less than zealous and well-prepared advocates.[33]

The critics castigate the juvenile system for not using juries[34] even though the United States Supreme Court has said the use of juries in juvenile courts is up to each state.[35] In fact, in the states which allow juries for juveniles, they are seldom used.[36] They are less used in the adult system.[37]

What About the Neglected and Dependent Children?

If the juvenile court were abolished, the neglected, the abused, and the status offenders would have no court designed to protect them. The reformers would have them handled administratively by social workers, where there would be no due process at all! Nor would there be any neutral authority to review the fairness of the social workers whose interest would be primarily in what they deemed to be best for the children, with only secondary regard for the rights of the parent(s). Children could be removed from their homes at the discretion of a social worker, and kept away for as long as the social worker saw fit. These reformers are the same people who inveigh against the lack of due process in the present juvenile system. Truancy could be overlooked by a staff already too busy with battered children, even though truancy is too often the first step to a lifetime of problems and criminality.[38] There would be no compulsory sanction for curfew, and persistent runaways could not be held even for a few days of analysis and reconciliation. A child could be taken from her mother, parental rights terminated, the little girl put up for adoption all on a social worker's decision! Maybe some court somewhere would be allowed to review the decision by a habeas proceeding, but this is not mentioned. To gain what they aver is a little more due process to some criminal offenders, they would deprive half the children now coming to the juvenile courts of all due process!

Is it a *Fait Accompli*?

There are those who say that with *Gault*[39] the adjudicatory stages of both the juvenile and adult systems have become about the same[40] and, with juvenile courts switching from rehabilitation to punishment, the dispositional stages have also become about the same. Therefore they say that the juvenile court can be abolished.[41] But, as to the adjudicatory stage, these are the same critics who condemn the juvenile system for having too little due process. As to the dispositional stage, they assume juvenile courts have become punishment-oriented even though the punishment orientation for juvenile courts has been adopted legislatively only in the State of Washington, and judicially only in a small number of the nation's three thousand juvenile courts and fifty-one appellate courts.[42]

Their concern is only with criminal offenses, yet half of juvenile court cases are neglect, dependency, and status offense matters which the reformers casually say can be handled administratively! And even after merging the two courts, the reformers would require an infancy defense[43] at the adjudicatory stage and a "youth discount"[44] at the dispositional stage. The juvenile court now considers both; the adult system considers neither. The infancy defense is of doubtful constitutional utility in the adult system.[45] The youth discount would be a factor of age and thus would apply arbitrarily to all youth, including those now certified and sentenced as adults. And if the purpose of abolition is to punish youth more harshly, why would you dissipate that harshness back to where it is now by a youth discount? If after abolition, the adult system would be redesigned to give the juveniles an infancy defense as special adjudicatory treatment and a youth discount as special dispositional treatment, would these be provided by a special "Juvenile Division"? As it is now?

Summary

There are many who think that juvenile violent crime will be better managed by abolishing the juvenile court. They think that the crueler punishment of the adult criminal system is needed, though they want to temper incarceration by using juvenile facilities. They want longer punishment, though the five-year average time now served by violent adults isn't much longer than for juveniles. They want adult procedural standards, though they would have the "infancy defense" at trial and the "youth discount" at sentencing. They want more due process, though they are quite ready to throw neglected children and status offenders to administrative handling with no due process.

They would do all this even though they offer no evidence that abolition of the juvenile court would reduce the violent crime rate—because the clear evidence is that it would not. The clear evidence is that while the juvenile rehabilitative approach of changing the influences which cause the juvenile to offend does not satisfy the public's thirst for retribution, it produces a lower recidivism rate than the adult punitive approach of making life miserable based on the plea bargained offense. The public might be safer if the adult system were abolished! Instead of merging the juvenile court into the adult system's sterile punishment-oriented approach, which does little to reduce crime, the public would face less crime if the adult courts were merged into the juvenile system where the reasons for committing crime would be reduced.

> Our prisons have failed their inmates. prisoners must endure a wasteful, if not destructive, period of their lives in an environment that makes it difficult to maintain dignity and self-esteem. Our prisons have failed society because they do not, generally, provide an experience that is likely to help offenders overcome the obstacles that led them to make mistakes for which they are now being punished. Instead they "reinforce the violence and exploitation that many offenders were sent to prison for in the first place." They have failed because they do not promote restoration [rehabilitation], a key to successful reintegration . . . "Offenders are more dangerous when they are released than when they entered prison."[46]

References

[1] David C. Anderson, " Retribution vs. Intervention" adapted from the May-June issue of the American Prospect by the *Star Tribune* [Minneapolis and St. Paul] June 5, 1997, page A24.

[2] Possibly the most persistent writer advocating abolition has been Professor Barry Feld; see his exposition, *Juvenile Justice,* 69 Minn. L.R. 141, 261 [1984].

[3] "A Justice Department survey of 11 states showed that 62½% of all released prisoners were arrested within 3 years—A Rand Corp. survey of former inmates, found that in California, 76 percent of former inmates were arrested within 3 years of their release—" *Correcting Revolving Door Justice: New Approaches to Recidivism,* Testimony at a Hearing before the Subcommittee on Crime and Criminal Justice of the Committee on the Judiciary, House of Representatives, One Hundred and Third Congress, March 1, 1994.

[4] *A Case for Reinventing Juvenile Transfer,* Elizabeth E. Clarke, Juvenile & Family Court Journal, Fall 1996, Vol. 47 No. 4, pg 19.

[5] "If the defendant's violence arises out of an irrational response to situations which will occur frequently in his lifetime or when he is under the influence of alcohol or drugs, or even if he is likely to strike out physically at others when he has an argument, he is probably one who comes within the concept of dangerousness. But . . . not every short-tempered person who gets into fights regularly is a serious threat. Relatively few are 'dangerous'." Model Sentencing Act 2nd Edition, Council of Judges of the National Council on Crime & Delinquency, "Crime & Delinquency" 1972, pg. 5.

[6] "There is no greater injustice than to treat unequal things equally." *Aristotle.*

[7] Structured sentencing, the so-called "guidelines," uses a grid devised by a legislative commission to make sentences in the adult system uniform by race and proportionate by the seriousness of the offense. The system now includes the federal government, nearly half the states, and some juvenile courts. It makes no claim that it will reduce recidivism. "—no state has formally claimed that guidelines will measurably reduce crime rates or set as one of its guideline goals the reduction of crime rates." U.S. Dept. of Justice, Bureau of Justice Assistance, Monograph [1996] page 115.

[8] Donna M. Bishop et al., The Transfer of Juveniles to Criminal Court: Does it Make a Difference?, 42 [2] *Crime & Delinquency* 171 [1996].

[9] U.S. Dept. of Justice, Office of Juvenile Justice and Delinquency Prevention, *Juvenile Offenders and Victims: A Focus On Violence,* May 1995 at 29, as quoted by Elizabeth E. Clarke, *A Case for Reinventing Juvenile Transfer,* Juvenile & Family Court Journal, Fall 1996, Vol. 47 No. 4, pg 11.

[10] Call it the 'back-end/front-end' debate. Back-enders focus on the retribution dispensed at the conclusion of the criminal justice process; front-enders look for earlier interventions: more creative policing, gun control, drug treatment and other alternatives to prisons. While the back-enders talk about the crime they prevent by incarcerating criminals, front-enders point out that eventually most criminals are released and return to crime." David C. Anderson, "Retribution vs. Intervention" adapted from the May–June issue of the *American Prospect by the Star Tribune* [Minneapolis and St. Paul] June 5, 1997 page A24.

[11] Adult prisons in 24 states have been declared constitutionally cruel, *Rhodes v. Chapman,* 452 U.S. 337, 353–354 [1981].

[12] Recidivism was inversely related to the age of the prisoner at the time of release: the older the prisoner, the lower the rate of recidivism. U.S. Dept. of Justice, Bureau of Justice Statistics, *Recidivism of Prisoners Released in 1983.* [1989].

[13] "Approximately 69% of a group of young parolees were rearrested for a serious crime within 6 years of their release from prison—Excluding violations of parole and probation, these parolees were rearrested for more than 36,000 felonies or serious misdemeanors, including approximately 6,700 violent crimes and nearly 19,000 property crimes." U.S. Dept. of Justice, Bureau of Justice Statistics, *Recidivism of Young Parolees.* [1988].

[14] As anecdotal evidence, the author has visited several state prisons in Minnesota, each offering excellent chances to learn well-paying marketable trades; but only a minority of the inmates are interested in learning. So they make license plates or do other menial work.

[15] "The purpose of the sentencing guidelines is to establish rational and consistent sentencing standards which reduce sentencing disparity and ensure that sanctions following conviction of a felony are proportional to the severity of the *offense* of conviction and the extent of the offender's criminal history." *Minnesota Sentencing Guidelines and Commentary,* Sec. 1 [emphasis added].

[16] See note 7, supra.

[17] "His hands stained with the blood of the woman he had just killed, Lawrence Stapleton is confronting America with a predicament: what to do about criminals who pay the price society imposes but still remain a danger." *Arizona Republic,* February 21, 1997, page 1.

[18] "Judges appear to be more adept than prosecutors or state legislatures in selecting serious, violent, and chronic offenders for transfer." James C. Howell, *Juvenile Transfers to Criminal Court,* Juvenile and Family Justice Today, Spring 1997, page 13.

[19] See note 8, supra.

[20] "Time served in prison had no consistent impact on recidivism rates—those who had served 6 months or less in prison were about as likely to be rearrested as those who had served more than 2 years." U.S. Dept. of Justice, Bureau of Justice Statistics, *Recidivism of Young Parolees* [1988]. See also, *Out of Sight, Out of Mind: Is Blind Faith in Incapacitation Justified?,* 105 Yale L.J. 1433 [1996] Book review of Incapacitation by Zimring, et al., Oxford Univ. Press 1995.

[21] "We must also remain vigilant about a juvenile's right to effective counsel and cognizant of the potentially harmful impact of placing juveniles in adult jails, lockups and correctional facilities, including problems associated with overcrowding, abuse, youth suicide, and the risk of transforming treatable juveniles into hardened criminals." *Combatting Violence and Delinquency: The National Juvenile Justice Action Plan,* Coordinating Council on Juvenile Justice and Delinquency Prevention, U.S. Dept. of Justice, Office of Justice Programs, Office of Juvenile Justice and Delinquency Prevention, Page 4.

[22] "On average, it takes less than two years to completely fill and empty State prisons of their approximate 750,000 inmates. That is, the average sentence of a State prisoner is 22 months—An average murderer serves 5½ years; a rapist, 3; a robber, 2¼; and someone convicted of assault, 1 year

and 3 months." David C. Anderson, "Retribution vs. Intervention" adapted from the May–June issue of the *American Prospect by the Star Tribune* [Minneapolis and St. Paul] June 5, 1997, page A24.

[23] *Parole Discharges in 29 States,* Sourcebook of Criminal Justice Statistics 1995, U.S. Dept. of Justice, 1996, Table 6.66, page 597.

[24] "Judges appear to be more adept than prosecutors or state legislatures in selecting serious, violent, and chronic offenders for transfer." James C. Howell, *Juvenile Transfers to Criminal Court,* Juvenile and Family Justice Today, Spring 1997, page 13.

[25] *Kent v. United States,* 383 U.S. 541 [1966].

[26] "— from November 9, 1992 through March 1, 1994—334 youth subject to automatic transfer passed through the Cook County detention center. *The data on these youth reveals that a significant proportion of the youth were not charged with a serious felony, and did not receive time in state corrections:* [emphasis in the original]—

- Nearly half the cases transferred were dismissed [23.6%] or resulted in a sentence of probation [24%].
- Of the 262 youth for whom racial data was available, 248 [94.7%] were African-American or Latino.

A Case for Reinventing Juvenile Transfer, Elizabeth E. Clarke, Juvenile & Family Court Journal, Fall 1996, Vol. 47 No. 4, pg 3.

[27] See note 15 supra.

[28] See note 17, supra.

[29] "— the reality of adult criminal proceedings is crowded courtrooms in which justice is dispensed through waivers and pleas negotiated by defense attorneys who are often less than zealous and well-prepared advocates." Irene Merker Rosenberg, *Leaving Bad Enough Alone: A Response to the Juvenile Court Abolitionists,* 1993 Wisc. L.R. 163 [1993] page 173, citing Michael E. Tiger, *The Supreme Court, 1969 Term: Waiver of Constitutional Rights: Disquiet in the Citadel,* 84 Harv. L.R. 1, 4–7 [1970]. Ms Rosenberg's paper is an excellent and fulsome review of the problems of abolition by a person who usually shares the philosophies of the abolition advocates.

[30] Although juvenile correction facilities are not as bad as adult prisons, they are not so consistently good that they provide an unquestionably therapeutic 'alternative purpose.'" Barry Feld, Juvenile Justice, 69 Minn. L.R. 141, 261 [1984].

[31] Currently, of the juveniles who are referred to the adult system, about 90% are incarcerated and are all treated the same as adults in the prisons except maybe for some extra food. *Juveniles Processed in Criminal Court and Case Dispositions,* U.S. General Accounting Office [1995], pages 24, 29.

[32] Irene Merker Rosenberg, *Leaving Bad Enough Alone: A Response to the Juvenile Court Abolitionists,* 1993 Wisc. L.R. 163 [1993] page 173, citing Michael E. Tiger, *The Supreme Court, 1969 Term: Waiver of Constitutional Rights: Disquiet in the Citadel,* 84 Harv. L.R. 1, 4–7 [1970].

[33] Barry Feld, *Juvenile Justice,* 69 Minn. L.R. 141, 261 [1984].

[34] *McKeiver v. Pennsylvania,* 403 U.S. 528 [1971].

[35] "Of the 148 cases which did proceed to trial and for whom information was available, it was reported that *the vast majority of the automatic transfers in Cook County [93.2%] waived their right to a jury trial* [emphasis in original]. Nearly three-quarters [72.3%] of the youth entered pleas of guilty. About 20% [20.3 %] of the youth were tried without a jury." *A Case for Reinventing Juvenile Transfer,* Elizabeth E. Clarke, Juvenile & Family Court Journal, Fall 1996, Vol.47 No. 4, pg 18.

[36] In state courts in 1988, only 5% of those charged with felonies went to trial by jury. *Sourcebook of Criminal Justice Statistics—1990* [1991], page 517.

[37] Irene Merker Rosenberg, *Leaving Bad Enough Alone: A Response to the Juvenile Court Abolitionists,* 1993 Wisc. L.R. 163 [1993], page 175.

[38] *Truancy: the First Step to a Lifetime of Problems,* Juvenile Justice Bulletin, O.J.J.D.P., U.S. Dept. of Justice, Oct. 1996.

[39] *In re Gault,* 387 U.S. 1 [1967].

[40] "The legal rules of procedure that govern the criminal and juvenile systems are virtually the same as a consequence of the due process decisions by the United States Supreme Court and the round of reform legislation that followed." Robert O. Dawson, *The Future of Juvenile Justice: Is It Time to Abolish the System?,* 81 Jour. Crime & Criminology 136, 149 [1990]. See also Irene Merker Rosenberg, *Leaving Bad Enough Alone: A Response to the Juvenile Court Abolitionists,* 1993 Wisc. L.R. 163 [1993], page 171.

[41] Barry Feld, *Juvenile Justice,* 69 Minn. L. R. 141 [1984].

[42] Irene Merker Rosenberg, *Leaving Bad Enough Alone: A Response to the Juvenile Court Abolitionists,* 1993 Wisc. L.R. 163 [1993], page 185, n. 141.

[43] Barry Feld, *Juvenile Justice,* 69 Minn. L. R. 141 [1984].

[44] Irene Merker Rosenberg, *Leaving Bad Enough Alone: A Response to the Juvenile Court Abolitionists, 1993* Wisc. L.R. 163 [1993], page 178.

[45] Irene Merker Rosenberg, *Leaving Bad Enough Alone: A Response to the Juvenile Court Abolitionists,* 1993 Wisc. L.R. 163 [1993], page 175.

[46] Leven, *Curing Americas Addiction to Prisons,* 20 Fordham L.J. 641 [1993], quoting from Morris, *Restorative Justice: Path to the Future,* Odyssey, Spring 1992 at page 90.